NUCLEAR PROLIF

Nuclear Proliferation
in South Asia

Nuclear Proliferation in South Asia

The Prospects for Arms Control

EDITED BY

Stephen Philip Cohen

Westview Press

BOULDER • SAN FRANCISCO • OXFORD

This Westview softcover edition is printed on acid-free paper and bound in library-quality, coated covers that carry the highest rating of the National Association of State Textbook Administrators, in consultation with the Association of American Publishers and the Book Manufacturers' Institute.

Copyright © 1991 by Westview Press, Inc.

Published in 1991 in the United States of America by Westview Press, Inc., 5500 Central Avenue, Boulder, Colorado 80301, and in the United Kingdom by Westview Press, 36 Lonsdale Road, Summertown, Oxford OX2 7EW

Library of Congress Cataloging-in-Publication Data
Nuclear proliferation in South Asia : the prospects for arms control /
edited by Stephen Philip Cohen.
    p. cm.
  ISBN 0-8133-8159-2
  Includes index.
  1. Nuclear arms control—South Asia. 2. Nuclear arms control—
South Asia—Verification. 3. Nuclear arms control—India.
4. Nuclear arms control—Pakistan. 5. Nuclear nonproliferation.
I. Cohen, Stephen P., 1936–   .
JX1974.7.N819 1991
327.1′74—dc20

90-24634
CIP

Printed and bound in the United States of America

The paper used in this publication meets the requirements of the American National Standard for Permanence of Paper for Printed Library Materials Z39.48-1984.

10   9   8   7   6   5   4   3   2   1

Contents

Tables and Figures

Preface

This book suggests new ways in which the United States can encourage the prevention, limitation, or containment of the proliferation of nuclear weapons in South Asia. For many years both scholarly and policy discussions of non-proliferation have asked: "What mix of incentives and disincentives might keep such states as India and Pakistan from going nuclear?" We pose a somewhat different question: "What combination of political agreements and technical arrangements would make it possible for India and Pakistan *not* to go nuclear?" I think there are subtle but important differences between the two questions. It suffices to say that there may be several answers to each, and that some would pose the questions differently. This book does not pretend to provide all the answers—it is an exploratory, as much as an explanatory, venture.

A Regional Approach

We take a frankly regional perspective. I recognize the problems of defining South Asia as a region; these are discussed in Chapter 1. There are also dangers associated with a reductionist, regional approach that attributes both the cause and the cure of regional conflict to an India-Pakistan arms race. Until recently few in the larger non-proliferation community understood the calculations that drove India and Pakistan towards weaponization and which led them to resist pressures to sign the Non-Proliferation Treaty. While we must be concerned with the impact of South Asian nuclear events upon proliferation elsewhere, with the preservation of the Non-Proliferation Treaty (NPT) and with the virtue of policy consistency, South Asia now constitutes so much of the proliferation problem and the regional outcomes are so uncertain that a strong case can be made for taking the narrow view. A different, a regional angle of vision has its utility. A consistent American non-proliferation policy that works only where there is no danger of proliferation and which has no impact or even accelerates the weaponization process in South Asia does not strike me as much of an accomplishment.

South Asia will demand close and constant attention in the next few years. We should not be optimistic just because India and Pakistan have not yet plunged into overt nuclear programs. Both states are not only driven by the logic of technology, their own interactive relationship, and other strategic and political considerations, they are also running out of alternatives to weaponization. The central goal of American policy should be to see that attractive alternatives exist. Failing that, there is an even chance that the slow, measured pace that has characterized nuclear decisions in the region will become increasingly interactive and threatening.

The Origins of This Book

This book is based on a regional nuclear verification study completed in 1990 for the Los Alamos National Laboratory.[1] But my own interest in applying diverse methodologies and approaches to the issue of proliferation predates that by many years.

As a graduate student in India in 1963-1965, I witnessed the first Indian debate on nuclear weapons—provoked by the Chinese test at Lop Nor. Jawaharlal Nehru had just died, and the Indian strategic community entered into a complex and sophisticated dialogue on the wisdom of becoming a nuclear weapons state.

However, Nehru's influence was still pervasive. When beginning this project I recalled Nehru's words, written in early 1954, in the Foreword to a study he commissioned from Indian scientists on the effects of nuclear weapons:

> I think this study will be of value even for non-scientific readers and the public generally. It will give some idea of the world we live in and even more so of what the fate of the world is likely to be if we start playing about with nuclear warfare. I suppose that no one, not

even the great experts in this new science, knows definitely what the full results of Hydrogen bomb explosions will be. Enough is known, however, to give us some kind of a picture of a war in which these weapons are used. War is associated with death. We have now to face death on a colossal scale and, what is much worse, the genetic effects of these explosions on the present and future generations. Before this prospect, the other problems that face us in this world become relatively unimportant.

And, in words which I hope apply to this book, Nehru concluded:

I trust that this study, brief and incomplete as it is, will be of some use in directing peoples' minds to the dreadful prospect of war in the nuclear age and to the dangers of continuing nuclear test explosions.[2]

Twelve years later I had an opportunity to discuss nuclear issues with some of Pakistan's senior civilian and military leaders, including Zia ul-Haq.[3] These experiences persuaded me not only of the regional roots behind the imperative to "go nuclear," but also of the strong economic, cultural, moral, and strategic arguments *against* weaponization.

I returned to the issue of regional proliferation in another guise when I served in 1985-1987 as a member of the U.S. State Department's Policy Planning Staff with special responsibility for South Asia and proliferation issues. I had innumerable conversations with American, Pakistani, and Indian officials; scholars; journalists; and scientists about regional nuclear proliferation. Invariably, my conversations were *tactical* in nature. Few Americans, Pakistanis, or Indians were interested in what lay more than a few months ahead.[4] Those who were worried about the future tended to have an apocalyptic view of proliferation—a view that is belied by the historical record, which is not all that bad. Others were content to let matters take their course.

This book—and the earlier project sponsored by Los Alamos—represents my attempt to understand and explain the technical and policy dynamics of regional proliferation that confront scholars and policymakers in a number of states. As a private citizen, a scholar, and a government official I came to the conclusion that a serious look beyond short-term issues would enrich the debate over nuclear proliferation in South Asia. Some of these long-term considerations were explored in a book published in 1987.[5] The generally favorable response to that volume reinforced my interest in a larger project. I am especially pleased that I did not have to look very far beyond the University of Illinois to bring together a number of highly qualified experts and scholars in an effort at a fresh approach to proliferation.

Finally, this study appears at a crucial moment in regional and global history. American policymakers are now fully aware that beyond the waning confrontation with the Soviet Union there lies a whole range of other issues and conflicts which could affect American security.[6] Nuclear proliferation in South Asia may not be the most dangerous or pressing of these issues, but it certainly ranks near the top. In Spector's phrase, we may be approaching the storm after the lull.[7]

Further, the movement of India and Pakistan towards weaponization will intersect with various dates and events: these include the annual U.S. presidential certification of Pakistan's nonnuclear status, the expiration of the second arms package for Pakistan (1992), the expiration of the U.S.-Indian agreement on the reactor and spent fuel at Tarapur (1993), and the completion of the Non-Proliferation Treaty's first twenty-five years (1995), which will necessitate a conference on extending the treaty.

In Whose Interest?

While this project is addressed to both American and South Asian policymakers, it is, quite frankly, an effort to advance important American interests. My own view is that "self-serving" policies are good policies: one would be foolish to advocate a policy which did *not* serve one's country's interests. On the other hand, policies which are merely self-serving are self-defeating when they do not address the enlightened self-interest of other states as well.

I believe that our preliminary survey of the prospects for a verifiable non-proliferation regime in South Asia meets this stiff test. It will, hopefully, address the interests of Americans, Indians, Pakistanis—and others—who seek a way out of the region's nuclear dilemma. Those who would argue that proliferation would enhance the interests and security of any individual regional state have yet, in my judgment, to make a persuasive case that one or more of the arrangements, agreements, policies, or "regimes" discussed below would not promote regional security at a far lower cost than a regional nuclear arms race. The following chapters explore a number of options that have been barely discussed in the professional arms control literature, let alone in South Asia. It is my hope that they will contribute to better understanding of new solutions to old problems.

Authorship and Acknowledgements

Each chapter in this book is entirely the responsibility of its author. No chapter in this book represents, in any way, the official views of the original sponsors of the Los Alamos study (the Department of State and the Department of Energy), or the Ford Foundation (which provided support for this revision), or the University of Illinois. The authors have relied entirely upon their own sources and both the Los Alamos project and this book are based upon publicly available, unclassified information. I have shaped the volume's overall structure and have chosen the individual chapter authors, but my own views should not be attributed to any other contributor to this book or to any of the participants in the workshops held in conjunction with the Los Alamos project.

This book owes much to the support and encouragement of a number of individuals and organizations. At the University of Illinois, Susan Burns (now at the RAND Corporation) served as Assistant Project Director for the Los Alamos study and made a substantial contribution to its revision and present form, above and beyond her two original and important chapters.

The Los Alamos study was made possible by the support of Edward Fei of the Department of Energy and Joseph De Thomas and Dr. Steven Aoki of the Department of State. The staff of the International Technology Division of the Los Alamos National Laboratory, especially Arvid Lundy, were helpful in their thoughtful administration of an unusual contract.

At the University of Illinois our work in South Asian security matters has been sustained by the continuing support of the Ford

Foundation. We are especially grateful to the New Delhi office of the Foundation and to Enid C. B. Schoettle of the International Programs Division. The participation of several of the South Asian participants in the workshops held in 1989 and 1990 was made possible by Ford support. This project has also benefitted indirectly from a major grant from the MacArthur Foundation to the Program in Arms Control, Disarmament, and International Security (ACDIS).

I have also received extraordinary support and encouragement (often in the form of much-welcomed criticism) from a number of individuals, especially Dr. Tom Graham, Harvard University, Leonard Spector, Carnegie Endowment for International Peace, Dr. Randy Rydell, Senate Governmental Affairs Committee, and the individuals who participated in the two workshops. I have not always accepted their suggestions and comments, but hope that they will not be displeased with the final result.

My colleagues and the staff at the University of Illinois were, as usual, highly supportive and helped me keep to a tight schedule; in this connection the three responsible University of Illinois at Urbana-Champaign (UIUC) administrators were Jeremiah D. Sullivan (Director of ACDIS), Marvin G. Weinbaum (Director, Program in South and West Asian Studies), and George T. Yu (Head, Department of Political Science). Of course, Janie Carroll and Alice Taylor kept this three-continent, thirty-person project together and deserve special thanks. Careful final editing and layout were provided by Benjamin B. Cohen and the indispensable Merrily Shaw.

Finally, although I cannot name them, a number of Indian and Pakistani officials have, in their skepticism, been oddly encouraging. Many have expressed grave reservations about any regional verification scheme and about this project, especially since it is "made in America," but they have listened and debated, partly because they do recognize that their strategic nuclear dilemma is different, but not unique. Americans can benefit from a closer understanding of that dilemma, but South Asians can benefit from both the failures and successes of others.

Stephen Philip Cohen
University of Illinois at Urbana

Notes

1. *Towards a Nuclear Verification Regime in South Asia*, Final Report, April 1, 1990. LANL Subcontract No. 9-XC9-C4353-1 to the Program in Arms Control, Disarmament, and International Security, the Program in South and West Asian Studies, and the Department of Political Science, all of the University of Illinois at Urbana.

2. Foreword to the first edition of *Nuclear Explosions and Their Effects* (New Delhi: Publications Division, 1954).

3. Some of these conversations were recorded in *The Pakistan Army* (Berkeley: University of California Press, 1984).

4. One important exception was Rodney Jones. See for example Jones and Steven A. Hildreth, *Modern Weapons and Third World Powers* (Boulder: Westview, 1984). Another significant effort at projection was sponsored by the CIA: John Kerry King, ed., *International Political Effects of the Spread of Nuclear Weapons* (Washington: GPO, 1979); the relevant South Asia chapter was by Richard Betts, "Regional Nuclearization and Political Tensions: South Asia."

5. Stephen Philip Cohen, ed., *The Security of South Asia: American and Asian Perspectives* (Urbana and Chicago: University of Illinois Press, 1987).

6. For an insightful survey of changes in the international security environment see Michael Vlahos, *Thinking About World Change* (Washington: Center for the Study of Foreign Policy, Foreign Service Institute, June, 1990). A military-oriented perspective is found in the *Report of the Commission on Integrated Long-Term Strategy* (Washington: Government Printing Office, 1989) and the report of the Future Security Environment Working Group, *The Future Security Environment* (Washington: Department of Defense, 1989).

7. Leonard S. Spector, "Nuclear Proliferation in the 1990s: The Storm after the Lull," in Bobby R. Inman, Joseph S. Nye, Jr., William Perry and Roger Smith, *New Threats: Responding to the Proliferation of Nuclear, Chemical, and Ballistic Missile Capabilities in the Third World* (Aspen: Aspen Strategy Group, 1990).

About the Contributors

Akhtar Ali is a professional engineer employed by a Pakistani corporation. The author of two books on regional nuclear programs, he was, in 1989-90, on a fellowship at the Center for Science and International Affairs, Harvard University.

Susan M. Burns received the Master of Arts degree in Political Science from the University of Illinois at Urbana-Champaign (UIUC) in 1990. She is currently a Graduate Fellow at the RAND Graduate School of Policy Studies in Santa Monica.

Brahma Chellaney is a freelance Indian journalist. Formerly employed by AP News Service, New Delhi, he received a two-year fellowship from the Social Science Research Council/MacArthur Foundation to study the spread of nuclear weapons in South Asia. In 1990 he was a visiting fellow at the Brookings Institution, Washington.

Stephen Philip Cohen is Professor of Political Science and Asian Studies at UIUC, and was a co-founder of the Program in Arms Control, Disarmament and International Security in 1978. He served on the Policy Planning Staff of the U. S. Department of State in 1985-87, and has been a consultant to the Department of State, the RAND Corporation, and Lawrence Livermore National Laboratory.

Arun P. Elhance is Assistant Professor of Geography, UIUC, and a specialist in operations research. After working for Hindustan Aeronautics Ltd. and Rolls Royce, Dr. Elhance received the Ph.D. degree from Boston University.

Nancy W. Gallagher is a member of the faculty of Wesleyan University. She received the Ph.D. degree in Political Science at UIUC, where her thesis was on conceptual models of arms control verification.

Vipin Gupta received the degree of Bachelor of Science in Aerospace Engineering from UIUC in 1990 and a Masters of Science in Remote Sensing from the Imperial College of Science and Technology, London, in 1990 where he is a Marshall Scholar.

S. Rashid Naim is a Fellow at St. Cross College, Oxford, Great Britain, and received the Ph.D. in Political Science from UIUC in 1990. He is a specialist on Islam and ideology in the Middle East and South Asia.

Jon Neuhoff is a graduate student in the Department of Nuclear Engineering at UIUC.

Clifford Singer is Associate Professor of Nuclear Engineering, UIUC, and a member of the ACDIS executive committee. Dr. Singer received the Ph.D. from the University of California at Berkeley.

1

Nuclear Neighbors

Stephen Philip Cohen

If rival states have the capacity to develop military nuclear systems but are not under a strategic imperative to do so, what technical and political arrangements might assist them in averting a nuclear arms race? This is the question addressed by this book. Implied in that question are two assumptions. The first is that India and Pakistan are not preordained to become nuclear weapons states; the second is that even if they do acquire some nuclear arms (or maintain their present option status) it is not inevitable that they enter into a nuclear arms race or pursue other policies which are detrimental to American (and, I would argue, their own) interests. Various arms control measures, including associated verification schemes, can assist regional states in pursuing what we regard as a shared interest in preventing, restraining, or managing a nuclear arms race. This applies equally to the India-China relationship.

The Situation in South Asia

The exact nuclear status of India and Pakistan is not publicly known. Some regard them as de facto nuclear weapons states. Others disagree.[1] Apparently, neither state has a working nuclear weapon but both could quickly convert existing stocks of fissile material into a deliverable device. In early 1988 a U.S. official stated that Pakistan has acquired the technical capabilities needed to possess a nuclear explosive device, but so far has not made the political decision to do so, and some essential steps remain to be taken, if the political decision were made.[2]

Given time, both could produce sufficient nuclear weapons to deploy a small first strike nuclear force. Certainly, India (with its large stocks of plutonium) has the capacity for a much larger force. Both states also possess adequate means for delivery in the form of advanced fighter-bombers. Both have recently tested short-range missiles, and on May 21, 1989, India launched the *Agni*, a medium range missile—offering no pretense that it was engaged in purely peaceful research or testing.

The overall Indian nuclear program is mature and well-developed. Indian nuclear research began in the 1940s, a bomb program was widely discussed and studied in the 1960s, and a so-called peaceful nuclear explosive (PNE) was tested in 1974. Despite this history of nuclear research—and predictions of imminent weaponization—the Indian leadership has crept very slowly along the nuclear path. This was not the perception of some Pakistani leaders. Misjudging Indian intentions, they pressed for a Pakistani program as early as 1964.

Thus there are two states in South Asia unconstrained by strong outside alliances, beset by a range of internal and external security problems, engaged in a long-term political struggle with each other. They have moved to the top of the global nuclear and proliferation agenda for the decade of the 1990s. Although possessing the means to acquire nuclear systems they have not done so. This provides American policymakers with both an insight into Indian and Pakistani nuclear politics and an entry point into their nuclear decisions.

In Whose Interest?

What are the different *interests* concerning regional proliferation held by important states?

American Nonproliferation Interests

These fall into or touch upon three different areas. First, there are purely *nuclear*-related concerns. These include slowing down or controlling regional military nuclear programs by stemming or stopping the flow of nuclear materials and technology to India and Pakistan; ensuring that India and Pakistan do not aid other states with their nuclear military programs; seeing to it that the South Asian example of creeping proliferation is not emulated or admired elsewhere; protecting the NPT (due for renewal in 1995), especially since it has come under recent Indian attack.

Second, there are two American *strategic/global* interests associated with regional proliferation. One is containment of Soviet (and, earlier, Chinese) influence in South Asia. This has always interacted with Washington's regional proliferation policy— sometimes to the detriment of the latter.[3] However, with the Soviet withdrawal from Afghanistan, proliferation becomes one area where further cooperation with the Soviets, and even the Chinese, makes sense, and might enhance both nonproliferation interests and the remnants of containment policy. Further, looking ahead to a world of five great powers (Japan, China, the U.S., the Soviet Union and the European Community—with its two independent nuclear systems) it is important to ensure that if regional proliferation occurs it will not destabilize what will already be a very complicated global order.

Finally, there are a number of *regional* American interests at stake. American policy has, since 1947, favored the emergence of a stable and cooperative South Asian regional system based upon Indian and Pakistani cooperation so that all regional states might better solve their pressing economic and developmental problems. The bilateral relationship with Pakistan has become something of a limited partnership. The U.S. has parallel interests with a moderate, Islamic, Pakistan in the Persian Gulf and Middle East; these interests will remain important even after the Afghan crisis is resolved, and justify a limited strategic connection. This connection will be endangered if Pakistan acquires an overt nuclear weapons capability.

India is a strategically unique state, more than a regional power but something less than a multiregional or global power. Not only will India dominate the rest of South Asia (raising particular problems for Washington's ties to Islamabad), it could challenge China and other large powers (including the U.S.) in the Indian Ocean and nearby regions if it feels its economic, political and strategic interests are threatened. Since Indian strategists are divided as to what those interests are, India's behavior could be especially unpredictable.

Soviet and Chinese Nonproliferation Interests

While Soviet participation in the nonproliferation regime may not be as strong as some have claimed (certainly, the possibility of cooperating with the Soviets on South Asian nuclear proliferation should not become the centerpiece of U.S. policy), the Soviets do have several important nonproliferation interests. They wish to prevent their complete encirclement by a ring of nuclear states.[4] To the degree that India and Pakistan do go nuclear, the Soviets want to ensure that they will not be drawn into a regional nuclear conflict, or that such a conflict will not entangle them indirectly with Chinese or American nuclear systems. Still, the Soviets are likely to continue to see India as a potential counterweight to China, especially after the recent crisis in the People's Republic, and in light of discontent in the southern regions of the USSR. If India *does* go nuclear, the Soviets will want to ensure that the Indians remain focussed on Chinese systems, and that Indian power will continue to balance Chinese power. The Soviet supply of civilian nuclear technology and the lease of a nuclear-powered submarine to India shows that for the Soviets, as for the U.S., nonproliferation interests can be subordinated to perceived strategic interests.

China, of course, has not pursued an active nonproliferation policy, and for many years argued that proliferation was part of the process by which great-power hegemony could be broken up. Like the Soviets (and most other nuclear weapons states), the Chinese are alleged to have provided significant support to one non-nuclear state (Pakistan) before they publicly adopted a tougher nonproliferation stance. Beijing's nonproliferation efforts are likely to remain limited.

India and Pakistan

While both states have very different nuclear programs and capabilities, they happen to have very similar nonproliferation interests. Both want to ensure that they will never come under a nuclear threat without the capacity to retaliate in kind. For both, the support of an external nuclear power (China, the U.S., and the Soviet Union) has, until recently, made such a threat very unlikely, and hence has made nuclear weapons unnecessary. Yet, their own interactive decisions of the late 1960s and early 1970s has forced their bilateral nuclear relationship to a new level. Now, they each have a strong need for assurances that they will not be surprised by the other, or betrayed by weak outside support.

Thus, both India and Pakistan agree that a nuclear option is necessary. Until now they have been united (for somewhat different reasons) in their opposition to the Non-Proliferation Treaty (NPT) and its associated verification regime (managed by the International Atomic Energy Agency), and even to serious discussions of verification or inspection arrangements that might lead to full-scope safeguards. Pakistan claims to support this regime, but only if India joins it; India has had deep reservations about the NPT quite apart from Pakistan's (or China's) participation in the NPT system.

Nevertheless, the NPT regime does serve the interests of both states to the degree that it restrains proliferation by others, and to the degree that the moral and political opprobrium associated with going nuclear might restrain the other. For this reason, Indian and Pakistani opposition to the NPT has been less vocal in recent years, and senior Indian nuclear policymakers have privately expressed (in March, 1990) their shock at the prospect of generalized proliferation in the Middle East or a transformed Europe.

The two states also have some shared *post-proliferation* interests. Both would exploit nuclear weapons for political, symbolic and strategic purposes. Pakistan would want to deter a conventional Indian attack and impress its Islamic neighbors, especially Iran and Saudi Arabia, while India would want to use its nuclear capability to enable it to meet China, the Soviet Union, and the U.S. on more or less equal terms—that of a middle-rank nuclear power. But even in such a post-proliferation world, where Delhi and Islamabad might head in different directions, they will still have a shared interest in avoiding a nuclear crisis between themselves.

Finally, India and Pakistan have a shared interest in not becoming the *target* of other nuclear systems, or allowing their own nuclear capabilities to entangle them in unnecessary conflicts. By going nuclear, they will automatically become part of the strategic political and targeting calculations of every other major nuclear power (and of Israel, in the case of Pakistan). While there are perceived advantages in becoming nuclear weapons states, India and Pakistan will share a whole new set of formidable dilemmas and dangers.

This brief summary of cannot do justice to the complexity of what is, after all, an unprecedented situation. This will be the first time in the short history of the nuclear world that two competing states, unrestrained by alliances, moved simultaneously to military nuclear status. Their nuclearization would, in fact, create four adjacent nuclear weapons states in South-central Asia—with a fifth nuclear state, the U.S., having significant regional naval nuclear capabilities. Such a world raises obvious problems for American and Soviet nuclear planners and it is likely to raise far more difficult problems for South Asian nuclear planners.

Regional Nuclear Dynamics

What are the most important elements of what is often referred to as an India-Pakistan nuclear arms race? One is that these two states cannot quite be characterized as "racing," that other factors account for their nuclear decisions. Three elements of the regional nuclear dynamic are important in this regard: the motives and nature of their so-called arms race, the internal politics of these programs, and the likely outcome of this competition.

Motives and Compulsions

There is a widespread belief that the Indian and Pakistani nuclear programs are competitively driven. It would be foolish to argue that these states do not influence each other, but it is wrong to characterize their relationship solely—or even primarily—as an arms race. American policy has recently been overly-influenced by this idea. Perhaps as a reaction to a decade or more of globalized nonproliferation policies, some officials and many proliferation experts have come to identify the India-Pakistan "arms race" as the cause of regional proliferation. In his testimony before the Governmental Affairs Committee in 1989 the Director of Central

Intelligence, William Webster, stated that a nuclear arms race was underway in South Asia, yet there "have been no real efforts in the international community to try to head off that race." The analysis received strong support from the committee chairman, Senator John Glenn.[5] While Glenn believes that nonproliferation is more than a regional issue ("a threat to international security") he also conceptualizes the problem as one of a local arms race, and argues that by using our leverage on one party to that race—Pakistan—the U.S. can influence Indian decisions, and thus bring a halt to regional proliferation process. Other Americans would not disagree with the analysis, except to argue that the U.S. should first pressure India, since a conciliatory gesture by the region's dominant power would have a greater impact on Pakistan; they envision a reciprocal, *negative* arms race.

But proliferation is driven by more than an India-Pakistan arms race. India's nuclear program has always been strongly influenced by the China factor and Pakistani strategists have come to see broader gains from a Pakistani nuclear program (which was, of course, stimulated by the Indian debates from 1964 onward over the nuclear option) than mere deterrence of an Indian conventional or nuclear attack.[6] Further, there is a large body of literature which persuasively argues that wars are not caused by arms races, but by their absence. Wars are caused by miscalculation, or when one side or another feels so secure (or insecure) that it can attack the other, or when one side or another misjudges its relative position vis-à-vis an antagonist. In South Asia wars have been caused by irredentist sentiments, by deeply held antagonisms, by territorial disagreements, by broader ambitions, by misjudgments about the strength, weakness, or intentions of the other side, not by an arms "race."[7] Horizontal nuclear proliferation has been a contentious issue in South Asia for over twenty-five years (since the 1964 Chinese test at Lop Nor), and there is an even sturdier regional interest in the vertical spread of nuclear weapons. A recent Indian Minister of Defense, K.C. Pant, was an important figure in the first Indian nonproliferation debate, and his maiden political speech at the 1964 session of the Indian National Congress persuasively made the case for the "option" strategy.

India's option strategy was, initially, a response to the Chinese test and subsequent weaponization. It was also a way to demonstrate to both the U.S. and the USSR that India was a power to be reckoned with (although most Indians now acknowledge that India's restrained response to China or even its 1974 Indian PNE did not do much to enhance India's reputation or image.

China has again figured in Indian strategic and nuclear calculations. Informed Indian hawks now speculate that the Sino-Soviet summit of June, 1989, means that the Soviet "umbrella" over India, epitomized in the Indo-Soviet Treaty of Peace and Friendship, has been furled.[8] The Pakistan program has been important in Indian calculations only since the late 1970s, and even then they were made in the context of the broader (if shifting) strategic picture.

While the Pakistan program *began* as a response to the Indian nuclear debate of the 1960s, and was accelerated by the 1974 Indian test, it also was conceived in larger terms.[9] First Zulfiqar Ali Bhutto, and then Zia ul-Haq (and thus the military, which was opposed to nuclearization under President Ayub Khan) saw Pakistan as a stable, advanced and Islamic state; a Pakistani bomb would not only deter the conventional and nuclear threat from India, it would put Pakistan in the forefront of the Islamic world. Also, the Pakistanis came early to an appreciation of extended deterrence; here they were following the Israeli and NATO examples, not India's.[10]

A Peoples' Bomb?

Outsiders have also consistently misjudged the intensity of support for nuclear weapons in India and Pakistan. This has led some to a fatalistic view of the inevitability of proliferation. But public opinion polls in India and Pakistan have consistently shown a majority against weaponization in both states. These figures were overwhelmingly anti-nuclear in the 1960s and 1970s, they are still marginally anti-nuclear. Yet, when asked whether India or Pakistan should possess a nuclear weapon if the other has it, or if their country were to be threatened by another outside power, virtually all respondents indicate strong support for a bomb. In other words, regional public opinion has doubts about nuclear weapons, but stronger reservations about being taken by surprise. This is, as one would expect, the view of most Indian and Pakistani politicians.[11]

If the public did not favor nuclearization, and the armed forces were neutral, at best,[12] then how did these two states move to the edge of a military nuclear capability? There are different answers to this question for India and for Pakistan.

In India's case, a coalition of hawkish scientists, bureaucrats, and strategists have kept the pressure on successive governments. All Indian leaders since Nehru's have resisted "the next step," but most have moved further down the nuclear path in the absence of a good reason to freeze or to dismantle their nuclear programs.[13] Since Lal Bahadur Shastri's term as prime minister (1964-66) this deferral of the go/no go decision, while simultaneously allowing research and development to move ahead, has acquired the label of the "option" strategy.[14] As a result, a wide range of programs have been authorized, started, and allowed to mature without a clear policy decision about their consequences.

In the 1960s the option strategy was invented in response to a perceived threat from China; in 1971 (when work on the PNE was authorized) India came under pressure from both the U.S. and the USSR in conjunction with the newly-minted NPT and in the context of heightened tension with Pakistan. By maintaining a nuclear option Delhi could at least assert its nuclear independence (even as its dependence on others for conventional arms was growing). By the late 1970s the option strategy was firmly embedded in Indian policy.

The news of Pakistan's nuclear program almost precipitated a weaponization decision (there was also talk of a take-out of Pakistan's enrichment facility at Kahuta), but it was decided to continue to broaden the technical base of the nuclear program and speed up missile development. Only in 1974 (and the actual decision to test the PNE) did domestic factors play a role: Indira Gandhi was in deep political trouble, and the test may have impressed some Indians. What is now evident (in the shape of the missile tests, statements about uranium enrichment, and other examples of a broad-based Indian program) are the consequences of decisions taken many years ago. Still, there is no strong evidence that the Indian leadership has committed itself to a full-scale, deployed nuclear and/or missile program.

Pakistan has been more purposive. From the beginning Bhutto wanted a nuclear weapon. He saw the bomb as a way of balancing India's conventional superiority, neutralizing the Indian nuclear threat, and reviving Pakistan's shattered strategic reputation. This policy met with near-universal support in Pakistan, and enabled Islamabad to operate one of history's most sophisticated industrial espionage programs.

The American connection may have modified Pakistan's plans, but it did not fundamentally alter them. Pakistan, also, wants to have an option, but one with a very short fuse. It models itself after Israel—ambiguity about its own nuclear program brings it many of the benefits of nuclearization yet allows it to retain a tie with its major outside weapons supplier, the United States.

Unlike India, where support for the nuclear program has broadened over the years, it has slightly weakened in Pakistan. When Pakistan was an isolated and threatened country the bomb seemed very attractive. But as Pakistan has emerged from the Zia years as a respected, reasonably stable, and militarily more impressive state, different Pakistani groups have had second thoughts about the nuclear program. The military at heart still regards it as problematic, the diplomats are fully aware of the strains that it has caused in Pakistan's relations with the U.S. and other Western states, and no Pakistani politician today has the experience and skill of Zulfiqar Ali Bhutto. They are more like their Indian counterparts—in the absence of a clear-cut alternative, they are willing to tolerate the nuclear program. Only the scientists involved in the program are true believers—although there are reports of a peace movement among some Pakistani scientists not directly engaged in the enrichment and weapons programs.

A Stable or Unstable Region?

Finally, outside observers have had trouble judging the stability of a proliferated South Asia. They tend towards two extreme views. One is the alarmist position that India and Pakistan, driven by racial and religious hatreds, are locked into a deadly arms race that could (at worst) lead to regional and/or global nuclear war, or (at best) produce a nuclear accident, nuclear theft, or the transfer of fissile material and sensitive technology to other near-nuclears such as Iraq and North Korea. The perception is widespread that regional governments are often unstable and cannot be trusted with nuclear weapons.

On the other hand there is a minority view that nuclear weapons themselves generate their own logic—that of deterrence. This position holds that any pair of nuclear antagonists, such as India and Pakistan, will replicate and evolve on a small scale the peaceful deadlock that has characterized the American-Soviet relationship.[15]

Perhaps the most honest conclusion we can reach about the stability of a proliferated South Asia is that we do not know what will happen. One of the unknowns about the future of proliferation is the degree of evolutionary congruence between technology and strategy. It took decades and billions of dollars for the West, the Soviet Union, and China to integrate strategy and military technology. But the new nuclear states (especially India) are likely to be born with fully mature military systems. Will their nuclear doctrine be as developed? What kind of doctrine will be adopted by nonaligned nuclear states that also have a complex conventional military threat? Looking at the problem in the abstract, Brito and Intriligator note that as the number of nuclear states increases there are more weapons, targets, and decision-centers. Further, the chances of an irrational leader appearing are also increased.[16] This may be balanced—once again, in the abstract—by the power of deterrence logic: increasing the number of nuclear states also increases the number of partners available for deterrence.[17]

But there is evidence about the crisis behavior of Indian and Pakistani decisionmakers. This evidence, like the theoretical analysis, is inconclusive. India and Pakistan have gone to war four times, and India fought a war with China in 1962; further, there have been a number of border crises, most recently in 1987, when India confronted both Pakistan and China. Pessimists can point to the growth of ethnic disturbances in all three states, to their propensity of such conflict to spill across borders, to the misperceptions and stereotypes held by leaders in each major state, and to the strong influence of domestic politics on the foreign policies of India and Pakistan.

Yet, South Asia's two major military powers have reached significant arms control agreements with each other. They have also managed to exclude outside states from their own bilateral relationship (formalized in the 1972 Simla agreement between Bhutto and Mrs. Gandhi), and regional leaders are increasingly aware of the impossible costs of a major war.[18]

My own view is that nuclear proliferation will stabilize the India-Pakistan relationship about to the degree that nuclear weapons have introduced caution into U.S.-Soviet and Soviet-Chinese relations—a judgment that does not imply much enthusiasm about proliferation's beneficial side-effects. India and Pakistan have, in fact, been engaged in a kind of nuclear diplomacy for several years, and there is strong evidence that in 1987 (during the height of the crisis caused by Operation Brass Tacks) both sides understood this perfectly. President Zia stated the obvious when he told visitors in 1988 that India and Pakistan had achieved deterrence stability because of uncertainty as to whether each possessed nuclear weapons and how many they might have. More recently, nuclear and conventional arms control agreements between India and Pakistan may have been made possible by the knowledge in both states that escalation could lead to nuclear war—or at least the overt display of nuclear capabilities. For these reasons, proliferation may have a calming, even stabilizing regional effect. It probably had this effect in 1990, during the worst crisis in India-Pakistan relations in twenty years.

On the other hand, there is the real possibility of accident, unauthorized acts, misunderstanding, or misperception. We know of at least one missed signal: during India's Operation Brass Tacks Pakistan sent a message to India via an Indian journalist who delayed publishing his story for purely commercial reasons. More recently, during the Kashmir crisis of 1990, Indian officials expressed their "exasperation" with the deletion (by a television producer) of key remarks on the nuclear issue uttered by General K. Sundarji (the retired chief of the army staff).[19] On a personal note, the Ministry of Defense Official and several other Indian officials and members of Delhi's strategic community have misread a passage in my own book on the Pakistan army.[20]

We also know that neither India nor Pakistan have done much work on nuclear doctrine, and both would face formidable command and control problems. How would they move beyond the present stage of nuclear ambiguity, bluff, and gamesmanship to the world of stable, second-strike deterrence? Would such a progression be as smooth as it apparently was for the U.S. and the Soviets?[21] Would the huge cost and complexity of a stable, mobile, and reliable deterrent be beyond their capacity (especially Pakistan's)? Will outsiders step in with technical assistance—possibly leading to a very slippery slope of the direct involvement of outsiders in regional nuclear calculations? Finally, will India and Pakistan duplicate the behavior of almost every other nuclear weapons state, and provide assistance to other states that wish to go nuclear?

These and other questions suggest how complex are the motives and processes which will determine whether or not India and Pakistan choose to acquire nuclear forces. They also suggest something of the difficulty the U.S. faces in constructing a policy that can cope with regional proliferation and its associated consequences.

The Regional Approach:
Advantages and Disadvantages

The 1964-65 Indian nuclear debate was closely watched by Pakistani officials who concluded—wrongly—that India was going to acquire a nuclear weapon. But even earlier, India had been in the forefront of global arms control and disarmament proposals. Even if it was not a major military power Delhi saw itself as a global actor, a moral force for good on the international level. There is a long Indian tradition, dating back to 1947-1948 of comprehensive Indian arms control proposals.[22]

The Pakistani approach has been more focussed, more regional in scope. While Pakistanis see themselves as a South Asian and a Middle Eastern power, Islamabad's formal arms control activities have been largely confined to the first region, although it pursued quiet diplomacy in attempting to resolve the Iran-Iraq war.

These divergent Pakistani and Indian approaches raise the question of which region we are examining in this book. South Asia is generally thought to include India, Pakistan and a number of small neighboring states, but *not* China. However, Indian strategists are correct when they argue for China's inclusion in discussions of South Asian security. Not only did India and China fight a war in 1962, and not only do China and Pakistan have a close military relationship dating back to 1965, but there are reports that China has supplied Pakistan with nuclear technologies. Further, China has played an important role in one regional conflict (Afghanistan), and has supported various Indian insurgency movements over the years. In turn, India has not been inactive in Tibet, and has collaborated with both the U.S. and the Soviet Union in monitoring Chinese strategic and military capabilities.[23]

There are also important linkages between South Asia—even narrowly defined—and nearby regions. Pakistan has close ties to several Arab states, Turkey and Iran. There are reports of nuclear assistance *to* Pakistan from several of these states, and strong fears of possible nuclear assistance *from* Pakistan to them—towards an "Islamic" or "Muslim" bomb. India has reached the point where it can project some military force outside of South Asia proper, mostly *via* its expanded and modernized navy and its fledgling missile program. And it must also be remembered that in the days of the British Raj the Indian Army was deployed throughout Asia, the Middle East, Africa, and Europe.

This book will therefore address itself to the Indian-Pakistani, and—in a very limited way—to the India-China nuclear relationship. The two cannot be separated, and any "regional" approach which does so will be crippled from the start. In a sense, therefore, we are looking at a region-and-a-half, South Asia plus a Central or East Asian power. We will not address the nuclear or strategic relationship between India, Pakistan, and the Soviet Union, although a proliferated South Asia will certainly affect Soviet nuclear calculations. We will, of course, examine the role of the Soviet Union in restraining or containing regional nuclear proliferation.

Nuclear Proliferation and Other Regional Conflicts

To what extent can the regional proliferation problem be examined without addressing regional territorial, political, and ideological disputes? Regional strategists have become adept at deflecting specific arms control proposals by arguing that a comprehensive settlement must precede discussion of specific measures; this is one reason why there is so little discussion of arms control, verification, and confidence building measures, even in India. [24]

No matter how one characterizes India—a dominant, or a regional great power, or a regional hegemon—and no matter how important or unimportant one regards Pakistan, the fact is that as far as each is concerned, India cannot make peace, Pakistan cannot make war. India sees itself as the aggrieved party, or as the eventually victorious party, and finds no reason to make concessions to a weaker Pakistan. Indians can hold contradictory images of Pakistan in their mind: that Pakistan is at fault, it is the provocateur, and also that Pakistan will eventually collapse because of its own internal contradictions. Both views imply waiting out Pakistan until some nebulous future: Pakistan will either concede to India its legitimate and dominant regional role, or it will simply fall under its own weight.

For Pakistanis, the problem is largely seen in military terms. India is a bully, bullies only understand force, Pakistan must possess enough force to be able to deter Delhi. But it is difficult to acquire such force, and in the absence of credible Indian concessions, stalemate is again the preferred policy.

The India-Pakistan conflict is thus about more than territory, and involves deep passions and suspicions. We must keep this in mind, even when dealing with technical dimensions of arms control. If two parties regard themselves as the victim, and that the other side is always at fault, they cannot bring themselves to *share* responsibility for the resolution of even a limited dispute.[25] An arms control proposal that deals with the production or deployment of nuclear weapons—or the level, deployment, and use of conventional forces, must also shape these deeper psychological and political perceptions. "Confidence-building measures" (CBM) is a clumsy title for the process by which two states learn to what extent they can (or cannot) trust each other. In this, verification of an arms control agreement is critical, as it may extend the boundaries of the area of trust, or—by detecting violations of an agreement—it may suggest areas where new agreements are needed.

A full-scale study of regional proliferation should examine such political, territorial, and ideological disputes, but the various contributors to this study have not been asked to do so in this preliminary venture.

Nonproliferation Strategies

Lewis Dunn divides nonproliferation efforts into three phases.[26] The first is the *prevention* of the spread of nuclear weapons to a region; the second is *containment* of that weapon in a region (and preventing its spread to other areas), and the third phase is the *management* of the strategic consequences of proliferation.

Until quite recently, American policy in South Asia has been to try to *prevent* the acquisition of nuclear weapons by India and Pakistan. While many South Asians have attributed this policy to a desire to contain or restrict their power, in reality it is rooted in deeply-held American national security interests. Nuclear proliferation is seen as troubling not because of the number of new weapons that it would produce, but because of the number of new decision-centers it would produce, subsequently increasing the risk of nuclear accident, nuclear theft, nuclear transfer, or nuclear war. Of course, on each count informed South Asian critics have pointed out that the existing nuclear weapons states have themselves engaged in the transfer of nuclear technology and, one way or another, are responsible for the Chinese, French, British, and presumed Israeli and South African nuclear capabilities. But, from an American (and Soviet, French, and British) perspective, the critical period is the years in which a new nuclear state is still absorbing the strategic implications of nuclear weapons, when it has not yet developed effective command and control arrangements, and when its neighbors and potential enemies have not yet absorbed the implications of nuclearization. The few theoretical studies examining this problem point to these early years as particularly dangerous.[27] The move from a nuclear device to a weapon without theory or doctrine or adequate command and control measures is not merely a matter of concern to a new proliferator's military and strategic elites, but is of vital importance to neighbors.

Second, American nonproliferation policy must also focus upon the assistance that India or Pakistan might provide to *other* states. Such assistance—vehemently denied at the moment by regional leaders—could follow the pattern set by the other nuclear weapons states (except Great Britain) which have apparently aided at least one other country's nuclear program.

Further, India and Pakistan need not become nuclear weapon states to assist others in their nuclear programs. Each could remain at the "option" stage and barter or sell nuclear technology to other states in exchange for political support, economic assistance, or conventional arms. If the partner country was distant enough

(North Korea, for example) the exchange might have no impact upon purely South Asian security relationships, although it might be devastating in the recipient region.

Finally, there has been increasing interest in recent years in *stabilizing* a potential Indian and Pakistani nuclear arms relationship, and some have suggested the provision of permissive action links (PALs) and other devices that would prevent unauthorized use of nuclear weapons.[28] The reason for concern in South Asia is self-evident. In the past, most new nuclear states were tied to a superpower in way way or another, or (in the cases of Israel and South Africa) might go nuclear in a region where no other states possess nuclear weapons. This would not be true of India or Pakistan; India and Pakistan would face each other, India would face China, Israel would be concerned about the Pakistani program, and both would have to be concerned about the U.S. and the Soviet Union.

The discussion over nonproliferation strategies appropriate to South Asia has already begun to move from considerations of prevention to considerations of management; there has yet to be more than guarded discussions of measures which might ensure that nuclear technologies do not *spread* from India or Pakistan to other states. We will elaborate these stages further in Chapter 11, but it is apparent that different phases of the nonproliferation problem require different strategies and resources. It is also evident that these strategies may conflict with each other, and that they carry different costs.

Purely technical measures (e.g. restricting the transfer of nuclear technology to proliferators) has been effective in slowing down India's and Pakistan's quest for nuclear weapons, and raised the cost of their programs (this strategy was especially effective in the case of India), but it is now known that Pakistan managed to overcome such constraints. Ironically, it may yet become necessary to provide technical assistance to Pakistan to ensure the safe disposition and control over any nuclear forces that they might deploy. The classic disarmers dilemma confronts us: would the prospect of such technical assistance at a later stage of proliferation negate earlier efforts to constrain or retard a program?

Similarly, increasing the economic cost of a nuclear program may slow it down in early stages but is likely to have little impact on deployment or transfer decisions. India and Pakistan both have invested huge amounts of money in their nuclear programs; if anything, they may come to see these programs as profit centers and will seek to recover some of their sunk costs by selling or bartering technology to other states.

Third, political arguments will have a varying impact at different stages of proliferation. An alliance or security commitment may be sufficient at an early stage to defer or suspend a particular nuclear program. This certainly was the case for India in 1964-1970, when that state had a tacit security guarantee from both the U.S. and the USSR vis-à-vis nuclear threats from China. The limited U.S. commitment to Pakistan after 1981 may have slowed that nuclear program down somewhat, and certainly provided the inducement to keep it at a pre-weapon stage. But in both cases, once a state has reached a certain level of nuclear technology these external political inducements diminish greatly. A nuclear or a near-nuclear state has achieved a high degree of strategic autonomy—it is a nuclear power, it has joined the nuclear "club" It comes to regard itself as a major power—this is one important *purpose* of going nuclear. It will also come to view the nuclear assurances of others as less than credible—this is the lesson of the French, Chinese, and even Israeli nuclear programs.

This latter trend will accelerate as the bipolar global structure further deteriorates and the technical engine of proliferation—the diffusion of a wide range of technologies to all parts of the world—speeds up. Research on explosive technologies, hydrodynamics, implosion, and advanced methods to produce fissile material is being conducted at a very high level in many regions.[29] In the past, a state had to do virtually everything itself to obtain a nuclear weapon; increasingly, much of the basic research is publicly available, engineering technologies are freely available on a commercial basis, and sunk costs are becoming a larger percentage of the total cost of a nuclear weapons program. Making a nuclear weapon is still a daunting enterprise, but the number of "nuclear overhang" states will grow within the next ten years.[30] This suggests that nonproliferation strategies designed to increase the financial cost or raise the technical barriers for a given proliferator will be of diminishing importance in years to come, and that increasing reliance will have to be placed upon persuasion and creating political disincentives.

Individuals and governments concerned with nonproliferation will also have to reexamine the role that military and strategic doctrine plays in the spread of nuclear weapons. One of the most powerful incentives for proliferation has been the growth of deterrence theory in Western and Soviet doctrine. Modern deterrence theory has given new life to an ancient idea: that it is acceptable to destroy another society in the course of fighting it. Indeed, it has given new life to another ancient idea: national suicide as strategic doctrine.[31] Of course, deterrence theory is always justified in terms of a second or retaliatory strike, but strategists and politicians have once again found acceptable the idea of the destruction of an enemy society. Although there have been doubters (notably, Indira Gandhi in India) these ideas have made headway in India and Pakistan; it is an open question as to whether they will gain acceptance.

Finally, the spread of nuclear technology to South Asia—no less than the spread of missile technology to Iraq and Iran—has implications for the entire field of arms control. So far, arms controllers have focussed on the Soviet-American nuclear relationship and the closely related European arms balance. With the prospect of proliferation to areas with very different histories and cultures—which also have their own conventional balances of power—we will see whether much of the theory, doctrine, and technology of arms control is relevant outside of its European and U.S.-Soviet context.

Notes

1. The status of both programs is discussed in subsequent chapters. For one survey see Leonard S. Spector, *Going Nuclear* (Boston: Ballinger, 1989).

2. Testimony of Robert Peck, Deputy Assistant Secretary of State for South Asia, before the U.S. House of Representatives, Subcommittee on Asian and Pacific Affairs, Feb. 18, 1988, pp. 11-12.

3. There is a paradox embedded in America's response to regional nuclear proliferation. The absence of U.S. involvement in a region makes U.S. interest in regional proliferation relatively low; but high American concern with a region creates an interest that competes with proliferation. Thus, U.S. policymakers generally tried to ignore both the Indian and Pakistani nuclear programs (although they were forced into attention by the nonproliferation community,

especially those in Congress); but when Pakistan's role in countering the Soviet presence in Afghanistan became important, and more high-level attention was diverted to the region, that issue tended to override proliferation concerns.

4. The 1973 U.S.-Soviet "Prevention of Nuclear War" agreement obliges both parties to consult immediately and undertake measures to avert the risks of nuclear war in the event of incidents involving other countries that could lead to nuclear weapons use.

5. See remarks by Senator Glenn, *Congressional Record*, November 17, 1989, "Nuclear Arms Race in South Asia." These continued remarks of November 16, 1989, which contain an excellent chronology and some pertinent documents.

6. See the discussion by Akhtar Ali on the question of an "Islamic bomb." He argues strongly for an India-derived motivation, but my conversations with many Pakistani military and civilian strategists clearly point to a secondary, Middle East and Gulf-related purpose. The Islamic bomb slogan is sensitive in Pakistan—and among Pakistan's supporters in the West—because it implies an anti-Israeli policy. In fact, Pakistan's hostility towards Israel has waxed and waned over the years; after Zia's assumed power in 1977 anti-Israeli statements and actions were sharply reduced. They could be revived, and a nuclear and missile armed Pakistan that pursued a hostile policy towards Israel would further link the Middle East and South Asia.

7. See the excellent survey of the three India-Pakistan wars by Sumit Ganguly, *The Origins of War in South Asia* (Boulder: Westview, 1986).

8. A leading Indian journalist, Inder Malhotra, states that the language of the joint communique invalidates Soviet obligations to aid India against China, since it commits the Soviet Union and China not to use force or the threat of force against each other in any manner including through the use of the "territory, territorial waters and air space of any third country adjacent to the other." *India Abroad*, June 16, 1989.

9. For discussions of Pakistani nuclear objectives see the two books by Akhtar Ali, *Pakistan's Nuclear Dilemma* (Karachi: Pakistan Economist Research Unit, 1984) and *South Asia: Nuclear Stalemate or Conflagration* (Karachi: Research on Armament and Poverty, 1987) and Stephen P. Cohen, *The Pakistan Army* (Berkeley: University of California Press, 1984).

10. The similarity between the Pakistani and the Israeli programs is by design. Whereas India defended its program and their option, on principles of self-reliance and national sovereignty Pakistani officials closely studied the Israeli-U.S. connection and utilized the loopholes created for Israel to shield their own program.

11. There is a substantial literature on the Indian nuclear debate, but, except for the *Defence Journal* of Karachi, only in 1989-90 did a public debate on nuclear weapons begin in Pakistan. For a recent sampling see the monthly *Globe* (Karachi), March, 1990.

12. In the past neither the Indian nor the Pakistani armies have pressed for the bomb. Ayub Khan rejected Bhutto's suggestion that Pakistan go nuclear and fired him as foreign minister. Pressure for a nuclear program came from

Pakistani civilians, not the armed forces. For a representative military view see Maj. Firzok Ataulla, "Pakistan's Nuclear Option," *The Citadel*, Command and Staff College, Quetta, Vol. 6, No. 2, 1989. The same was true of India. None of the Indian armed services favored going nuclear until strong evidence of a Pakistani program became available. Even today the Indian military are concerned that a nuclear program might divert resources from conventional arms purchases or that another service might gain control over the bomb.

13. Even Nehru left the option open by approving an experimental reprocessing facility; this facility produced the plutonium used in the 1974 Pokhran test.

14. This was discussed fully over twenty years ago, in the midst of a major Indian debate over nuclear strategy. For a survey see G.G. Mirchandani, *India's Nuclear Dilemma* (New Delhi: Popular Book Service, 1968).

15. This position has been most fully articulated by Pierre Gallois, Kenneth Waltz, and, in South Asia, by K. Subrahmanyam.

16. K. Subrahmanyam has ridiculed this Western fear.

17. Michael Intriligator and Dagobert Brito, "A Possible Future for the Arms Race," in N.P. Gleditsch and O. Jnolstad, eds., *Arms Races: Technological and Political Dynamics* (London: Sage Publications, 1989), Intriligator and Brito, "Nuclear Proliferation and Stability," *Journal of Peace Science*, Vol. 3, No. 2, Fall 1978, pp. 173-183 and Brito and Intriligator, "Proliferation and the Probability of War: Global and Regional Issues," in Brito, Intriligator, and Adele Wick, eds., *Strategies for Managing Nuclear Proliferation: Economic and Political Issues* (Lexington: Lexington Books, 1983).

18. For one estimate, widely discussed in India and Pakistan, see Rashid Naim, "Asia's Day After," in Stephen P. Cohen, ed., *The Security of South Asia: Asian and American Perspectives* (Urbana and Chicago: University of Illinois Press, 1987); for a revised and expanded version, see Chapter 2 of this book.

19. *The Hindu*, Feb. 28, 1990.

20. *Ibid.* See also K. Subrahmanyam, "A Nuclear Doctrine for India?" *The Hindu International Edition*, June 9, 1990.

21. One important exception was the 1962 Cuban missile crisis, which in President Kennedy's estimation, brought the risk of nuclear war to one chance in two or three. Theodore Sorensen, *Kennedy* (New York: Harper and Row, 1965), p. 705.

22. For a narrative account of this history see J. P. Jain, *India and Disarmament: Volume 1: An Analytical Study* (New Delhi: Radiant, 1974). For a selection of documents outlining India's position on a number of arms control issues see A. Appadorai, *Select Documents on India's Foreign Policy and Relations, 1947-1972; Volume II* (Delhi: Oxford University Press, 1985).

23. But it must be remembered that the India-China conflict is even more asymmetrical than the India-Pakistan conflict. India regards China as a major strategic threat, especially in view of Beijing's support for Islamabad; the Chinese do not view India as an equivalent threat, but regard Delhi as a surrogate

for larger states, e.g. the U.S. (from 1953 to 1965) and the Soviet Union (from 1962 to very recently).

24. Another reason, of course, is that many of those regional experts who understand the value of such measures in ameliorating political conflict are themselves partisans in such conflicts, and do not wish to see them resolved.

25. I am grateful to Judith Kipper for drawing my attention to the dual-victim image.

26. See Dunn, "Four Decades of Nuclear Non-Proliferation: Some Lessons from Wins, Losses, and Draws," in Joseph S. Nye, ed., *New Threats: Responding to the Proliferation of Nuclear, Chemical, and Ballistic Missile Capabilities in the Third World* (Aspen: The Aspen Strategy Group, 1990).

27. See the work of Brito and Intriligator, cited above.

28. Richard Haass, "South Asia: Too Late to Remove the Bomb?" *Orbis*, 32: 4, Winter, 1988, pp.107-118 and Haass, *Conflicts Unending: The United States and Regional Disputes* (New Haven: Yale University Press, 1990), p. 91. Recent revelations about U.S. help to the French nuclear establishment have also stimulated discussions about helping India or Pakistan move their nuclear programs to a more stable and secure level of weaponization. See Richard H. Ullman, "The Covert French Connection," *Foreign Policy*, Spring, 1989, pp. 3-33.

29. With considerable assistance from the U.S. See: United States General Accounting Office, *Weapons-Related Information and Technology Controls* (Washington, D.C.: GAO, RCED-89-116, 1989).

30. Shai Feldman discusses the prospects for overhang states, and regional and global stability, in "Managing Nuclear Proliferation," in Jed C. Snyder and Samuel F. Wells, Jr., eds., *Limiting Nuclear Proliferation* (Cambridge: Ballinger, 1985).

31. The speech of the Athenians to the Melians, recorded in Thucydides' *The Peloponnesian Wars* is an example of the first doctrine, the response of the Melians—resistance and destruction—an example of the second.

2

Aadhi Raat Ke Baad
("After Midnight")

S. Rashid Naim

The Bulletin of Atomic Scientists has a clock on which midnight would signal the outbreak of nuclear war between the superpowers. Tension between the superpowers is reflected by the minutes left to midnight. This study evaluates the likelihood of such a dreaded midnight occurring in South Asia, discusses the likely scenarios in a nuclear exchange between India and Pakistan, and estimates the likely subsequent damage.

It is imperative that those making decisions on the acquisition and use of nuclear weapons in South Asia should understand both what is known *and unknown* about the consequences of the use of nuclear weapons. Indeed, it may be more important to be aware of the extent to which the impact of the use of nuclear weapons cannot be predicted. This study discusses both the predictable and unpredictable effects of the use of nuclear weapons.

The Immediate Effects of Nuclear Weapon Use

An atomic explosion releases three forms of energy: blast, nuclear radiation, and thermal radiation (heat). Blast is a high-powered wind that is forced away from the point of explosion and is caused by a sudden increase in pressure around the area of blast leading to overpressure. Although it lasts for only a short time after an explosion, overpressure causes, directly or indirectly, most of the

23

material damage on the surface, or at low or moderate altitudes in the air. The magnitude of the blast effect depends on the yield of the weapon and the height of burst.

A second type of destructive energy released by a nuclear explosion is thermal radiation. Actually all the energy released by a nuclear explosion, including residual radiation from weapon debris, is thermal energy (heat), but what we define as thermal radiation is the part that can cause fire damage and personal injury.[1] Approximately 35 percent of the energy of a typical nuclear explosion at up to a height of 100,000 feet is in the form of thermal energy of this kind.[2]

Thermal radiation causes damage in two ways. First, it results in dangerous burns on human flesh. Second, depending upon the amount of combustible material in the area of the explosion, it can lead to massive fires. A single megaton weapon can cause third degree burns up to five miles away, second degree burns up to distances of six miles, first degree burns similar to sunburn up to seven miles away.[3] The distances up to which burns are caused depend upon weather conditions; the behavior pattern of thermal energy is similar to that of sunlight. Thermal radiation also results in massive fires. According to some estimates, up to 10 percent of the buildings within the 5 psi (pounds per square inch) ring may catch fire, whereas within the 2 psi ring, about 2 percent of the buildings may sustain fire damage.[4] The vertical updraft of heated air may cause a firestorm which can be made worse by existing winds.[5] Temperatures can exceed 1,000°C.

A nuclear explosion also releases two forms of radiation: direct nuclear radiation and fallout. Direct nuclear radiation is a stream of atomic particles which may be injurious or fatal to a human being, depending upon the extent of exposure. Fallout is nuclear radiation caused by contaminated debris lifted by the explosion and carried by the wind to other areas. A dose of 600 rem (Roentgen Equivalent Man) within a short period of time (six to seven days) could result in fatal illness among 90 percent of the population exposed. A dose of 450 rem within a short period of time could cause up to 50 percent fatalities. A dose of 300 rem would kill about 10 percent of those exposed.[6]

Long-Term Effects of Nuclear Weapon Use

Besides the long-term impact that would be caused by the destruction of structures and resources in the target area there are other long-term effects, both calculable and those which cannot be estimated. Among the long-term effects which can be calculated with reasonable precision are the effects of low-level ionizing radiation and damage to the ozone layer. Incalculable or unpredictable long-term effects which are possible include irreversible damage to the ecological system, impact on food production, and other unknown physical and biological effects.

Calculable Effects

Among the long-term effects of the use of nuclear weapons that can be calculated with some degree of precision is the effect of low-level ionizing radiation. We have already discussed the effects of intensive radiation above. Doses of ionizing radiation that are too small to cause immediate death or incapacitate those exposed can, nevertheless, have harmful effects in the long-term. Such exposure to low-level radiation can be caused by sublethal doses from the nuclear blast itself, by being on the fringes of the fallout zone of a nuclear blast, or by delayed fallout from debris deposited in the troposphere and stratosphere. Low-level radiation could continue to be accumulated in body organs in harmful quantities for as long as forty years after the initial explosion.[7] Such exposure can cause increased risk of cancer of all types.[8] It is also expected to cause chromosomal damage leading to increased abortions and genetic defects among newborns.[9] Calculations based on the effect of a large nuclear exchange between the United States and the Soviet Union predict an increase by several millions in cancer deaths. These figures are for attacks not specifically aimed at civilian areas and not using weapons designed to release high levels of radiation. If the latter were the case, much higher levels of cancer increases may be expected.[10]

Large nuclear explosions would also inject quantities of nitrogen oxide into the stratosphere. This is likely to contribute towards the thinning of the ozone layer.[11] Though nuclear exchanges of the intensity discussed here are unlikely to inject large quantities of nitrogen oxide into the stratosphere the impact of smaller amounts cannot be ignored.

Then there are the effects that nuclear war would have on the economic, social and political order in India and Pakistan. These too can be classified as long-term effects, some of which can be predicted and others cannot. The extent to which nuclear war would affect society in these areas is dependent upon the nature of the exchange and will be discussed under each of the scenarios below.

Incalculable Effects

The effects of nuclear war that cannot be predicted or calculated are as important as effects for which calculations can be attempted. Among the expected effects of nuclear weapons that cannot be calculated are irreversible changes in the weather pattern and environment,[12] mutations in plant and animal life,[13] and unpredictable changes in the social and political order which cannot be predicted. Though such effects would only be significant in a nuclear exchange of massive proportions, exchanges of the type likely to occur in South Asia could still have some impact in these areas.

Prediction of Effects

Any prediction of the effects of a nuclear war must be prefaced by a statement on the problems of making such predictions and their imprecise nature. This applies in particular to the long-term effects of nuclear war. For instance death and destruction caused by fires from explosions cannot be calculated with precision because they will be dependent on such variables as weather conditions, details of building construction, time of day, precise point of detonation of the nuclear device and the extent to which emergency services remain operational.

Similarly the number of casualties from fallout would depend upon variables such as size and nature of the attack, population distribution, population posture during and after an attack, wind speed and direction, time of day when attack occurs, etc.

Precise calculation of the number of deaths caused by cancer over a period of several decades is complicated by such uncertainties as age breakdown of the population, degree of protection available, population posture following an attack, and the time of year when the attack occurs.

Predictions about deaths caused by economic, social and political disruption are heavily dependent on the nature of the attack, warning time prior to attack, the psychological impact of the attack, and other unpredictable factors.

The rate and efficiency of political and economic recovery cannot be predicted with certainty. It is possible to calculate direct economic damage by assuming the size and location of the explosions, and the hardness of economic assets; however, the issues of bottlenecks and synergy cannot be addressed by such assumptions. Similarly economic and political recovery would be influenced by whether the war ended or continued after a nuclear exchange.

In calculating the damage from fallout we have assumed that the season is Monsoon/Winter, the wind direction is Northeast and wind speed 10 Mph, that the populations are unprotected, and that there is either very little or no warning time.

This study uses two sizes of weapons—20 kilotons and 1 megaton—to calculate the immediate effects of nuclear weapons. Several reasons dictate these sizes. First, a 15 to 20 kiloton bomb is within India's manufacturing capability. Second, if a fission-fusion-fission device (hydrogen bomb) is developed by either or both countries, the likely size will be 1 megaton, because weapons with larger yields would have a diminishing, marginal effect, given the size of likely targets. Large nuclear weapons are likely to be used against civilian targets as part of a countervalue strategy, and given the size of most urban centers in South Asia, a one megaton weapon would be of sufficient strength to achieve the objective of destroying them.

Because we only discuss the use of 20 kT or 1 MT weapons (and because some of the data on effects are available only for one of these sizes or for a different size altogether), a scaling formula is used to convert the area of a psi ring from an explosion of one size to the area of a psi ring of the same strength from an explosion of another size. This formula is:

$$\frac{D}{D'} = \left[\frac{W}{W'^{\circ}}\right]^{1/3}$$

Where W' is the kT yield from an explosion of known size, D' is the distance from the point of explosion of W' yield where a given overpressure occurs, W is the kT yield from another explosion, and D is the distance from the point of explosion of W yield where the same level of overpressure as in a W' yield explosion will occur.[14]

The psi ring is useful because some investigators calculate death and injuries by assuming that all people inside the 5 psi ring will die, and nobody outside it will die.[15] The same method is used in this study to predict deaths and injuries. The area (square miles) within the 5 psi ring is designated the lethal area, that is, the area within which all persons are killed. The lethal area is computed by means of the following formula: $A = \pi r^2$ where A is the area within the 5 psi ring, r is the radius of the 5 psi ring, and π is 3.1416. The number of deaths caused by a weapon Td is determined by multiplying the given population density Pd by the lethal area A (Td = Pd x A).

A study of casualty figures from the Hiroshima and Nagasaki bombings and projected casualties in simulated nuclear exchanges between the U.S. and the USSR[16] shows that in nuclear explosions injuries generally do not exceed deaths, and when they do so it is only by a small fraction. In this study, just as we have used the 5 psi ring as the limit of the lethal area, we have also used the 2.2 psi ring as the outer limit of the injury zone; all persons outside the 5 psi ring but within the 2.2 psi ring are injured, and none outside the area of the 2.2 psi ring are injured. This formulation is based on the following reasoning: a study of the casualty figures, real and projected, in the above sources showed that the number of deaths declines sharply beyond the 3.25 psi ring and becomes relatively negligible beyond the 1.2 psi ring, whereas the number of injured survivors is the highest within the area between these two rings. Taking the median point between the 3.25 and 1.2 psi rings, we have therefore estimated that everyone between the 5 psi ring and the 2.2 psi ring will be injured, and no one beyond the 2.2 psi ring will suffer injuries. Like the use of the 5 psi ring to determine the lethal area, the use of the 2.2 psi ring to determine the zone of injury will make the task of calculating casualties easier without making too great a sacrifice in accuracy.

Property damage is defined in terms of square miles of built-up area destroyed. The 2 psi ring is used to determine property damage.[17] Using the calculation system in Glasstone and Dolan,[18] the area likely to be destroyed is shown in Table 2.1. Variations in terrain and the possibility of a firestorm could affect these property damage figures by a factor of up to five.[19] As we shall see, certain features peculiar to South Asia would sharply increase the number of fatalities and injuries and amount of property damage implied by the method of calculation used in Table 2.1. Casualty and damage figures projected by the above means are somewhat optimistic; actual figures are likely to be higher. Finally, it should be remembered that the figures generated by the above method are only approximations.

Long-term effects from fallout have been calculated using the method described in Glasstone and Dolan.[20] The debris raised by the size and type of explosion (20 kT surface or 1 MT air) was calculated for each target. A wind speed of 10 mph is assumed and the amount of fallout descending over various distances from the explosion was calculated (See Table 2.2). Idealized unit-time dose-rate patterns created were then superimposed over a map of the area. Population density in the affected area was calculated to arrive at the number of people exposed to fallout radiation.

Factors Peculiar to South Asia

Some factors peculiar to the South Asian region could affect the extent of damage and number of casualties caused by a nuclear exchange between India and Pakistan. First, in terms of numbers the casualty figures in a South Asian nuclear exchange would be much higher than those likely to occur in a nuclear exchange in Europe, North America or the USSR. This is because of the higher population density in South Asia. However, lower levels of urbanization would mean that in percentage terms a smaller proportion of the total population would be destroyed in a South Asian nuclear exchange than in one in Europe, North America or the USSR.

TABLE 2.1 Property Damage from Nuclear Blasts

Weapon Yield	Type of Burst	Radius of 2 psi Ring (miles)	Area Destroyed (mi.²)*
20 kT	Air	2.2	15.2
20 kT	Surface	1.4	6.1
1 MT	Air	8	200.9
1 MT	Surface	5	78.5

*$A = \pi r^2$ = column 3

TABLE 2.2 Calculations for Idealized Unit-Time Reference Dose-Rate Contours for 20 Kilotons, 50% Fission, Surface Burst, 10 mph Effective Wind Speed

1 Reference Dose Rate (rad/hr)	2 Downward Distance (miles)	3 Max Width (miles)	4 Ground Zero Width (miles)	5 Scaled Down Distance Col. 2 x F
3,000	3.66	0.10	0.15	3.05
1,000	6.93	0.35	0.33	5.77
300	0.94	0.85	14.43	17.33
100	2.30	1.40	28.54	34.56
30	4.07	1.80	51.31	61.60
10	6.85	2.32	77.00	92.40
3	9.83	3.04	96.20	115.50
1	14.00	5.12	128.30	154.00

Wind scaling factor = $v = 1 + \dfrac{v - 5}{30} = 0.833$

Contour Calculation based on Table 9.93 in Glasstone and Dolan, *Effects of Nuclear Weapons*.

Note: Wind scaling neglected in calculation of width of contours.

Average width of 30 rad/hr Contour = 3.0 miles
Average length of 30 rad/hr Contour = 51.31 miles
Average area of 30 rad/hr Contour = 154 sq miles
Average width of 1 rad/hr Contour = 9.6 miles
Average length of 1 rad/hr Contour = 128.3 miles
Average area of 1 rad/hr Contour = 1227 sq miles

Second, the damage caused by thermal effects is likely to be more severe than in Europe, North America, or the USSR because of the limited firefighting capabilities in the two South Asian countries.

Third, burn injuries would be a more severe medical problem. The high death rate among burn victims who do not receive prompt treatment and the relatively sparse medical resources available could lead to very high mortality rates among the initial survivors of the attack. There are only 48 physicians and 61 hospital beds per 100,000 persons available in Pakistan and only 35 physicians and 74 hospital beds per 100,000 persons in India.[21]

Fourth, although in more economically developed countries post-attack casualties could be limited by relying on the medical, shelter, and economic resources of small- and medium-sized cities, this may not be true in South Asia. Except for a few large cities, neither India nor Pakistan (and especially the latter) has the necessary resources. In fact, it is very doubtful that post-attack recovery is possible for either country without massive outside assistance. Consequently, one more point should be borne in mind: it is misleading to compare nuclear wars involving countervalue attacks (strikes against cities) with natural disasters. Nuclear attacks focus on the destruction of industrial, technological and administrative structures; those very institutions and assets that allow recovery from the effects of a natural disaster would themselves be totally destroyed.

Fifth, in economically less-developed countries a very high percentage of national value (administrative, technical, and industrial infrastructures) can be destroyed with relatively few warheads, since these are concentrated in small areas. Further destruction would require a large number of warheads. Only a few populated centers have to be hit to destroy what a nation values. The positive aspect, if there is any, is that such concentration of infrastructure will keep civilian casualties confined to a few areas. This point should be kept in mind when discussing effects of a nuclear exchange between India and Pakistan and is especially applicable to the latter.

There are political and social factors peculiar to South Asia which are likely to affect casualties and destruction. These include the "soft" nature of both India and Pakistan as states and, in the case of India, communal violence. Both states have within their borders linguistic and ethnic minorities which may not share war objectives and may see in the destruction caused by the war the chance to break away from the state. Regional and ethnic tensions are also likely to be exacerbated by disagreement over the regional priority in allocation of scarce resources for recovery. In the case of India communal rioting between Hindu and Muslims on a large scale is a possibility. Such riots are likely to be the result of Hindu anger towards "Muslim" Pakistan. These political crises are likely to further hamper the task of post attack recovery. It is conceivable that the political crises following a nuclear exchange may lead to the breakup of both India and Pakistan.

Weapon Systems and Their Impact on Strategy

Certain basic characteristics of any future Indo-Pakistani nuclear balance should be noted. In a nuclearized South Asia India's greater resources and higher level of technological achievement would probably allow it to develop and maintain a substantial lead over Pakistan in the number of warheads. In the absence of a weapons manufacturing program in either country, it is not possible to project accurate figures about the number of warheads likely to be possessed by the two countries at a given future point in time. A recent study of small nuclear forces estimates that in 1982, India had the potential to produce enough fissile material for a maximum of 53 warheads per year. Similarly Pakistan's potential production capacity would be 21 warheads per year in 1990.[22] It must be noted that these figures are upper boundary estimates that assume efficient production and use of fissile material. The yield of these warheads would be the smallest possible needed to achieve an explosive chain reaction. Therefore these figures should be considered a loose general estimate rather than a precise measure of the equivalent megatonnage (EMT) or throw-weight capacity that the two nations are capable of producing.

The second chief feature of an India-Pakistan nuclear balance would be the relative vulnerability of the two countries. Pakistan's smaller size and greater accessibility to Indian attack aircraft make it more vulnerable than India in case of a nuclear exchange. Even one-way suicide attack missions which would substantially increase the range of Pakistani aircraft would not cover all of India.

What about delivery systems?. At this time both countries have modern aircraft capable of delivering nuclear weapons. India has the MiG-23, MiG-25, and MiG-27, Jaguar, and Mirage 2000, while Pakistan has the Mirage III and V and the F-16. Whereas all of Pakistan is within range of Indian aircraft, only the Northwestern and Western regions of India are within range of Pakistani aircraft unless Pakistan launches one-way suicide missions. However, there are other delivery systems. It is well within India's capability to develop IRBMs by the end of this decade. It already has successfully carried out tests of the medium range *Agni* missile which has a range of 930 miles (see maps 2.1 and 2.2). India has developed the capability to put reconnaissance satellites into orbit, and the INSAT satellites, now in orbit, substantially upgrade India's command and control capabilities. India is currently designing a powerful liquid-fuel rocket which could also serve as a delivery vehicle for nuclear warheads.[23] If India were to deploy IRBMs with a range of about 930 miles, it could maintain a nuclear strike force out of the range of Pakistani aircraft, yet capable of hitting almost all of Pakistan. Thus if and when the two countries acquire nuclear weapons, they will also have delivery systems; there need not be a time lag between the acquisition of the two.

Use of Nuclear Weapons in South Asia

The crucial issue remains: What are the chances of actual use of nuclear weapons by India and Pakistan against each other? Assuming that rationality and perspective are retained by regional decisionmakers during a period of crisis, an examination of the constraints and incentives involved leads us to the conclusion that such use is very unlikely for a series of pragmatic reasons— domestic, regional, international, and geographic.

Deterrence

Pakistani debate on nuclear doctrine seems to have followed the line of thinking associated with the evolution of nuclear strategy elsewhere; that is, to adopt the general principles of deterrence, the main adversary being India. Advocates of nuclear weapons in India also justify their demands on the basis of the deterrence value of nuclear weapons against both China and Pakistan./

For Pakistan, the threats to strategic and military security are permanent and lethal. Most of these threats are associated with Pakistan's security dilemma vis-à-vis India, and until recently, the Soviet occupation of Afghanistan. These external threats are compounded by internal instability and inadequate resources.[24] For Pakistan, the possession and use of nuclear weapons for deterrence is very attractive and the idea could become even more acceptable as the imbalance in conventional military strength between Pakistan and India increases in favor of the latter. Indeed, it is possible to stand the proliferation chain argument on its head. The argument has been that if China acquired nuclear weapons, India would acquire them and this in turn would lead to a Pakistani bomb. We can instead argue that Pakistan needs nuclear weapons to offset India's conventional military superiority. In order to prevent Pakistan from using these nuclear weapons for compellence (for example, in Kashmir) rather than deterrence, India needs nuclear weapons. As K. Subrahmanyam puts it (although in a different context), "nuclear weapons can be deterred only by nuclear weapons."[25] The proliferation of nuclear weapons into South Asia may follow this pattern.

If the two nations develop striking power to the extent that their respective nuclear forces serve only to cancel each other out, diplomatic, political, and perhaps even conventional military interactions may proceed in much the same manner as before. There would be, however, one important difference. Direct external threats from India to the very existence of Pakistan as a state could no longer exist. On one hand, this could lead to fewer restraints on adventurist tendencies among Pakistani leaders; on the other hand, it would remove what is felt by many to be the root cause of the continuing conflict between the two countries, the widespread feeling in Pakistan that India is bent on dismembering their country. The possession of nuclear weapons could enable Pakistan to inflict unacceptable punishment on India should the latter threaten its very existence. The positive effects of an increased sense of security among the Pakistani elite might outweigh any negative impact caused by increased adventurism in its leadership. Although both nations have committed acts of brinkmanship in the past, policy formation and crisis behavior have on the whole been pragmatic and sober. Indeed, the acquisition of nuclear weapons by both sides may prevent even conventional wars between the two countries as leaders exercise extra caution for fear of starting a nuclear conflagration.

The successful maintenance of a credible deterrence posture by the two countries against each other would, however, not be a simple matter. First of all it would require superior Pakistani technical ability to offset India's larger nuclear arsenal (which is inevitable given India's greater resources and the threat it faces from a nuclear China), and the fact that, whereas all of Pakistan is within strike range of Indian planes and missiles, all of India, including potential missile launching areas is not within range of Pakistan (see Figures 2.1 and 2.2). Thus Pakistan would need superior technology to prevent India from carrying out a preemptive first strike against Pakistani nuclear forces. Given India's current technical superiority, it is hard to envisage Pakistan acquiring the needed. In the absence of such security for a Pakistani force, acquisition of nuclear weapons would be more destabilizing than stabilizing, because the temptation to use the weapons before they are destroyed would be great.

A related factor that could lead to similar premature use is Pakistan's possible inability to deliver a nuclear weapon under certain wartime conditions. It has been pointed out that if Pakistan were in such dire military straits that it actually decided to use nuclear weapons against an attacking enemy, it might have already lost the military ability to deliver the warheads.[26] As in the case of insufficiently protected nuclear weapons, such a situation would be very destabilizing. Since it alone would be capable of determining when the capability to deliver warheads is about to be lost, the decision when to use nuclear weapons in a conventional war could be left solely to the military.

A third problem with nuclear deterrence in the India-Pakistan dyad is that of command and control. Unless both countries developed strong C^3I (command, control, communications, and information), Pakistan, and to a more limited extent, India, would face a trade-off between viability and stability. In Pakistan's case weak C^3I might encourage the adoption of Launch on Warning

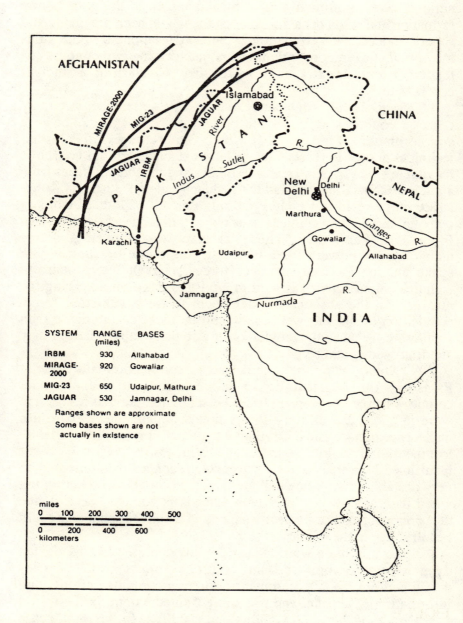

FIGURE 2.1 Range of Indian Delivery Systems.

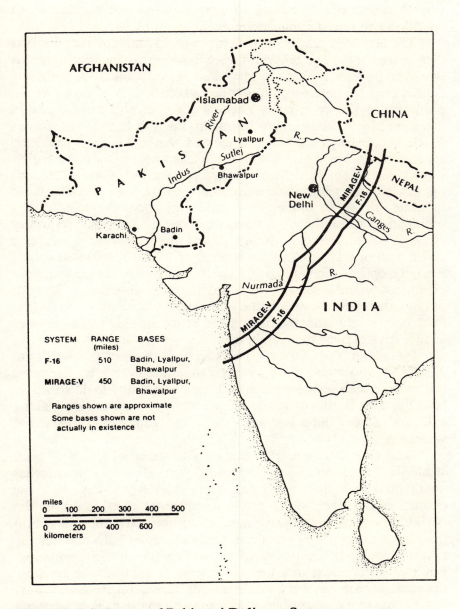

FIGURE 2.2 Range of Pakistani Delivery Systems.

(LoW) postures. Needless to say, LoW is not conducive to confidence in robust mutual deterrence.

These three major problems would destabilize nuclear deterrence. If the two countries were to acquire nuclear weapons, it would be imperative that steps be taken to overcome these problems so that credible deterrence might be established. We have already pointed out the conditions necessary for establishing credible deterrence by Pakistan and the problems that it is likely to encounter in meeting them. It must be asserted here that unless these problems are overcome, the introduction of nuclear weapons into the region would be extremely destabilizing. If Pakistan were to acquire nuclear weapons but not the necessary technology to make them invulnerable to an Indian first strike, the incentive to launch a preemptive strike during a crisis or adopt a Launch-on-Warning strategy would be great. Such vulnerability of Pakistani weapons could also provide India with incentives to use nuclear weapons. First, the option of neutralizing Pakistani nuclear weapons with little or no loss would be available to Indian decision makers. Second, the fact that, being aware of the vulnerability of their weapons, the Pakistanis might launch a preemptive strike would in turn serve as an incentive to India to preempt them.

Protection is not enough. Pakistan must develop a capability to deliver such weapons during a crisis situation, even after its armed forces have been severely mauled. Lack of an ability to do so would have the same impact on the deterrence strategy and decision-making calculus of both India and Pakistan as the vulnerability of actual warheads.

Adequate C^3I is needed not only to deter adoption of such strategies as Launch on Warning, but also to ensure that unauthorized use does not occur. Both sides would have to know enough about each other's C^3I to promote confidence in the unlikelihood of preemptive and unauthorized use. It would therefore be necessary to establish communication links between the two that are specifically geared to such exchange of information. Finally, other measures are necessary to establish a credible deterrent. These measures would include successful communication by one side to the other of an ability and will to use nuclear weapons if the security of the state is threatened beyond a certain point. It would also be necessary for both countries to enunciate a clear deterrence doctrine that would inform the other side about the conditions under which a non-nuclear conflict situation would escalate into nuclear conflict.

Compellence

Compellence—forcing another state to do something by threatening a nuclear strike—would only work if one side were to have a monopoly of nuclear weapons or a military superiority that would make it impossible for the "compellee" to retaliate against the "compellor." At the very least, the demands made by the "compellor" should not be viewed as so outrageous or so destructive to the nationhood of the "compellee" as to make these demands unacceptable even under threat of nuclear attack. If the "compellee" had a nuclear force of its own, chances of successful compellence would be very low indeed. One of our assumptions has been that both sides acquire nuclear weapons and the means to deliver them. Under such conditions, using nuclear weapons for compellence is impractical.

Let us take the example of Kashmir. It is hard to imagine either India or Pakistan giving up the areas of Kashmir under their control to the other side because of nuclear threats, especially if both had nuclear weapons. Both countries consider control over their part of Kashmir vital to their national character, albeit for different reasons. Neither would give up control in the face of nuclear threats that could be countered by nuclear weapons in its own possession.

The successful use of nuclear weapons for compellence by one side would lead to a rapid escalation of such use, a situation equally unacceptable to both sides because of the destabilizing effects it would have and the risk of a subsequent nuclear exchange. Thus constraints on use of nuclear weapons for compellence are strong, and it is doubtful if attempts at such use would succeed.

Tactical Use

Nuclear weapons may also be used to attack field formations during battle. It is our contention that differentiating between the tactical and strategic uses of nuclear weapons in the South Asian context is fallacious because of the number of civilian casualties that would occur on both sides. The situation here is different from that in Europe, where the use of "tactical" nuclear weapons would not kill Russian and American civilians. European civilians would of course die, and it is for this reason that the Europeans don't see much difference between strategic and tactical weapons. The damage and loss of life that would occur in South Asia from "tactical" use makes distinctions between tactical and strategic a cruel and dangerous joke. Escalation of tactical use into counter-city strikes is almost inevitable, given the extent of damage that would be caused by tactical use. Any quick, decisive result in a war is likely to come out of a battle in Punjab or Kashmir. It is this sector of the India-Pakistan border that has the highest level of troop deployment, and it is in this area that tactical nuclear weapons are most likely to be used. Given the high population density along both sides of the border in the Punjab-Kashmir sector, collateral civilian casualties and damage are likely to be very high. Once nuclear weapons, even tactical ones, have caused extensive damage and casualties in such border urban centers as Amritsar, Gujranwala, Ferozpur, Gurdaspur, Pathankot, Srinagar, Fazilka, Baramula, Lahore, Sialkot, Kasur, Gujarat, and Jhelum, the chances of escalation into counter-city strikes are very great. Using tactical nuclear weapons against field formations in the Punjab-Kashmir sector would be tantamount to a large scale exchange between the two parties.

Use of tactical nuclear weapons further south along the Rajasthan and Gujarat border would not cause widespread collateral civilian casualties because of the relatively sparse population along both sides of the border in that sector. Therefore tactical use of weapons in this sector would not necessarily escalate into counter-city strikes. The danger remains, however, that once the nuclear threshold is crossed, such escalation would occur.

This discussion on use of tactical weapons has assumed that such use would be made against military formations of the other side before they cross the border. Once forces of one side have crossed the border and occupied populated areas of the other side, the latter would face a situation where use of tactical nuclear weapons against the enemy would cause the deaths of large numbers of its own population. Under such circumstances a country might choose to use nuclear weapons in a warning or symbolic attack to force the enemy to stop his advance, vacate occupied territory, or both. The dangers of escalation from such use to counter-city strikes have already been discussed. On the other hand if a country decides to use tactical nuclear weapons against enemy forces on its own territory and incurs substantial civilian casualties in the process, it may launch attacks on some of the enemy's population centers to compensate for its losses. The chance of an escalation to large-scale attacks on civilian targets in such a situation is self-evident.

Besides the danger pointed out above, two additional factors add to the risks of actual use of nuclear weapons if "tactical" weapons are developed and deployed. First, tactical nuclear weapons would provide policymakers with what could be perceived as an intermediate option between no-use and annihilation: this would undermine deterrence. Second, and because of the first, it would be easier to make the decision to use nuclear weapons in the hope that "tactical" use against military targets would limit retaliation by the other side to similar levels. As we have seen, however, once nuclear weapons have been used in any form, rationality and restraint are likely to be weakened, creating a situation that could lead to counter city strikes. Such escalation might result from miscalculation about the enemy's real intentions, or a steady escalation of use of smaller yield weapons into use of larger yield weapons.

The development of tactical nuclear weapons by India and Pakistan is not unlikely and is the main danger that would arise from acquisition of nuclear weapons by the two countries.

Other Constraints

The ultimate constraint on using nuclear weapons in a situation where both sides have them is of course Mutual Assured Destruction (MAD). However, other international, regional, domestic, and geographic constraints, some fairly strong, also exist in South Asia.

Use of nuclear weapons in any but the most extraordinary situation is unlikely because of several international and regional factors. For India, the main regional constraint is the China factor. Any use of nuclear weapons against Pakistan would have to take into consideration the impact on Chinese-Indian relations. Even if China were to stand by and do nothing, such an attack would be likely to lead to a nuclear arms race with China.

Then, of course, devastation from a nuclear war would open the door for the penetration of outside powers—China, the Soviet Union, and the United States—into the subcontinent. There is also the problem of setting a precedent. Small and medium-sized powers do not want to legitimize the use of nuclear weapons because they would then be open to similar attacks or threats from the big powers, with whose huge arsenals of nuclear weapons they cannot hope to compete.

Another constraint on the use of nuclear weapons might be the composition of India's population. Any strikes on major urban centers in India would cause many casualties among India Muslims (who are intermixed with the non-Muslim population). Table 2.3 shows the percentage of Muslims in the populations of towns likely to be hit in a counter-city strike of the sort outlined in Scenario C.

It is not my contention here that the Indian Muslim factor would prevent an attack on Indian cities; rather, for several reasons, it would be a major constraint on Pakistani behavior in all but the most severe of crises, e. g., where the very existence of Pakistan was at stake. The more important of these reasons are: the ideology behind the creation of Pakistan, the maintaining of which is essential for the continued existence of the state; the role that Pakistan has sought to play in the Muslim world; the support and concern, at least rhetorical, for the Muslims of India expressed by all sections of the Pakistani elite; the likely rise in influence of Hindu communal organizations in India which would take advantage of heightened anti-Muslim sentiments, and, last but not least, close familial ties between Indian Muslims and Pakistanis of Indian origin (*Muhajirs*). The latter are an important force in Pakistani politics and hold key political and bureaucratic positions. Here it is important to note that, contrary to the arguments made by some Indian analysts,[27] the more conservative, religious, and Jihad-oriented a Pakistani government is, the less likely it is to use nuclear weapons against India because of the impact, both direct and indirect, such an attack would have on Indian Muslims, and on Pakistan's own position within the Muslim world. It must be noted that once the decision to use nuclear

TABLE 2.3 Percentage of Muslims in Projected Population of Indian Towns Likely to Be Targets in a Pakistani Counter-City Strike

City	Population (1990)*	Percentages Muslim	Muslim Pop. (col 1 x col 2)
Bombay	11,914,900	14.12	1,682,400
Delhi	9,118,600	7.40	674,800
Ahmedabad	3,164,100	14.58	461,300
Agra	1,041,800	16.34	170,200
Gwalior	944,300	15.00	141,600
Jaipur	904,600	18.71	169,300
Baroda	821,400	12.00	98,600
Amritsar	813,500	0.42	3,400
Indore	798,900	12.41	99,100
Ludhiana	775,800	0.10	800
Surat	693,500	24.00	166,500
Jalandhar	590,900	0.08	500
Meerut	528,400	39.00	206,100
Jodhpur	467,000	20.00	93,400
Ghaziabad	174,700	24.00	41,900
TOTAL	32,752,400		4,009,900

* Based on 1971 or 1981 census. The prevailing growth rate in each city has been used to project the 1990 population.

Source: *Statistical Pocket-Book of India 1980* (New Delhi: Ministry of Planning, Government of India, 1981), pp. 5, 10-12; N. A. Siddiqui, *Population Geography of Muslims of India* (New Delhi: S Chand & Co., 1976), pp. 66-98.

weapons is taken, targeting is unlikely to be influenced by these considerations.

On the other hand, Indian Muslims would also be a factor in the Indian government calculations if that government ever planned to launch a nuclear strike against Pakistan. It should be understood clearly that although the loyalty of Indian Muslims to India is not in question, at the same time the fact that Indian Muslims have close familial ties with a large percentage of the population of Pakistan's largest urban center, Karachi, cannot be ignored. Again, such considerations might restrain rather than prevent Indian decision makers from using nuclear weapons. In this regard it is worth noting that in past conflicts between the two countries, some of them very bitter, neither side has resorted to indiscriminate attacks on population centers. In the case of the 1971 civil war in Pakistan, atrocities were committed against fellow Muslim South Asians by the Pakistani army. Given the consequences that followed, the likelihood that this will occur again is not very high.

There are also regional meteorological and geographical constraints on the use of nuclear weapons. The "heartland" of Pakistan—the Indus Valley region of Pakistani Punjab—runs parallel to the strategic, rich, and now restless state of Punjab in India. Any attack on Pakistani cities in this heartland would mean deaths and damage from fallout in Indian Punjab. Similarly, attacks on Indian Punjab cities, indeed even on Delhi, would result in some fallout deaths and damage in Pakistani Punjab. The extent of damage would depend on wind direction and force, which varies during the year. During the period of the Northeast Monsoon (December to March), fallout would be carried back to India. Similarly, during the Southwest Monsoon (June to September), fallout would be carried back to Pakistan. (See Figure 2.3) Therefore, to prevent damage to itself from fallout from its own weapons, India would have to attack during the months of April through October, whereas Pakistan would have to attack during the months of October through May. Even without strong winds, damage to the border regions of the two countries would be substantial. Fallout damage to the two Punjabs would be of great economic and political significance if the two countries were to survive as states after a nuclear war.

It is thus clear that besides Mutual Assured Destruction, other constraints exist on use of nuclear weapons in general and on their use for any other purpose than deterrence. These constraints would play an important restraining role. At the same time the importance of these constraints should not be overestimated. The best and most effective constraint would still be MAD.

As already noted, the chances of a strategic nuclear exchange between India and Pakistan (provided the conditions necessary to achieve nuclear stability outlined above are met) are very low. The probability of such an exchange is about the same as that of a

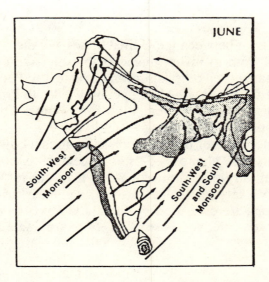

FIGURE 2.3 Seasonal Wind Patterns in South Asia.

Source: J. Bartholomew, *Oxford School Atlas of India, Burma, and Ceylon* (London: Oxford University Press, 1968), p. 15

strategic exchange between the United States and the Soviet Union. The ability of both to inflict unacceptable damage on the other, indeed, to threaten each other's survival as states and even societies, is deterrence enough. It would compel both sides to limit ambitions at the expense of the other, and force both elites to end exaggerations of external threats to security.

The development of tactical nuclear weapons, however, would sharply increase the chances of use of nuclear weapons. Even if such use is initially of a limited nature, it is, for reasons already discussed, very likely to escalate into major nuclear strikes. Thus if nuclear weapons are ever used by India and Pakistan against each other on a large scale, such use is likely to originate in a tactical exchange.

Scenarios

One can create scores of different scenarios likely to occur in a nuclear exchange between India and Pakistan. Three of the most likely ones are discussed here: attacks on military targets (Scenario A), attacks on military targets, energy and transportation centers (Scenario B) and counter-city strikes (Scenario C). All assume a political decision to use nuclear weapons. The dynamics and likelihood of such a decision are discussed later.

We will take up each of these scenarios, briefly identify the goals and targets, and calculate the estimated damage likely to result from each. For reasons already discussed, *the projected casualty figures in each scenario are necessarily only general estimates.*

Scenario A

This scenario envisages an attack by India and Pakistan on military targets and formations. Such an attack would hit major cantonments within striking range and would be a part of a strategy of compellence or would be designed to fulfill tactical military purposes. The goal would be the destruction of the enemy's major military formations either to preempt a conventional attack, or as a prelude to military action by the attacking side.

Since the aim would be to destroy concentrated military personnel and equipment, 20 kT weapons are likely to be used. These would fulfill the purpose of the attack and minimize collateral damage. For the same reason surface bursts are likely to be used which would result in 5 psi rings of a radius of .8 miles, 2.2 psi rings of a radius of 1.3 miles, and 2 psi rings with a radius of 1.4 miles.[28]

Tables 2.4 and 2.5 identify targets and summarize casualties likely to be caused by such an exchange. They also show the number of persons likely to be exposed to dangerous levels of fallout from the blasts. The contours showing areas likely to be affected by delayed fallout are shown on Fig. 2.4. The targets listed are mainly army cantonments. A nuclear attack by either country would also seek to destroy both nuclear weapons and delivery systems and would involve attacks on air fields and on missile sites. These attacks are likely to be carried out using 20 kT weapons set for surface burst. The number of airfields targeted would depend upon the deployment policy adopted by Pakistan. Two broad options are available. Given the accessibility of almost all of Pakistan to Indian aircraft, Pakistan might choose to concentrate its nuclear weapons and aircraft committed to a nuclear attack mission on a few air bases, concentrating its defenses on protecting these bases from a surprise attack. On the other hand, a strategy of dispersal might make it more difficult for India to carry out a preemptive strike. Whatever deployment policy is adopted, the location of nuclear weapon air bases is likely to optimize distance from the frontier (the farther away the better, giving more warning time in case of an attack) with penetrability of Pakistan's own air strikes (the shorter the distance from the frontier, the better). Given the above, the airfields likely to be used as bases for nuclear weapons include Badin, Bhawalpur, Peshawar, and Lyallpur. These would be targets of an Indian attack.

The greater range of Indian nuclear capable aircraft along with the fact that all of India cannot be reached by Pakistani aircraft (at least the new modern sophisticated aircraft—Canberra bombers, which have greater range, are slow and vulnerable) makes the Indian task of deployment less complicated. Likely air bases include Delhi, Mathura, Gwalior, Udaipur, and Jamnagar. Air bases located close to the frontier would not be used because they would be more

TABLE 2.4 Casualty and Damage Projections: Limited Attack on Military Centers of Pakistan

Target Cantonments	Population of City (1990)*	Immediate Estimated Deaths	Estimated Injuries** From Blast	Property Destroyed (sq mi)	Population of Area affected by 30 Rad/Hr Fallout ****	Population of Area Affected by 1 Rad/Hr Fallout ****
Karachi	8,337,100	128,900	211,541	6.16	30,000	206,000
Lahore	4,599,900	66,100	10,800	6.16	236,000	165,000
Rawalpindi	1,427,100	68,300	11,200	4.12	177,000	1,240,000
Hyderabad	1,088,000	44,600	73,200	4.12	118,000	825,000
Peshawar	383,100	27,500	45,100	3.08	138,000	962,000
Sialkot	283,200	20,400	33,400	6.16	217,000	1,513,000
Quetta	282,600	35,500	58,300	6.16	16,000	110,000
Bhawalpur	261,900	18,800	30,900	6.16	59,000	413,000
Wah Cantt.***	222,100	148,000	74,000	6.16	59,000	413,000
Gujrat	212,500	15,300	25,100	6.16	118,000	825,000
Sahiwal	51,600	3,700	6,100	6.16	138,000	962,000
TOTAL	17,149,100	577,100	579,641	60.60		

* Based on the 1972 census, the prevailing growth rate in each city has been used to project the size of the 1990 population. The exception is Wah, which grew by 194% between 1962 and 1972, because of the establishment of a major arms production center. The growth rate between 1972 and 1990 for Wah has therefore been calculated at 5.92%, the average growth rate of Pakistani cities. The 1962 and 1972 population figures are from *The Statistical Abstract of Pakistan 1980* (Government of Pakistan: Islamabad 1981), pp. 5-7. Figures have been rounded off. Population density and city area figures are from K.U. Kureshy, *A Geography of Pakistan* (Karachi: Oxford University Press, 1979), pp. 86-96. The population density throughout the area of each city is considered to be uniform. Figures have been rounded off.

** Population density throughout the area of each city is taken as being uniform. Figures have been rounded off.

*** 100% of the population of Wah cantonment will be affected because the large military contingent is located in the cantonment.

**** Based on Table 2.2 above.

TABLE 2.5 Casualty and Damage Projections: Limited Attack on Military Centers in Northwest India

Target Cantonments	Population of City (1990)	Immediate Estimated Deaths*	Estimated Injuries From Blast	Property Destroyed (sq mi)	Population of Area Affected by 30 mRad/Hr Fallout **	Population of Area Affected by 1 Rad/Hr Fallout **
Bombay	11,914,900	136,900	224,600	6.16	120,000	822,000
Delhi	9,118,600	40,700	66,900	4.62	240,000	1,624,000
Ahmedabad	3,164,100	153,500	251,900	3.08	120,000	822,000
Gowaliar	944,300	18,000	25,400	6.16	120,000	822,000
Baroda	821,400	4,200	6,900	6.16	120,000	822,000
Amritsar	813,500	15,500	21,900	6.16	240,000	1,624,000
Ludhiana	775,800	14,800	20,900	6.16	120,000	822,000
Jullandhar	590,900	11,300	15,900	6.16	120,000	822,000
Rajkot	529,100	10,10	14,200	6.16	59,000	431,000
Meerut	528,400	10,100	14,200	6.16	240,000	1,624,000
Jamnagar	408,400	79,300	13,000	6.16	30,000	206,000
Jhansi	337,300	6,400	9,100	6.16	30,000	206,000
Ajmer	334,300	6,400	9,000	6.16	30,000	206,000
Jammu	273,400	5,200	7,400	6.16	240,000	1,624,000
TOTAL	30,554,400	503,310	701,300	81.62		

Based on 1971 or 1981 census, the prevailing growth rate in each city has been used to project the size of the 1990 population. The figures are from *The Statistical Pocket Book of India 1980* (New Delhi: Ministry of Planning, Government of India, 1981), pp. 5, 10-12.
* Ground Zero is located at the center of each city. Population density and city area figures are from various sources, including Statistical Pocket Book. Figures have been rounded off.
** Based on Table 2.2.

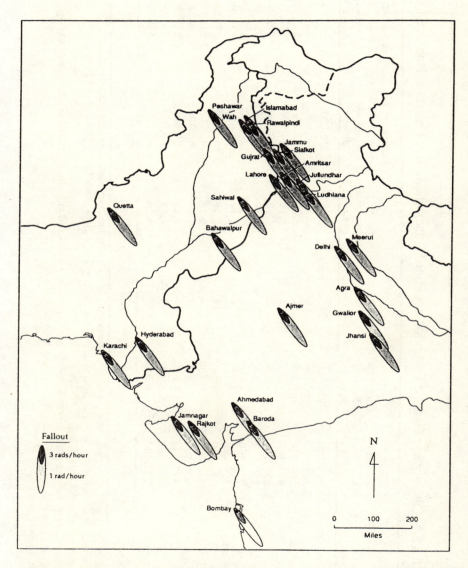

FIGURE 2.4 Fallout Contours from an Attack upon Selected Military Targets in Pakistan and Northwest India.

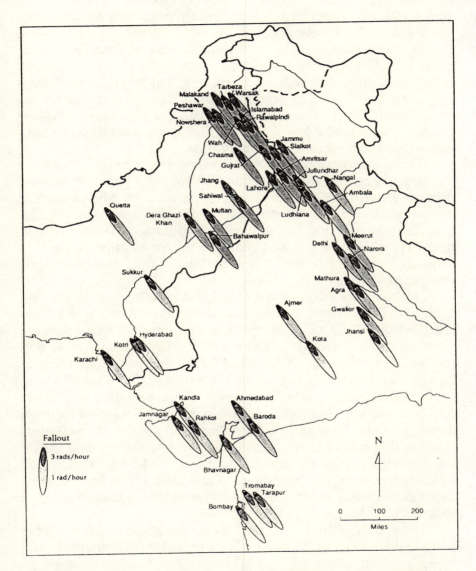

FIGURE 2.5 Fallout Contours from an Attack upon Selected Military, Energy and Transport Targets in Pakistan and Northwest India

vulnerable without any payoff in terms of increased penetrability of aircraft based there. India could deploy its IRBMs as far east as Allahabad and still cover the core areas of Pakistan. These missile sites could only be reached by Pakistani aircraft if they were to carry out one way attack missions.

Both countries might locate their nuclear attack forces at new air bases. Such bases may be built away from population centers to reduce casualties in case they are attacked. On the other hand, they might be built close to civilian centers and thus signal to the opposing side that an attack on these bases would cause so many civilian casualties that any chance of limiting the war and preventing more destructive scenarios was an illusion.

The discussion here has concerned itself with attacks on military targets in cantonments and on some air bases; it has not discussed attacks on units deployed on the frontier. Use of nuclear weapons against the latter would constitute tactical use. The probability of such use has already been discussed. Because of the mobility of these targets and changing deployment postures, it is difficult to project targets and casualties if field formations are threatened. No such attempt is made here.

It is clear from the above discussion that even an attack limiting itself to military targets in cantonments and airfields using relatively small weapons (20 kT), and trying to minimize collateral damage (surface bursts) would produce substantial death, injury, and destruction of property. Approximately 577,000 people are likely to be killed and about 580,000 injured in Pakistan (See Table 2.4). In India approximately 604,000 people would be killed and about 850,000 injured (See Table 2.5). Some of the reasons for high casualty figures have already been discussed above. An additional factor is that many major cantonments which would be targeted are located within or adjacent to cities. Some of the reasons for high casualty figures have already been discussed above. An additional factor is that many major cantonments are located within or adjacent to cities.

Long term effects are also likely to be as serious as the immediate effects. In Pakistan a total of 1,306,000 persons would be exposed to fallout of over 30 rad/hr and 7,634,000 would be exposed to fallout between 1 and 30 rad/hr (See Table 2.4). In India a total of 1,829,000 persons would be exposed to fallout of over 30 rad/hr and 12,477,000 would be exposed to fallout between 1 and 30 rad/hr. (See Table 2.5) Such exposure will lead to a sharp increase in cancer caused by radiation. Besides this large parts of the manufacturing and agricultural area of Northwest India and Northern Pakistan will be contaminated by fallout (See Figures 2.4 and 2.5). This will lead to major reduction in industrial and agricultural production.

Scenario B

This scenario envisages attacks by India and Pakistan on not only military targets but also on major transportation and energy centers. Such an attack would again aim at achieving compellence goals. The attacks on economic targets would be more harmful to Pakistan for several reasons. First, whereas India can attack almost any economic target within Pakistan, large parts of India's industrial heartland—central Uttar Pradesh, most of Maharashtra, and West Bengal—will be out of range of Pakistani aircraft (unless one-way suicide missions are undertaken). Second, attacks on economic targets would mean a decision to fight a prolonged war, which would enable India to mobilize its superior resources and wear down Pakistan's ability to resist.

The military targets in this scenario would be the same as in the first scenario. Tables 2.6 and 2.7 list likely economic targets in an exchange aimed at major transportation and energy centers.

Successful attacks on the targets listed in Table 2.6 would result in severe damage to Pakistan's economic infrastructure. For example, the destruction of the four hydroelectric and thermal power stations listed would reduce Pakistani thermal and hydroelectric power production from 1,583 to 715 million watts. The destruction of the Mangla and Tarbela dams would reduce water storage capacity by 16.6 million acre feet. The collateral damage caused to irrigation and water control systems would lead to major flooding in Southern Punjab. The destruction of railway centers would paralyze rail transport. Destruction of Karachi's port would lead to total disruption of sea communications. Large areas of Pakistan's Punjabi heartland would be exposed to fallout (see Figure 2.5). Much of the best agricultural land in the country would be contaminated.

TABLE 2.6 Energy and Transport Targets in Pakistan*

A. Energy	1) Hydroelectric power stations
	a) Mangla
	b) Warsak
	c) Tarbela
	d) Malakand
	2) Thermal power stations
	a) Multan
	b) Sukkur
	c) Sahiwal
	d) Gudu
	e) Hyderabad
	f) Kotri
	3) Nuclear power station
	a) Karachi
	4) Gas
	a) Sui gas fields
	5) Oil refineries
	a) Multan
	b) Attock
B. Nuclear Facilities	1) Heavy water
	a) Multan
	b) Karachi
	2) Enrichment
	a) Kahuta
	b) Sihala
	3) Fuel fabrication
	a) Chashma
	4) Reprocessing
	a) Chashma
	b) Rawalpindi
	5) Research reactor
	a) Rawalpindi
C. Transportation	1) Jhang Railway Junction
	2) Hyderabad Railway Junction
	3) Mianwali Railway Junction
	4) Karachi Railway Junction
	5) Karachi Port

* Choice of target is based upon economic value and size.

Although all economic targets in India will not be within range of Pakistani weapon systems, the damage there would still be grave. The fertile agricultural states of Punjab and Haryana as well as western Uttar Pradesh would be contaminated (see Figure 2.5). The

TABLE 2.7 Energy and Transport Targets in Northwest India*

A. Energy	1) Hydroelectric power stations

A. Energy   1) Hydroelectric power stations
   a) Trombay
   b) Bhakra
   c) Kotla
2) Thermal power stations
   a) Bhavnagar
   b) Agra
   c) Ahmedabad
3) Nuclear power stations
   a) Narora
   b) Tarapur
   c) Kota

4) Petroleum
   a) Bombay
   b) Baroda
   c) Mathura

B. Nuclear Facilities   1) Heavy Water
   a) Nangal
   b) Baroda
   c) Kota
2) Reprocessing/Enrichment
   a) Trombay
   b) Tarapur
3) Research Reactor
   a) Trombay

C. Transportation   1) Railways
   a) Agra Junction
   b) Delhi Junction
   c) Amritsar
   d) Ambala Cantt
   e) Bombay Central V.T.
   f) Baroda
2) Ports
   a) Bombay
   b) Kandla
   c) Jamnagar

*These targets are within range of Pakistani Mirage III and Mirage V and F-16 aircraft.

substantial industrial base of these parts of the country would also be wiped out or severely damaged. As in Pakistan collateral damage to dams and irrigation control systems would lead to widespread flooding.

Besides the deaths and injuries that would result immediately, the long-term impact of attacks on economic targets could include widespread famine, rampant epidemics, and the destruction of the two countries as viable economic systems.

The weapons used to achieve these results could have small yields. The civilian casualty figures in both countries would, of course, be much lower if attacks were limited to military targets only. Casualty figures for an exchange involving attacks on military, energy and transport targets have not been calculated because data is unavailable on the size and density of population in some of the areas listed in Tables 2.6 and 2.7.

A more widespread attack on military and economic targets could occur, but this would be a case of overkill because damage done by destroying targets listed in Tables 2.6 and 2.7 would be enough to cause total economic disruption in both countries. Such a scenario involving attacks on more targets could evolve, however, as a result of steady escalation during a war in which retaliatory strikes would gradually lead to attacks on relatively minor economic or military targets. Such a development is unlikely, if only because the number of nuclear warheads that will be available to the two countries in the near future is limited. In case of a really savage war, the following scenario is likely to occur.

Scenario C

A more deadly use of nuclear weapons would involve strikes aimed primarily at civilian population centers. This is possible if deterrence fails. Unlike the other scenarios, this would involve the deliberate destruction of urban centers and the infliction of the maximum possible civilian casualties. Therefore, weapons with higher yields and air, rather than surface, bursts are likely to be used. Either a 1 MT weapon or several weapons with smaller yields could be used against each target.

The 5 psi ring from a 1 MT air burst would have a radius of 4.4 miles, the 2.2 psi ring radius of 7.6 miles, and the 2 psi ring a radius of 8.1 miles.[29] Given the nature of most South Asian cities, very high casualties would result. For example, the entire area of the city of Lahore would fall within the "Lethal Zone." Tables 2.8 and 2.9 give likely targets in a counter-city strike scenario. It is estimated that a total of 17,508,000 people would die from the immediate effects of such an exchange in Pakistan and a total of 29,414,000 would die immediately in India.

Casualties are likely to be very high because of the congested nature of South Asian cities, the limited fire-fighting capabilities in most cities, limited medical facilities, and the total disruption of the administrative infrastructure on a national scale. More deaths are likely over the long term as many of the injured are unlikely to survive. Unlike the more developed countries, India and Pakistan would not be able to rely on the medical, administrative, and economic resources of the small- and medium-sized towns not hit in a nuclear war for relief operations.

The breakdown of political authority which is likely to follow such a widespread use of weapons could trigger an upsurge of secessionist activity in both India and Pakistan. Such events are likely to further slow the rate of economic and political recovery. Certainly, democratic political processes would be threatened.

Assuming that a fifteen mph wind is blowing over each city, fallout of 3,000 rem would cover a downwind area of 140 sq mi. (Exposure to more than 300 rem per week is likely to be fatal.) Thus eight such patterns covering an area of 1,120 sq. mi. would hover over Pakistan. Similar fallout patterns would cover an area of 2,100 sq mi in India, which would cause additional deaths from exposure to radiation. These deaths are not included in the estimates in Tables 2.8 and 2.9. Given the population density of some of the areas surrounding the major cities targeted in this scenario, the number of such deaths would be very high.

Conclusions

We reach the following conclusions about the usability of nuclear weapons in South Asia:

- The introduction of nuclear weapons into South Asia would not necessarily be destabilizing, provided that it was not too rapid and asymmetrical in nature.

TABLE 2.8 Targets in a Counter-City Strike against Pakistan

City	Projected Population(1990)*	Immediate Estimated Deaths
Karachi	8,337,100	6,252,000
Lahore	4,599,900	4,500,000
Lyallpur	2,064,300	2,000,000
Rawalpindi	1,427,100	1,400,000
Hyderabad	1,088,000	1,088,000
Multan	1,007,200	1,000,000
Gujranwala	885,300	885,000
Peshawar	383,100	383,000

* Populations have been calculated by projecting the growth rate for each city between 1962-72 to 1990. The 1962 and 1972 population figures are from *The Statistical Abstract of Pakistan 1980* (Islamabad: Government of Pakistan, 1981), pp. 5-7. Figures have been rounded off. Ground Zero is located at the center of each city. Population density and city area figures are from Kureshy, pp. 86-96. Figures have been rounded.

TABLE 2.9 Targets in a Counter-City Strike against India

City	Projected Population (1990)*	Immediate Estimated Deaths
Bombay	11,914,900	8,936,000
Delhi	9,118,600	9,100,000
Ahmedabad	3,164,100	3,100,000
Agra	1,041,800	1,020,000
Gwalior	944,300	940,000
Jaipur	904,600	900,000
Baroda	821,400	800,000
Amritsar	813,500	810,000
Indore	793,900	790,000
Ludhiana	775,000	770,000
Surat	693,500	690,000
Jalandhar	590,900	500,000
Meerut	528,400	500,000
Jodhpur	467,000	390,000
Ghaziabad	174,700	168,000

* Based on 1971 or 1981 census, the prevailing growth rate in each city has been used to project the size of 1990 population. The figures are from *The Statistical Pocket Book of India 1980* (New Delhi: Ministry of Planning, Government of India, 1981), pp. 5, 10-12. Ground Zero is located at the center of each city. Population density and city area figures are from various sources. Figures have been rounded.

- Nuclear weapons would probably be used to maintain a deterrence posture by both countries. However, four potential problems exist with regard to Pakistan's ability to maintain a stable and credible deterrence posture: its technical backwardness compared to India. The danger that Pakistan might lose the ability to deliver nuclear weapons because of losses suffered during conventional warfare; the relatively greater vulnerability of Pakistan to Indian attack than of India to Pakistani attack, and the need for the two sides to develop C^3I. These problems will have to be overcome to establish credible deterrence.
- The use of nuclear weapons for compellence would be impractical unless only one side had nuclear weapons. If both have nuclear weapons, their use to compel compromise on vital issues of national interest would not be possible.
- The major destabilizing effect of nuclear weapons would be caused by any policy to use them as tactical weapons. The adoption of such policies and the development of tactical nuclear weapons must therefore be prevented, if and when the two states acquire nuclear weapons.
- Besides MAD, other international, regional, domestic, and geographic constraints exist on use of nuclear weapons for any purpose besides deterrence. These constraints are significant.

The following conclusions can be reached about the nature and extent of damage caused by a nuclear exchange between India and Pakistan and the degree of confidence with which such effects can be predicted:

- Any use of nuclear weapons in the region, even on a small and limited scale, would cause very high civilian casualties and collateral damage and would be likely to cause escalation from a limited nuclear exchange into a major counter-city strike.
- The delayed effects of the use of nuclear weapons are as likely to be as important as the immediate effects.
- These delayed effects are difficult to calculate with precision, and decision makers must keep these incalculable effects of the use of nuclear weapons in mind when making decisions on the acquisition and use of weapons.

Thus the acquisition of nuclear weapons by India and Pakistan will not necessarily lead to instability in the region. If both sides acquire nuclear weapons, a policy of using them for deterrence would be established and, if rationality and perspective were retained by decision makers in times of crises, acquisition of nuclear weapons might actually lead to more stable relations between the two states. But if nuclear weapons are introduced into the region, it is imperative that this introduction be gradual and symmetrical and that the conditions necessary for a credible and robust deterrence be established.

Notes

1. S. Glasstone and P.J. Dolan, eds., *The Effects of Nuclear Weapons* 3rd ed. (Washington, D.C.: Department of Defense and Department of Energy, 1977), p. 276.

2. Office of Technological Assessment (OTA), Congress of the United States, *The Effects of Nuclear War* (Washington, D.C.: OTA Congress of the U.S., 1979), p. 20, and Glasstone and Dolan, *The Effects of Nuclear Weapons*, p. 277.

3. OTA, *Effects of Nuclear War*, p. 21.

4. *Ibid.*

5. K.N. Lewis, "The Prompt and Delayed Effects of Nuclear War," *Scientific American* , July, 1979, p. 40.

6. OTA, *Effects of Nuclear War*, pp. 19-20.

7. *Ibid.*, pp. 110-111.

8. *Ibid.*, pp. 111.

9. *Ibid.*

10. *Ibid.*, pp. 112.

11. *Ibid.*, pp. 112, 114.

12. See E.S. Batten, *The Effects of Nuclear War on the Weather and Climate* (Santa Monica: RAND Corporation, 1966); R.U. Ayers, *Environmental Effects of Nuclear Weapons* (Hudson Institute, 1965).

13. OTA, *Effects of Nuclear War*, pp. 114-115.

14. Glasstone and Dolan, p. 101.

15. OTA, *Effects of Nuclear War*, p. 19.

16. See Glasstone and Dolan, *Effects of Nuclear Weapons*, p. 544; OTA, *Effects of Nuclear War*, p. 37; and J H Barton & L D Weiler, *International Arms Control* (Stanford: Stanford University Press, 1976), p. 47.

17. OTA, *Effects of Nuclear War*, p. 35.

18. These calculations were made on the "Nuclear Bomb Effects Computer" in Glasstone and Dolan.

19. Lewis, Prompt and Delayed Effects, p. 38.

20. Glasstone and Dolan, chapter 9.

21. Figures based on Federal Bureau of Statistics, Government of Pakistan, *Pakistan Statistical Yearbook 1990* (Karachi: Manager of Publications, Government of Pakistan, 1989), p. 387 and Department of Statistics, Ministry of Planning, Government of India, *Statistical Abstract of India, 1985* (New Delhi: Department of Statistics, Ministry of Planning, Government of India, 1987), pp 547-48.

22. From Rodney W Jones, "Small Nuclear Forces," *Washington Papers*, No. 103 (Washington, D.C.: CSIA, 1984), p. 17.

23. J.F. Elkin and B. Fredricks, "Military Implications of India's Space Program," *Air University Review*, Vol. 34, No. 4, May-June, 1983, pp. 56-63.

24. See Stephen Philip Cohen, "Nuclear Issues and Security Policy in Pakistan," Paper delivered at the Annual Meeting of the Association of Asian Studies, Washington, D.C., March 1980, pp. 3-13.

25. K. Subrahmanyam, "Implications of Nuclear Asymmetry," in Subrahmanyam, ed., *Nuclear Myths and Realities* (New Delhi, 1981).

26. Cohen, p. 13.

27. See, for example, Maj.-Gen. D.K. Palit and P.K.S. Namboodiri, *Pakistan's Islamic Bomb* (New Delhi: Vikas Publications, 1979), pp. 114-115.

28. These have been calculated on the "Nuclear Bomb Effects Computer" in Glasstone and Dolan.

29. These have been derived using estimating methods in OTA, Chapter 2.

3

The Design of Verification Regimes

Nancy W. Gallagher

To aid development of successful, stable India-Pakistan[1] arms control accords, this chapter addresses four questions:

- What is the nature and logic of verification?
- What are the main steps in the verification process?
- What key considerations should be taken into account when designing verification regimes?
- How should verification proposals and regimes be evaluated?

Verifying a nuclear agreement requires more than knowledge of the relevant technologies and institutional arrangements. It also demands thorough understanding of the nature of verification and the politics of verification design. Arms control efforts have been stymied in the past because key players agreed to verification in principle, only to disagree radically over verification in practice. Furthermore, it will be shown that the success and stability of arms control endeavors can be undermined by verification designs which promote unilateral rather than cooperative approaches to security, and which may reduce, rather than enhance, the security of both sides.

Drawing on logical analysis and practical lessons from previous superpower verification experience, this chapter summarizes the logic and politics of verification and suggests implications for South Asia. It begins by determining what all forms of verification have in common, regardless of the participants or the substance and form of their agreement. Viewing verification as the political process of making decisions regarding the occurrence of cooperation points to four critical components: (1) determination of principles, (2) information gathering, (3) analysis and (4) projection. Verification arrangements differ primarily in regards to how effectively and by whom these four stages are carried out.

This abstract understanding of verification aids development and analysis of specific verification proposals for South Asian arms control in a number of ways. It provides a checklist of components that must be included and choices that must be made when designing verification regimes. It offers insight into controversies that have complicated superpower verification negotiations and will likely plague South Asian efforts at regional arms control as well. Finally, it shows that verification arrangements not only measure, but also change, the degree of cooperation. This suggests a number of oft-ignored considerations that should be taken into account when designing and evaluating regional verification regimes for South Asia.

The Nature of Verification

Verification negotiations are more likely to be productive when participants speak the same basic arms control language. Unfortunately, we currently lack a universally accepted definition of verification and a common conception of what constitutes a "good" verification regime. Contemporary articles on verification use such widely varying definitions as the "*action* of demonstrating *compliance*,"[2] the *technological* and *intelligence process* that establishes the *fact* of *compliance*,"[3] and a "shorthand *expression* both for alleged instances of Soviet *non-compliance* and for U.S. *reactions or inactions*."[4] (Emphasis added.)

Behind this confusion lies a long history of controversies and changes in American verification policy. At the beginning of this century, the U.S. opposed international inspection as an unnecessary infringement on sovereignty and never mentioned the word verification. After World War II, though, international "control" and "foolproof safeguards" were deemed essential for successful arms control. "Verification," used narrowly to refer to the authentication of exchanged data,[5] was one means of substantiating compliance. However, American plans relied most on international inspection and direct operational involvement in nuclear facilities to ensure their peaceful nature.

In the 1960s and 70s, American policy shifted again. The word verification acquired the broad connotations common today. However, what was actually being sought was much more limited than before. The objective changed from policing and preventing violations to deterring and detecting them. The primary means were no longer cooperative arrangements. Instead, verification was to occur mainly by "national technical means"(NTM). Furthermore, due to the belief that perfect verification was both impossible and unnecessary, a new standard was adopted which required only that verification systems be "adequate" to detect militarily significant violations in a timely fashion.[6]

The Reagan Administration reinforced some of these trends and reversed others. It retained the emphasis on deterring and detecting arms control violations, but insisted that only rigorous and intrusive systems capable of uncovering all militarily and political violations can protect American security interests.[7] Critics, however, charge that this approach makes a number of unrealistic assumptions about what constitutes a militarily or politically significant violation, that it places political and economic demands on the Soviets that we would be unwilling or unable to accept ourselves, and that it stalls or undercuts arms control progress in a variety of other ways.[8]

Verification is certainly not "strictly an American concern."[9] While Soviet thinking about verification differs significantly from American approaches, they do have a coherent policy and legitimate verification needs. The traditional Soviet position has been that verification is a political, rather than a technical issue and that decisions about verification should be based on the political and military significance of what is being limited rather than on "facts" about system capabilities and technically possible cheating scenarios. Moscow maintains that negotiations should focus on the principles for agreement first, leaving verification details until the substance of limitations has been decided. Historically, the Soviets have preferred to minimize verification, largely because they have been less concerned about undetected American cheating than about Americans spying or interfering with the Soviets' internal affairs under the guise of verification.

However, Soviet leaders have definitely wanted some verification capabilities. They have used verification to reassure their own population.[10] They have also expressed particular interest in designing verification systems to prevent Americans from using their technical prowess to circumvent treaty limits.[11]

The current Soviet position on verification maintains some of its traditional elements, but reflects significant changes in others.[12] It still stresses that significant non-compliance is unlikely to be concealable and that the extent of verification should be proportionate to the amount and significance of arms control occuring. The principle of verification over disarmament rather than permitted arms remains, although it has not blocked tacit Soviet acceptance of national technical means of verification (NTM) nor prevented explicit agreement to observation of military maneuvers in the Stockholm Accords. The greatest change is a much greater willingness to allow inspectors access to Soviet territory, including some militarily sensitive locations and an increasingly positive attitude toward international verification.

Still other perspectives on verification can be found by looking beyond the superpower arms control context. The French, for example, were early proponents of the confidence-building function of verification. They were concerned that arms control without verification of compliance would create an atmosphere of mistrust in which defensive non-compliance was likely. As the French delegate to one interwar disarmament conference put it:

> Do you not feel that without a system of verification you will have created a state of mistrust and that, in the absence of detailed information and with a prevailing impression that the Convention is not being scrupulously applied in one quarter of another, other parties will be tempted to embark on the same course?[13]

On the whole, the other members of international disarmament bodies, such as the Geneva Conference on Disarmament, have taken a middle position on verification. They tend to agree that some verification is necessary for states to have confidence in an agreement, but reject many American verification demands as extreme and suggest that the verification issue has often been used by both superpowers to avoid serious arms control.[14] When arms control talks have stalled or broken down, these bodies have tried to pressure the superpowers to make meaningful progress and have provided fora in which talks could be resumed without loss of face. They have also contributed by offering resources for inspection teams, seismic stations and satellite monitoring, and by resolving some sticky verification issues such as the impasse over invitational versus mandatory on-site inspections (OSIs) of suspicious events under a Comprehensive Test Ban Treaty (CTBT).

Is it possible to find a way of thinking about verification that is broad enough to encompass this diversity of perspectives, but precise enough to avoid confusion and miscommunication during verification debates, negotiations and implementation? A context-independent conception of verification can be developed by determining what is similar about all problems in international life where verification is desired. After discovering the role that verification plays in these situations, one can determine what steps must necessarily occur for verification to function effectively. This provides a working definition of "verification in the abstract" and an understanding of the key components of a complete verification system.

Many definitions of arms control verification require that it be applied to and legitimated by a formal treaty. This criterion for differentiating verification from intelligence gathering does not reflect how the term verification is actually used. Current American policy seeks pre-agreement verification, such as the 1988 Joint Verification Experiments and President Bush's "try before you buy" approach to START verification.[15] Leaders also speak of verifying compliance with unratified treaties, such as the Threshold Test Ban Treaty (TTBT), and with unilateral arms control declarations, such as the recent Soviet moratorium on nuclear testing. The basic verification problem also exists for tacit arms control, such as mutual restraint concerning the use of chemical weapons or attacks on each other's satellites.

All of these situations have three things in common that make the use of the word "verification" appropriate. First, a problem exists which creates *incentives to seek cooperation*. These are of several types:

- Mutual cooperation is essential to success
- Mutual cooperation is most efficient route to success

- Cooperation by others will promote one's goal even if one secretly fails to reciprocate fully

Protecting the continental environment, handling population exchanges humanely, and allocating water resources are Indian and Pakistani problems that require mutual cooperation. Preventing a unintended nuclear war also falls in this category because there is no way for a nation to advance that objective by cheating on agreements regarding safety mechanisms, hotlines, or escalation controls. For other types of regional problems, such as providing communication links between India and Pakistan, mutual cooperation would be most efficient, but it is not the only solution. There are also situations where one has incentives to seek the other's cooperation, but not always to cooperate fully oneself. Managing an arms race to get maximum security and political leverage with minimum cost and risk falls into this category. Since it takes two to create an arms race, convincing one's opponent to observe restraints while doing some undetected cheating of one's own would not, in the short run, be the same as shooting oneself in the foot to make oneself run faster.

A second characteristic of verification problems is that *incentives to behave unilaterally* are present alongside pressures for cooperation. To behave unilaterally is to take independent actions that are motivated by one's own needs, interests and capabilities, but that do not take other's wishes and well-being into account. Like incentives to cooperate, incentives to act unilaterally can take several forms: incentives to defect, incentives for insurance, and internal incentives.

Incentives to defect arise whenever states believe the benefits of unilateral action will outweigh the likely costs. "Realists" often believe that cooperation is merely a pause in competition while both sides jockey for a better position from which to seek unilateral gain. This view assumes that incentives to defect dominate international life. However, states that choose to defect on a regular basis must either see themselves as self-sufficient or believe that they can use threats and deceit to ensure others' cooperation without reciprocation.

Incentives for insurance occur when states prefer lasting mutual cooperation, but feel compelled to take unilateral actions to protect themselves in case others try to take advantage of them. When the U.S. Senate ratified the Limited Test Ban Treaty (LTBT), conservatives required that a number of safeguards be adopted to make sure that the Soviets could not gain a significant advantage by cheating or suddenly abrogating the treaty. Some of these, such as expanding the U.S. underground testing program, undermined the objective of slowing the arms race. Others, such as maintaining facilities and staff capable of resuming atmospheric testing on very short notice, could have threatened the stability of the LTBT itself by giving the Soviets the impression that the United States was positioning itself to break out of the treaty regime. This shows that "security dilemmas"—i.e. situations where unilaterally buying an insurance policy actually makes one less secure—exist in the realm of arms control as well as in the area of arms races.

Internal incentives to act unilaterally occur when cooperation requires significant and costly changes in such things as ideology, resource allocation, or bureaucratic structure. Because of internal incentives, non-adversarial unilateral actions may still occur even in situations where cooperation would seem more rational. Internal counter-cooperative pressures have received little attention from international relations theorists, but politicians and policy-makers are usually very sensitive to them. Because President Ronald Reagan's Administration had depicted the Soviet Union as an "evil empire" and a country which would "lie, cheat and steal" at every opportunity, ratifying the Intermediate-range Nuclear Forces Treaty (INF) was more costly and complicated for him than it might have been otherwise. Bureaucratic pressure against cooperation also came from those who worried that allocating resources for INF verification would reduce funds for alternative goals such as national intelligence gathering and weapons modernization. And a number of minor noncompliance issues have arisen, not because the U.S. and the Soviet Union do not want to uphold the treaty, but because they lack the organization and oversight necessary to make sure that those carrying out dismantling and verification activities clearly understand all the details of what they may and may not do.

The third characteristic of situations requiring verification is that states *need to know whether cooperation or unilateral action has occurred.* Accurate assessments are important for states that wish to respond appropriately to other's actions; they are even more essential for states that wish to influence or control that behavior. If international politics were a pure self-help system, then it would be essential to be able to distinguish between cooperative and non-cooperative action. Otherwise, how could states deter or punish hostile actions and reward friendly behavior? In practice, international life is constrained by formal or informal norms and international institutions. Distinguishing between cooperation and unilateral action is also essential for these constraints to be effective and for stable expectations to be formed. The 1960 Indus River Treaty would not likely have survived two India-Pakistan wars if those two countries had been unable to determine whether tacit understandings regarding acceptable behavior were being observed.

From these three characteristics—incentives for cooperation, conflicting incentives for unilateral action, and need to make decisions about which type of behavior has or will occur—one can define arms control verification as: *the political process of making decisions regarding the degree to which cooperation is occurring and/or is likely to occur in an arms control regime.*

This definition emphasizes several points that have already been raised. Since verification can occur prior to or outside of the signing and ratifying of a particular treaty, the context for verification decision making is best described as an *arms control regime.*[16] Furthermore, because verification involves subjective, political judgement which can rarely be absolutely objective and clear cut, it make sense to speak of *the degree* of cooperation rather than its existence or non-existence. Focusing both on cooperation that *is occurring* and that which *is likely to occur* underlines the observation that successful initiation and stable maintenance of arms control regimes are a function not only of perceptions regarding past and present actions, but also of expectations concerning future behavior.

It is clear that, by this definition, *India and Pakistan are already involved in a significant amount of verification even without many formal arms control accords.* As former CIA director William Colby has observed, those who argue that the United States lacks the means to verify agreements forget that American leaders need similar information about other states' armaments, testing patterns and force levels whether they are assessing threats for unilateral security planning or evaluating cooperation for arms control.[17] The same is certainly true for Pakistan and India. In fact, Benazir Bhutto made precisely this point when she observed that if U.S. intelligence is capable of detecting Pakistani efforts to enrich uranium and acquire bomb components, it should suffice to verify a Pakistani pledge not to do so.[18] Therefore, the key question is not "Do India and Pakistan have the means to verify arms control accords?," but rather "How can India and Pakistan design their verification systems so that they support cooperative rather than unilateral approaches to regional security problems?"

The Verification Process

Maximizing verification's ability to support arms control requires a clear understanding of the steps involved. From activities that do, or logically should, occur in conjunction with verification, one can discern four distinct types of activities necessary to make decisions regarding whether cooperation is occurring: Determination of Principles, Information Gathering, Analysis, and Projection. For simplicity, these components will be referred to as "stages" in the verification process, although they can be pursued simultaneously, sequentially or cyclically.

Determination of Principles

Like scientists, arms control verifiers require the guidance of a set of principles which tell them what to look for, where to seek it, what tools to use, and how to interpret what they find. Unlike most scientists, though, arms control verifiers lack a pre-existing shared paradigm. Since they operate in a divided and changing political and technological context, arms controllers must compose the rules as they proceed. These principles may be determined jointly, they may be declared unilaterally, or they may be draw from unspoken assumptions and perceptions inside participants' heads—but without them, verification is both a logical and a practical impossibility.

Many works on verification assume that if others' actions were perfectly visible, states would automatically recognize cooperation when they saw it.[19] This presumes that verifiers have an abstract idea of what constitutes cooperation against which observed behavior can be compared. Differentiating between cooperation and non-cooperation can be more difficult than one might think. "No nuclear tests above 150 kilotons" seems straight-forward enough until one has to decide what constitutes a "slight, unintended breach" of the threshold or even what, precisely, defines a nuclear "test."[20]

Unless all parties to an arms control accord agree about what principles to use, compliance concerns are likely to arise. One of the thorniest U.S.-Soviet compliance problems stems from the fact that while both sides agree that missile test telemetry encryption is occurring, they have different ideas of what it means to undertake "deliberate concealment measures" that "impede verification" of SALT II. When political relations sour, agreeing about abstract standards of cooperation becomes even more complicated. The radical reassessment of Soviet compliance behavior that occurred in the Reagan Administration illustrates that the worse relations are between two adversaries, the more likely the same behavior is to be perceived as hostile.[21]

Standards establishing the legitimacy of different forms of information-gathering and the weight of various types of evidence are also essential. Some information-gathering techniques, such as on-site inspection (OSIs) and in-country seismic monitoring, are highly impractical unless subject countries acquiesce to their use. NTM can be employed without consent for unilateral decision-making purposes. However, to avoid accusations of spying, only information gathered by mutually legitimated means can be publicly used to justify compliance concerns and verification decisions. Bargaining about enhancing (or decreasing) the effectiveness of verification technologies or about techniques of analysis such as calibration or extrapolation is also part of the principle determination stage of verification.

Negotiations can be seen as a formal, joint decision-making approach to the first stage of verification. Treaty provisions paint a partial picture of cooperation: what would and would not occur or exist, what would be legitimate techniques of verification information gathering, how disputes would be handled, even how long the cooperative experiment would last and how it could be amended or ended. Less formal arms control cooperation, such as refraining from interference with reconnaissance satellites or use of poison gas, necessarily also involve tacit or explicit bargaining over broad norms and expectations.

No matter how carefully participants define principles prior to implementation, standards for "positive results" in arms control experiments are likely to continue being debated throughout the life (and perhaps long past it) of the cooperative regime. Some policy makers believe that a "good" treaty would have such detailed brush strokes that there would be no room for ambiguity or interpretation, no uncertainty over whether another country's nuclear testing program or handling of non-compliance concerns constituted cooperation or not. But arms control agreements are often left deliberately fuzzy on critical points, and even a portrait with photographic clarity will look different to each viewer.

Information Gathering

One verification technology, seismic monitoring, distinguishes between information gathering for three different purposes: (1) detection, (2) identification, and (3) estimation.[22] It is useful to broaden this distinction to consider the different types of information gathering necessary for verification in general.

Detection is often treated as the cornerstone of verification. However, this immediately begs the question of what, precisely, a verification regime should seek to find. Perceptions of cooperation and confidence in arms control will differ depending on whether one designs a verification system solely to deter and detect violations or also to provide appropriate reassurances and rewards. "Negative" forms of verification, such as challenge inspections of suspicious activities, zero in on possible evidence of cheating. "Positive" verification, such as routine observance of permitted nuclear tests, also aims to collect evidence that arms control is working. Treaty language typically legitimates positive verification for providing assurances of compliance, while the rhetoric of American verification debates focuses more on negative verification capabilities for catching cheating. Actual verification regimes usually do a mixture of both. In seismic monitoring, for example, the detection of a seismic event indicates that a noncompliant action may have occurred, while information about compliance comes in the form of non-events (i.e. uncovering no signs of suspicious seismic activity).

High "detection capability" is not enough. Once an interesting event has been found, correct *identification* must occur. In the case of seismic monitoring, the difference between detection and identification is the difference between knowing that a suspicious seismic activity has occurred and determining whether it was caused by a nuclear explosion, a chemical explosion or an earthquake. Identification problems that have arisen in other areas of arms control include determining whether the 1979 Sverdlovsk anthrax epidemic was evidence of biological-weapons production or contaminated meat[23] and deciding whether a sea-launched cruise missile is conventional- or nuclear-armed.[24] Since it is possible to detect events that cannot be identified, but not to identify events that cannot be detected, a country's detection ability will always surpass its identification capability.

The third step, *estimation*, is primarily a problem for verification of quantitative limits. Disagreement over estimation practices, not inadequate detection and identification capabilities, underlie the controversy over Soviet compliance with the TTBT's 150 kT. limit. The need to gather estimation information is one of the reasons why quantitative agreements are generally considered harder to verify than qualitative ones for equivalent systems. Detecting and identifying one intermediate range missile of a forbidden type in Europe after the INF elimination procedure was supposedly complete would itself be strong evidence of non-compliance. No such conclusion could be reached on the basis of sighting one new Trident submarine, though, unless one could simultaneously account for the existence of enough other strategic launchers to show that the SALT II limits had been exceeded.

Analysis

After the data has been gathered, the next step is to determine what it means for cooperation. Determining the degree to which cooperation has occurred requires comparing this information with principles, norms and expectations regarding the meaning of cooperation. Satisfactory verification requires a good match between the principles for cooperation and the technical capabilities of the verification systems. For example, analyzing seismic data for a low-yield threshold test ban will be easier and more reliable if the principles for cooperation include measures to help differentiate chemical from nuclear explosions. These could include agreements to notify others before conducting chemical explosions, to invite outsiders to observe legal blasts, and to use ripple-firing techniques that give multiple chemical explosions a unique seismic signature. Likewise, agreement on counting rules or "functionally-related observable differences" could facilitate limitations or bans on nuclear warheads without requiring verifiers to have the technology to determine precisely what is inside each nose cone.

Saying that verification has produced either "ambiguous" or "clear-cut" evidence of cooperation/non-cooperation really means that one is either satisfied or dissatisfied with one's ability to decide what the nature of that event is. Willingness to be satisfied by evidence of compliance or non-compliance depends, in part, on numerous political and psychological factors, such as political climate and significance of the arms control regime, that have little to do with the capabilities of the verification system itself. Skeptics charge that American leaders are unlikely to admit that the verification provisions they have negotiated are unsatisfactory,[25] while arms control advocates claim that conservatives are so philosophically opposed to cooperation with the Soviets that no verification system could satisfy them.[26]

When a country is satisfied that cooperation either has or has not occurred, it will move out of the true verification process and begin deciding how to respond. Participants who are dissatisfied with their ability to decide whether the other is cooperating or not, however, can seek clarification of principles and/or improved information. The dialogue between India and Pakistan on their no-attack on nuclear facilities agreement has not even reached this stage, as they have yet to provide each other with a list of their nuclear facilities.

Theoretically, participants in an arms control verification regime could cycle through the first three stages of the verification process indefinitely. They could continuously refine principles, extend information gathering, and reanalyze the fit between norms and observed behavior without ever being completely satisfied with their ability to decide whether or not cooperation has occurred. It is doubtful, however, that this type of limbo will be acceptable when agreements are more politically or militarily significant. A state's confidence in its own ability to make decisions about whether or not cooperation is occurring may actually be more important to the success of arms control than its confidence in the good intentions of the other side. If that is true, one would expect there to be great pressure on leaders to either declare that they were satisfied with their analysis of current events or to give up and let the arms control regime break down.

Projection

The verification process does not end with a decision about one instance of cooperation or non-cooperation. The fourth stage is the projection of the results of the analysis to form expectations about the probability of future cooperation. As long as countries see themselves in an ongoing relationship characterized by conflicting incentives for and against cooperation, projection will occur. Only when one party has come to believe that unilateral security is both possible and preferable to continued attempts at cooperation will projection be unimportant. But under those circumstances, verification will be unnecessary altogether.

Projection is particularly obvious in pre-agreement forms of verification. Then, the objective of discussing standards and demonstrating information-gathering capabilities is to influence choices about entrance into a more formal arms control regime. Eisenhower's Open Skies and Bush's proposal to begin continuous monitoring of some ballistic missile factories before a START treaty is signed[27] are examples of pre-agreement verification designed, in part, to aid the U.S. and the Soviet Union in making accurate assessments and projections of intentions.

Before or after a treaty has been signed, the projection stage of verification includes both extrapolation from past events and consideration of whether the arms control regime can be restructured so that cooperation is more likely to occur. Debating what the Soviet's compliance record predicts about the risks of new agreements assumes that extrapolation provides a reliable guide to the future. Specifying limitations and obligations in ever-greater detail, on the other hand, implies that future problems can be avoided by reducing ambiguity as much as possible.

The Design of Verification Regimes

The stages of verification can be handled unilaterally, consultatively or in collaboration. Does it matter how the job is done? If verification were a purely technical matter, any arrangements providing the desired degree of accuracy would be acceptable. This view underlies the argument that verification is "neutral" and that Soviet satisfaction of American verification demands is a "litmus test" of their commitment to arms control[28] that should require no substantive concessions by Americans in return.[29]

Because arms control verification is highly political rather than purely scientific, though, design choices affect both the acceptability and stability of verification regimes in two key ways. First, arms control paradigms are provisionally constructed by participants. How this is done shapes what will be evidence of cooperation and how sensitive the system is to signs of cooperation relative to those of non-cooperation. Second, the tools of arms control verification change the system they measure. Design choices at each stage significantly affect whether a country's incentives and abilities to cooperate are greater or less than pressures and possibilities for defection, insurance seeking and internally-generated unilateral actions. In short, actual verification regimes are not neutral, but rather play an important role in determining the amount of cooperation that is perceived and the amount that actually occurs.

The types of verification design choices that are most likely to affect Indian and Pakistani decisions to seek regional security through unilateral or cooperative means boil down to two types of issues—how effectively and by whom will each step of the verification process be handled? Important, yet often conflicting, considerations exist on both of these dimensions. The politics of verification seeks to determine how these concerns should be prioritized and balanced.

General Monitoring Capabilities. Those evaluating verification regimes would like a simple answer to the question "will it tell us enough about what is actually happening for us to be comfortable and secure in an arms control regime?" Unfortunately, this question is often translated into a probabalistic assessment of detection capabilities. To aid decision makers, the U.S. intelligence community assigns a "confidence level" to each potential treaty provision. This reflects their estimate of the likelihood that the United States will detect Soviet non-compliance given U.S. monitoring systems, current Soviet practices and potential evasion scenarios.[30]

However, there are a number of advantages to thinking about the "how much?" dimension of verification in terms of overall system sensitivity, rather than just detection capabilities. It serves as a reminder that verification regimes should be designed and evaluated as a whole. After all, detection is only one of three types of information gathering, and information gathering is just one of four critical stages of verification. Also, a broader approach emphasizes that more is not always better when it comes to verification regimes for a number of reasons.

Negotiability. The more complicated or controversial a verification provision is, the more difficult it will be to negotiate. One of the most common reasons given for failure to include or to significantly limit something in an arms control treaty is the fear that trying to negotiate the needed verification would prevent any agreement from being reached at all.

Useful Ambiguity. As recent controversies over the Antiballistic Missile Treaty demonstrate, over-specification of definitions and limitations can destabilize a treaty regime by allowing participants to design around restrictions or by making the treaty obsolete in the face of strategic, technological, or political change.

Information Overload. This is of particular concern for countries with more limited technological and human resources. If verifiers cannot process the data that they receive and sort out the relevant from the irrelevant input, decision making is likely to become distorted, or even paralyzed. Numerous detectable seismic events occur each year in India and Pakistan. Unless test ban verification systems focus only on those events that could be nuclear blasts, regional verification resources would be quickly overwhelmed.

Collateral Information Collection. This is another problem for indiscriminate verification systems that obtain a high detection rate by picking up information on everything under the sun. Cooperation may be threatened when verification systems gather extra intelligence that is irrelevant or unnecessary for evaluating cooperation, but potentially useful for unilateral security gains. For many proposed forms of verification—such as CORRTEX,[31] on-site inspections of military facilities, and restrictions on encryption—it is unclear whether benefits to arms control exceed the risks that military secrets will be compromised.

False Alarms. Detectability is concerned only with making sure that leaders are unlikely to wrongly believe that cooperation is occurring when others are actually cheating.

A "system sensitivity" approach, however, recognizes that verification schemes with high probabilities of wrongful accusations are equally inaccurate and problematic. False alarms create unnecessary friction, waste resources, and may undermine attempts to cooperate that both sides actually want to support.

The politics of verification design aim, in part, at influencing how system sensitivity considerations such as detection, ease of negotiation, collateral information collection and false alarm reduction are balanced. A second set of design issues, those relating to decision-making style, are also important. As noted above, stages in the verification process can be handled jointly, consultatively, or unilaterally. When deciding how each step of the verification process should be handled, competing concerns relating to resource availability, sovereignty, reciprocity, reliability, and arms control stability need to be considered.

Resource Availability. When weighing the costs, benefits and risks of arms control under various types of verification regimes, analysts often overlook the economic and human costs of the verification systems themselves. For countries that lack the necessary technologies and institutional arrangements, the start- up costs of verification can be high. Furthermore, each additional seismic monitoring station, satellite, or inspection team has a price; returns diminish relative to costs as the incremental improvement in decision-making abilities decreases. However, both resource availability and verification costs are likely to depend not only on "how much" verification is sought, but also on "what type" of decision-making is adopted. Start-up costs can be reduced by convincing outsiders with the relevant technologies to lend equipment, assist with technical development, or join in verification decision making.[32] Needless duplication can be avoided and cost redistribution promoted if participants accept some joint verification measures instead of insisting on their own, completely independent, verification system.

Sovereignty. A second decision-making style consideration that runs counter to incentives for sharing verification resources is the desire to preserve national sovereignty. Western nations have been no less concerned about arms control verification infringing on their sovereignty than India and Pakistan. However, when leaders seriously desire accords, ways have been found to reconcile the demands of sovereignty and verification. This is possible because impact on sovereignty relates less to effectiveness of verification than it does to verification style. Agreement that SALT I and II be verified by NTM represented a change in both the type of verification sought by the U.S. and the Soviet attitude toward the legitimacy of satellite reconnaissance. The Peaceful Nuclear Explosions Treaty (PNET), the Stockholm Accords and the INF Treaty have shown that on-site inspections are less likely to conflict with sovereignty when the host country retains as much control as possible over the timing, location, and execution of the inspections.

Equality of information is another sovereignty-related consideration. Countries such as India that find the Non-Proliferation Treaty (NPT) discriminatory are also likely to reject accords which permit the use of verification technologies available to some participants and not others.[33] For bilateral agreements, it may be Pakistan that insists on international and/or joint bilateral verification arrangements since India has a greater unilateral capacity to both detect certain Pakistani violations and to shield their own.

Finally, the United Nations principles for verification specify that arrangements should interfere as little as possible with national economic life.[34] The less interested South Asians are in PNEs, the easier it will be to verify the absence of nuclear tests.

Reciprocity. This has become an important way to reconcile the demands of verification decision making and of sovereignty. It seems easier for the superpowers to negotiate reciprocal privileges than to give verification rights to international inspectors whose own countries are not all similarly limited and inspected. Norms of reciprocity are symbolically important because they reinforce the notion of agreement between sovereign equals. They have practical value by putting natural restraints on verification demands. During negotiation, norms of reciprocity remind all parties that whatever they request will be required of them, too. Realization that abuses and misuses of verification provisions can be reciprocated is likely to reduce spying, unwarranted challenge inspections, and other mischief- making. These considerations help explain Indian and Pakistani insistence on reciprocal forms of bilateral verification. They also suggest that they may be reluctant to allow non-signatory states, especially China, to be involved in verification decision-making.

Reliability. For verification to succeed, decisionmakers must be satisfied that information-gathering, analysis, and projection methods are reliable. American verification specialists usually maintain that decisions should rest on information and analysis that is independently conducted or confirmed; otherwise, the regime amounts to nothing more than unreliable "self-verification."[35] This assumes that competitors will seek advantages whenever possible by providing misleading information or distorted analysis. However, it is equally plausible that unilateral verification will be unreliable precisely because it utilizes only one set of resources and perceptions. Developing procedures now to evaluate and improve the reliability of information gathered jointly or provided by a third party would make future South Asian arms control agreements more likely.

Secrecy/openness. In the U.S.-Soviet case, advocates of unilateral information gathering and analysis maintain that verification will be a more effective deterrent to cheating if the other side is uncertain about the extent of U.S. detection gathering capabilities and unable to design around or impede the particular techniques being employed. They also prefer unilateral verification because it facilitates using the same resources (satellites, human intelligence, etc.) for both arms control verification and military intelligence gathering. The obvious, but often ignored, drawback of this is that it undercuts the ability of arms control verification to reduce tensions by promoting openness and preventing unpleasant surprises.

Arms Control Stability. Just as different verification decision-making designs can increase or decrease the economic costs of arms control cooperation, they can also change incentives and abilities to cooperate, as well as perceptions that cooperation is occurring. American verification policy recognizes that verification can reduce incentives to cheat by increasing the risks of being caught. But little attention is given to the possibility that highly unilateral verification systems which involve much collateral information collection may increase abilities to defect from an arms control agreement by providing data needed for targeting or weapons design. Also, attempts to compensate for verification weaknesses through unilateral "insurance policies" (preparing to resume the prohibited activities on short notice, developing alternative ways to accomplish the same military goals, or secretly cheating oneself "just in case") may force one's opponent to do likewise and cause the breakdown of cooperation. Internal pressures for non-cooperation may also be reinforced by highly unilateral approaches to verification. These can institutionalize the expectation of cheating, as occurred when conservatives in the Senate began requiring the President to provide a report each year on Soviet noncompliance.

An alternative to unilateral verification is "joint" verification. In joint verification, there is a preference for consultation and collaboration at each of the four stages of verification decision making. This preference arises from a view of verification that sees it functioning to do much more than simply detect and deter violations. A second objective is to provide appropriate reassurances and rewards when cooperation is occurring. Third, joint verification aims to lessen internal obstacles to cooperation by increasing channels for communication and decreasing misperception, and offering opportunities for adversaries to gain insight into each other's security concerns and practices, as well as practical experience working side by side.

Although the U.S. and the Soviet Union have little actual experience with fully joint decision-making forms of verification, it is logical to expect that since verification regimes change the system that they are applied to, joint verification designs would be more likely to promote significant and lasting cooperation than unilateral designs would. We have already seen a number of reasons why arms control is more likely to succeed if participants determine the principles for cooperation together rather than each using their own definitions, measuring sticks, etc. At the information gathering stage, the PNET and INF verification provisions show the importance of designing inspection procedures carefully, so that the guests believe that the information gathered is a reliable guide for verification and hosts are reassured that it will be used for nothing more sinister. And for analysis and projection, most supporters of arms control believe that bodies like the Standing Consultative Commission can promote the stability of arms control when used to promote understanding and quiet resolution of disputes rather than to score unilateral propaganda advantages, and lay the groundwork for treaty abrogation.

These decision-making style considerations are particularly important for those designing regional, rather than superpower, verification regimes. Technological, economic, and human resource constraints are even tighter for countries like India and Pakistan than for the United States and the Soviet Union. Careful thought must be given to maximizing the efficiency of national verification resources and to weighing the costs and benefits of seeking outside help. Furthermore, whereas the United States and the Soviet Union have focused primarily on unilateral or bilateral forms of verification in recent treaties and negotiations, India and Pakistan have a broad menu of decision making options. Among them are verification by the United Nations or some other broad international body, by a committee of regional states, or by the United States and the Soviet Union as guarantors of compliance.

Evaluating Verification Regimes

Realizing that designing verification regimes is politically as well as technically complex does not mean that verification is hopelessly difficult or that arms control is unlikely to be worthwhile. In order to promote their own security, India and Pakistan already engage in extensive decision-making regarding what type of behavior is occurring in those areas of regional life where incentives to act unilaterally and cooperatively exist. The very fact that this type of decision-making involves a variety of conflicting political considerations is a strong argument for thinking carefully and explicitly about the extent to which different types of verification designs are capable of promoting *both* national security and stable arms control cooperation.

In order to do this, it is important to give some thought to standards for evaluating the degree to which specific verification designs can support particular arms control objectives. In the United States and the Soviet Union, the debate over verification standards has focused on deciding "how much?" verification is necessary for the benefits to outweigh the costs and risks of arms control agreements.

Traditionally, American conservatives seek *absolute* verification. They use legalistic arguments to insist that all treaty violations are militarily or politically significant, and must be detectable for an agreement to be in America's security interests. The Reagan Administration standard of *effective* verification initially called for near perfection, although it softened considerably once they became more serious about concluding the INF agreement. In general, arms control supporters maintain that absolute verification is impossible and unnecessary. Instead, verification regimes are *adequate* if they detect militarily significant violations in time to negate any advantage the other might gain. Of course, analysts differ as to what is a "militarily significant violation," "timely warning" and "appropriate response."

The standard Soviet position is that countries do not sign treaties while intending to cheat; therefore, *minimal* verification should be adequate to ensure that obligations are being met. Recently, Moscow has been willing to accept more verification in order to get an agreement, but still considers the extra to be unnecessary.

American debates over the evaluation of verification can be summarized by saying that proponents of varying standards think in similar terms, but have different opinions as to what values should be assigned to the following variables:

A should accept provision **X** if the benefits of **X** outweigh **P** (the probability that **B** will cheat) times **C** (cost to **A** of undetected cheating)
where
P is determined by comparing **D** (the value to **B** of cheating) with **T** (the threatened punishment) times **V** (probability that **A**'s verification system will detect noncompliance with **X**).

From the foregoing analysis, it is easy to ascertain that this way of evaluating verification is inadequate on a number of counts. An obvious one is that it assumes that nations make verification decisions as if they were unitary rational actors. However, the one systematic study that has been done of the determinants of American verification policy making found that the seemingly contradictory governmental decisions made regarding different aspects of the Natural Resources Defense Council's joint seismic monitoring project with Soviet scientists are best explained by an organizational/bureaucratic politics model rather than a rational actor approach.[36] This is definitely borne out by participant memoirs and other studies of American arms control policy-making, and is likely to be true of any complex democracy. There is also evidence that key Soviet verification decisions have been shaped by domestic political considerations.[37]

This type of assessment focuses only on verification's impact on incentives to defect from arms control regimes because it assumes that all state behavior is the product of rational, self-interested calculation. While verification can certainly make important contributions in this regard, one must also remember that incentives for insurance seeking and internal incentives can also pressure states to take unilateral actions. Evaluating verification regimes only in terms of their deterrent capabilities misses important opportunities to use verification for reassurance, both that the other is complying *and* that one's own cooperation will be recognized and rewarded. It also overlooks possibilities for using verification negotiation and implementation to enhance communication, correct misperceptions, convey useful knowledge, and otherwise decrease internal impediments to successful cooperation.

Another way to understand the inadequacies of current standards for evaluation is to recognize that proponents of "perfect," "effective," "adequate," and minimal" detection capabilities debate only "how much?" They overlook the equally important issues relating to "what type" of verification would be most likely to support successful agreement and stable implementation of arms control accords.

Elsewhere, I argue that this is because policy-makers have adopted an increasingly unilateralist approach to verification without recognizing the impact that different types of verification decision-making designs can have on the relative balance between unilateral and cooperative incentives, abilities and perceptions.[38] The more significant the arms control agreement and the more delicate the balance between unilateral and cooperative pressures, though, the more critical verification decision-making design questions become.

To maximize verification's ability to promote cooperative approaches to South Asia's security problems, regime designers must be sensitive to the politics of verification on two different levels. Naturally, when putting together a verification package, one must continually ask, "will it play in Islamabad and Delhi?" In other words, arms control will be improbable and any agreements reached will be unstable unless participants believe that the specific verification provisions provide a satisfactory ability to make decisions about whether or not cooperation is occurring. This involves using means that are appropriate given their countries' concerns about security, resource allocation, and status. However, the logic of verification is such that it is not sufficient simply to find a least common denominator solution to questions of verification design. For verification to promote the development of stable cooperative solutions to regional security problems, consultative and collaborative approaches to the determination of principles, information collection, analysis and projection should be included whenever possible as positive components of verification regime design.

Notes

1. See the chapters by Burns, Chellaney, and Cohen for some discussion of the India-China relationship.

2. Allan Krass, *Verification: How Much is Enough?* (London and Philadelphia: Taylor and Francis, 1985), p. 6.

3. Richard Scribner and Kenneth Luongo, *Strategic Nuclear Arms Control Verification: Terms and Concepts*, AASS Pub. No. 85-2, January, 1985, p. 38.

4. Mark Lowenthal and Joel Witt, "The Politics of Verification," in William Potter, ed., *Verification and Arms Control* (Lexington,: D.C. Heath and Company, 1985), p. 153.

5. See, for example, The United States' 1952 proposal for "Disclosure and Verification" of information relating to conventional and nuclear armaments, in United Nations Disarmament Commission, *Official Records*, Special Supplement No. 1, pp. 22-27.

6. For the formulations used during the Kennedy, Nixon and Carter Administrations, see Michael Krepon, "The Political Dynamics of Verification and Compliance Debates," In William Potter, ed., *Verification and Arms Control* (Lexington: D.C. Heath, 1985), pp. 137-139.

7. Michael Krepon, "The Political Dynamics of Verification and Compliance Debates," in Potter,*Verification and Arms Control*, pp. 139-141; Lowenthal and Wit, pp. 162-163.

8. Allan Krass, "The Politics of Verification,"*World Policy Journal*, Vol. 2, No. 4, Fall, 1985, pp. 731-753.

9. The view that verification is "for all practical purposes . . . strictly an American concern" is one shared by many American arms control analysts. See W. Slocombe, quoted in Allan Krass, "The Soviet View of Verification," in Potter, *Verification and Arms Control*, p. 37.

10. S.A. Cohen, "The Evolution of Soviet Views on Verification," in William Potter, ed., *Verification and SALT: The Challenge of Strategic Deception* (Boulder: Westview Press, 1980), p. 68.

11. The Eastern Bloc's concern of using verification to ensure that Western states are not gaining destabilizing advantages through technological developments is a basic theme in Andrzej Karkoska, *Strategic Disarmament, Verification and National Security* (London: Taylor and Francis, 1977).

12. William Potter, "The Evolution of Soviet Attitudes Toward On- Site Inspection" pp. 185-206 in Lewis Dunn, ed., *Arms Control Verification: the New Role of On Site Inspection* (Lexington: Lexington Books, 1990).

13. Quoted in Philip Towles, *Arms Control and East-West Relations* (New York: St. Martin's Press, 1983), pp. 134-135.

14. Alva Myrdal, *The Game of Disarmament* (New York: Pantheon Books, 1976).

15. Robert Scott, "Joint Nuclear Tests Raise Questions About Administration Policy,"*Arms Control Today*, Vol. 18, No. 8, Oct. 1988, p. 26; Richard Lugar, "Verify and Then Trust," *New York Times*, June 27, 1989.

16. I am using Stephen Krasner's definition of a regime as the "principles, norms, rules and decision-making procedures around which actor expectations converge" regardless of whether or not they are codified in a treaty. Stephen Krasner, ed., *International Regimes*, (Ithaca, N.Y.: Cornell University Press, 1983) p. 1.

17. William Colby, "The Intelligence Process," in Kosta Tsipis, David Hafemeister, and Penny Janeway, eds., *Arms Control Verification: The Technologies That Make It Possible* (Washington, D.C.: Pergamon-Brassey's, 1986), p. 11.

18. Peter W. Galbraith, "Nuclear Proliferation in South Asia: Containing the Threat," A Staff Report to the Committee on Foreign Relations, United States Senate, August 1988 (Washington, D.C.: U.S. Government Printing Office), p. 17.

19. The most obvious example of this are the game-theoretic analyses that only allow players two choices of action, conveniently labeled something like "cooperate" and "defect" or "tell the truth" and "lie." Any treatment of

verification, though, that focuses primarily on improving detection capabilities, though, falls into this trap.

20. Neither the LTBT nor the TTBT give an explicit definition of a nuclear test. According to Herbert York, chief U.S. negotiator at the CTBT talks during 1979-1980, the United States never tabled a definition of a nuclear test because the delegation could not get internal agreement as to the standard that should be used to distinguish between prohibited and permitted nuclear explosions. Interview with Herbert York, San Diego, CA, Oct. 13, 1989.

21. Robert Jervis, *Perception and Misperception in International Politics* (Princeton: Princeton University Press, 1976).

22. U.S. Congress, Office of Technology Assessment, *Seismic Verification of Nuclear Testing Treaties* OTA-ISC-361 (Washington, D.C.: U.S. Government Printing Office, 1988), (Hereafter, OTA study.)

23. Gloria Duffy, Project Director, *Compliance and the Future of Arms Control*, (Cambridge: Ballinger, 1988), pp. 51-52.

24. Rose Gottemoeller, "Finding Solutions to SLCM Arms Control Problems," *International Security*, Vol 13, No.3, Winter, 1988-89, pp. 175-183.

25. Carnes Lord, "Verification: Reforming a Theology," *The National Interest*, Spring, 1986, p. 58.

26. Allan Krass, "The Politics of Verification," *World Policy Journal*, Vol. 4, Fall, 1985, pp. 743-4.

27. R. Jeffery Smith, "U.S. to Propose Monitoring Arms Plants Prior to Treaty," *Washington Post*, June 20, 1989.

28. Eugene Rostow, Statement before the Committee on Armed Services, U.S. Senate, July 24, 1983.

29. Walter Pincus, "U.S. Devising New Verification Terms for Talks on Missiles," *International Herald Tribune*, July 23, 1983.

30. William Rowell, *Arms Control Verification: A Guide to Policy Issues for the 1980s* (Cambridge: Ballinger, 1986), p. 17.

31. CORRTEX stands for "Continuous Reflectometry for Radius Versus Time Experiments," the name used for the particular form of hydrodynamic nuclear test yield verification favored by the Reagan Administration and demonstrated in the Joint Verification Experiments. "U.S. Policy Regarding Limitations on Nuclear Testing," Special Report No. 150 (Washington, D.C.: U.S. Department of State, Bureau of Public Affairs, August, 1986).

32. See, for example, the chapter in this book by Neuhoff and Singer.

33. Bhupendra Jasani and Frank Barnaby,*Verification Technologies: The Case for Surveillance by Consent* (Leamington Spa, U.K.: Berg Publishers, 1984).

34. "Principles of Verification Affirmed by the Disarmament Commission," (May 2-20, 1988, New York), Text in Serge Sur, *A Legal Approach to Verification in Disarmament or Arms Limitation* (New York: United Nations, 1988), pp. 67-68.

35. In describing PNET negotiations, Warren Heckrotte says that one Soviet proposal would have involved U.S. and Soviet personnel working

together on some monitoring procedures. The U.S. resisted any forms of cooperation, however, that would raise questions about the integrity of the data because "verification that was not solely the responsibility of the verifying side would amount to self-inspection." Warren Heckrotte, "Verification of Test Ban Treaties," in William Potter, ed., *Verification and Arms Control*, p. 67.

36. Philip Schrag, *Listening for the Bomb: A Study in Nuclear Arms Control Verification Policy* (Boulder: Westview Press, 1989).

37. See, for example, Christer Jonsson, *Soviet Bargaining Behavior* (New York: Columbia University Press, 1979) and Glenn Seaborg, *Kennedy, Khrushchev and the Test Ban* (Berkeley: University of California Press, 1981).

38. Nancy Gallagher, *The Politics of Verification and the Control of Nuclear Tests,* Ph.D. Dissertation, The University of Illinois at Champaign-Urbana, (forthcoming, 1990).

4

Preventing Nuclear War: Arms Management

Susan M. Burns

Verification—a means of monitoring a counterpart nation's military activities and assessing whether these activities are in compliance with the terms of a negotiated agreement—cannot be considered in isolation from its essentially arms-controlling function. The verification of compliance with a negotiated arms control agreement, based on information collected through various monitoring methods, is fundamentally a task of determining whether the goals of the *agreement*, not the verification regime itself, are being met.

This and the following chapter survey a range of arms control options, including many *not* requiring verification, of greatest relevance to South Asia. The liberal emphasis here on Western, primarily U.S.-Soviet, conceptions and examples should *not* imply that these are the only "correct" kinds of arms control measures that might be adopted by South Asia or that they could be transferred to other regions without modification. But U.S.-Soviet efforts to define and refine arms control comprise the most extensive body of arms control experience to date. The lessons of forty years of "nuclear learning," including several serious crises cannot be ignored.

Arms Control Approaches and Definitions

Americans and Soviets have long recognized the importance of managing a relationship of mutual and stable deterrence, in which the disincentives to initiate military conflict outweigh the incentives, even in a crisis. For example, a premise of the 1972 Antiballistic Missile Treaty (ABM) is that ABM systems could seriously threaten a counterpart's ability to retaliate after a strategic first strike, weakening mutual deterrence.[1] We opt for a similarly broad view of arms control objectives as the avoidance of military conflict (i.e., war prevention), reducing the destructiveness of military conflict should it occur, and reducing the economic and other costs associated with preparing for military conflict.[2]

Arms control measures are of two major types: first, reducing incentives to engage in military conflict by enhancing deterrence and crisis stability and, second, weapons reductions, eliminations prohibitions, or renunciations of the ability to make certain kinds of, weapons. The first type will be referred to here as *arms management* and comprises the subject of this chapter. The second type, referred to as *arms limitations*, is discussed in Chapter 5. Both kinds of arms control are intended to meet the three objectives above, but represent two very distinct approaches to doing so. Either could be unilateral or negotiated, though most arms limitations are negotiated because they generally require participant states to relinquish something.

Some Provisos

We make no assumptions regarding Indian or Pakistani possession of nuclear weapons or intentions to to develop them. We do contend, however, should both countries opt for deployment of nuclear weapons, that deterrence and crisis stability is best enhanced by mutual acknowledgement of such capabilities within an arms control framework aimed at the objectives stated earlier. Nor is this discussion intended to imply that India and Pakistan should or even will use nuclear weapons under any circumstances. We assume that the political leaders of a nuclear-weaponized India or Pakistan will be as rational in their crisis decision-making as the leaders of *any* nuclear weapons state.

Rationality, moreover, should not be confused with morality; it can be justifiably argued that the extreme magnitude of destructiveness peculiar to nuclear weapons makes any use of them immoral. But decisionmakers severely constrained by time and erroneous perceptions of adversary behavior and capabilities could quite "rationally" conclude that striking first with nuclear weapons is their best or rather, only, option. Understanding the circumstances that could inspire such decisions is vital to ensuring, or at least maximizing the probability, that a nation's leaders are never put in a position of having to make them. Encouraging efforts to prevent nuclear war and institutionalize a stable and mutual deterrence should no more promote Indian or Pakistani use of nuclear weapons, than providing clean hypodermic needles to prevent the spread of AIDS "encourages" the use of heroin.

Nuclear Deterrence and South Asia

Defining Deterrence Stability

Deterrence stability forms the foundation on which war prevention rests. Thomas Schelling and Morton Halperin provide a definition that is relevant to the South Asian context:

> A "balance of deterrence"—*a situation in which the incentives on both sides to initiate war are outweighed by the disincentives*—is described as "stable" when it is reasonably secure against shocks, alarms, and perturbations. That is, it is stable when political events, internal or external to the countries involved, technological change, accidents, false alarms, misunderstandings, crises, limited wars, or changes in the intelligence available to both sides, *are unlikely to disturb the incentives sufficiently to make deterrence fail.*[3] (Emphasis added.)

Deterrence stability is considered to be composed of three essential elements: crisis stability, arms-race stability, and political stability. The first refers to absence of incentives to strike first with nuclear weapons in a crisis, the second to absence of incentives for rapid qualitative or quantitative expansion of a state's nuclear arsenal vis-à-vis that of an adversary, while the last refers to "the effectiveness of deterrence in reducing incentives for major coercive political changes."[4] Deterrence is as much a product of politics and perceptions as technology; this is likely to hold true in South Asia as elsewhere.

Deterrence Stability and Covert Nuclear Forces

In the absence of significant perturbations in each state's perceptions of the security threats posed by extra-regional states and each other, India and Pakistan are likely to continue their pursuits of military nuclear capabilities covertly; the current state of nuclear ambiguity may well persist for the next few years. Presently, no evidence of Indian or Pakistani nuclear weapons deployments exists. Yet some contend that mutual awareness of abilities to produce air-deliverable fission weapons in a short period of time enables a crude deterrence relationship between these countries.[5]

Before assessing the efficacy and stability of such a crude deterrence system, however, it is essential to distinguish between two types of "nuclear ambiguity." The first type is characterized by pairs of potentially hostile states, such as India and Pakistan, which demonstrate no evidence of actual deployment of militarily meaningful (i.e., deliverable) nuclear weapons, but do show a continuing pattern of limited, unacknowledged nuclear weapons research and fissile materials production. Potentially hostile states officially disavowing possession of nuclear weapons but for which some evidence exists that one or the other has actually deployed them comprise the second type of ambiguity. For states of the first type, such as India and Pakistan, a deliberate and mutual nuclear ambiguity, marked by "tacit bargaining,"[6] may be quite stable as long as neither side possesses sufficient incentive to move toward the latter form of nuclear ambiguity. Should India, Pakistan or both make the transition to covert deployment of nuclear weapons,[7] there is ample reason to believe that their "nuclear relations" will be characterized by a great deal of instability in crisis situations. Crisis misperceptions could have a way of feeding on themselves, of magnifying threats in the absence of confirmatory evidence regarding an adversary's true capabilities or intentions. Further, uncertainties about adversary capabilities may provide impetus for arms racing. The U.S. bomber and missile gap hysteria of the late 1950s is illustrative.[8]

Uncertainty about the *outcome* of military conflict (for example, being unsure about whether one's probable losses will outweigh any potential gains) may enhance deterrence. Uncertainty about an adversary's ability to carry out deterrent threats, in contrast, most likely does not. Inaccurate assessment, particularly underestimation, of a counterpart's true retaliatory capabilities vis-à-vis one's own has been implicated as a likely motive for surprise attack.[9] Much deterrence theory analysis justifiably centers on how states can credibly *communicate* their possession of sufficient capability to back up deterrent threats. If a state is to successfully deter its adversaries from undertaking actions that threaten its most vital interests it must effectively communicate both a willingness and capability to respond in ways that would make such adventurism unprofitable for its initiator. Nuclear ambiguity, by definition, entails a lack of formal communication about just what constitutes "vital interests," willingness to retaliate with nuclear weapons against threats to vital interests, and most importantly, possession of the capability to do so.

Even if India and Pakistan were to declare nuclear weapons status, the transitional phase to mutual deterrence is likely to be characterized by significant deterrence *instability*.[10] However, the prospects for evolution of a stable system of mutual deterrence in a situation of covert nuclear weapons deployments are doubtful. *Because secrecy would preclude communicating the adoption of deterrence and crisis stabilizing measures, keeping nuclear weapons covert would effectively freeze in place any existing incentives for preemption during a serious crisis or conventional war.* For example, Pakistan could secretly adopt measures to ensure the survivability of a larger fraction of its nuclear delivery systems (most likely aircraft) under attack. But it would have to credibly communicate its ability to retain retaliatory sufficiency in order to successfully deter preemption by an adversary, even under conditions of a serious crisis.

In either the case of covert deployment or post-declaration of nuclear weapons status, both India and Pakistan may well perceive strong incentives to strike first in a severe crisis or conventional war in anticipation of preemption by the other, given two factors: first, significant asymmetries in capabilities and vulnerability will exist between India and Pakistan in the early stages of nuclear weapons deployments and second, each country is very likely to be aware of such asymmetries between them. In a crisis or conventional war, incentives to use nuclear weapons first could arise under two conditions. First, the country with "inferior" capabilities (in terms of vulnerability to preemption and retaliatory insufficiency)

anticipates preemption of a significant fraction of its nuclear
capabilities by its adversary. This would most likely comprise
Pakistan's situation. Second, the country with "superior"
capabilities is aware of its counterpart's vulnerabilities and, in a
crisis, has reason to believe the latter is anticipating preemption and
thus likely to use its nuclear weapons first. India could well be
confronted with this dilemma.

A nuclear Pakistan may thus give serious consideration to
adopting a launch-on-warning policy. Air distances from Indian
bases to potential targets are so short that Pakistan may not wait to
absorb an Indian preemptive strike before acting, especially if
preemption could destroy most of Pakistan's retaliatory capability.
A policy of launch-on-warning under these circumstances would be
dangerously hair-trigger.[11]

Again, such incentives may continue to exist even if nuclear
weapons status is declared, especially if such declaration was made
in the absence of arms control aimed at reducing vulnerability to
preemption and enhancing crisis stability. But, because of the
greater certainty regarding the capabilities of an overtly nuclear
adversary, a much stronger element of caution would be introduced,
substantially decreasing incentives to engage in provocation that
might lead to lead to the kind of serious crisis that inspires nuclear
first-use. Overt status may thus enhance pre-crisis deterrence
stability. The explicit unilateral and bilateral adoption of arms
management measures, however, would be essential to enhancing
deterrence stability under crisis conditions.

Arms management can be both a means of mitigating many of
the uncertainties that feed threat perceptions and of recognizing the
requirements of a stable deterrence relationship, should Indian and
Pakistani nuclear weaponization and deployment become a *fait
accompli*. By formalizing, in December, 1988, an agreement not to
attack each other's nuclear facilities, Rajiv Gandhi and Benazir
Bhutto recognized that the destruction of one state's nuclear option
by the other is a highly probable action in a war, or even a less
serious crisis. By doing so, both also acknowledged the logic of
instability inherent in an ambiguous nuclear relationship. Each also
seemed to implicitly accept the right of the other to retain a nuclear
option (mutual recognition of the right to exercise the option—go
nuclear—may be another matter altogether). A regional nuclear

monopoly, as Israel attempted to impose on the Middle East with its destruction of Iraq's OSIRAK reactor, is probably not in the long term interests of either state, even if in the form of an ambiguous option.[12]

Arms Management and Covert Nuclear Forces

Mutual acknowledgement of military nuclear capabilities would be essential for arms control efforts that aim to institutionalize a stable relationship of mutual deterrence. If India and Pakistan should decide to deploy nuclear weapons, declarations of such intent would permit the explicit adoption of measures to ensure nuclear weapons safety, security, and survivability under attack. Moreover, admitting military nuclear capabilities would enable each side to communicate clearly the circumstances under which it would resort to the use of nuclear weapons, and the will and capability to do so or retaliate in response to nuclear first use. Without such communication one or the other side may be tempted to press on in a crisis, believing its opponent incapable of initiating the use of nuclear weapons or retaliating should the aggressor initiate their use. This would be especially likely if an aggressor were to initiate the use of tactical nuclear weapons in the mistaken belief that it could keep a conflict limited because its victim lacked the means to respond in a similar fashion.[13]

It has already been noted that covert nuclear status impedes the adoption of arms management measures aimed at remedying deterrence instabilities. There are a number of persuasive reasons in favor of a covert nuclear weapons state declaring its status, *if it has deployed militarily usable nuclear weapons*. Shai Feldman describes four principal reasons why secretive nuclear weapons capabilities are more dangerous than overt nuclear status:[14]

First, the circle of relevant decisionmakers is necessarily kept small in the interests of secrecy. Little or no accountability thus exists in the formulation of strategic doctrine or nuclear targeting plans. Only during a crisis could the existence and plans for use of nuclear weapons become known to those outside the limited circle of decisionmakers.

Second, doctrine for covert nuclear forces is likely to be formulated exclusively by the military. Consequently, doctrines and plans for use of nuclear weapons are likely to be of an offensive, warfighting nature, increasing the probability that the weapons will actually be used in a serious crisis or conflict. Command and control capabilities are likely to be limited because of secrecy, severely impeding efforts to terminate the use of nuclear weapons, especially tactical, once begun. It is improbable that technical and procedural mechanisms to guard against premature or unauthorized use of nuclear weapons will have been implemented.

Third, covert nuclear weapons states cannot communicate the intentions regarding circumstances likely to provoke the use of nuclear weapons that are the basis of stable deterrence. NATO's doctrine of willingness to initiate the use of nuclear weapons in the event of imminent conventional defeat, whatever its merits on other grounds, conveys an unambiguous message about what actions by a potential adversary could well provoke the use of nuclear weapons. The intentions/capability communications function of arms control has been discussed earlier. Of this Feldman writes that "[t]he transmission of messages regarding capabilities and intentions must be an ongoing activity; if it is delayed until the actual occurrence of war escalation may be unavoidable."[15]

Finally, widespread domestic awareness of the existence of nuclear weapons capabilities sensitizes elites to the dangers of aggression. Knowledge of the existence of such weapons is likely to induce considerable trepidation among both elites who might otherwise encourage policies of aggression and naively overconfident adversaries.

These are not arguments in favor of "going nuclear." Rather, they are strong cautionary notes to states with an extant covert nuclear weapons capability (such states already gone nuclear) about the obligations of safely maintaining such an arsenal. If India and Pakistan are currently *in possession of nuclear weapons,* effective arms management undertaken in the interests of deterrence and crisis stability demands that the bombs be brought up from the basement.

Reasons for Keeping Covert

Certainly, states which have yet to deploy nuclear weapons should be encouraged to abstain from doing so. For states that have covertly deployed nuclear weapons, there are several compelling strategic justifications for not declaring commitment to nuclear weapons-state status.

Most significantly, covert status can itself be an implicit form of arms control, because its successful maintenance imposes severe restraints on weapons development and size of arsenals. Obviously, only zero-yield and non-nuclear component testing is permissible under such conditions, constraining the development of tactical nuclear weapons and the mating of warheads to ballistic missiles because the former require confidence in expected yield and the latter requires that warheads be relatively miniaturized.[16]

Covert status can preserve diplomatic and domestic political flexibility by enabling quiet retreat from commitment to nuclear weapons-state status.[17] Once nuclear weapons status is declared, reversal of commitment and renunciation of nuclear weapons may prove impossible. However, if renunciation is done unilaterally in a context of secrecy, rival states may continue to hold now-erroneous perceptions that the "renouncing" state still possesses some form of nuclear weapons capability. Ideally, covert nuclear rivals would mutually renounce commitment to nuclear weapons status, though this may be extremely difficult to effect in practice, if "negotiated" tacitly.

Declaration of nuclear weapons status may inspire states considering nuclear weapons to push ahead with developing them. Even states which had given little thought to a nuclear weapons program prior to another's declaration of status might be encouraged to undertake such a program. In the case of rival "threshold" states, such as India and Pakistan, which have not yet deployed nuclear weapons, a declaration of commitment to status as a nuclear weapons state by one would most certainly be followed by a similar declaration by the other.

Before considering the compatibility between effective arms control and "nuclear ambiguity," however, we must first distinguish between declaration of nuclear weapons *possession* and declaration of *commitment* to nuclear weapons-state status. Conceivably, both India and Pakistan could declare possession within the context of an arms control regime, while refraining from *official commitment* to nuclear weapons-state status. Declaration of capabilities within an arms control context need not commit threshold nuclear states such as India and Pakistan to the straight-line nuclear evolution of the established nuclear weapons states (i.e., ever-expanding nuclear arsenals, and the development of advanced nuclear weapons designed for warfighting). Such states could just as well negotiate verifiable restrictions on the size of arsenals, modes of deployment and technical characteristics of existing nuclear weapons while abstaining from additions to military nuclear capabilities. By refraining from additional testing after Pokhran, India demonstrated that states can indeed control the rate at which they acquire nuclear weapons capabilities, and postpone official commitment to nuclear-state status.

Alternatively, arms control measures may be aimed solely at reducing the opportunities for initiation of conventional military conflict and its subsequent escalation to nuclear weapons use, rather than at the existence of the weapons themselves. Such confidence building measures (CBMs) would permit each country to retain nuclear weapons covertly while attempting to eliminate motivations for their use in a conflict. But if a serious crisis or conventional military conflict did develop in the absence of arms control aimed at explicit management of nuclear weapons capabilities, the uncertainties surrounding each country's covert nuclear options and will to use them may overshadow the best of crisis management efforts. Indian temptations to preemptively attack possible warhead storage depots, air bases, or vulnerable missile launchers, and Pakistani incentives to use nuclear weapons in anticipation of a preemptive strike would be no less. Conventional arms confidence building measures are nonetheless a valuable starting point. They may also be easier to negotiate than arms control agreements that necessitate detailed and intrusive verification measures. Trust is an essential element of mutual commitment to arms control regimes requiring verification; confidence building and conventional war prevention measures could provide positive steps toward its development.

Arms Management Measures

Arms management should enhance deterrence stability. In the U.S.-Soviet arms control context, deterrence stability primarily means reducing the incentives to resort to the use of nuclear weapons in a crisis situation, but it can also refer to reducing the incentives to initiate a conventional military conflict that may lead to the use of nuclear weapons. Making such a distinction permits arms controllers to focus on establishing "firebreaks" between political conflict and the initiation of conventional military conflict as well as between the initiation of the latter and escalation to nuclear weapons use. For reasons discussed previously, mutual nuclear deterrence between India and Pakistan may not be so robust as to withstand serious crises such as conventional war. *South Asian nuclear war prevention measures should therefore focus on reducing the incentives for the initiation of conventional military conflict as the "first line of defense" against the potential use of nuclear weapons.* Measures to prevent the escalation of conventional conflict to the nuclear level comprise a crucial second line of defense.

Conventional War Prevention

In the U.S.-Soviet-European context, arms management aimed at preventing the outbreak of conventional war generally refers to the use of confidence-building measures (CBMs).

The importance of CBMs as a potential means of war prevention cannot be understated. The Indian Working Paper submitted to the 1983 session of the United Nations Disarmament Conference disparaged CBMs as being of "marginal significance" and a distraction from the more urgent task of global nuclear disarmament.[18] Rather than mere distractions, however, CBMs can mitigate the factors that could lead to the use of weapons (conventional or nuclear). Furthermore, institutionalizing "mutual reassurance," which might be achieved through a system of CBMs, is probably essential for maintaining long-term deterrence stability.[19] In a related vein, Richard K. Betts notes that "[w]ar is never absolutely inevitable. The challenge to . . . deterrence is to cover the situation where war seems almost inevitable."[20]

Johan Holst and Karen Melander have defined *confidence building* as "The communication of credible evidence of the absence of feared threats."[21] Confidence building *measures* have been defined by Jonathan Alford as "measures that tend to make military intentions explicit."[22] CBMs aim to prevent the initiation of war either through accidental miscalculation and misperception, or by surprise attack. Preventing the latter results primarily from the use of CBMs as a means of removing the element of surprise. Enhancing states' abilities to detect deviations in adversary military actions that may be indicative of war preparations, or accurately interpret adversary military actions not intended as war preparations are thus the most important objectives of CBMs. In other words, CBMs increase predictability (or transparency) about the actions of the other side by "Facilitat[ing] recognition of the 'normal' pattern of military activities."[23] They attempt to do so by constraining the actual or potential use of weapons in three ways: communications and information exchange, observation and inspection, and restraints on operations and deployments. Table 4.1 presents examples of these major types of CBMs.

For a region-specific illustration of the potential usefulness of CBMs for moderating war incentives, consider the crisis precipitated by India's extensive Brass Tacks maneuvers along the India-Pakistan border in 1986-87. By January, 1987 India had placed its troops on full alert, citing a massive buildup of Pakistani troops along the border. Reportedly, each side had together amassed more than 200,000 troops in the area.[24] The Pakistani troop buildup represented a classic "action-reaction" escalation response to the massive Indian maneuvers. The existence of a crisis hotline linking New Delhi and Islamabad seems to have done little good: H.K. Dua, an editor of the *Hindustan Times,* remarked that "no one [had] even tried to talk on the hotline with the other."[25] Compounding the lack of accurate information available to either side were exaggerated figures and misleading maps of the Pakistani troop buildup printed in the Indian press. The source of such distorted information was reportedly "high-level defense briefings."[26] Moreover, there were indications that the Indian maneuvers were undertaken at least partly as a way to warn Pakistan not to acquire AWACs radar aircraft from the U.S. The gravity of the crisis was evinced by former Pakistani President Zia ul-Haq's remark that, "Neither India or Pakistan wanted to go to war but we could have easily gone into war."[27]

The escalation of fears and misperceptions and the resultant massing of troops by both sides most likely could have been avoided had certain kinds of CBMs been adopted by India and Pakistan prior to the initiation of the Brass Tacks maneuvers. At least four types of CBMs might have contributed to averting this near blunder into war:

- Prior notification of forthcoming maneuvers above a specified ceiling, in particular those held near sensitive border areas. Notification well in advance would prevent the use of military maneuvers for political intimidation, a potential precipitant of military conflict, especially if the intimidation is blatant. Notification data should include: general purpose of the maneuver, numerical strength of forces involved, area, and duration of the exercise.[28]
- Ceilings on the size of maneuvers near sensitive border areas.
- The presence of Indian observers or inspectors at Pakistani military exercises and vice versa, to confirm data provided by notification.
- Active, early use of the crisis hotline by each side to clarify intentions should evidence of misperception by a counterpart become evident. Obviously for communications measures to be effective, communication must take place.

A subsequent incident involving India and China later in 1987 resulted in the massing of a total of 400,000 troops by both countries along the Chinese border with Arunachal Pradesh in northeastern India.[29] China claimed that Indian troops had crossed into the Chinese-controlled Tibetan Autonomous District. The basis for such conflict between India and China stems from contested territory along the border, a dispute that has its origins in Anglo-Chinese treaties of the 19th century and contributed to the 1962 China-India war. India and China may be reluctant to implement CBMs until such territorial issues are resolved to the satisfaction of both sides. However, establishing a crisis hotline between Beijing and New Delhi, and verifiable agreement to abstain from conducting military exercises in contested territory might be two useful measures that both countries could adopt for the duration of negotiations to resolve border claims.

Lessons from the Sinai. A non-European context in which CBMs have been especially successful is the inspection and monitoring regime established by the Israeli-Egyptian Sinai Disengagement Agreement of 1975. Verification of this agreement involved the use of unmanned sensor fields located at the entrances to the Giddi and Mitla Passes, Egyptian and Israeli manned

TABLE 4.1 Types of Conventional Confidence Building
Measures[30]

Communications and Information Exchange	Observation and Inspection	Restrictions on Deployment and Operations
Disclosure of military budgets, major unit and command location and organization, force levels and doctrine	Exchange of observers at major maneuvers	Maneuver/movement /exercise ceilings
Notification of conventional weapons accidents or unauthorized use that could adversely affect security of other side	On-site inspections (OSI)	Thinning of forces within designated border zones
Notification of major military maneuvers, especially those near sensitive border areas	Remote and manned permanent monitoring and observation posts	Ban on forward basing of offensive conventional weapons support equipment
Ban on coded radio traffic	Non-concealment/ transparency measures (to enhance observation by inspectors or NTM)	Designated troop entry/exit points
		Ban on "simulated attack" maneuvers
Crisis "hotline" communications links		Agreement not to use maneuvers for political signalling and intimidation

surveillance posts at opposite ends of the Giddi Pass, and a
demilitarized buffer zone monitored by the United Nations
Emergency Force.[31] The unmanned sensor fields provided an
electronic early warning system capable of detecting and identifying
intruding vehicles and even people. Monitoring technology for the
sensor fields was provided by the U.S. as a guarantor of the
agreement. The United States also conducted SR-71 reconnaissance
overflights of the area on a weekly basis. Information obtained by
U.S. aerial surveillance was relayed directly to Egypt, Israel, the
U.S., and the UNEF command. U.S. on-site inspection teams
performed an additional verification function.

The success of the Sinai verification and monitoring regime is evident in the lack of reported or detected treaty violations considered serious enough jeopardize the accord. Nor were any significant complaints of attempts to collect collateral military intelligence registered with the Egyptian-Israeli Joint Military Commission, a mechanism established by the agreement for consultation purposes. Apparently, all compliance questions were resolved satisfactorily by the Commission.

In South Asia the obvious candidates for a similar confidence-building and verification regime would be disputed territories and boundary lines in Kashmir, such as the Siachen Glacier, Aksai Chin, and the Kashmir cease-fire "line of actual control" established in 1972. Territory in dispute between India and China in the northeast is an added possibility. The most serious political obstacle to implementing such a monitoring regime is, of course, the need for agreement to militarily disengage from disputed areas; neither India or Pakistan officially recognizes the line of control as the status quo in Kashmir, and China rejects India's interpretation of the McMahon Line as the latter's international border. Nonetheless, a monitoring and inspection regime could serve to effectively verify temporary disengagement agreements during negotiations over contested territories. Such an arrangement could effectively avert hostilies or "accidents" that might derail a delicate negotiating process. It could also provide a trial run of verification systems for a more permanent settlement. In addition to demonstrating the merit of rather low-cost, low-maintenance CBM monitoring technology, the Sinai disengagement experience illustrates a number of lessons with relevance to South Asia:[32]

- Successful verification can itself contribute to easing political tensions between adversaries.
- Trusted third-party states can provide significant technical and administrative assistance for implementing a verification regime.
- On-site inspections can be intensive, yet not offensively intrusive.
- A joint, high-level military (or civilian) commission can act effectively as a compliance and consultation mechanism.
- Formal treaties and agreements provide a legal framework for implementing effective verification.

• A graduated thinning of military forces closer to sensitive border areas reduces the opportunities for military conflict.

The Limitations of Conventional CBMs. CBMs do not ultimately remove the deep causes of conflict between adversarial states even if, as demonstrated by the Sinai experience, effectively verifiable agreements can contribute to a process of political confidence-building. Ascribing to CBMs a lofty goal of cessation of all or even most conflict is a prescription for disappointment and cynicism about any type of arms control.

CBMs can certainly help to confine unresolvable political conflict to the political and diplomatic arena by curtailing its transformation to military action. Their success in doing so, however, is at least as dependent on the political willingness of adversaries to make them work as they are on effective verification.

Whether CBMs actually prevent surprise attack is questionable; any state determined to undertake offensive military action will likely find clever routes of deception.[33] In any arms control situation states intent on violating the terms of an agreement will ferret out whatever opportunities may exist for evasion. What CBMs can do, for states committed to the avoidance of war, is remove the most gratuitous reasons for initiating it, namely, accident, miscalculation, and misperception. They can also inhibit the deployment of military forces for political intimidation by obligating each side to notify the other of impending maneuvers. Even if a state is intent on initiating a military attack under cover of an announced maneuver, the need to overcome CBM-induced obstacles in order to maintain true deception will likely present the target state with several clues indicative of an impending attack. This assumes, of course, that the target state interprets clues correctly. U.S. military intelligence certainly had sufficient evidence of a probable attack on Pearl Harbor but fell victim to its own disbelief. To quote Betts again: "Inadequacies in warning are rarely due to absolute failure to ring an alarm. Usually the problem is a conceptual consensus that rejects the alarm."[34] An added value of CBMs in denying the element of surprise to an attacker is that they can help focus the prospective victim state on where it should look for signs of impending attack.[35] Military officers train to recognize deception (Pearl Harbor notwithstanding); they could just as well train to recognize evidence of deviations from CBM procedures.

Care must be taken by the drafters of CBM accords to prescribe in sufficient detail the conditions under which observation and inspection activities will take place, and what information shall be collected.[36]   Otherwise, observation/inspection CBMs might degenerate to exercises in guided tourism, restricted to "maneuvers" staged for the benefit of inspectors.   Provisions for challenge inspections might allay some of these difficulties but, as will be seen later, challenge OSI is not without significant political risk.

CBMs must also avoid interference with defensive preparedness. Perhaps the most significant objection to CBMs involving demilitarization of border zones is that troops are denied the opportunity to gain familiarity with the ground they must defend. Unfamiliarity with ground puts a defender at a much greater disadvantage relative to a prospective attacker. Jonathan Alford suggests one solution to this problem: limit exercises to single divisions in border areas. Under such an arrangement, careful planning would allow successive generations of divisions to gain familiarity with border territory over time.[37] Deceptive attack would be extremely difficult to carry out with only a single division.

In the South Asian context, an India-Pakistan or India-China CBM regime would also have to allow for a limited military presence along borders for management of internal unrest. A significant potential for secessionist rebellion and communal unrest in border areas exists in all of these countries (in India, the Punjab and Kashmir primarily; in Pakistan, Sind; in China, Tibet). A South Asian CBM regime must incorporate procedures for distinguishing between troops deployed for external offensive action and those dispatched to quell domestic disturbances. Finally, Indian, Pakistani, and Chinese leaders may question the value of restrictions on their military movements within their own territories. Though CBMs require some limitation of sovereignty in this regard, each country would likely experience a net gain in security if the military activities of potential adversaries are similarly restrained.

Nuclear Arms Management Measures

The earlier discussion of conventional CBMs was examined ways to ultimately reduce the probability nuclear conflict by effectively blocking one route to its inception: conventional military conflict. But this represents only one possible path to nuclear war:

- What if, despite conventional war prevention measures, it nevertheless occurs? Can its escalation to the nuclear level be averted?
- What if misperceptions deriving from a political conflict, a nuclear weapons accident, or terrorist nuclear threat inspired one country to strike preemptively with nuclear weapons, skipping the conventional war-escalation step altogether?

Both of these questions imply a need for measures to reduce the incentives for nuclear weapons use by increasing the disincentives, i.e. institutionalizing a "balance of stable deterrence." We do *not* presume possession of nuclear weapons by either India or Pakistan, nor do we wish to speculate here about the technological sophistication or size of Indian and Pakistani nuclear arsenals, should they exist. Rather, the attempt here is to anticipate potential arms control needs if these countries decide to actively deploy nuclear weapons.

Some potential nuclear weapons management measures (e.g., EMP-hardening of command, control and communications centers) may well be beyond the current technological and economic capabilities of either country (Pakistan especially) and thus cannot be considered short-term remedies. Longer-term capital and technology intensive measures are considered briefly; emphasis is otherwise on rather low-technology actions that can be implemented fairly readily to mitigate the transitional instability inherent in the initial stages of nuclear weapons programs.

Preventing Nuclear War—Unilateral Measures

One measure, requiring relatively little technical and economic investment, that each country can implement promptly is to *adopt enhanced security procedures at nuclear facilities*. Paul Leventhal and Brahma Chellaney report that current security measures, with the exception of the most sensitive facilities (Pakistan's Kahuta and India's BARC nuclear complexes) are generally lax.[38] The possibility of unauthorized access to materials usable in nuclear explosive devices is significant. Secessionist, ethnic, and communal interests have been sources of terrorist activity in the past and will continue to be so in the future. Nuclear terrorism is thus a threat that cannot be discounted by either Indian or Pakistani political authorities; a terrorist device exploded in an urban area might, through confusion about its source, be interpreted as the opening round of an adversary nuclear strike. More probable is the accusation of a counterpart government of having sponsored the terrorists that detonated the device, should a determination be made that it was indeed a terrorist weapon. Prevention of these or similar incidents demands rigorous protection of nuclear facilities from insider sabotage or unauthorized possession and diversion of sensitive nuclear materials. A strict national system of nuclear material accounting and control is imperative (the U.S. Nuclear Materials Management and Safeguards System required of U.S. civilian nuclear facilities provides a good example). Additionally, both countries should implement IAEA guidelines for physical protection and security of nuclear facilities.[39] These are measures that can be adopted regardless of current or anticipated nuclear weapons status. Apparently, neither India or Pakistan has undertaken such measures to date.[40]

Prevention of unauthorized access to and use of nuclear weapons themselves will pose a problem of correspondingly greater magnitude as increasing numbers of these are deployed. The unauthorized or accidental explosion of a military nuclear device on foreign territory would undoubtedly appear to carry the imprimatur of an adversary government, much more so than a crude terrorist device. Dispersal of weapons to enhance survivability in war could conversely degrade their security by increasing opportunities for unauthorized access. Indian and Pakistani civilian and military authorities are certainly conscious of the imperatives of averting terrorist access to nuclear weapons. But unauthorized access to or use of nuclear weapons by mutinous military personnel or enemy seizure in war pose equally hazardous threats.

For both countries then, should they commit to deployment of nuclear weapons, the development of technical and procedural mechanisms to *divorce nuclear weapons access from use* must be a top priority. Permissive Action Links (PALs), electromechanical combination locks incorporated into the arming circuitry of most

U.S. warheads, require the entry of correct enabling codes before warhead arming can proceed. Newer U.S. PALs have a "limited try" feature; a few attempts at insertion of invalid codes triggers a locking mechanism that disables the warhead. U.S. strategic bombers employ a Bomber Coded Switch System (BCSS) which locks the bomb-bay release mechanism until the aircraft commander enters a valid code.[41]

While such technical mechanisms are designed to control warhead enablement, procedural safeguards aim to restrict the actions of those having access to nuclear weapons. Sensitive U.S. nuclear weapons operations are guided by a two-man rule; nuclear weapon enablement additionally requires the simultaneous execution of a strict sequence of actions by two individuals of similar training and authority.[42] U.S. ICBM launch procedures illustrate the concept most vividly. Not only must each of the two launch officers in a Minuteman launch capsule insert and turn launch keys simultaneously but so also must the two man crew of another capsule within the same squadron before any missiles can launch. Each capsule within a squadron is equipped with inhibit switches that can be used to veto an unauthorized launch by crews in other capsules.[43]

American nuclear weapons operations are further predicated on centralized civilian control over decision-making. Emergency Action Messages (EAMs) containing warhead and weapon enablement codes (such as might be received by a Minuteman launch crew, who must then decode and authenticate its validity) are released only by the highest civilian authorities: the National Command Authority is composed only of the President and Secretary of Defense, or their authorized deputies or successors.[44] In India and Pakistan, similar highest-level civilian control over decisions regarding nuclear weapons use and release of authorization would be integral to both precluding unauthorized use and consolidating escalation firebreaks between conventional and nuclear conflict. We can expect that much of the same debate about compromising security versus inhibiting readiness that accompanied initial U.S. implementation of of PAL mechanisms and code-release procedures will arise among Indian and Pakistani nuclear decisionmakers. While force readiness and survivability are given high priority in the U.S. (e.g., naval nuclear warheads, considered to be in an environment providing almost no opportunity for unauthorized use, are   not equipped with PAL devices), the President retains final authority over decisions regarding employment of U.S. strategic forces.[45]

Electrical and mechanical safeguards against accidental detonation of a weapon exposed to fire, mishandling, or aircraft crashes, have also been incorporated into U.S. nuclear warheads. The use of insensitive high explosives (IHE), and the design of warheads for "one-point safety"[46] are two examples of U.S. warhead safing mechanisms. Arming mechanisms are also designed for weapon safety. For example, gravity bombs utilize sensors that detect the presence of an external environment characteristic of a released weapon; arming will proceed only if sensors indicate that the weapon is following a trajectory identical to that of a bomb in free fall. Once arming is "okayed" by PAL and safing devices, fuzing mechanisms ensure that the warhead detonates at its pre-programmed destination or point in space.[47]

Two other unilateral measures for prevention of nuclear weapons use entail political, rather than technical or procedural, decisions by nuclear-weapon policymakers. First, use of nuclear alerts or threats of nuclear weapons use for political signalling or intimidation should be scrupulously avoided. Such actions would tend only to exacerbate tensions and crisis misperceptions more than encourage accommodation.[48] Second, both India and Pakistan should abstain from adoption of launch-on-warning systems or policies. Bombers might be be recalled if scrambled in response to a false alarm but determination that the alarm was indeed false would not likely be made before the planes had penetrated adversary airspace, given the short flight times between Indian and Pakistani targets. Time constraints for missile launch decisions would be even more severe. Missiles, of course, could not be recalled.[49]

Finally, reducing the vulnerability of missiles and aircraft to preemptive attack would decrease incentives for such attack while concurrently relieving pressures for adoption of a launch-on-warning policy. Aside from dispersal of weapons, reinforced concrete shelters for aircraft and underground silos for missiles are options. Egypt employs concrete shelters for aircraft protection.[50] Construction of hardened missile silos and underground launch control facilities, while not an impossibility for either India or

Pakistan, are capital and technology intensive options not likely to be available for a number of years following decisions to overtly deploy nuclear weapons. An inexpensive partial solution might be to adopt the Chinese example of basing some missiles in caves[51] or on ships at sea. Mobile basing of missiles on trucks, railcars, submarines or surface ships, presumes, of course, the implementation of stringent technical and procedural safeguards against unauthorized access and use. Maintaining a certain percentage of nuclear-armed aircraft on a high alert level (U.S. SAC bombers maintain a 30% rate of alert[52]), prepared for dispersal in the event of an attack, is a further alternative. Mass dispersal of aircraft, especially in a crisis, however, can be provocative if an adversary perceives such action as prelude to preemptive attack. Abstaining from co-locating warhead storage depots with bomber or missile bases would additionally reduce the attractiveness of the latter as targets for preemption.

Preventing Nuclear War—Bilateral Measures

For communication of concerns about strategy and doctrine, collaborative efforts toward prevention of nuclear terrorism, or exchanging baseline data on nuclear forces, *nuclear risk reduction centers* (NRRCs) linking Indian and Pakistani capitals might be established. In September, 1987, the U.S. and Soviet Union agreed to the establishment of similar centers in Moscow and Washington, primarily for the purpose of exchanging information and notifications required by various arms control agreements.[53]

In the South Asian context, however, arms control verification data and compliance questions might be more profitably dealt with by compliance-arbitration and consultative mechanisms established by agreement for such purposes. NRRCs should instead function as additional communications links between counterpart policymakers in the absence of crisis, as conduits for relaying concerns about nuclear weapons or civilian nuclear activities that could be potential sources of conflict. In other words, the primary function of NRRCs is to identify and permit collaboration on mitigating concerns *before* they reach the crisis level. Nevertheless, NRRCs might also serve as a clearinghouse for exchange of CBM notifications and data.

The original U.S. proposal for NRRCs, introduced as an amendment to the 1982 Defense Authorization Act by Senators John Warner and Sam Nunn, called for the centers to "maintain a 24 hour watch over any events with the potential to lead to nuclear incidents."[54] NRRCs linking Islamabad and New Delhi could be staffed by military and civilian liaison officers having direct access to the counterpart country's highest civilian authorities. Nunn and Warner envisioned several functions for U.S.-Soviet NRRCs,[55] with direct relevance to the South Asian context:

1. Discuss and establish procedures for coping with such incidents as a missing nuclear weapon, unexplained nuclear explosions, terrorist nuclear incidents and the like.
2. Facilitate close communications during incidents of nuclear terrorism in order to implement collaborative action to deal with them. Collaborative efforts might include exchange of technical and intelligence information regarding acquisition of nuclear weapons or weapons materials and equipment by subnational groups.
3. Exchange information about military nuclear activities that could be subject to misinterpretation by the other side; Provision of such information would be voluntary and procedures must be implemented to avoid the use of NRRCs for transmitting deliberately deceptive information.
4. Discuss nuclear doctrines and strategic practices that elicit suspicions or anxiety.

The second function, that of maintaining close contact during terrorist nuclear incidents, is really a crisis control measure. The suspicions and confusion likely to be generated by a nuclear terrorist incident in South Asia would demand that the top leadership of both India and Pakistan maintain constant communications until the nature of the incident is clarified by NRRC technical staff. Upgrading any existing crisis hotline links between regional heads of government to include high speed facsimile transmission would facilitate crisis resolution efforts. Upper-echelon military commanders could maintain contact through NRRC liaison officers if decisions regarding potential military action are involved. They should especially do so if the incident concerns unauthorized use or hijacking of nuclear weapons by military personnel.

Other negotiated nuclear war prevention measures might include notifications of missile test and space vehicle launches, and multiple take-offs of dual-capable aircraft above a threshold number in the direction of the other country.[56] Depending on the type, sophistication, and coverage provided by early warning systems employed by South Asian states, either of these activities could trigger alarm in a counterpart country. Exchange of observers at missile test and space vehicle launches, or military nuclear training maneuvers, much like the observation and inspection activities of conventional CBMs, might be additional means of allaying misinterpretations and preventing false alarms. A related measure could be a negotiated ban on encryption of missile test and space vehicle telemetry data.

Preventing Escalation—Unilateral Measures

Much of our earlier discussion about prevention of nuclear war by decreasing the chances of its initiation via routes other than conventional war escalation is equally germane to the latter context. The peacetime implementation of the series of measures just described could certainly foster moderation of the escalatory "action-reaction" spiral that could lead to nuclear weapons use in a crisis.

It is arguable that, in a military conflict that has remained strictly conventional, relevant decisionmakers would continue to hold strong psychological aversions to initiating the use of nuclear weapons. The precedent created by the first use of nuclear weapons, however, could seriously weaken inhibitions against subsequent use by either side.[57] The most important conventional war escalation-prevention measures will be those that strengthen the aversions, or disincentives, to initiating the first use of nuclear weapons.

Deescalation Procedures. It is a truism that climbing back down the escalation ladder is much more difficult than climbing up.[58] Nevertheless, Indian and Pakistani strategic planners and leaders should seriously contemplate devising procedures for deescalation and early termination of conventional military conflict. Much of the literature on war termination (nuclear or conventional) is necessarily speculative and theoretical: instances of deescalation are rarer than those of escalation and, of course, no example of nuclear conflict deescalation exists. Deescalation in the case of conventional war, at least, appears to hinge on the communication by each side of thresholds it will not cross, i.e., on the establishment of ground rules of engagement both prior to and during conflict. No India-Pakistan war has been especially prolonged; both sides appear, tacitly at least, to acknowledge a need for "damage limitation" in conventional conflict.[59] Certainly, leaders and relevant policymakers of both countries are aware that possession of nuclear weapons magnifies the imperative of limiting future conventional conflict. Any damage Pakistan might inflict on India with nuclear weapons, however limited, would be far more devastating than might be achieved with a strictly conventional attack. Under such circumstances, traditional notions of conventional military superiority enabling the kind of decisive victory that ends conflict quickly, are tenuous at best.

No Early Use vs. No First Use. One doctrinal measure is to avoid strategies that demand early use of nuclear weapons in an as-yet conventional war. A general policy of no *first* use of nuclear weapons in the face of imminent conventional defeat would be far more acceptable to India than Pakistan, because of the former's superior conventional military capabilities.[60] Pakistan might consider any uncertainty surrounding its willingness to initiate nuclear weapons use in the event of conventional conflict with India as enhancing deterrence of Indian military adventurism. For similar reasons NATO has resisted officially adopting a policy of nuclear no-first use.[61] Pakistan could commit to a policy of no early use of nuclear weapons without degrading the credibility of its nuclear deterrent. However, no early use or no first use policies entail much more than simple declaration. Effective communication of such policies requires a commensurate structuring of military forces and doctrine such that the worst of an Indian conventional assault could be staved off long enough to buy time for crisis resolution and negotiation of a ceasefire. In sum, the aim here is to raise the conventional "tripwire" to a height where moves toward early termination of a conventional war become both plausible and worth pursuing. Ideally, no-early or no-first use policies would be coupled with negotiated conventional arms limitations and CBMs aimed at addressing or rendering unimportant the perceived disparities in conventional military capabilities that motivate adoption of first-use strategies.[62]

Emphasize Distinction Between Nuclear and Conventional Weapons. Indian and Pakistani military planners should avoid the trap of treating nuclear weapons as simply more powerful conventional weapons, i.e., abstain from assigning to nuclear weapons the achievement of conventional military objectives but only on a larger scale. The fundamental difference between nuclear and conventional weapons must be emphasized at all levels of military doctrine and operations. Tactical nuclear weapons, as noted earlier, are especially dangerous in this regard because they make such thinking possible, as do highly accurate, relatively low-yield, nuclear ballistic missiles designed for counterforce missions. Concepts of fighting a purposefully limited nuclear war are dubious and fraught with uncertainty; the nature of South Asian geography and population distribution virtually ensures that collateral damage resulting from even limited tactical nuclear weapons use could be extreme.

Command, Control, and Communications. One of the most significant unilateral escalation-prevention measures is the development of stringent command, control, and communications capabilities (C^3) for guiding the use of both conventional and nuclear weapons. This can be defined as "a system of input processing, decision-making and execution for military forces and operations."[63] Tight control over the release and use of nuclear weapons is crucial. Field commanders should not be granted discretionary power regarding even tactical nuclear weapons; lower-level commanders and officers need not be excluded from the nuclear weapons chain of command, but the final authorization for use should originate with the highest levels of civilian authority.

Preventing Escalation—Bilateral Measures

Tactical nuclear weapons pose perhaps the greatest threat to conventional war escalation-prevention. If India and Pakistan were to "go nuclear" a negotiated ban on the forward deployment of tactical nuclear weapons, if not a total prohibition of their production and deployment, would help prevent escalation.

Other than negotiated restrictions on deployments of particularly destabilizing weapons, bilateral escalation prevention measures consist primarily of enhancing communications essential for crisis resolution and war termination. A direct communications link (DCL, or "hotline") between heads of government is an obvious measure. Crisis hotlines function best, however, when used sparingly and not for routine communications. Paul Bracken states it succinctly: "Messages sent over [The U.S.-Soviet DCL] will be taken seriously because the line is used *only* in emergencies."[64] A crisis hotline must also be designed such that messages will always get through; the hotline design must preclude "the possibility that the other side does not answer the telephone."

Nuclear risk reduction centers might provide a second tier of contacts. Though crisis management was not the intent of NRRCs as proposed by Nunn and Warner,[65] facilitating their control could comprise a legitimate activity of an India-Pakistan (or India-China) NRRC. Knowledgeable technical staff could provide data and information. While the highest civilian officials would retain authority to finalize cease-fire agreements and the like, NRRC staff could be empowered to offer suggestions to counterparts on the other side. The working relationships established during peacetime between Indian and Pakistani military and civilian NRRC staffs could potentially expedite crisis management and, ultimately, resolution.

Measures for Early Termination of Nuclear Conflict

The possibility of deterrence failure would exist in a nuclear South Asia as it does elsewhere. Some analysts believe, moreover, that the geographical proximity of India and Pakistan, and the intense, protracted nature of their rivalry implies a high likelihood of nuclear weapons use in a crisis.[66] A legitimate question then, is whether nuclear deterrence failure inevitably demands that nuclear armed adversaries fulfill the threats of deterrence credibility, that is, "do their worst" in response to the first use of nuclear weapons by a counterpart. The answer seems dependent on two factors: the intentions underlying use of nuclear weapons (e.g., preemptive attack, "demonstration shot"), and the extent of initial use of nuclear weapons. Even in the South Asian context, there would be a magnitude of difference between the initial detonation of one or two nuclear weapons and an all-out "strategic" exchange. A massive first strike would leave its victim little option but to respond in kind, assuming the capability to do so still exists. The initial use of one or two or even three, especially tactical, nuclear weapons may still allow room for mutual de-escalatory action. Deescalation requires that, first, decisionmakers of both sides, authorized to negotiate and implement termination of nuclear weapons use, have survived the initial detonations and second, they continue to possess the C^3 capabilities to do so.

However, active peacetime planning for early termination of a nuclear conflict walks a very delicate line between maintaining the credibility of massive retaliatory threats (essential for peacetime deterrence) and enhancing confidence in the ability to deliberately wage a "limited" nuclear war.[67] To an adversary, peacetime unilateral planning for war termination mechanisms might look suspiciously like planning for a purposefully damage limiting—for the side that starts it—war. Yet, planning, in the sense of each side recognizing its counterpart's interest in damage limitation, needn't imply planning for deliberate war. It could also mean the unilateral and bilateral adoption of measures encouraging mutual restraint in the event nuclear weapons are used. Such measures are really an acknowledgement that, despite the best preventive efforts, deterrence could fail.

Unilateral Measures. Effective command, control, and communications procedures are absolutely vital to halting the use of nuclear weapons. Neither India nor Pakistan is likely to possess the technical and economic resources required for adequate protection of C^3 centers and linkages from such effects as electromagnetic pulse (EMP) for several years following a decision to deploy nuclear weapons.[68] If a decision to deploy is nevertheless made, each country should assign a high priority to research and development of EMP- and blast-hardening technology.

The small nuclear arsenals likely to be possessed by India and Pakistan would require much less demanding C^3 capabilities than do the massive and complex arsenals of the U.S. and Soviet Union.[69] This situation is likely to hold as long as the numbers of nuclear weapons remain limited to less than several hundred. However, the relatively restricted geography encompassed by even a limited India-

Pakistan nuclear war implies the extreme vulnerability of whatever C^3 capabilities might exist in these countries. Even if weapons were targeted to explicitly avoid major C^3 centers, collateral damage, including vast numbers of civilian casualties, would be extensive.[70] Both India and Pakistan should eschew nuclear strategies based on "decapitation" strikes, but neither should rely on the benevolence of its counterpart to refrain from attacking its C^3 centers in conflict.[71]

Collateral damage to C^3 capabilities in a nuclear conflict that begins in a very limited way might be reduced by not co-locating major C^3 centers with nuclear weapons bases. Separating major C^3 centers and nuclear weapons bases would potentially facilitate an adversary's deliberate abstention from decapitation strikes. For similar reasons, no U.S. ICBMs are deployed near U.S. Strategic Air Command headquarters in Nebraska.[72] However, it is far more difficult to avoid reliance on civilian telecommunications switching centers, which are necessarily located in or near large cities, for military communications even if major C^3 centers themselves are located away from urban areas. The U.S. Department of Defense, for example, relies heavily on domestic telephone switching centers for emergency communications with strategic nuclear forces.[73] Destruction of switching centers either deliberately or collaterally would fragment communications and isolate C^3 centers.[74]

Adequate command, control, and communications capabilities must endure on *both* sides in order that termination proceed in a timely and effective manner. Robert Leahy has described five necessary (though not sufficient) conditions for "efficient" war termination:

- Command authority is possessed by informed decisionmakers who have *authenticated* authority to initiate and consummate war termination actions.
- Command centers [exist to] provide command support facilities for use by decisionmakers.
- Communications allow decisionmakers to obtain and exchange information at both the intranational and international levels and provide the means by which they direct the forces under their command.
- Attack warning and assessment capabilities to provide information on enemy attacks, to monitor cease-fire

compliance and also to assess damage done in previous attacks.

- Intelligence data, its collection, assessment, and dissemination are essential. Information on the military, political, industrial, and civil state of allies, neutrals, and adversaries will be needed as well.[75]

Even in a very limited India-Pakistan nuclear conflict, the chances are high that the capabilities required for these functions (assuming they exist prior to the initiation of nuclear conflict) will sustain considerable damage. The first of Leahy's prerequisites is nonetheless something both countries can plan for prior to or following a decision to deploy nuclear weapons. Both it and the third prerequisite merit some elaboration as they apply to the South Asian context.

Indian and Pakistani requirements for nuclear weapons security conflict with reducing wartime vulnerability of C^3 centers; a centralized C^3 center staffed by the most senior civilian officials would be destroyed if hit by a single adversary nuclear weapon. Not only would retaliatory capability be paralyzed as a result but war termination would be effectively made impossible. Both countries will thus require a more decentralized chain of civilian command for devolution of authority in war.[76] Authorized successors could disperse to alternate command posts in the event of serious crisis to await word of the status of senior level decisionmakers. For war termination, time is especially crucial; news of an attack on Islamabad or New Delhi, for example, might not be available for hours, during which time many more nuclear weapons might be launched by either side. A successor-designation system must be capable of ascertaining on a frequent, periodic basis the status and location of all in the line of succession. The U.S. Federal Emergency Management Agency (FEMA) has developed a "central locator system" which monitors the hour-by-hour location of the President and all Presidential successors.[77] This information is also provided to all command centers. Furthermore, the system must be capable of both authenticating the identity of individuals claiming authority and determining that their superiors in the chain of command are in fact dead or incapacitated.

Bilateral Measures. Assuming the survivability of key officials or their designated successors and adequate C^3 capabilities, India and Pakistan might have to negotiate an end to nuclear conflict in the midst of fighting it. To save vital minutes each side could transmit simple preformatted messages through crisis communications links indicating a willingness to cease fire.[78] The U.S.-Soviet Direct Communications Link similarly uses preformatted messages for communications during certain kinds of crises.[79] The content of such messages should be negotiated by mutual agreement during peacetime, perhaps through NRRC staff.[80] Additionally, India and Pakistan could agree to mutually identifiable actions to be undertaken as demonstrative of serious desire for termination of conflict. Such "intent demonstration" actions would have to be characterized by simultaneity (or near simultaneity) of implementation, verifiable limitation of capabilities to resume war, and interactive communications. Ideally, crisis communications would have been initiated during earlier phases of the crisis that led to use of nuclear weapons. All three actions are essential to facilitating a climate of mutual restraint. Otherwise, one side may mistakenly interpret a momentary lull in the fighting as an effort by its counterpart to regroup and resume attack.

Notes

1. The preamble to the ABM Treaty states, "effective measures to limit anti-ballistic missile systems . . . would lead to a decrease in the risk of outbreak of war involving nuclear weapons." ABM Treaty reprinted in Jozef Goldblat, *Arms Control Agreements: A Handbook* (New York: Praeger, 1983), pp. 166-171.

2. Thomas Schelling and Morton Halperin, *Strategy and Arms Control* (New York: Twentieth Century Fund, 1962), p. 2. For recent restatements of these objectives and discussion of types of arms control see also Michael Intriligator and Dagobert L. Brito, "On Arms Control," in Edward A. Kolodziej and Patrick Morgan, eds., *Security and Arms Control, Vol. I* (New York: Greenwood Press, 1989), pp. 213-232, and Patrick Morgan, "Elements of a General Theory of Arms Control," in Paul Viotti, ed., *Conflict and Arms Control: An Uncertain Agenda* (Boulder: Westview, 1986), pp.283-310.

3. Schelling and Halperin, p. 50.

4. Joseph P. Nye, Jr., "The Impact of Technology on Nuclear Deterrence and Strategic Arms Control," in F. Stephen Larrabee, ed., *Technology and Change in East-West Relations, East-West Monograph Series, no. 6* (New York: Institute for East-West Security Studies, 1988), pp. 65-71.

5. For example, see P. R. Chari, "How to Prevent a Nuclear Arms Race Between India and Pakistan," in Bhabani Sen Gupta, ed., *Regional Cooperation in South Asia: Vol. 1* (New Delhi: South Asia Publishers, 1986), p. 141 and Akhtar Ali, *South Asia: Nuclear Stalemate or Conflagration?* (Karachi: Research on Armament and Poverty, 1987), p.107.

6. According to Neil Joeck India-Pakistan nuclear relations are characterized by a tacit communication of thresholds which each is unlikely to cross as long as the other similarly refrains, because each ultimately desires to avoid an uncontrolled nuclear arms race. This may explain why India has thus far conducted only one nuclear test, and apparently has not deployed nuclear weapons. See Joeck, "Tacit Bargaining and Stable Proliferation in South Asia," *CISA Working Paper no. 66* (Los Angeles: UCLA Center for International and Strategic Affairs, April, 1989).

7. It is very probable that "covert" deployment of nuclear weapons would be covert only as a matter of official policy. Evidence of such activities would be difficult to suppress indefinitely, though it would be relatively easy to suppress information crucial to the development of deterrence stability, such as numbers and survivability of weapons. Why states should chose to deploy a *militarily meaningful* nuclear weapons capability in secrecy is not entirely clear; the above discussion implies that "secret" nuclear weapons actually have less credible deterrent value.

8. These events demonstrate the utility of even unilateral monitoring arrangements for moderating misperceptions of adversary capabilities. A new strategic reconnaissance satellite, launched in 1960, revealed previous estimates of Soviet ICBM numbers to have been grossly exaggerated. For a detailed discussion of the genesis of the U.S. bomber and missile gap controversies see Fred Kaplan, *The Wizards of Armageddon* (New York: Touchstone Books, 1983), chapters 10 and 19.

9. Robert Jervis, "Deterrence Theory Revisited," *ACIS Working Paper no. 14* (Los Angeles: UCLA Center for Arms Control and International Security, May, 1978), pp. 39-40 and Patrick Morgan, "The Opportunity for a Strategic Surprise," in Klaus Knorr and Patrick Morgan, eds., *Strategic Military Surprise: Incentives and Opportunities* (New York: National Strategy Information Center, 1983), pp.196-197.

10. For a more detailed examination of the technical requirements of maintaining a stable deterrence relationship between India and Pakistan, see Zalmay Khalilzad, "Proliferation and Stability in Southwest Asia", in Dagobert L. Brito, Michael D. Intriligator, and Adele E. Wick, eds., *Strategies for Managing Proliferation* (Lexington: Lexington Books, 1983) pp. 189-197.

11. Khalilzad, "Proliferation and Stability," p. 194. There is some question as to whether a Pakistani "anticipatory" strike would target Indian cities, military capabilities, or some combination of both; striking Indian cities would most certainly trigger a similar Indian response. Pakistani countervalue attacks would be militarily useful only to the extent that Indian command and control capabilities are disrupted or destroyed. Counterforce attacks would be limited to targets within range of Pakistani aircraft, and Indian air defense superiority would

make such attacks a dubious prospect. It is thus doubtful that Pakistan would initiate large-scale attacks with nuclear weapons, *unless* it received warning of an imminent Indian attack. Pakistani early-warning systems could not, of course, ascertain whether incoming Indian planes were nuclear or conventional armed; decisions would likely be made on the assumption that Indian aircraft carried nuclear weapons.

12. "Unilateral" deterrent systems are prone to crisis instability because they are highly dependent on the intentions of the state possessing a preponderance of deterrent capabilities, i.e., on whether or not that state is a status quo power. Such states may be tempted to settle every score in their favor, giving lesser rivals strong and unremitting incentive to match the capabilities of their more powerful adversary in order to move toward a system of mutual deterrence. Arms racing is thus a likely consequence of unilateral deterrent systems, with the transition to a system of mutual deterrence being characterized by strong incentives for preemption on the part of the more powerful state. See Patrick Morgan, *Deterrence: A Conceptual Analysis* (Beverly Hills: Sage Publications, 1983), pp. 84-92.

13. Because they blur the line between conventional and nuclear warfare, the initial use of tactical nuclear weapons in a conflict that started out conventional, even for demonstration shot purposes, makes escalation to a strategic nuclear exchange much more likely, especially if command and control is limited. See Richard Rosecrance, "Strategic Deterrence Reconsidered,"*IISS Adelphi Papers,* 116, 1975, pp. 22-23. Moreover, for reasons of geography, climate, and population distribution the use of tactical nuclear weapons in an India-Pakistan war is unlikely to be limited to "tactical" consequences. See Naim's chapter this volume. For discussion of possible Indian military strategies involving the use of tactical nuclear weapons in a conventional war with China or Pakistan, see Rodney Jones, "India's Nuclear Strategy," *Nuclear, Biological, and Chemical Defense and Technology International,* Vol. 1, No. 2, May, 1986, pp. 66-72.

14. Shai Feldman, "Managing Nuclear Proliferation," in Jed C. Snyder and Samuel F. Wells, eds., *Limiting Nuclear Proliferation* (Cambridge: Ballinger, 1985), pp. 304-307.

15. *Ibid.* p. 306.

16. A. F. Mullins, "Proliferation in South Asia: The Military Dimension" (Livermore: Lawrence Livermore National Laboratory, Manuscript, n.d.), p. 6.

17. Joeck, p. 2.

18. Charles C. Floweree, "CBMs in the UN Setting," in John Borawski, ed., *Avoiding War in the Nuclear Age: Confidence Building Measures for Crisis Stability* (Boulder: Westview,1986), pp.107-108. The Indian view of deterrence is equally disparaging; the Indian government professes not to abide by a doctrine of deterrence. See speech by Indian Minister of Defense K.C. Pant at Massachusetts Institute of Technology, Boston, "Comments on Philosophy of Defense," reprinted in FBIS-South Asia, July 21, 1989, p. 39. As with CBMs, concepts of deterrence are considered as justification for superpower evasion of nuclear disarmament obligations under the NPT. Deterrence should not,

however, be thought of as a matter of choice, or even doctrine, motivated by any particular cultural, political or ideological position. For the purposes of this study, deterrence is considered a condition that results from the existence of a mutual desire to avoid military conflict, arising from a mutual awareness that the potential destructiveness of war for *both* sides outweighs any possible benefits to be gained from it by *either* side.

19. Edward A. Kolodziej, "Limits of Deterrence Theory," *Journal of Social Issues,* Vol 43, No. 4, 1987, p.132.

20. Richard K. Betts, "Hedging Against Surprise Attack, "*Survival,* July/August,1981, p.155.

21. Johan Holst and Karen Melander, "European Security and Confidence Building Measures," *Survival,* July/August, 1977, p.147.

22. Jonathan Alford, "The Usefulness and Limitations of CBMs," in William Epstein and Bernard Feld, eds., *New Directions in Disarmament* (New York: Praeger, 1981), p.134.

23. Johan Holst, "Confidence Building Measures: A Conceptual Framework," *Survival,* Jan./Feb., 1983, p. 2.

24. Matt Miller, "Tensions Escalate Between Old Enemies, India and Pakistan," *Wall Street Journal,* March 4,1987 For a detailed account of the Brass Tacks episode see Ravi Rikhye, *The War That Never Was* (Delhi: Chanayaka Publications, 1988).

25. Sanjoy Hazarika, "India Puts Military on Full Alert, Citing a Pakistani Troop Buildup," *New York Times,* Jan. 24, 1987.

26. Miller, "Tensions Escalate."

27. *Ibid.*

28. See, for example, 1986 Stockholm Accords, past NATO CSCE proposals.

29. Sanjoy Hazarika, "Border of China and India is Tense," *New York Times,* May 8, 1987.

30. From various sources: J. Borawski, ed., p.11 and Appendix A: "A CBM Handbook"; J. Alford, "The Usefulness and Limitations of CBMs," in Epstein and Feld, eds., p.136.

31. David Barton, "The Sinai Peacekeeping Experience: A Verification Paradigm for Europe," in *1985 SIPRI Arms and Disarmament Yearbook* (Oxford: Oxford University Press, 1985), pp. 541-563.

32. *Ibid.,* p.551-556.

33. Jim E. Hinds, "The Limits of Confidence," in Borawski.

34. Betts, "Hedging Against Surprise Attack," p. 147.

35. Alan Vick and James Thompson, "The Military Significance of Restrictions on the Operations of Strategic Nuclear Forces," in Barry Blechman, ed., *Preventing Nuclear War* (Washington, D.C.: Georgetown Univ.,1985), pp.101-102.

36. Effective OSI and observation provisions should specify: extent of inspector or observer access, freedom of movement, size of area covered, number of inspectors and frequency of inspections, "sensitive areas" to be excluded, obligations of the inspected party to accept inspection teams, and how far in

advance notification of inspection must be given. Additionally, provisions to prevent harassment of inspectors should be implemented as well. See Hinds, "The Limits of Confidence," for this and related discussion pertaining to Soviet treatment of Western military liaison officers and observers.

37. Jonathan Alford, "CBMs in Europe," *IISS Adelphi Papers No. 149, 1979* p.12.

38. Paul Leventhal and Brahma Chellaney, "Nuclear Terrorism in South Asia," Paper presented to the Institute for Defense Studies and Analysis, New Delhi, Oct. 10, 1988, pp. 15-16.

39. For a comparison of IAEA safeguards with the U.S. NMMSS see Sidney Moglewer, "IAEA Safeguards and Nonproliferation,"*Bulletin of the Atomic Scientists*, Oct., 1981, pp.24-29. For a discussion of IAEA physical protection and security guidelines see *Nonproliferation Issues* (Washington, D.C.: Congressional Research Service: Library of Congress, 1977), pp. 328-329.

40. Leventhal and Chellaney.

41. See Donald R. Cotter, "Peacetime Operations," in Ashton B. Carter, John D. Steinbruner, and Charles A. Zraket, eds., *Managing Nuclear Operations* (Washington, D.C.: Brookings Institution, 1987), pp.46-51; Peter Stein and Peter Feaver, "Assuring Control of Nuclear Weapons: The Evolution of Permissive Action Links," *CSIA Occasional Paper no. 2* (Cambridge: Harvard University Center for Science and International Affairs, 1987), for discussions of PAL development and technologies.

42. Cotter, p. 50; Stein and Feaver.

43. See Daniel Ford, *The Button* (New York: Simon and Schuster, 1985), pp.117-119 for a brief description of Minuteman launch procedures and operations.

44. William Arkin and Richard Fieldhouse, "Nuclear Weapons Command, Control and Communications," in Marek Thee, ed., *Arms and Disarmament: SIPRI Findings, 1986* (Oxford: Oxford University. Press, 1986), p. 118.

45. Security and control of use of NATO nuclear weapons is the joint responsibility of NATO allies and the U.S.

46. "One-point safety" is defined as "the probability of achieving a nuclear yield greater than four tons of TNT equivalent shall not exceed one in a million in the event of a detonation initiated at the single most sensitive point in the high explosive system," Thomas B. Cochran et. al., eds., *Nuclear Weapons Databook, Vol. II: U.S. Nuclear Warhead Production* (Cambridge: Ballinger, 1987), p. 48, note 42.

47. See Cotter, in Carter, et. al., pp. 42-46 for details.

48. Graham T. Allison, Albert Carnesale, and Joseph P. Nye, Jr., eds., *Hawks, Doves, and Owls: An Agenda For Avoiding Nuclear War* (New York: W.W. Norton, 1985), p. 234; chapter 7 provides a good overview of nuclear war prevention measures.

49. In theory at least, devices for receiving a "self-destruct" code could be installed on missiles to thwart accidental or unauthorized launch. Alternatively, such a device could be designed to initiate destruction of a missile automatically

in the event of launch, unless a coded transmission were simultaneously received at the time of launch disenabling the self-destruct mechanism. Sherman Frankel, "Unauthorized and Accidental Launch of Nuclear Systems," Talk presented to University of Illinois-Urbana-Champaign Program in Arms Control, Disarmament, and International Security, March 30, 1990.

50. Khalilzad, p. 194.

51. Alistair I. Johnston, "China Enters the Arms Control Arena," *Arms Control Today* , July/August, 1987, p. 13.

52. Vick and Thomson, p.105.

53. David K. Shipler, "U.S. and Russians Sign Pact to Limit Nuclear War Risk," *New York Times,* Sept. 16, 1987; See also David K. Shipler, "Shevardnadze-Shultz Talks Started," *New York Times,* March 23, 1988, for additional discussion of arms control functions of U.S.-Soviet NRRCs.

54. "Interim Report of the Nunn-Warner Working Group on Nuclear Risk Reduction," in Blechman, ed., p. 169.

55. *Ibid* , pp.170-171.

56. In 1970 the Soviet Union had proposed, during the SALT negotiations notification of mass aircraft take-offs but difficulty over defining "mass" led to U.S. rejection of the proposal. See Raymond L. Garthoff, "The Accidents Measures Agreement," in Borawski, ed., pp. 61-62.

57. Herman Kahn, *On Escalation: Metaphors and Scenarios* (New York: Praeger, 1965), p. 98

58. Kahn warns of the limits of the escalatory ladder metaphor; crisis escalation and deescalation do not consist of a simple sequence of stopping points. "In many ways, escalation is an irreversible process. Moreover, there are aspects of deescalation that do not correspond in any way to 'escalation in reverse'"(pp. 230-231). For similar criticisms of the ladder metaphor, see Colin S. Gray, "Strategic Deescalation," in Stephen Cimbala and Joseph Douglas, Jr., eds., *Ending a Nuclear War: Are the Superpowers Prepared?* (Washington, D.C.: Pergamon-Brassey's, 1988), pp. 60-78 and Fred C. Ikle, *Every War Must End* (New York: Columbia University Press, 1971), pp. 39-58. For a more general critique of the idea that nuclear crises can be successfully managed, see Richard Ned Lebow, *Nuclear Crisis Management: A Dangerous Illusion* (Ithaca: Cornell University Press, 1987).

59. See Sumit Ganguly, *Origins of War in South Asia* (Boulder: Westview, 1986), for a discussion of past India-Pakistan military conflicts. Some may argue, however, that Indian conventional military superiority has ensured quick and decisive victories in all cases of war with Pakistan.

60. India might, however, find itself in such a position vis-à-vis China.

61. Carl H. Amme, *NATO Strategy and Nuclear Defense* (New York: Greenwood Press, 1988), pp. 11-17.

62. Daniel J. Arbess and Andrew M. Moravcsik, "Lengthening the Fuse: No First Use and Disengagement," in Joseph P. Nye, Jr., Graham Allison, and Albert Carnesale, eds., *Fateful Visions: Avoiding Nuclear Catastrophe* (Cambridge: Ballinger, 1988), p. 83.

63. Arkin and Fieldhouse, "Nuclear Weapons Command, Control and Communications," p.115.

64. Paul Bracken, "War Termination," in Carter, et. al., eds., p. 204. The U.S.-Soviet DCL does not use a telephone, or any other form of voice communications. Voice communications are thought to be more easily subject to misinterpretation or mistranslation. Moreover, printed messages permit heads of state to confer with advisors prior to sending a reply, and provide a permanent record of communications.

65. Crisis management functions would inevitably be expropriated by upper-echelon executive decisionmakers and their staffs. See Richard K. Betts, "A Joint Nuclear Risk Control Center," in Blechman, ed., p. 73.

66. *Report of the Carnegie Task Force on Nuclear Weapons and South Asian Security* (Carnegie Endowment for International Peace, 1988), p.63.

67. George Quester, "War Termination and Nuclear Targeting Strategy," in Desmond Ball and Jeffrey Richelson, eds., *Strategic Nuclear Targeting* (Ithaca: Cornell Univ. Press, 1986), p. 291.

68. Some relatively "low-tech" EMP hardening measures are possible: for example, vacuum tubes are less susceptible to EMP than solid-state transistors. Moreover, it is technically easier to design hardened equipment from scratch than to retrofit unhardened equipment. See Samuel Glasstone and Philip Dolan, *The Effects of Nuclear Weapons* (Washington, D.C.: Department of the Army pamphlet no. 50-3, 1977), pp. 524-526.

69. See Paul Bracken, *The Command and Control of Nuclear Forces* (New Haven: Yale University Press, 1983) pp. 179-188 for a discussion of early U.S. nuclear command and control arrangements and procedures.

70. Should either country possess the capability to launch high altitude bursts (this capability could shortly be within Indian grasp) the resulting EMP damage to communications equipment and links would be substantial for *both* countries. Glasstone and Dolan, pp. 518-520.

71. Clark C. Abt, *A Strategy for Terminating a Nuclear War* (Boulder: Westview, 1985), pp. 40-41.

72. Paul Bracken, "War Termination," in Carter, et. al., eds.; William Arkin and Richard Fieldhouse, *Nuclear Battlefields* (Cambridge: Ballinger, 1985), pp.146-147.

73. See Ashton B. Carter, "Communications Technologies and Vulnerabilities," in Carter, et. al., pp. 250-252.

74. In the United States the construction of a Nationwide Emergency Telecommunications System, with switching centers hardened against blast and EMP, is underway. Robert Leahy, "The Mechanics of War Termination," in Cimbala and Douglass, pp.104-105.

75. *Ibid.*

76. See Bracken, *The Command and Control of Nuclear Forces,* pp.191-192 for a discussion of the management difficulties and vulnerabilities of a highly centralized command and control system.

77. Leahy, p. 97.

78. *Ibid.*, p.121.

79. In 1985, the U.S. proposed in the SALT Standing Consultative Commission, and the Soviet Union agreed, the use of hotline "crisis codes" and preformatted messages in the event of nuclear incidents involving terrorism, accidental or unauthorized use, or third-party nuclear threats. Raymond L. Garthoff, "The Accidents Measures Agreement," in Borawski, ed., p. 68.

80. The importance of having mutually agreed stopping points in place *prior* to the initiation of war is discussed by Thomas Schelling in *Arms and Influence* (New Haven: Yale University Press, 1966), pp. 204-220.

5

Arms Limitations

Susan M. Burns

The primary purpose of limiting arms is to remove the existence of *weapons* as a potential cause of conflict. Further, negotiated limitations on especially pernicious weapons may limit the destructiveness of wars that do occur. Given the requisite technologies and political will, what kinds of arms limitations regimes could India and Pakistan implement? Before surveying these regimes, it is essential to examine those features distinguishing the South Asian arms control context from that of the U.S. and Soviet Union or other regions. Three features are especially significant: the covert nature of military nuclear activities, their integration with ostensibly civilian power and space programs, and small (if any) nuclear weapons stockpiles.

Arms Limitations and Nuclear Covertness

Arms limitations agreements anticipate the existence of something to limit. Parties to such agreements must at least implicitly acknowledge whether they possess the objects or engage in the activities that the agreement aims to control—and submit to verification procedures capable of detecting whether they do. For India and Pakistan, the most comprehensive forms of regional arms limitations aimed specifically at nuclear weapons could obligate them to do one of the following, depending on what stage of development each is at in its military nuclear programs:

1. Agree not to produce any nuclear warheads in the future, assuming none now exist.
2. Agree to dismantle such warheads as already exist and not produce any more.
3. Explicitly recognize the other's possession of a limited number (the number that exist at the signing of the agreement) of warheads and weapons (warheads mated to delivery vehicles) while agreeing not to produce more warheads or deploy more weapons. Unilateral and negotiated measures are necessary in this case to manage deployments of existing weapons to enhance crisis and deterrence stability.
4. Explicitly recognize the nuclear status of the other while mutually working toward controlling both quantitative and qualitative aspects of current and future weapons deployments to enhance crisis and deterrence stability.

Any of these approaches essentially means an end to the possession of a nuclear option. Either India and Pakistan will have renounced a nuclear capability (approaches 1 and 2) or explicitly accepted each other's possession of such a capability (approaches 3 and 4).

One of the most compelling reasons for keeping covert nuclear weapons covert[1] is that such status imposes severe restraints on both the quantitative and qualitative development of arsenals.[2] Were India and Pakistan to declare nuclear weapons status, a close and interactive linkage between arms control efforts and weapons technology development would be essential to manage their nuclear forces through a potentially very precarious transition from newly emergent status to a relationship of stable deterrence, while limiting the incentives to arms race. In lieu of retaining covert status, arms imitations measures aimed specifically at production and testing could serve an essentially similar restraining function.

Arms Limitations and Small Nuclear Forces

What do small, or even nonexistent, nuclear forces imply for arms limitations measures aimed at restricting their production and deployment? The most important consequence is that the potential military significance (in terms of gaining a strategic advantage) of noncompliance is much greater than for similar noncompliance against a background of very large forces. Small absolute numbers mean that the relative significance of incremental additions to force size is potentially very large. Figure 5.1 illustrates mathematically the relationship between absolute force size (in terms of stockpiled warheads) and the relative significance of incremental increases. Here, "relative significance" is defined as the percentage change resulting from incremental additions of 10 to an existing stockpile of **n** warheads. What is apparent from Figure 5.1 is that, as **n** grows very large, the relative significance of additional increments of 10 warheads approaches zero, i.e., grows very small.[3]

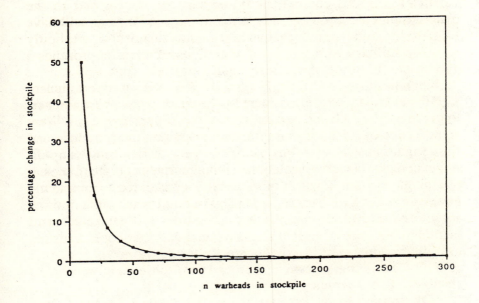

FIGURE 5.1 Percentage Change (Relative Significance) of Incremental Additions of 10 to a Stockpile of n Warheads.[4]

   Representative of this situation are proposals for a superpower fissile materials production ban. Frank von Hippel and Barbara Levi contend that verification capable of detecting at least a 10% clandestine increase in the size of current fissile materials stockpiles over a ten year period would be sufficient for such purposes. Diversions over a ten year period comparable to 10% of the current U.S. stockpile, von Hippel and Levi contend, would amount to a diversion of six metric tons per year of weapons-grade uranium or one metric ton per year of plutonium.[5] Von Hippel and Levi note that fissile materials diversions of such magnitude could conceivably enable the clandestine production of hundreds of warheads but conclude that "measured against the existing stockpiles such increments could not be considered [strategically] significant." In contrast, the South Asian case demands that verification for fissile materials production limitations be capable of detecting with a reasonable probability the diversion of kilogram quantities of fissile materials over a period of weeks to months. In other words, verification in this context should be capable of detecting fissile materials diversions on the same order of magnitude as specified for IAEA safeguards "significant quantities" and "timely detection."[6]

   The military importance of violations of an arms-limitation agreement is somewhat more easily defined (but still rather problematic) than is "political" significance.[7] Generally, militarily significant violations are considered to be those that enable a violator to gain a military advantage over a counterpart. Defining the military significance of violations of agreements banning the production of fissile materials for weapons use is not very difficult in the South Asian context (detecting violations is another matter) if the diversion of a single weapon's worth of material is considered to enable the development of a military advantage by permitting the production of a nuclear warhead. Looking again at Figure 5.1, it can be inferred that the production of even a single nuclear warhead could translate to military advantage if existing stockpiles of warheads are small enough—assuming, of course, warheads are subsequently mated to suitable delivery vehicles.[8]

   Obviously, arms limitations aimed at halting the future production of warheads in the context of small or nonexistent nuclear forces require much more intrusive and stringent verification measures than in the context of large nuclear arsenals, where the production of a single warhead, or even tens or hundreds, is "trivial" by comparison. In 1961, Jerome Weisner postulated an inverse relationship between the extent of necessary inspection and levels of armaments in a situation of progressively deeper reductions in force levels.[9] The premise from which Weisner derived this relationship is that, as progressive reductions in the absolute numbers of armaments proceed, the *minimum acceptable* compliance uncertainty similarly decreases. The phenomenon depicted by Figure 5.1 can be said to represent a restatement of this premise; if small increases have a larger relative significance for smaller arsenals, parties to an agreement covering such arsenals will require (and expect) more accurate evidence of compliance. Weisner proposed his model before the advent of sophisticated satellite reconnaissance capabilities enabled non-intrusive observation of nuclear weapons deployments, but its essence remains relevant to the case of fissile materials production bans for countries possessing limited stocks of such materials or nuclear warheads.

Arms Limitations and Dual-Use Nuclear Programs

The production of weapons-usable fissile materials in covert nuclear weapons states poses particular verification and monitoring difficulties. Dual use pervades the nuclear programs of such states. Military nuclear production activities as might exist are necessarily closely integrated with civilian nuclear energy, space, and conventional military production activities. Figure 5.2 represents a generic flowchart of nuclear weapons production in a covert nuclear state and illustrates the extent of integration between civilian nuclear, conventional military and space program activities with clandestine nuclear weapons production.

Figure 5.2 also indicates the most obvious points of application of arms limitations agreements: production, testing, and deployment. These points constitute the most effective monitoring foci of arms limitations, relative to "hidden" processes such as design, research and development. The following discussion approaches possible South Asian arms limitations regimes in terms of these three foci. Finally, provisions for the effective implementation of a regional nuclear weapons free zone are considered.

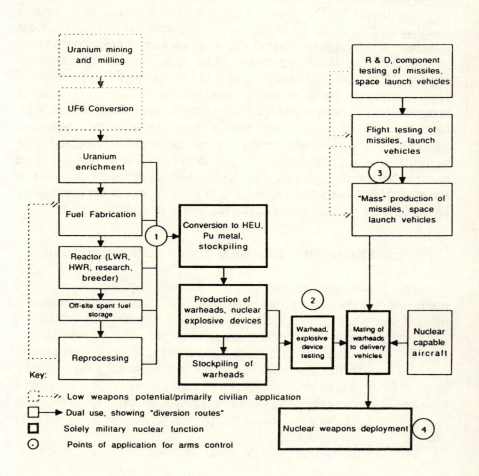

Uranium mining and milling

UF6 Conversion

Uranium enrichment

Fuel Fabrication

Reactor (LWR, HWR, research, breeder)

Off-site spent fuel storage

Reprocessing

Conversion to HEU, Pu metal, stockpiling

Production of warheads, nuclear explosive devices

Stockpiling of warheads

Warhead, explosive device testing

Mating of warheads to delivery vehicles

Nuclear capable aircraft

R & D, component testing of missiles, space launch vehicles

Flight testing of missiles, launch vehicles

"Mass" production of missiles, space launch vehicles

Nuclear weapons deployment

Key:

- ⋯⋯⟋ Low weapons potential/primarily civilian application
- ☐ → Dual use, showing "diversion routes"
- ☐ Solely military nuclear function
- ⊙ Points of application for arms control

FIGURE 5.2 Nuclear Weapons Production in a Threshold State.[10]

TABLE 5.1 Ease of Monitoring Various Weapons Systems and Activities[11]

Easier to Monitor	Example	Harder to Monitor	Example
Elimination of complete weapons systems	INF Treaty	Numerical limits or thresholds	SALT Treaty specifications on launcher or "platform" numbers
Numerical Limits or thresholds	Aircraft or missile numbers, TTBT	Qualitative limits	Guidance accuracies, MIRVed missiles, missile flight range
Testing	Missile flight testing, nuclear explosive testing	Production, R&D	Fissile materials production, warhead design and assembly, design and production of missiles
Deployment	Ban on missile deployments	Production, R&D	
Single function platforms	Silo-based missiles	Dual function platforms	Some nuclear capable aircraft, possibly IRBMs, cruise missiles
Large weapons systems	ICBMs, IRBMs, nuclear capable aircraft	Small weapons systems	Tactical nuclear weapons, cruise missiles

Table 5.1 compares in a very general way the relative ease of monitoring restrictions on specific kinds of weapons systems and activities. Those listed in the left-hand column are easier to monitor relative to the entry opposite on the right. Ease of monitoring is defined here in terms of the presence of "direct observables," i.e., how amenable certain kinds of restrictions on weapons or related activities are to less intrusive means of monitoring such as satellite surveillance.[12] Harder-to-monitor restrictions, in contrast, demand greater counting or measurement accuracy, or rely on the observation and inference of hidden characteristics or activities. For

monitoring situations of this nature more intrusive methods such as on-site inspection (OSI), or on-site automated sensors, are often necessary.

Eliminations of complete weapons systems (but not their parts, such as warheads) are usually easiest to monitor. Though the possibility of clandestinely produced or residual hidden weapons remains, compliance determination in this case is straightforward. The observance of a single weapon of the banned category suffices as evidence of noncompliance. Monitoring and compliance for comprehensive nuclear explosive testing bans, however, is not necessarily easier than for threshold testing bans.[13] Testing and deployment restrictions, whether involving complete bans or numerical thresholds, are in turn more directly monitored than are restrictions on warhead or delivery-vehicle production. But compliance determination for testing and deployment restrictions is not always more straightforward than it is for production limitations.[14]

Production Monitoring Agreements

Fissile Materials Production Restrictions

In the South Asian context, the intent of an agreement prohibiting the production and use of fissile materials for nuclear explosive devices would be to ensure that materials usable in such devices are not diverted from legitimate civilian purposes. The IAEA, of course, has accumulated a vast experience with inspecting specific kinds of nuclear facilities and safeguarding fissile and source materials from diversion. Though the IAEA need not necessarily perform the monitoring and verification functions of regional or bilateral fissile materials restrictions, on-site inspection regimes for these agreements should logically employ IAEA materials accounting, containment, and surveillance methodology. However, because the IAEA system is designed to accommodate an extensive multilateral application, employing its methodology in a bilateral or regional context necessitates some modification.

The Dual-Use Problem. As a flowchart of a generic covert nuclear weapons program, Figure 5.2 (above) illustrates the linkage between discrete *processes* rather than specific facilities in which these processes take place. In a covert nuclear weapons state, several of the processes illustrated here as distinct may actually take place within one or two facilities having ostensibly peaceful functions. Verification regimes for negotiated restrictions on use and production of fissile materials (other than complete shutdowns of designated nuclear facilities) in this context must simultaneously account for both civilian and potential nuclear explosive production activities. Because of the NPT and IAEA mandates to facilitate the development of peaceful nuclear technology in non-nuclear weapons states, IAEA safeguards have been designed as such a means of simultaneous accounting. The purpose of OSI and materials accounting methods employed by a South Asian regional or bilateral fissile materials restriction regime would be fundamentally identical to that of IAEA safeguards implemented under both the NPT (INFCIRC/153) and non-NPT (INFCIRC/66) systems. However, both of the IAEA safeguards systems leave open a number of potential "loopholes."[15] Closing them would be a prerequisite for effective verification of a regional or bilateral fissile materials production-restriction agreement.

Closing Loopholes. First, the language of a regional or bilateral South and Mid-Asian agreement must explicitly prohibit the diversion of fissile materials for the fabrication of nuclear *explosive devices*. The IAEA's original model non-NPT safeguards document, INFCIRC/66, provided only that safeguards be administered to ensure that "special fissionable materials" are "not used in such a way as to further any military purpose."[16] Such wording allowed states to claim exemption of the development of "peaceful nuclear explosives," even though there is essentially no difference, in terms of technology and fissile materials required, between a nuclear explosive device for peaceful use and one for military purposes.[17]

A second ambiguity in the IAEA's safeguards systems relates to the extension of safeguards to materials produced from safeguarded source, or fertile, materials. The terms of INFCIRC/66 state only that the extension of safeguards to subsequent production of fissile materials from or modifications of source materials is "desirable."[18] A regional or bilateral fissile materials production restriction regime should include provisions for the continuance of safeguards regardless of subsequent transformation of treaty-limited fissile materials production potential. Provision should likewise be made for extending inspections and controls to new facilities constructed during negotiations or after the conclusion of an agreement.

No provisions exist for applying safeguards to facilities constructed indigenously on the basis of technology transferred under INFCIRC/66 agreements. The analogue of this situation, in the context of a regional or bilateral fissile materials production restriction regime, would be secret facilities constructed to circumvent comprehensive monitoring of declared facilities or a more limited regime designating certain facilities for inspection. INFCIRC/153 (NPT) safeguards agreements, in contrast, obligate NPT signatories to place all nuclear facilities under safeguards. IAEA inspectors, however, can legally inspect only declared facilities—they cannot search for and inspect suspected clandestine plants. A verification regime for a fissile materials production restriction agreement must additionally be capable of detecting clandestine nuclear production facilities and responding to the existence of such treaty violations, perhaps through the use of "challenge" or on-demand inspections.

Effective verification of a limited, designated-facility on-site inspection and materials accounting regime would have to encompass more than simply accounting for the production of fissile materials within the facilities designated for inspection.[19] Ensuring no diversion to nuclear explosive use entails a capability to account for the disposition of any nuclear materials that have passed through designated facilities at every point of potential use or diversion in the nuclear fuel cycle. A designated facility agreement should consequently provide for limited inspections and materials accounting at any facility whenever materials originating from or modified by the primary designated facilities are used. Some uncertainty also exists regarding IAEA rights to inspect inoperative facilities in NPT signatory states.[20] Both the extent of inspector access within certain facilities (e.g., access to the commercially sensitive cascade area of uranium enrichment plants) and the inspection status of inoperative plants are issues that must be resolved during the negotiation of a regional fissile materials production restriction regime.

Two additional factors relevant to such a regime, whether limited or comprehensive must be considered by its drafters. First, upper limits on the annual number of inspections should derive from an assessment of the diversion potential of the kind of nuclear facility subject to inspection as well as total facility throughput, or inventory. Current IAEA inspection limits are based on the latter. David Fischer and Paul Szasz point out that threshold nuclear weapons states have most frequently used research reactors in combination with pilot-scale reprocessing facilities to produce weapons-usable fissile materials.[21] India used its Canadian-supplied CIRUS research reactor to produce the plutonium for its 1974 Pokhran nuclear explosion.[22] The use of small research and test facilities is probably both more economical and amenable to secrecy than are commercial scale nuclear production facilities, for the clandestine production of small amounts of fissile materials for nuclear explosive use.

Finally, nonexplosive military uses of fissile materials, primarily production and use of HEU for nuclear submarine propulsion, must be addressed under a fissile materials restriction regime. India currently leases a nuclear submarine from the Soviet Union, which provides the HEU fuel required for its operation (under the agreement spent fuel is returned to the Soviet Union).[23] India may wish to produce its own fuel in the future, should it develop a uranium enrichment capability. The use and transfer of HEU for submarine propulsion is covered by neither IAEA safeguards system. Reportedly, India is conducting research on laser isotope separation methods and has built a pilot scale gaseous centrifuge enrichment plant at Trombay.[24]

Negotiated Shutdowns of "Sensitive" Nuclear Facilities. The 1988 Carnegie Task Force proposed that India and Pakistan negotiate temporary shutdowns of their most proliferation-prone nuclear facilities.[25] The most useful targets of a facility shutdown agreement would be Pakistan's Kahuta uranium enrichment facility and India's largest reprocessing plant at the Bhabha Atomic Research Complex (BARC). The non-operational status of these plants could probably be ascertained rather effectively by satellite surveillance technologies. Detection of noncompliance would be virtually assured if periodic inspections were carried out in conjunction with NTM monitoring. Because India has an active breeder reactor research program it will likely object to any restrictions that significantly slow or halt its plutonium production capability. Since Pakistan has no apparent civilian need for a uranium enrichment capability it has less justification for objecting to a facility shutdown agreement applying to Kahuta. Mutual and verifiable (through baseline on-site inspection) data exchanges on stockpiled nuclear materials would facilitate assessment of Indian annual civilian plutonium production requirements. Additionally, materials accounting and inspection of India's smaller PREFRE reprocessing plant would be essential to ensure nondiversion from legitimate civilian use. "Sensitive" Pakistani research or pilot scale nuclear facilities other than Kahuta (inoperative under a facility shutdown agreement) could be similarly placed under a limited accounting and inspection regime.

Production Monitoring of Missile "Factories"

The U.S. Soviet Intermediate and Shorter Range Nuclear Forces (INF) Treaty, which aims to eliminate an entire class of ballistic missiles, provides the most salient verification model for a regional or bilateral agreement banning or restricting production of missiles for nuclear weapons use. The phrase "for nuclear weapons use" is significant; in the South Asian context a complete ban on missile production (or R&D and testing) would be infeasible if it were to imply a simultaneous ban on development of civilian space and conventional military technology. Dual use of missile technology is an especially significant problem in the region because, as with fissile materials production, "nuclear" missile research and development and, testing, exist side by side with civilian space and conventional military technology. A regional missile production monitoring regime must be capable of distinguishing among production for nuclear weapons, non-nuclear weapons, and civilian space applications.

The production of missiles or civilian space launch vehicles involves large scale, distinctive manufacturing processes that take place at specialized facilities amenable to both INF-type production monitoring and observation by NTM. For example, the static firing of solid rocket motors is performed at special outdoor test sites. Production monitoring is most effective for primarily hand made strategic and intermediate-range missiles with large components manufactured in limited production runs.[26] Tactical nuclear delivery vehicles, such as artillery shells or cruise missiles, are especially difficult to monitor at the production stage because first, components are produced in great quantities and are small in size, and second, such weapons are dual-capable with few outwardly distinguishing characteristics between conventional and nuclear armed variants. Tactical munitions factories might be used to produce weapons adaptable to either a conventional or nuclear warhead.[27]

To be effective, a missile production monitoring regime must do two things: (1) ensure nonproduction of treaty limited items (or only production of agreed numbers at declared facilities) and (2) ensure nonproduction of treaty limited items elsewhere or at clandestine sites. Detection of the latter implies provisions for short-notice challenge inspections applicable at least to acknowledged potential sites, in conjunction with NTM monitoring. The INF commits the U.S. and Soviet to noninterference with each other's NTM capabilities, prohibits concealment measures that might impede monitoring by NTM or on-site inspection, and permits each side an annual quota of challenge inspections at sites other than primary missile elimination and production facilities subject to routine OSI.[28] Both the Soviet Union and the U.S. have found INF inspection arrangements satisfactory and useful, despite their intrusiveness. In addition to challenge inspections, the INF Treaty specifies four types of OSI: baseline inventory, routine production monitoring, elimination, and closeout. These are discussed more fully in the subsequent section.

The INF Treaty provides for the continuous presence of counterpart inspectors at missile production facilities in the U.S. and Soviet Union. Inspectors patrol the facility perimeter (which may encircle several buildings) and also observe the movement of objects and vehicles through designated portals of facilities within the perimeter. Inspectors are permitted to examine the interiors of containers or vehicles with dimensions greater than or equal to those of complete treaty limited missiles or their smallest stages. Covered objects of similar dimensions are only partly unshrouded for inspection, but it is the inspected party's responsibility to demonstrate to the satisfaction of the inspectors that the covered object is not a treaty limited item. Other items are subject only to external inspection, weighing, and linear measurement. INF inspectors carry out their tasks without benefit of actual access to the plant's interiors—they only monitor the movement of objects through designated portals or the facility perimeter.[29]

The INF Treaty delimits an extensive protocol for the conduct of inspections for two reasons: to restrict information gathered to that necessary only for treaty verification purposes, and to permit the use of inspected facilities for the production of missiles or missile components not covered by the treaty.[30] The Soviet missile factory designated for inspection, the Votkinsk Machine Building Plant, currently manufactures and assembles SS-25 missiles, which are not limited by the treaty. INF Treaty inspection procedures are thus particularly relevant to the South Asian context, where missile production facilities designated for inspection might be concurrently used to produce components for conventional military munitions or shorter-range missiles, and space launch vehicles, items likely to be permitted under a negotiated regime of missile production restrictions. In addition to human inspection, continuous monitoring could be supplemented with automated sensors, such as cameras, motion or infrared detectors, capable of detecting the passage of objects of certain dimensions or characteristics through designated portals.[31]

Testing Restrictions

Nuclear Test Bans

In addition to fissile materials production restrictions one of the more effective routes to blocking the development of missile-deliverable nuclear warheads could be the implementation of a complete ban on nuclear explosive testing. For states in the early stages of developing a nuclear weapons capability, a ban on nuclear testing would significantly impede the development of all but first-generation fission devices deliverable by aircraft and not requiring certainty of yield.[32] For development of boosted-yield fission devices utilizing small amounts of thermonuclear materials, fusion devices ignited by fission primaries, relatively miniaturized missile deliverable warheads or tactical weapons requiring predictable yields and substantial reductions in weight, some level of nuclear field-testing is necessary.[33]

The range of yields essential for assuring a reasonable reliability of design refinements beyond early 1950s fission explosive technology, while not wide, has significant implications for a comprehensive South Asian nuclear test ban. The minimal yield at which successful thermonuclear boosting will occur has been estimated as ranging from 0.4 kT to 1 kT.[34] For a fusion device ignited by a fission primary the minimum yield necessary for successful ignition ranges, depending on whether the fusion secondary is designed for a low or high total yield, from less than 1 kT up to 15 kT.[35] A significant fraction of U.S. nuclear testing from 1980-1984 falls within the 10-15 kT range, indicating that much testing in the U.S. is concerned with assessing the reliability of fission primaries for new or modified thermonuclear warhead designs.[36] Some analysts believe, however, that even the smallest nuclear explosions may have military and scientific significance, especially for "beginner" states.[37]

To effectively halt, or at least significantly slow, the refinement of warhead size and predictability of yields, and the development of boosted and thermonuclear weapons, a regional test ban would require monitoring methods capable of detecting (and identifying) very low yield underground nuclear tests. Three negotiated provisions would be integral to enhancing the effective use of seismic monitoring of very low yield nuclear testing:

- Emplacement of in-country seismic monitoring systems in both India and Pakistan (or possibly third countries).
- Characterization of the geology of regions in which testing is likely to be conducted. While accurate yield estimation would not be necessary for a complete nuclear test ban, this provision would enable more accurate *identification* of low-magnitude seismic events. However, accurate identification might not be possible without calibration tests.[38]
- Short-notice on-site inspection provisions to clarify ambiguous seismic events, or for examining the site of a suspected clandestine test. For the former, inspections might be conducted by joint India-Pakistan inspection teams.

The uncertainties inherent in detecting and identifying ambiguous seismic events at low magnitudes (e.g., distinguishing large chemical explosions or small earthquakes from low yield nuclear tests) make provisions for OSI imperative for effective compliance determination for a comprehensive regional nuclear test ban. Additional negotiated cooperative measures for enhancing seismic detection and identification under a *comprehensive or very low-yield* nuclear test ban regime could include:[39]

- Limitations on the size and nature (e.g., salvo or ripple-fired) of chemical explosions. Ideally, advance notification of such explosions would be given and provisions made for short-notice inspections in the event of possible evasion by conduct of a low yield nuclear explosion simultaneously with or immediately following a chemical explosion.
- Jointly-conducted large chemical explosions in several potential nuclear testing sites for calibration purposes.

Missile Flight Testing Ban

Production monitoring regimes employing on-site inspections would likely be an essential means of accounting for the end uses of space launch and missile production activities. But production monitoring alone cannot entirely ensure that end use is restricted to permitted civilian space program applications. Production monitoring would be most effective if complemented with negotiated restrictions on testing.

Indian, and especially Pakistani, ballistic missile technology is still fairly embryonic; if implemented in the near term, a regional comprehensive flight test ban could effectively forestall the development and deployment of reliable IRBMs or ICBMs. Reliability would be prerequisite to confidence in ballistic missile performance. In addition to the research and development required for new models of IRBMs and ICBMs, periodic assessment of reliability necessitates operational flight testing of a statistically significant "sample" of deployed missiles. A single test, or even a few, of India's *Agni* IRBM provides an insufficient database for both assessing reliability and for developing methods of evaluation that could potentially substitute for subsequent operational flight testing. New types of U.S. ICBMs typically undergo some two dozen or more research and development flight tests prior to deployment. For continuing reliability assessment 1-2% of the deployed Minuteman II and III missile force is operationally tested each year.[40] Even if India need not conduct this large a number of R&D and operational flight tests to assess reliability, establishing *confidence* (a subjective measure) in missile performance would likely require many more than one test. But many refinements of guidance and control system technology in Minuteman ICBM technology have been evaluated by testing of subsystem components, rather than through full flight tests.[41] Realistically, however, such alternative means of evaluating reliability of incremental improvements in its IRBMs will not be available to India for a number of years because that country lacks a broad base of experience with ballistic missile technology.

A comprehensive ban on flight testing of ballistic missiles would certainly be easier to monitor than a regime permitting some testing. The latter would be primarily relevant to arms control that aims to impede the development of missile accuracy and new models of IRBMs and ICBMs and will not be discussed here. A comprehensive ban would not be free of monitoring and compliance difficulties, however, mainly because of the potential dual use of missile technologies. Verification of compliance with a missile flight test ban in countries with an active civilian space research and launch program must be capable of both distinguishing between the testing and launch of space launch vehicles and ballistic missile flight tests and detecting the transfer of technology developed under the aegis of civilian space programs to the military sector.

Such distinctions, and hence their monitoring, are more easily made for nuclear energy and materials production than for rocket technologies. The U.S. used Titan II ICBMs for launching Gemini spacecraft in the early 1960s; the first stage of India's *Agni* IRBM was a modification of an indigenously produced satellite launch vehicle booster.[42] The Missile Technology Control Regime (MTCR) exemplifies the dual use problem. A set of guidelines agreed to by seven industrially advanced nations in April, 1987 for restricting export of key ballistic missile technologies, the MTCR, while "not designed to impede national space programs" inevitably defines as "sensitive" many components equally essential for civilian space program applications.[43]

Civilian space launches can be distinguished from their ballistic missile counterparts by both their trajectory and the absence of a reentry vehicle containing one or more warheads.[44]   An effective missile flight test ban that permits civilian space program activities might thus include:

- A specific ban on the testing of reentry vehicles. Adequate verification of a missile flight test ban would require at least a capability to detect and track reentry vehicles released from longer range missiles.[45]
- A means of monitoring the trajectory of a missile or space launch vehicle. Consequently, a missile flight test ban agreement must include a provision prohibiting encryption of flight test telemetry.
- Advance notice of all missile and space launches, specifying time, purpose, and characteristics of the launch vehicle. Because monitoring short range or tactical missile flight tests is decidedly more difficult than for longer range missiles, testing of the former (which have conventional military applications and are unlikely to covered by a missile flight test ban) could be restricted to a specified test range, as could civilian space launches. Restricting tests of permitted short range or tactical missiles and space launches to designated sites, in addition to requiring advance notification of tests, would facilitate their detection and identification.

Bans on Deployment of Nuclear Weapons

Deployment comprises the third most practical point of application for nuclear arms limitations. The most effective deployment restriction measures, however, are those implemented in conjunction with bans on production and testing of nuclear explosive devices (warheads) and ballistic missiles or other delivery vehicles. If the objective of regional nuclear arms limitations is a ban on possession of nuclear explosive devices of any kind for any purpose, the most effective verification regime would be one that focuses on all three nodes in the nuclear weapons life cycle. Monitoring is a synergistic processes; the more varied the foci and means of monitoring the higher the overall probability of detection and identification of noncompliant activities. The application of arms limitations to several stages in the nuclear weapons production cycle requires the potential violator of an agreement to successfully evade detection at each monitored stage. The probability of successful evasion of detection consequently decreases with the number of monitored stages. "Redundant" verification is especially necessary for arms control agreements that are difficult to monitor at one or more stages but easier at another.

Monitoring the possible deployment of nuclear capable aircraft in South Asia clearly illustrates the importance of verification synergism. Neither India or Pakistan has a dedicated force of nuclear-armed heavy bombers easily distinguished from dual capable fighter-bomber aircraft. Arms control monitoring of potentially dual capable aircraft must be able to detect (primarily through NTM) direct observables indicative of a nuclear role. The SALT II Treaty specifies the use of "functionally related observable differences" (FRODs) as a means of determining whether an aircraft "can carry out the mission of a heavy bomber."[46] Even in the seemingly straightforward case of identifying dedicated nuclear heavy bombers, however, FRODs are few and their presence difficult to discern with certainty through NTM.[47] In the U.S.-Soviet context, the presence of bomb bay doors or wing-root extensions for carriage of cruise missiles are probably the most obvious FRODs identifying aircraft as capable of performing a nuclear heavy bomber role.

In the South Asian context, dual capable fighter-bombers are the norm, not the fairly distinctive heavy bombers that are more appropriate for strategic nuclear missions. While the observation of aircraft external attachment points (pylons or "hardpoints") would permit the assumption of a bomb carriage capability, determining whether a bomb is conventional or nuclear is virtually impossible without on-site inspection. A possible nuclear role for such aircraft must be inferred from the detection of such rather ambiguous indicators as special C^3 links essential for nuclear weapons operations or the observation of alerting procedures.[48] Ensuring the nondeployment of nuclear weapons on South Asian dual capable fighter-bombers would be most effectively attained through a ban on production and testing of warheads, activities that are considerably easier to monitor, though production monitoring entails the use of more intrusive OSI methods.[49] Nonetheless, a deployment restriction agreement should include a ban on aircraft deployment of nuclear weapons; the detection of apparent noncompliance could then legitimately be brought to the attention of the violator, and subject to clarification through treaty compliance and dispute arbitration mechanisms.

A South Asian agreement banning the deployment of IRBMs or similar nuclear capable ballistic missiles in fixed launchers such as silos can be monitored with high confidence using fairly modest NTM capabilities.[50] India and eventually Pakistan may deploy IRBMs on mobile launcher platforms such as trucks or railcars to enhance the survivability of their nuclear forces. The detection and identification of these would be considerably more difficult than for fixed-base missiles.[51] Partly in recognition of these verification difficulties, the SALT II treaty bans mobile deployments of heavy missiles.[52] Production monitoring of missile factories primarily and verification of a missile flight test ban secondarily would constitute more effective routes to ensuring nondeployment of mobile missiles.

Because of their small size and similarity to conventional munitions the deployment of tactical nuclear weapons would prove the most difficult of all to monitor.[53] Fissile materials production monitoring and nuclear testing bans (the latter capable of detecting very low yield testing) would comprise the most feasible means of ensuring nondeployment of tactical nuclear weapons. Additionally, because effective integration of tactical nuclear weapons into military strategy and planning would require the training of large numbers of soldiers in their use, the existence of tactical nuclear weapons might be inferred from the detection and observation of certain maneuvers or exercises. Both unilateral NTM (including, for example, the monitoring of radio traffic to detect C^3 associated with tactical nuclear weapons operations) and observation by NTM or OSI legitimated by negotiated arms control provisions could be employed for detection of tactical nuclear weapons training and deployment.

Nuclear Weapons Free Zones

We have discussed bilateral nuclear arms control arrangements between India and Pakistan, and, to a lesser extent, India and China. Multilateral regional arms control initiatives, specifically nuclear weapons free zones (NWFZ) are a third possibility. Shortly after India's nuclear test in 1974, Pakistan submitted to the UN General

Assembly its proposal for a South Asian NWFZ, and has subsequently resubmitted it on an almost yearly basis.[54] With similar persistence India has repeatedly rejected Pakistani NWFZ overtures, not least because they fail to include China within their ambit.[55]

An exploratory survey of the mechanics of South Asian NWFZ implementation, notably its provisions for verification, is worthwhile even if the near-term probability of concluding such an agreement is remote. By examining UN deliberations and the records of implementation for the two NWFZs established in populated areas (the Treaty of Tlatelolco and the South Pacific Nuclear Free Zone) some general guidelines for devising an effective South Asian NWFZ regime may be derived.

Considering a South and Mid-Asian NWFZ

Nuclear Weapons Free Zone or Nuclear Free Zone? Multilateral regimes seeking to proscribe nuclear weapons or nuclear weapons related activities within a geographically defined perimeter may also seek to restrict nonmilitary nuclear activities. The Treaty of Raratonga aims to prohibit certain nonmilitary nuclear activities (hence the official appellation South Pacific Nuclear Free Zone rather than Nuclear Weapons Free Zone[56]), notably Japanese disposal of low level radioactive wastes within the region.[57] The Treaty of Tlatelolco, in contrast, does not restrict peaceful nuclear activities, other than to ensure nondiversion of fissile materials to nuclear weapons use.[58] A NFZ or NWFZ may also impose restrictions on zonal state export of potentially dual-usable nuclear technologies or materials. The Treaty of Tlatelolco enjoins its parties "to refrain from engaging in, encouraging, or authorizing, directly or indirectly, or in any way participating in the testing, use, manufacture, production, or possession or control of any nuclear weapon."[59]

Even if it did not require its parties to conclude full-scope IAEA safeguards agreements (which it should), a South Asian NWFZ or NFZ agreement should obligate non-NPT zonal states exporting nuclear materials and technologies to impose IAEA safeguards on non-NPT recipient states. Ideally, zonal parties would also be obligated to adhere to the 1977 London Nuclear Suppliers Group guidelines for the export of nuclear technology, a code which is considerably stricter with regard to the extension of safeguards to nuclear technology replicated on the basis of imported and safeguarded technology than is the INFCIRC/66 system.[60]

Role of Extrazonal States. Both the Treaties of Tlatelolco and Raratonga mandate the exclusion of extrazonal state nuclear weapons or related activities from their zones of application. The 1975 UN expert group report on NWFZs stated in its list of recommendations for the effective administration of NWFZ regimes, "when a zone covering a region is envisaged, the participation of all militarily important states, and preferably all states, would reinforce the efficacy of the zone."[61] The only existing NWFZ adjacent to a nuclear weapons state, the Treaty of Tlatelolco, excludes U.S. continental territory and territorial waters from its zone of application. All five nuclear weapons states have ratified Additional Protocol II of the treaty, which obligates them not to use or threaten to use nuclear weapons against zonal parties to the Treaty (so-called "negative security guarantees").[62]

The inclusion of China would most certainly be a precondition for Indian accession to an NWFZ regime. As an extra-regional nuclear weapons state adjoining South Asia, China's potential role in a South Asian NWFZ is significant. As a declared nuclear weapons state, China could hardly be included as a zonal state unless it were to renounce nuclear weapons. China could, however, adhere to a South Asian NWFZ negative security guarantee protocol, much as it has for the Treaties of Tlatelolco and Raratonga. Neither of these treaties, however, significantly impinges on possible Chinese plans for ocean deployments of nuclear weapons; a South Asian NWFZ substantially incorporating the Indian Ocean within its zone of application most probably would.

Assuming the acceptance and recognition of a South Asian NWFZ by all nuclear weapons states through the granting of negative security guarantees, several formidable questions complicate the implementation of all NWFZ agreements. Among these are: the disposition of existing security arrangements between zonal states and nuclear weapons states (e.g., ANZUS, the 1971 Indo-Soviet Treaty of Friendship), and conflicts with the International Law of the Sea (ILOS) conventions regarding military vessels' freedom of navigation on the high seas, rights of innocent passage and the granting of transit and port calls to nuclear armed vessels. Though rather ambiguous on this point, the Treaty of Tlatelolco appears to permit transit of shipborne nuclear weapons through the zone subject to permission of states whose territorial waters may be involved.[63]

Peaceful Nuclear Explosions. Article XVIII of the Treaty of Tlatelolco permits its parties to "carry out explosions of nuclear devices for peaceful purposes," subject to IAEA oversight.[64] As previously noted, however, no practical means exists of verifying distinctions between peaceful and military nuclear explosives because the technological base for both is essentially the same. In recognition of this, the South Pacific Nuclear Free Zone prohibits acquisition or testing of any form of nuclear explosive device. Because of the intractable verification and compliance difficulties involved, a South Asian NWFZ agreement should similarly impose a blanket prohibition on nuclear explosive devices of any type, for any purpose.

Verifying a South and Mid-Asian NWFZ

The 1975 UN expert group report recommended an "effective verification system as integral to a meaningful NWFZ regime."[65] During the UN General Assembly debate on the creation of the Treaty of Tlatelolco, the U.S. had similarly stipulated "effective verification coupled with provisions for resolution of noncompliance allegations" as requirements for establishment of an NWFZ.[66] Both the Treaties of Raratonga and Tlatelolco establish safeguards as the means of verifying compliance by zonal state parties, with routine on-site inspections to be performed by the IAEA.

Five of the seven zonal states which would fall within the ambit of a South and Mid-Asian NWFZ are party to the NPT.[67] A NWFZ would likely obligate zonal states, regardless of NPT status, to conclude full-scope safeguards agreements with the IAEA but only upon NWFZ treaty ratification. Obviously, India and Pakistan could thus remain outside a NWFZ verification regime simply by withholding signature, ratification, or entry-into-force requirements should the agreement include a waiver provision. The effectiveness of any NWFZ regime for ensuring nonproduction and nonpossession of nuclear weapons by all zonal states is doubtful as long as India and Pakistan were excluded from treaty verification mechanisms.

A South Asian NWFZ treaty, assuming one is concluded, need not rely on IAEA safeguards as the sole means of verifying compliance, though they or something very similar would be the primary means. A "two-tiered" South Asian NWFZ is conceivable, in which states rejecting IAEA safeguards could accede to an "alternate verification protocol" until such time as they deem IAEA safeguards politically acceptable. An alternative verification protocol might employ relatively non-intrusive seismic and NTM monitoring, on a regional basis, for detection of nuclear or ballistic missile testing, and nuclear weapons deployments. More intrusive measures could include OSI, conducted by an acceptable regional verification body, of nuclear facilities, space launches, or suspect nuclear test sites. The usefulness of an alternative verification arrangement in bringing non-NPT states into the NWFZ fold assumes, of course, that a non-NPT state's rejection of IAEA safeguards is predicated on a rejection of the IAEA, rather than an ultimate intention to build nuclear weapons or retain an option to do so. In the latter case, the state will likely reject *in toto* any agreement or arrangement which aims to thwart its nuclear ambitions or retention of a nuclear option. Additionally, a two-tiered verification scheme might be politically difficult to implement because it would seem to sanction asymmetries in application, in conflict with the nondiscriminatory tradition of NWFZ regimes.

For extrazonal nuclear weapons states adhering to negative security guarantee protocols of the Treaties of Tlatelolco and Raratonga, no truly satisfactory means of verifying their compliance exists.[68] Short of on-site inspection, the presence of nuclear weapons aboard suspect ships cannot be ascertained with any reasonable certainty. A recent U.S. Natural Resources Defense Council-USSR Academy of Sciences experiment has apparently shown gamma ray monitors to be inadequate for *off-ship* detection of the presence of nuclear weapons. However, helicopter-borne neutron detectors were able to detect neutron emissions at distances up to 70 meters from cruise missile warheads on a Soviet surface ship.[69]

Negotiated Provisions for Verification

Cooperating to Enhance Monitoring Effectiveness

The application of arms limitations measures to early stages (i.e. production) in the nuclear weapons life cycle can help thwart noncompliance with measures applied to later stages (testing and/or deployment). Analogously, various unilateral and negotiated measures can facilitate the monitoring of specific kinds of nuclear weapons activities. In the U.S.-Soviet arms control context cooperative measures have historically been considered supplementary to NTM, intended as they are to facilitate monitoring by such non-intrusive means. This preeminence of NTM in U.S.-Soviet arms control verification evolved both out of necessity and circumstance.[70] Prior to the INF Treaty, on-site inspection measures were a largely non-negotiable issue in U.S.-Soviet arms control efforts. Extensive deployment of nuclear weapons, moreover implied that the counting of *launchers* via satellite observation might provide an effective substitute for the counting of warheads. SALT I, and more particularly SALT II, incorporated cooperative measures for the purpose of facilitating accurate satellite reconnaissance counts of weapons as deployed on launchers.

While some cooperative measures are designed mainly to enhance monitoring of compliance with quantitative limitations of deployed weapons (e.g., counting rules for MIRVed missiles) and are of little relevance to South Asia, others (e.g., baseline data exchanges, transparency measures) are potentially very important. On-site inspection, considered by some to be an "active" cooperative measure designed to collect information unattainable through NTM is, as alluded to previously, a verification tool with special significance for a South Asian arms limitations regime.[71]

Baseline Data Exchanges. The primary purpose of the mutual exchange of data relevant to the provisions of an arms control agreement is to create a baseline for comparison with data collected through subsequent monitoring. SALT II required the U.S. and Soviet Union to exchange data on existing numbers of treaty limited weapons as well as "maintain an agreed data base" by notifying each other of changes in these numbers.[72] The Peaceful Nuclear Explosions Treaty (PNET) requires provision of information on the purpose of a PNE, its location in geographical coordinates, geological characteristics of the explosion site and certain technological features of the device. The 1988 India-Pakistan agreement banning attacks on nuclear facilities obligates each party to annually "inform the other. . .of the latitude and longitude of its nuclear installations and facilities and whenever there is any change."[73]

The mutual provision of data and its periodic updating can itself be a significant confidence building measure, subject to two provisos.[74] First, databases do not stand alone as effective verification measures. Parties to an agreement should be able, either independently or through other cooperative measures such as OSI, to confirm the validity of data provided by a counterpart. Second, precise definition of what information is to be provided is essential. Vague or ambiguous descriptions not only facilitate exploitation of "grey areas" but can also encourage spurious charges of dishonesty or unwarranted suspicions.

Transparency Measures. These are mainly intended to enhance the visibility of treaty limited items or activities to NTM observation. Examples are provisions for advance notifications of military exercises or missile flight testing, uncovering missile silos during the periods of time when surveillance satellites pass overhead, and restrictions on missile telemetry encryption. Beginning with the 1972 Anti-Ballistic Missile (ABM) Treaty, U.S.-Soviet arms control agreements have incorporated a standard provision enjoining the signatories "not to interfere with the national technical means of verification of the other party" and "not to use deliberate concealment measures which impede verification by national technical means."[75] Because of its implications for mobile ICBM basing the proscription of "deliberate concealment" (inherent in the concept of mobility) was an especially contentious issue for SALT II.[76]

In the South Asian context, transparency measures might be applied to agreements banning the production of ballistic missiles but permitting the production of space launch vehicles. The final assembly of space launch vehicles could be required to take place in open construction halls, or such vehicles could be purposely displayed at optimal times for satellite observation.[77] Restricting the encryption of space launch vehicle telemetry could comprise an important cooperative verification measure for assuring the peaceful intent of Indian or Pakistani space programs.

Designation Measures. If transparency measures enhance the "brightness" of what is observed by NTM eyes, designation measures focus them by localizing treaty limited items or activities. Designation measures have been employed in U.S.-Soviet arms control regimes primarily to facilitate counting of weapons. For example, designated deployment areas (DDAs) have been proposed as a way out of the land-mobile ICBM verification impasse; the concealment afforded by mobility is preserved because missiles are counted only as they pass through well defined DDAs.[78]

For South Asia, designation measures are relevant for agreements covering civilian space program activities, permitted conventional weapons, such as tactical munitions or very short range missiles having a dual capability (designation measures might facilitate the counting of these if deployed in relatively large numbers), and confidence building measures restricting military exercises or troop deployments to areas circumscribed by agreement.[79]

The occurrence of even permitted items or activities outside the perimeter of an agreed deployment area would constitute noncompliance. Moreover, restricting space program activities, for example, to well-defined designated sites could substantially ease the monitoring essential for discerning whether these activities are in compliance with a ban on IRBM production or testing.

Seismic Monitoring Cooperative Measures. There are several means of enhancing the identification of ambiguous seismic events. These are described in the previous discussion of bans on nuclear explosive testing.

On-Site Inspection. India and Pakistan nuclear weapon activities are still largely confined to the production stage. Pragmatic and effective South Asian arms control aimed at ensuring nonpossession of nuclear weapons then, must logically focus on this stage. Detecting the diversion of fissile materials from peaceful application entails both accounting for rather small quantities of these materials and the isolation of restricted from unrestricted activities within the confines of buildings that are opaque to NTM. Ensuring nonproduction of ballistic missiles, while more amenable to NTM monitoring in many respects, would also be enhanced by an ability to look where NTM cannot. In the South Asian context, for production agreements other than complete shutdowns of nuclear materials or ballistic missile factories, on-site inspection would afford rather high monitoring confidence, especially if coupled with NTM. Though it can effectively compensate for many NTM shortcomings, on-site inspection carries with it potentially serious political risks because of its intrusive nature.

Routine OSI. Routine inspections are *expected* inspections; they are limited to declared facilities and are carried out in accordance with a predetermined, mutually agreed schedule.[80] In other words, participants in a routine OSI regime have advance knowledge of when and where counterparts intend to conduct inspections. Routine OSI are primarily for demonstrating continuing compliance with an agreement, rather than a means of confirming suspected noncompliance. Treaty parties needn't furnish evidence to justify initiating routine inspection of a counterpart. Unlike inspections conducted on a challenge basis, routine inspections generally do not proceed from an *a priori* assumption of noncompliance.[81] Of all possible OSI regimes then, routine inspections are least prone to politically motivated abuse and the easiest to negotiate.

Nevertheless, routine OSI, like any cooperative venture obligating a degree of surrender of sovereignty, is not immune to political abuse. Scheduled inspections may be subject to delays by the inspected state, inspectors harassed or their duties obstructed. Moreover, lack of cooperation in a routine OSI regime does not necessarily stem from a desire to see an agreement fail. The presence of foreign inspectors in sensitive facilities raises legitimate security concerns for any state.[82] A major objection advanced by the Soviet Union to past U.S. OSI proposals was that inspections would be used as intelligence "fishing expeditions." Detailed specification of OSI procedures, inspector access and rights, permitted inspector equipment, escort arrangements, permitted time of arrival, and inspection duration, are essential if opportunities for obstruction and collateral information collection are to be lessened. These are issues that must be resolved by mutual agreement, preferably at the negotiation stage.

Depending on the goals of a South Asian production (of fissile materials or ballistic missiles) restriction agreement or any other arms limitation regime necessitating inspections, several types of routine OSI can be implemented.[83]   Though described in terminology derived from the U.S.-Soviet INF Treaty, the following are equally relevant to a variety of South Asian production monitoring or other arms limitations regimes requiring OSI:

- *Baseline inspections* authenticate mutually exchanged data or establish an initial database of treaty limited items. Baseline inspections can also be used to refine and elaborate subsequent inspection procedures. The IAEA, for example, conducts "initial inspections" to verify facility design information provided by the safeguarded state, establish material balance areas, and assess monitoring equipment needs.
- *Elimination inspections* confirm the destruction or disassembly of treaty limited items. Though negotiated shutdowns of specified production facilities can be fairly confidently monitored by NTM, provision might be made for initial and periodic elimination inspections to confirm observations made by NTM.
- *Closeout inspections* verify that a specified facility has ceased production or storage of treaty limited items. In contrast to elimination inspections, closeout inspections are carried out in operative facilities that may continue to produce items or house activities not restricted by agreement.
- *Continuous monitoring* can be accomplished either through the continuous presence of human inspectors and/or the installation of automated sensors and surveillance devices. The INF Treaty establishes a permanent inspector presence at designated U.S. and Soviet missile production sites. IAEA containment and surveillance devices (e.g., seals and video cameras) permit continuous observation and access prevention in the absence of inspectors.

Undeclared facilities, even if used for entirely legitimate purposes, are obviously not subject to inspection under a routine OSI regime and can thus be a valid source of compliance concerns. Treaty provisions for periodic updatings of databases and declared site lists would permit the incorporation of new facilities, including those detected by unilateral NTM, within the verification regime. Whether agreement can be reached about the inclusion of new or as-yet unacknowledged facilities would depend largely on the owner state's commitment to the overall success of the agreement. If a state is resolute in its use of clandestine facilities to violate the terms of an agreement while maintaining a pretext of compliance at declared sites, it will hardly be a willing negotiator. In such a situation both sides might reasonably question the value of the agreement as a whole and its breakdown may be unavoidable.

Special Inspections—Short Notice or Challenge Inspections. By definition, special inspections are those conducted on a nonroutine basis. Advance notification, if given at all, is measured in hours or days, and both declared and undeclared sites might be subject to inspection depending on treaty provisions. The sensitivity of short notice or challenge inspections to the prevailing political climate derives from their nonroutine nature. Whether or not a state is required to furnish justification for its request to inspect a counterpart, such a request may be perceived as implying guilt or noncompliance. Furthermore, security concerns about loss of sensitive collateral or proprietary information are intensified by the prospect of inspectors arriving at potentially any site with little warning.

Requiring justification for an inspection request could mitigate some of the most adversarial aspects of special inspections. The lack of such a requirement could encourage harassment by inspection. But capricious demands for inspection will likely be met in kind. Annual inspection quotas could discourage unwarranted inspection demands, though an especially imaginative and uncooperative state might contrive to exhaust its counterpart's inspection quota by provoking it with "apparent" violations. Additionally, if the need to furnish evidence in order to justify an inspection request entails the revelation of sensitive intelligence assets, a state might be reluctant to request an inspection even if it possesses solid evidence of significant noncompliance.

Some special inspection regimes do not require justification of inspection requests. The INF Treaty, for example, accords the U.S. and Soviet Union the right to request without justification short notice inspections (to be implemented within four to 24 hours after arrival of inspectors at "key entry points") of sites other than primary missile production facilities, which are covered by a continuous inspector presence. The 1986 Stockholm CSBM

Accords contain similar provisions for unjustified short notice inspections.[84] The workability of both short notice OSI regimes appears to derive from the use of annual inspection quotas, ensuring that parties use inspections wisely. Most importantly, the parties to these agreements seem to genuinely desire to cooperate. The record of the usefulness of requiring justification for inspection requests thus appears to be mixed. Furthermore, the need to justify inspection requests could seriously hamper timely access, if this is important for effective verification.

In addition to quotas, two other negotiated qualifications can serve to mitigate potential political abuse of special inspections and allay fears of sensitive information loss. INF short notice inspections apply only to an extensive list of declared sites drawn up by mutual agreement. Such a provision ensures that inspection requests are limited to facilities relevant to treaty compliance issues. Again, for declared-site inspections to be maximally effective, provision must be made for periodic revision and expansion of declared-site lists as warranted by new developments.

For short notice or challenge inspection regimes applying to any suspect site, the inclusion of a right of refusal could obviate a potential source of harassment and discourage intelligence fishing expeditions of facilities with little direct treaty relevance. The inspection regime could additionally require a state refusing an inspection request to furnish alternative evidence or means of demonstrating compliance.[85] Such an arrangement, however, could pose a significant hindrance to timely-access requirements.

Invitational inspections comprise a type of special inspection useful for compliance diplomacy purposes. Voluntary invitations to inspect can be extended by states desiring to allay compliance concerns about facilities not covered by routine or short notice inspection regimes. An example frequently cited in this regard is the Soviet Union's 1986 invitational tour, extended to a U.S. Congressional delegation, of the Krasnoyarsk radar facility. While the visit ultimately failed to resolve U.S. concerns about ABM Treaty compliance, it may have served significant confidence building purposes.[86] While the public diplomacy aspects of invitational inspections are especially susceptible to exploitation, these kind of inspections might be employed as an important compliance-dispute resolution mechanism.

On-site Inspection in Perspective. Lewis Dunn and Amy Gordon have identified four factors which influence the ease of clandestinely producing treaty limited items or carrying out prohibited activities under an OSI regime: the ease with which other sites could be reconfigured to produce, service, or house treaty limited items or activities; how readily undeclared facilities or activities could be disguised, how much effort would be needed to avoid detection if an attempt were made to misuse an inspected facility or site, and the extent to which dual use items are limited.[87]

Even if no OSI regime is capable of detecting all instances of noncompliance at every possible site, all types of OSI can certainly impede the efficient conduct of noncompliant activities. As can be said of any arms control agreement, whether or not a state cares about being caught depends upon its commitment to at least maintaining the appearance of compliance. If commitment is sufficiently strong, a state will be deterred, at a minimum, from blatantly violating the terms of an agreement. Skirting legality or loophole-stretching may be less indicative of imminent treaty breakout than of a desire to impose unilateral interpretations of treaty language while on the whole remaining committed to the arms control regime. OSI certainly complicates the more obvious attempts at treaty violation, assuming, of course, that the facilities of greatest arms control significance fall within the ambit of an OSI regime.

Facilitating Compliance

Monitoring, which consists of the collection of data pertinent to arms control agreements, comprises the technical portion of the verification process. The verification process also involves compliance assessment, or using the solid data generated by monitoring to assess whether parties to an agreement are abiding by its terms. Compliance assessment is an unavoidably political pursuit, dependent as it is on judgements about the consonance between monitoring data and human interpretations of what a treaty requires its signatories to do or not do. Compliance, in short, "is the actual practice of arms control."[88]

Just as an agreement may incorporate negotiated provisions for enhancing technical monitoring capabilities, it might also establish mechanisms for resolution of noncompliance charges or disputes over treaty language, and specify sanctions in the event of treaty breaches. Multilateral experience with compliance mechanisms, such as the Agency for the Prohibition of Nuclear Weapons in Latin America (OPANAL) of the Treaty of Tlatelolco, and the U.S.-Soviet bilateral experience, the SALT Standing Consultative Commission (SCC) in particular, offer valuable lessons in compliance diplomacy. Additionally, whether an agreement is a formal treaty or tacit understanding, the specificity of treaty language, or its adaptability to new technological developments are all factors which impinge on the efficacy of compliance.

Treaties or Tacit Understandings? All of the negotiated arms control measures discussed earlier entail rather detailed provisions for verification procedures. Informal or tacit agreements, in contrast, are appropriate for arms control situations in which noncompliance is fairly obvious or evidence for it is easily obtainable through unilateral monitoring or intelligence methods.[89] "Parallel unilateral actions" (or inaction) might also be considered a form of tacit understanding.[90] India and Pakistan have both abstained from conducting nuclear explosive tests since 1974. R.V.R. Chandrasekhara Rao contends that the incentives for abstention from testing are such that each country wishes to avoid being the first to break the "moratorium."[91] Perhaps, but as neither India or Pakistan has made a formal commitment to abstain from nuclear explosive testing, each retains the incentives to continue its nuclear weapons research, albeit short of detectable nuclear testing. Tacit understandings, or apparent parallel unilateral actions provide no means of resolving compliance disputes; rules that are not mutually defined and acknowledged can hardly be broken. Moreover, evidence of noncompliance obtained through unilateral intelligence cannot legitimately be considered anything other than espionage.

In addition to delineating rights, obligations, procedures for monitoring and compliance, and definitions of noncompliance, formal treaties also establish baselines for comparing subsequent compliance behavior. Mutually agreed and defined ground rules facilitate predictability in arms control and military relations.[92] The existence of formal, contractual obligations can promote observance of the rules by institutionalizing commitment to the arms control process. By institutionalizing commitment, especially if mechanisms for consultation and amendment are included, formal arms control agreements can foster continuity of cooperative action.

Treaty Language: Precise or Ambiguous? Precision of definition would seem essential for promoting compliance with treaty provisions. Clearly defined terms and narrowly circumscribed obligations can certainly help discourage the unilateral "reinterpretations" which often inspire compliance disputes. But an effective arms control regime also maintains a delicate balance between precision and "flexible ambiguity" that extends a treaty's reach to future technological and strategic developments. Adherents to a strict interpretation of the 1972 ABM Treaty contend that it precludes testing of Strategic Defense Initiative systems and component technologies; the Reagan Administrations "new interpretation" of the treaty argued that post-1972 technologies do not come under the aegis of the treaty's bans on testing and deployment of ABM systems or components.[93]

A country's negotiators may also prefer some ambiguity in treaty language if it preserves some flexibility in military activities. The U.S., for example, argued for a less-than-precise definition of launchers during the SALT II negotiations because a more restricted definition would likely preclude certain MX basing options.[94] In a South Asian arms control regime this kind of creative ambiguity would ideally be avoided, but the regime should be sufficiently flexible if it is to be capable of accounting for modes of nuclear weapons deployment not presently available to either India or Pakistan, such as mobile IRBM systems. Simultaneously, a South Asian arms control regime must define what is restricted in terms precise enough to minimize exploitation of grey areas.

Treaty Adaptability. Obviously, no arms control negotiators can foresee every potential strategic or technological contingency, nor can any agreement be completely free of interpretation disputes as its provisions are put into practice. The achievement of the proper mix of precision and flexibility of language is difficult between even the most cooperative of parties. The effective use of consultative fora and procedures for treaty amendment can help compensate for shortcomings in treaty language. Treaties lacking such provisions are prone to obsolescence. They are also highly vulnerable to "tit for tat" noncompliance spirals because no formal, confidential channel for mutual resolution of conflicting interpretations of treaty obligations exists. Article XIII of the ABM treaty established the Standing Consultative Commission, one of the functions of which is to "consider, as appropriate, possible proposals for further increasing the viability of this treaty, including proposals for amendments in accordance with the with the provisions of this treaty."[95] To date, the SCC has not been used for treaty amendment purposes. Rather, it has been employed primarily as a means of implementing SALT agreements and resolving compliance questions.[96] The SCC has also been given responsibility for the ABM Treaty's formal review procedures established by Article XIV.[97] During the Nixon, Ford, and Carter Administrations the SCC was an effective problem solving forum in which several rather contentious compliance disputes were resolved to the apparent satisfaction of both sides.[98] Successful SCC resolution of U.S. allegations of Soviet testing of SA-5 radars "in an ABM mode" is frequently cited as an example of the utility of consultative mechanisms for clarifying ambiguous treaty language.[99] The effectiveness and limitations of bilateral consultative mechanisms, using the SCC as a model, is discussed subsequently.

Unilateral Clarifications. A statement by one party clarifying its interpretations or position regarding certain treaty provisions can serve to establish the bounds of what is considered acceptable treaty behavior and may help encourage compliance by a counterpart.[100] The beneficial aspects of unilateral clarifications are most likely realized if they are presented during treaty negotiations or as part of a mutual post-treaty effort to secure accommodation of conflicting views.

If consultation and negotiation has failed to render a mutually satisfactory reading of treaty language, subsequent submission of unilateral statements is more likely to widen the rift than to promote acquiescence by the other side. This is especially so if unilateral clarifications represent an effort to undo previously agreed but ambiguous treaty provisions.[101]

If a treaty lacks a mechanism for consultation in the event of such disputes, or if one is established but a negative political atmosphere precludes its effective use, unilateral clarifications provide the most obvious option for parties to communicate their views regarding treaty obligations to counterparts. But the incentives in such a situation to reinterpret treaty provisions to accommodate military planning and new weapons programs, or to respond reactively to a counterpart's reinterpretations are great. If treaties are to retain any meaning as cooperative ventures parties must abide by their provisions as negotiated, unless amended by mutual agreement.[102]

Public or Private Diplomacy? The Reagan Administration's "public confrontation" style of SALT compliance diplomacy stands in marked contrast to the quiet SCC "problem solving" approach of its predecessors.[103] The risks of public compliance diplomacy are well illustrated by this contrast; intransigence and a spiraling downturn in arms control relations are the more likely consequences, especially if noncompliance charges are presented in a polemical and accusatory manner. No country wants to be seen by the world as bowing to a rival's presumptions of guilt.

Equally important is the confidentiality afforded to sensitive military information by a private consultative forum. Public release of sensitive information would exacerbate any reluctance of parties to exchange data vital to resolving compliance disputes.

Nevertheless, there is some justification for making less sensitive information about the results of consultative sessions available to the public. The executives of parliamentary democracies such as India and Pakistan are obliged to inform their constituents and parliaments about treaty implementation matters. An informed electorate is integral to sustaining domestic support for current or future arms control efforts. Unclassified summaries of India-Pakistan or regional treaty consultative commission activities and net assessments of *both* sides' compliance records presented in an objective, problem-solving style would help to dispel the mystery and misconceptions likely to arise from arms control secrecy.[104] Detailed, classified versions can be provided to relevant parliamentary committees. In the U.S., classified accounts of substantive SALT SCC agreements and issues are sent by the President to six Congressional committees.[105] Regulation 8 of the SCC Memorandum of Understanding stipulates, however, that the actual proceedings of the SCC are not to be made public unless expressly agreed by the SCC Commissioner.

Compliance Sanctions and "Safeguards." In contrast to decisions rendered by domestic courts of law, no arms control police exist to enforce bilateral treaty parties to comply with their obligations. The conspicuous lack of effective sanctions and enforcement mechanisms in the event of a counterpart's noncompliance is perhaps one of the most intractable weaknesses of bilateral arms control efforts. Multilateral arms control agreements, such as the NPT, permit more options for applying sanctions to violators. Noncompliant NPT parties may lose their status as an IAEA member state[106] and other parties might agree to embargo exports of nuclear technology or assistance to the offending state.

In the bilateral arms control case, unilateral action is the only viable sanction. Arms control safeguards have been suggested in the U.S.-Soviet context as "measures designed to encourage compliance with arms control agreements and/or to provide for a party's security against violations or the collapse of an accord."[107] Proponents of safeguards contend that the fear of detection is an insufficient deterrent to noncompliance; the U.S. must be prepared to respond with concrete, compensatory actions capable of negating any military gains accruing from Soviet noncompliance. Regarding the ABM Treaty and concerns of potential Soviet noncompliance, in 1979 Secretary of Defense Harold Brown proposed "an aggressive [ABM] R&D program to guard against Soviet [ABM Treaty] breakthrough . . . and to encourage their compliance with the treaty."[108] However, responding in kind to perceived violations, especially if changes in treaty-limited military activities are called for, is likely to generate tit-for-tat noncompliance exchanges that may quickly spiral out of control. As Stephen Flanagan states, "[i]t has proved very difficult in practice to identify military safeguards that genuinely encourage compliance with various limitations rather than simply drive the other parties to undertake hedges that ultimately undermine the goals and purpose of an accord."[109]

Bilateral Consultative Fora. In light of the previous discussion, the most fruitful means of resolving compliance and interpretation disputes is mutual consultation within a treaty-mandated institution established for such a purpose. The U.S.-Soviet Standing Consultative Commission comprises the preeminent example of the structure and functioning of a consultative mechanism for implementing bilateral arms limitations agreements.

Useful guidelines for enhancing the effectiveness of bilateral consultative fora also derive from the U.S.-Soviet SCC experience.

As well as considering compliance questions and potential treaty amendments the SCC was mandated by the ABM treaty as a forum for the voluntary provision of data by either party considered "necessary to assure confidence in compliance," consideration of questions "involving unintended interference" with NTM, proposals for additional arms control measures and possible "changes in the strategic situation" that may affect treaty provisions. A consultative commission established by an India-Pakistan or India-China arms limitations agreement could perform similar tasks with perhaps added responsibilities for mutual oversight of the procedural implementation of cooperative verification measures as OSI. The depository and analysis of IAEA-like material accountancy reports required for verifying fissile materials production restrictions might be undertaken by a special consultative commission technical advisory group. The Memorandum of Understanding implementing the SALT SCC provides for the creation of working groups composed of technical advisers for addressing specific issues. Some of the advisory groups established by the SCC have dealt with topics unrelated to the SALT agreements; chemical weapons, a comprehensive nuclear test ban and conventional arms transfers are some examples.[110]

In general, identical databases on treaty limited items and activities might be maintained and upgraded by consultative commission staff in each country. This would create a technical library available for commissioners' reference during compliance resolution negotiations. Discussion and negotiation of common understandings regarding nuclear and conventional conflict prevention or CBMs is another potential function of an India-Pakistan SCC. One function such a consultative commission should avoid, however, is crisis management. Linking arms control and crisis resolution processes in this manner is likely to exacerbate the former's vulnerabilities to the prevailing political climate.

Sidney Graybeal and Michael Krepon and others[111] have posed a number of recommendations for enhancing effective functioning of the U.S.- Soviet Standing Consultative Commission. Most of these suggestions derive from the apparent breakdown of SALT consultative mechanisms in the early 1980s with the advent of the

Reagan Administration's confrontational approach to U.S.-Soviet arms control. These lessons are equally relevant to countries, such as India and Pakistan, considering potential arms control measures.

First, compliance questions should be addressed by the SCC first, rather than at higher levels or in other fora. India is likely to be especially sensitive to the latter, as evinced by its irritation with Pakistan's ritual raising of the Kashmir issue in other than strictly bilateral contexts.

Second, issues should be brought to SCC attention in a routine and timely manner, before they spiral out of control. If at all possible, the counterpart SCC commissioner should be notified of upcoming issues in advance. Advance notification can facilitate more timely resolution of disputes.

Third, the expertise of the SCC delegation can be used to help prevent ambiguous language in future arms control agreements that can engender compliance disputes.

Fourth, compliance disputes should not be characterized as violations until such disagreements have been adequately examined and discussed within the SCC. Prior to raising an issue in the SCC, delegations should be thoroughly prepared and the factual basis of their positions as accurate as possible.

Finally, unrelated compliance issues should be kept separate—address each issue individually on its own merits. Linking bilateral issues irrelevant to the arms control regime to progress in SCC negotiations should be especially avoided.

Multilateral Consultative Fora. Multilateral arms limitations regimes generate a peculiar set of compliance concerns, if only because of the greater administrative complexities involved. In a multilateral context compliance issues and disputes are more visible, lending greater opportunities for politicization of consultative mechanisms. Wide disparities in capabilities and influence between parties to a multilateral agreement can create an imbalance of incentives to abide by treaty obligations.[112]

For a South Asian regional nuclear arms limitations regime, such as an NWFZ, this imbalance is significant. If Bangladesh were to justifiably request an inspection of India's BARC reprocessing plant, would India feel compelled to cooperate? An Indian commitment to an NWFZ regime would hopefully carry with it a desire to maintain at least an appearance of cooperation. As the largest, most militarily powerful regional state (other than China) India may be concerned that a South Asian NWFZ would provide smaller states a forum for ganging up against it,[113] perhaps by harassing it with frivolous inspection requests. Because India and Pakistan are the only specifically South Asian states with any significant nuclear technological infrastructure, the bulk of NWFZ routine and special inspection efforts will be aimed at them. In such a context of asymmetries, a South Asian NWFZ must incorporate procedural and administrative mechanisms to ensure an equality of incentives to comply.

Very little practical experience with the implementation of compliance and consultation procedures exists for the two established NWFZs: special inspections have not commenced under the Tlatelolco regime, and no apparent compliance questions have yet arisen within the South Pacific NFZ. Nevertheless, these regional nuclear arms limitations regimes provide models for the possible structure of South Asian NWFZ compliance and consultation mechanisms.

While the IAEA performs routine inspections for both the Treaties of Tlatelolco and Raratonga, each treaty has established rather different mechanisms for reporting, coordinating compliance concerns of parties, and for the administration of special inspections.[114]

For the Treaty of Tlatelolco, the Organization for the Prohibition of Nuclear Weapons in Latin America (OPANAL) performs the task of receiving and disseminating biannual compliance reports submitted by treaty parties. Parties can request that OPANAL carry out special inspections, of either counterparts or of their own nuclear facilities if deemed necessary to allay compliance concerns. Copies of special inspection reports are forwarded by OPANAL to both the UN and the Organization of American States (OAS). The OPANAL Secretary General can request a party to submit a special report regarding compliance concerns as well. A treaty party may also request OPANAL to convene a General Conference if thought warranted by the findings of a special inspection. The General Conference in turn makes recommendations to the inspected state. In the event that treaty violations have been found, the General Conference will report its concerns to the UN, the OAS, and where appropriate, the IAEA.

The Raratonga Treaty, in contrast, establishes no permanent agency for verification and compliance administration. Instead, the Director of the South Pacific Bureau for Economic Cooperation and Development, the Secretariat to the South Pacific Forum, a regional organization established in the 1970s, receives and circulates routine compliance reports submitted by treaty parties. The Director also compiles annual reports on the status of the treaty and other matters, including noncompliance charges and investigations. The Treaty of Raratonga provides for a Consultative Committee, convened by the Director at the request of any party "for consultation and cooperation on any matter arising in relation to [the] treaty or for reviewing its operation."[115]

Unlike the Treaty of Tlatelolco, complaints procedures under the South Pacific NFZ require parties with compliance concerns to first make them known to the offending state. Only after that state has had an opportunity to respond and explain are noncompliance charges taken to the Director for consideration by the Consultative Committee. The Consultative Committee will then provide the state a further opportunity to resolve compliance concerns. If still unsatisfied, the Committee will appoint three special inspectors, after consulting with the states involved in the dispute. Inspection reports are then distributed to all treaty parties. In the event of a definitive treaty violation a South Pacific Forum meeting of all parties is promptly called.

James Schear has suggested several guidelines to facilitate the effective functioning of multilateral arms control compliance and consultation arrangements.[116] The following discussion adapts Schear's guidelines to the South Asian context.

Under a multilateral treaty regime, compliance diplomacy is probably best facilitated by a permanent verification and consultation institution, especially if significant disparities exist between parties with regard to items or activities that the treaty aims to control. The South Pacific NFZ may be an exception to this rule; a high degree of regional consensus regarding the goals of a South Pacific NFZ,[117] and a general absence of nuclear capabilities have permitted the use of a previously established regional cooperation organization. The South Asian Association for Regional Cooperation (SAARC) is probably too fragile politically to contend effectively with the extra burdens of NWFZ verification and compliance in the manner of the

South Pacific Forum. Furthermore, the member states of SAARC have explicitly agreed to exclude "bilateral and contentious" issues from discussion in SAARC fora.[118] However, SAARC technical and scientific committees might contribute regional expertise and training of inspectors.

Permitting bilateral consultation between parties outside the permanent verification and compliance institutions may help to prevent politicization of these institutions. In particular, India and Pakistan may in some instances be more amenable to resolving alleged noncompliance through this quiet, less public route.

Exposure to the higher visibility of multilateral compliance and consultation mechanisms might act as an effective sanction in the event of actual treaty violations, and discourage harassment by inspection. Annual reports, available to all treaty parties, might detail the number of inspections and the states requesting them, and inspection findings. However, the use of public diplomacy as a sanction against treaty violators must be done prudently. For example, participants in fact-finding sessions should be barred from publicly announcing their positions on a counterpart's compliance behavior before a judgement is rendered.

Treaty parties should agree, at the negotiation stage, to guidelines, rules and procedures for the content and presentation of evidence when justifying inspection requests. Parties charged with noncompliance should be allowed to offer evidence and explanations before special inspections are carried out, though in some instances timely access may be compromised. Invitational inspections to allay compliance questions might be encouraged, but specific procedures regarding the conduct of these are necessary to avoid intentionally misleading "guided tours."

Notes

1. For discussions of why covert nuclear weapons capabilities should remain covert see Lewis A. Dunn, *Controlling the Bomb* (New Haven: Yale Univ. Press, 1982), pp. 135-138; Alan Dowty "Going Public With the Bomb: The Israeli Calculus," and Gerald M. Steinberg, "Deliberate Ambiguity: Evolution and Evaluation," in Louis Rene Beres, ed., *Security or Armageddon: Israeli Nuclear Strategy* (Lexington: Lexington Books, 1986).

Going nuclear is often used to describe states which announce their nuclear weapons status by demonstrating a nuclear explosive capability, such as by conducting a test. Here, it will be used to refer to states that have acquired a militarily meaningful nuclear weapons capability (i.e. a warhead mated to an appropriate means of delivery) whether or not they have overtly demonstrated their status as a nuclear weapons state. *Proliferation* will refer here to the acquisition of the technology and materials necessary to enable development of a nuclear weapons capability by states other than the five declared nuclear weapons powers (the U.S., USSR, China, France, and Britain). A state can be a "proliferator" without having gone nuclear. India, Pakistan, Israel, and South Africa are examples of states that have either gone nuclear, or are very close to doing so.

A more formal term for such states is *threshold nuclear weapons state*. Even if, as in the Indian case, a threshold nuclear weapons state has demonstrated a nuclear explosive capability, it is not a *declared* nuclear weapons state unless it has made an overt, official commitment to deployment of nuclear weapons. Threshold nuclear weapons states might therefore also be called *covert* nuclear weapons states.

2. A. F. Mullins, "Proliferation in South Asia: The Military Dimension" (Lawrence Livermore National Laboratory; n.d.), p. 6.

3. Figure 5.1 represents a purely mathematical expression of relative significance as percentage change; it says nothing about changes in actual military usefulness of incremental additions to force size, nor does it presume to measure the perceived political significance of evidence of noncompliance with arms-limitations agreements. Further, it assumes that new warheads are added to existing stocks in constant increments of 10 (in reality, additions are likely to be variable) and that no dismantling of previously added warheads occurs. Nonetheless, Fig. 5.1 can be said to represent a quantification of the perception that a small numerical increase in a small weapons stockpile is much more significant militarily than a comparable, or even somewhat larger, increase in an already large arsenal.

4. Values for percentage change in stockpile resulting from incremental additions of 10 warheads were calculated according to the following:

Percentage change $= \left(\dfrac{n}{n+10} - \dfrac{n-10}{n} \right)$ x 100 where n = number of warheads

This allows for a comparison of the percentage change resulting from an addition of 10 to a stockpile of n warheads *relative* to the percentage change resulting from an addition of 10 to a stockpile of n-10 warheads. For example, in a stockpile of 40 warheads:

Percentage change $= \left(\dfrac{40}{50} - \dfrac{30}{40} \right)$ x 100 = 5%. With smaller constant

incremental additions, the percentage change approaches zero more rapidly. With greater constant incremental additions the percentage change approaches zero more slowly. In general,

$\left(\dfrac{n}{n+k} - \dfrac{n-k}{n} \right)$ x 100 = percentage change resulting from constant incremental additions of k units to a "stockpile" of n units.

5. Frank von Hippel and Barbara Levi, "Controlling Nuclear Weapons at the Source: Verification of a Cutoff in the Production of Plutonium and Highly Enriched Uranium for Nuclear Weapons", in Kosta Tsipis, et. al., eds., *Arms Control Verification: The Technologies That Make It Possible* (Washington, D.C.: Pergamon-Brassey's; 1986), pp. 356-357.
6. IAEA "significant quantities" and "timely detection" criteria are given in "The Present Status of IAEA Safeguards on Nuclear Fuel Cycle Facilities," *IAEA Bulletin* , August, 1980, pp. 4, 6.
7. Allan Krass, *Verification: How Much is Enough?* (London: Taylor & Francis; SIPRI, 1985), pp. 202-204.
8. This situation illustrates the verification principle that violations are much more clearly defined for outright bans of specified weapons systems or agreements obligating parties not to do something (e.g., production of nuclear explosive devices, atmospheric nuclear testing) than for agreements specifying numerical limitations. See Herbert Scoville, Jr., "Verifying a Nuclear Freeze," in William T. Parsons, ed., *Arms Control and Strategic Stability* (Lanham: University Press of America, 1986) p.88. This concept is more fully discussed below.
9. The "Weisner curve" is discussed in Krass, pp. 167-169.
10. The placement of the number "1" at the "exit" of the fissile material production process is not meant to imply that monitoring should take place only at the exit of fissile material production facilities; rather, it signifies the application of monitoring and verification activities at all points of the fissile material production cycle for which diversion could take place including, for example, uranium enrichment, reactor, and reprocessing facilities. Again, Figure 1 is intended to illustrate *processes* in the nuclear weapons life-cycle, rather than specific *facilities* housing such processes.
11. Adapted from discussion in Wilkening, pp. 107-124.
12. Dean A. Wilkening, "Monitoring Bombers and Cruise Missiles" in William C. Potter, ed., *Verification and Arms Control* (Lexington :Lexington Books, 1984), pp. 107-124. See also Vipin Gupta, "Sensing the Threat," this volume.
13. The detection and identification of very low magnitude seismic events for the purposes of monitoring compliance with a complete nuclear testing ban is more difficult than is the detection and identification of larger nuclear explosions under a limited test ban regime specifying a relatively high threshold.
14. In some situations compliance might be monitored with greater certainty if more intrusive OSI measures are employed.
15. David Fischer and Paul Szasz, *Safeguarding the Atom* (London: Taylor & Francis; SIPRI, 1985), pp. 75-86.
16. INFCIRC/66 in Fischer and Szasz, p.187.
17. This loophole has since been eliminated, however, for all safeguards agreements based on the original INFCIRC/66 document. Personal communication, Robert Rochlin, U.S. Arms Control and Disarmament Agency.
18. INFCIRC/66 in Fischer and Szasz, p.187.

19. There have been at least two proposals for an India-Pakistan limited or designated facility inspection regime. Peter Galbraith, a staff member of the U.S. Senate Foreign Relations Committee has proposed that India and Pakistan each submit one currently unsafeguarded nuclear facility to safeguards, with Pakistan designating the Indian facility to be inspected, and India designating the Pakistani facility. See Galbraith, "Nuclear Proliferation in South Asia: Containing the Threat," *Staff Report to the Committee on Foreign Relations, U.S. Senate* (Washington, D.C.: U.S. Government Printing Office, 1988), p. 22-23; the Carnegie Task Force on Nuclear Proliferation and South Asian Security proposed that India and Pakistan negotiate a regime of limited duration inspections of designated facilities. "Nuclear Weapons and South Asian Security," *Report of the Carnegie Task Force on Nonproliferation and South Asian Security* (Washington, D.C.: Carnegie Endowment for International Peace,1988), pp. 88.

20. Fischer and Szasz, p. 80

21. *Ibid.*, p. 82.

22. Leonard Spector, *Going Nuclear* (Cambridge: Ballinger, 1987), pp. 84-85.

23. Leonard Spector, *The Undeclared Bomb* (Cambridge: Ballinger, 1988), pp. 100-101.

24. *Ibid.*, p. 113.

25. *1988 Report of the Carnegie Task Force on Non-Proliferation and South Asian Security*, p. 89.

26. Ivan C. Oelrich, "Production Monitoring for Arms Control," in Michael Krepon and Mary Umberger, eds., *Verification and Compliance: A Problem-Solving Approach* (Cambridge: Ballinger, 1988) pp. 118-119.

27. Because of the relatively short geographic distances involved, distinctions between tactical and strategic-range missiles in South Asia may be merely semantic; here, tactical nuclear delivery vehicles refers primarily to weapons likely to be used on a conventional battlefield, e.g. artillery shells, atomic demolition mines, etc., manufactured in rather large numbers. Though dual-capable short-range missiles as the Indian *Prithvi* (described as a "battlefield support missile," with a range of 150 km) and the Pakistani *Hatf* I and *Hatf* II missiles (with ranges of 80 and 300 km respectively) can be considered as tactical weapons, they could also be used strategically, i.e., targeted at cities or military targets well beyond battlefield limits.

28. "Summary and Text of the INF Treaty and Inspection Protocols," *Arms Control Today*, Jan./Feb., 1988, pp. 1-16.

29. INF Treaty Inspection Protocol; Serge Sur, "Verification Problems of the Washington Treaty on the Elimination of Intermediate Range Missiles," *UNIDIR Research Papers No. 2* (New York: United Nations, 1988), p. 11.

30. Sur, p.11-12.

31. Oelrich, pp. 114-117.

32. The reliability of implosion mechanisms for first generation fission devices could be assessed with laboratory testing using flash x-ray and "pin sensor" equipment. Field testing of implosion mechanisms, substituting chemical high explosives for fissile materials, is another alternative to full-scale

nuclear testing. Uncertainty of yield for a fission device tested in these ways could be great, however. See Donald R. Westerveldt, "The Role of Laboratory Tests," in Jozef Goldblat and David Cox, eds., *Nuclear Weapons Tests: Prohibition or Limitations?* (Oxford: Oxford University Press; SIPRI, 1988) pp. 47-58.

33. J. Carson Mark, "The Purpose of Nuclear Test Explosions," in Goldblat and Cox, pp. 31-46.

34. Frank Von Hippel, Harold Fieveson and Christopher Paine, "A Low Threshold Nuclear Test Ban," *International Security*, Fall, 1987, p. 141

35. *Ibid.*, see also Mark, pp. 32-34.

36. Steve Fetter, *Toward a Comprehensive Test Ban* (Cambridge: Ballinger, 1988) p. 112; also Thomas Cochran, et. al., *Nuclear Weapons Databook Vol. II: U.S. Nuclear Warhead Production* (Cambridge: Ballinger, 1987), p.43

37. Ray Kidder, " Degree of Verification Needed," in Goldblat and Cox, pp. 267-269.

38. Willard J. Hannon, "In-Country Seismic Stations for Monitoring Nuclear Test Bans," in Goldblat and Cox, p. 202.

39. U.S. Congress, Office of Technology Assessment, *Seismic Verification of Nuclear Testing Treaties,* OTA-ISC- 361 (Washington, D.C.: U.S. Government Printing Office,1988), pp. 106-107.

40. Farooq Hussain," The Impact of Weapons Test Restrictions," in James Schear, ed., *Nuclear Weapons Proliferation and Nuclear Risk* (Hampshire: Gower; International Institute for Strategic Studies, 1984), pp. 134-135.

41. *Ibid.*, p. 144.

42. Pushpindar Singh, "India's *Agni* Success Poses New Problems," *Jane's Defense Weekly*, June 3, 1989, pp. 1052-1053; Dilip Bobb, "*Agni:* Chariot of Fire," *India Today*; June 15, 1989, pp. 10-13.

43. U.S. Arms Control and Disarmament Agency, *World Military Expenditures and Transfers, 1987* (Washington, D.C.: ACDA, 1987), p. 26; David Silverberg, "MTCR Imperfect, But Only Organized Attempt to Limit Proliferation,"*Defense News*, Sept. 4, 1989, p. 30 ; Aaron Karp, "The Frantic Third World Quest for Ballistic Missiles," *Bulletin of the Atomic Scientists,* June, 1989.

44. The final boost stage of ballistic missiles is terminated earlier, before the payload has enough velocity to enter orbit. See Kosta Tsipis, *Arsenal: Understanding Weapons in the Nuclear Age* (New York: Simon & Schuster, 1983) pp.102-129 for a description of ballistic missile technology.

45. Even if flight tests of longer range missiles were prohibited, reentry vehicles could conceivably be tested on smaller, less detectable missiles which drive the reentry vehicle out of the atmosphere and return it to earth, simulating the conditions of reentry from a longer range missile. See Hussain, p.140.

46. SALT II Treaty, Art. II, reprinted in Jozef Goldblat, ed., *Arms Control Agreements: A Handbook* (New York: Praeger, 1983), p. 213.

47. Wilkening, p. 110; Michael Krepon, "Counting Rules," in Krepon and Umberger, pp. 127-128.

48. Wilkening, p. 114. Also see Vipin Gupta, Chapter 8, for discussion of monitoring radio traffic for evidence of military nuclear operations.

49. Roger Harrison, *Verifying a Nuclear Weapons Freeze* (Leamington Spa, U.K.: Berg, 1986)

50. The commercial SPOT satellite system was able to detect and identify a French IRBM silo complex using a 10 meter resolution capability. William A. Kennedy and Mark G. Marshall, "A Peek at the French Missile Complex," *Bulletin of the Atomic Scientists,* September, 1989, pp. 20-23.

51. For discussions of verification problems associated with mobile missiles see Paul. K. Davis, "Land Mobile ICBMs: Verification and Breakout," in Potter, ed., *Verification and SALT: The Challenge of Strategic Deception* (Boulder: Westview, 1980), pp.143-162; Harry Saurwein, "Mobile ICBMs," in Schear, ed., *Nuclear Weapons Proliferation and Nuclear Risk,* pp. 169-175; Albert Gore, "Verifying Mobile Missiles," in Krepon and Umberger, pp. 3-16.

52. SALT II Treaty, Art.IX.

53. Harrison, p. 40.

54. William Epstein, "Nuclear Free Zones," *Scientific American,* November,1975, p.32. Pakistan presented its latest South Asian NWFZ proposal to the UN in November, 1989. For details of the 1988 proposal see *United Nations Disarmament Yearbook: 1988* (New York: United Nations, 1989), pp. 250-252.

55. For a summary of Indian objections to Pakistani NWFZ proposals see *United Nations Disarmament Yearbook: 1986* (New York: United Nations, 1987) pp. 208-209.

56. Greg Fry, "Toward a South Pacific Nuclear Free Zone," *Bulletin of the Atomic Scientists,* June/July, 1985, p.16.

57. David Freestone, "Nuclear Weapons Free Zones," in Istvan Pogany, ed., *Nuclear Weapons and International Law* (New York: St. Martin's, 1987), p. 195.

58. Treaty on the Prohibition of Nuclear Weapons in Latin America, Art.I, in Goldblat, p. 148.

59. *Ibid.*

60. London Nuclear Suppliers guidelines for report of nuclear materials and technologies transfers reprinted in Fischer and Szasz, pp. 217-223.

61. Edmundo Fujita, "The Prevention of the Geographical Proliferation of Nuclear Weapons: Nuclear Weapons Free Zones and Zones of Peace in the Southern Hemisphere," *UNIDIR Research Paper No. 4* (New York: United Nations, 1989), p. 14.

62. UN Resolution 3472B calls upon nuclear weapons states to affirm the following obligations regarding established NWFZs "in a solemn international instrument having full legally binding force": 1. To respect in all its parts the statute of total absence of nuclear weapons defined in the treaty; 2. To refrain from contributing in any way to the performance in the territories forming part of the zone of acts which involve a violation of the . . . treaty; 3. To refrain from using or threatening to use nuclear weapons against the States included in the zone. Cited in Fujita, p.45

63. See discussions in Goldblat, pp. 64-65; Miguel Marin Bosch, "The Treaty of Tlatelolco and the NPT," in David Dewitt, ed., *Nuclear Nonproliferation and Global Security* (New York: St. Martin's, 1987), pp. 180-181. For discussion of the International Law of the Sea Convention see Patricia Birnie, "Law of the Sea and Nuclear Weapons: Legal Aspects," in Pogany, ed., pp. 160-161.

64. On this issue see Julio Cesar Carasales, "The Future of Tlatelolco 20 years After its Signature," p. 81 and Alfonso Garcia Robles "20th Anniversary of the Treaty of Tlatelolco," p.71 in *Disarmament,* Winter, 1987/1988 and Goldblat, p. 64 for relevant discussion of this issue. That the Treaty of Tlatelolco expressly permits the development and use of PNEs is disputed by the U.S. and Soviet Union; both of these countries construe the Treaty's definition of a nuclear weapon (Art. V) as precluding PNEs (Leonard S. Spector, personal communication).

65. Fujita, "The Prevention of the Geographical Proliferation of Nuclear Weapons," p. 14.

66. Freestone, "Nuclear Weapons Free Zones," p. 184; Epstein, "Nuclear Free Zones," *Scientific American,* p. 26.

67. Bangladesh, Bhutan, Nepal, Maldives, and Sri Lanka. An eighth "regional" state, China, is a non-NPT nuclear weapons state but has concluded safeguards agreements with the IAEA applying to some of its civilian nuclear facilities.

68. Carasales, "The Future of Tlatelolco," pp. 82-83.

69. Bill Keller, "Rare Test by U.S. Scientists of Soviet Missile at Sea,"*New York Times,* July 6, 1989; Thomas B. Cochran, "Black Sea Experiment Only a Start," *Bulletin of the Atomic Scientists,* November, 1989, p. 15. For a discussion of the technical and political difficulties associated with monitoring to ascertain the presence of nuclear weapons on ships see "Potential Verification Provisions for Long-Range, Nuclear-Armed, Sea-launched Cruise Missiles," The Center for International Security Workshop Report, Stanford University, July 1988.

70. The Soviet Union has not always accepted the legitimacy of satellite reconnaissance as a verification tool. In 1962, the Soviet delegation to the UN sought to ban all spaced-based intelligence collection. See Stuart A. Cohen, "The Evolution of Soviet Views on SALT Verification," in Potter, ed., *Verification and SALT,* p. 57.

71. James Schear, "Cooperative Measures for Verification," in Potter, ed., *Verification and Arms Control,* p. 16.

72. SALT II Treaty, Art. XVII.

73. India-Pakistan no-attack agreement reprinted in *Programme for Promoting Nuclear Nonproliferation Newsbrief,* July, 1989, p. 12.

74. Krass, pp. 208-210.

75. Both quotations from the ABM Treaty, Art. XII, para. 2 and 3; see also SALT II, Art. XV, para. 2 and 3; INF Treaty, Art. XII.

76. Paul. K. Davis "Land-Mobile ICBMs," in Potter, ed., *Verification and SALT,* p. 147.

77. Schear, "Cooperative Measures for Verification," in Potter, ed., *Verification and Arms Control*, p. 21.

78. *Ibid.*, pp. 16-18.

79. Restricting these to designated, easily observed areas, however, could facilitate adversary targeting during military conflict.

80. Krass, pp. 213-214.

81. Sidney Graybeal and Michael Krepon, "On-Site Inspection," in Krepon and Umberger, pp. 93-94.

82. Schear, "Cooperative Measures for Verification: How Necessary? How Effective?"; Lewis A. Dunn and Amy E. Gordon, "On-Site Inspection for Arms Control Verification: Pitfalls and Promises," *Harvard University Center for National Security Negotiations Occasional Paper*, No.1, Vol. 2, May, 1989, pp. 34-36.

83. Dunn and Gordon, p. 3.

84. See Document of the Stockholm Conference on Confidence Building and Security Measures and Disarmament in Europe, excerpts reprinted in *Disarmament*, Fall, 1986, pp. 62-77.

85. Dunn and Gordon, p. 9.

86. Graybeal and Krepon, "On-site Inspection," pp. 104-105. The Soviet Union has recently admitted that the Krasnoyarsk facility is indeed an ABM treaty violation.

87. Dunn and Gordon, p. 24.

88. Gloria Duffy, *Compliance and the Future of Arms Control* (Stanford: Stanford University Center for International Security and Arms Control, 1988), p. 2.

89. Richard Bilder and Russell Hardin, "Formal Treaties and Tacit Agreements: An Exchange," *Bulletin of the Atomic Scientists*, April, 1985, p. 51.

90. *Ibid.*

91. R.V.R. Chandrasekhara Rao, "India, Pakistan Racing to be Last," *Bulletin of the Atomic Scientists*, November, 1987, p.33

92. Bilder and Hardin, p. 52.

93. Duffy, Chapter. 6.

94. Robert Einhorn, "Treaty Compliance," *Foreign Policy*, No. 45, Winter, 1981-1982,p. 39.

95. ABM Treaty, Article XIII.

96. Sidney Graybeal and Michael Krepon, "Improving the Utility and Effectiveness of the Standing Consultative Commission," in Krepon and Umberger, p. 241.

97. Dan Caldwell, "The Standing Consultative Commission: Past Performance and Future Possibilities," in Potter, ed., *Verification and Arms Control* p. 222.

98. Duffy, Chapters 8 and 10.

99. *Ibid.*, pp. 172-173; Graybeal and Krepon, "Improving the Utility and Effectiveness of the Standing Consultative Commission," pp. 245-246; Caldwell, pp. 223-224.

100. Schear, "Cooperative Measures for Verification," in Potter, ed., *Verification and Arms Control*, pp. 23-24.

101. Stephen Flanagan, "Safeguarding Arms Control," in Krepon and Umberger, p. 234.

102. Robert W. Bucheim and Dan Caldwell, "The U.S.-USSR Standing Consultative Commission: Description and Appraisal," in Paul Viotti, ed., *Conflict and Arms Control* (Boulder: Westview, 1986), p. 138.

103. Duffy, Chapter 8.

104. Einhorn, pp. 44-46; Graybeal and Krepon, "Improving the Utility and Effectiveness of the Standing Consultative Commission," pp. 254-256.

105. Duffy, p. 164; Mark M. Lowenthal, "U.S. Organization for Verification," in William Potter, ed., *Verification and SALT*, pp. 83-89.

106. Julie Dahlitz, *Nuclear Arms Control With Effective International Agreements* (London: George Allan & Unwin, 1983), p. 185. To date, however, there has been no case of IAEA application of such sanctions to any NPT party state or any non-NPT Agency member state.

107. Flanagan, p. 215.

108. Report of Secretary of Defense Harold Brown to the Congress with FY 1980 Budgets, FY 1981 Authorization Request and FY 1980-84 Defense Programs (Washington, D.C.: U.S. Government Printing Office, Jan., 25, 1979) pp.126-127, cited in William R. Harris, "A SALT Safeguards Program," in Potter, ed., *Verification and SALT*, p. 132.

109. Flanagan, p. 223.

110. Dahlitz, p. 151.

111. Graybeal and Krepon, "Improving the Utility and Effectiveness of the Standing Consultative Commission," pp. 248-256; Duffy, Chapters. 8 & 10; Einhorn, pp. 39-47.

112. James Schear, "Compliance Diplomacy in a Multilateral Setting," in Krepon and Umberger, pp. 262-263.

113. The Indian government expressed similar concerns about Bangladesh President Ziaur Rahman's 1980 proposal for a South Asian regional cooperation organization. The resulting South Asian Association for Regional Cooperation incorporated a "unanimity principle," whereby no decisions will be taken by SAARC without a vote of unanimous consent among member states. See Pran Chopra, "From Mistrust to Cooperation," in Pran Chopra, et. al., eds., *The Future of South Asia* (New Delhi: Macmillan; Centre for Policy Research, 1986), p. 41.

114. The following discussion is derived from the Treaty of Tlatelolco and The South Pacific Nuclear Free Zone Treaty; David Freestone, "Nuclear Weapon Free Zones," in Pogany, pp. 190-192, pp. 199-201. For a concise comparison of the Treaties of Tlatelolco and Raratonga, see the *Arms Control Reporter*, Sept.,1985, pp. 456 D1-D2. South Pacific Nuclear Free Zone Treaty reprinted in same issue, pp. 456. D3-D9.

115. South Pacific Nuclear Free Zone Treaty, Article X.

116. Schear, "Compliance Diplomacy in a Multilateral Setting," pp. 273-278.

117. Greg Fry, "A Nuclear Weapons Free Zone for the Southwest Pacific: Prospects and Significance," *Strategic and Defense Studies Centre Working Paper no. 75* (Canberra: Australian National University, Sept. 1983), pp. 6-11.

118. Imtiaz H. Bokhari, "South Asian Regional Cooperation,"*Asian Survey*, Vol. 25, No. 4, April, 1985, p.376; for a discussion of scientific and technical cooperation within the SAARC framework see R.R. Subramaniam, "A Technological Base for South Asia Regional Cooperation," in Bhabani Sen Gupta, ed., *Regional Cooperation and Development in South Asia: Vol I* (New Delhi: South Asia Publishers; Centre for Policy Research, 1986), pp. 210-225.

6

A Geographical Perspective

Arun P. Elhance

It is space, not time, that hides consequences from us.
John Berger, The Look of Things

When confronted with a real problem, a geographer is apt to ask—*where* is the problem? How is it manifested in concrete space? And, what can a truly spatial perspective illuminate about the different aspects of the problem? In keeping with this tradition, an attempt is made in this chapter to elucidate the various spatial dimensions of the problem of achieving a nuclear weapons agreement in South Asia.

Our contention here is that geography, more than most other factors, lies at the heart of all past conflicts and hostilities within and between the two potential nuclear powers in the region, Pakistan and India.[1] Created artificially from the same subcontinental land mass only four decades back, these two countries are destined to be irrevocably interlinked and intertwined with one another in social, cultural, economic, military-strategic and political arenas, both externally and internally.

Kashmir and Punjab, the two subnational regions—once again artificially divided between the two countries—are at the heart of most bilateral tensions between these countries. They continue to be constant sources of domestic conflicts within these countries also.

It was the spatial separation of West and East Pakistan across a potentially hostile Indian territory that had dictated Pakistan's political and security problems since its creation in 1947, and led to the creation of an independent nation, Bangladesh, in 1971. And, territorial claims have continued to be the main instigators of all major conflicts in the region between India and Pakistan, and India and China.

All wars are fought in geographical terrain and have spatial outcomes. The three wars between Pakistan and India in 1948, 1965 and 1971, and the one between China and India in 1962, have all left spatial legacies which continue to dictate relations among these countries. From the occupation of a piece of some obscure glacier to the occupation of large disputed territories, spatial claims and drives lie at the very heart of the South Asian regional security subsystem.

Finally geography has strongly influenced all weapons acquisitions, war fighting plans and military infrastructure build ups in the region. If South Asia does go overtly nuclear, all decisions regarding the number of weapons, types of delivery systems, basing and targeting, C^3I and verification system(s) must take into consideration the unique geography of the subcontinent.

If the above observations/assertions are accepted, then a geographical perspective on the nuclear problem in South Asian is both a worthwhile and an interesting endeavor. This chapter aims to fulfill this expectation. While India and Pakistan are our focus, we must inevitably draw in other South Asian countries and at least one other from outside the region, the PRC, because of the unique geography (and history) of this conflict-ridden area.

The historical, cultural and political geographies of South Asia are interesting in themselves, but we will focus only on physical and economic geography. The primary objective is to draw out implications of the latter geographies for the achievement and verification of a nuclear agreement in South Asia.

The Geography of South Asia

South Asia is clearly dominated by India on all measures of population, area and economic strength. The population, area and GDP of India are many magnitudes higher than the combined measures for all the other six countries. However, the growth rate of the Pakistani economy (1980-87) is 2% higher than India's. The 1987 per capita GNP in Pakistan and Sri Lanka are also approximately 16% and 33% higher than India's, respectively.[2]

The distribution of manufacturing value added in India for the three major sectors—machinery and transport equipment, chemicals and other industries—shows India to be much more industrialized than the other South Asian countries. India clearly dominates the region in the number of large cities with more than 0.5 m population, while Pakistan and Bangladesh score higher on rates of urbanization in the large cities. Overall, only Pakistan has a higher percentage of urban population than India. Higher overall urbanization rates are noted for all countries, except Sri Lank, with data for Afghanistan not available. India also leads all countries for per capita availability of physicians and, except Sri Lanka, for a smaller population per nursing person.

For other economic measures, India's external debt is larger than all six countries combined, yet due to the much larger size of its economy, the annual debt service payments are a very small percentage of its GNP and only the third largest percentage—after Pakistan and Bangladesh—of its exports. At the same time, India's external reserves are almost twice as large as the combined reserves of the other six countries. These reserves enable India to cover nearly six months' worth of exports as compared to five months for Pakistan, and only one and a half months for Sri Lanka.

India's regional dominance is likely to continue into the next century also. Comparisons along measures of poverty and deprivation, not included here, are likely to moderate this picture somewhat, but not radically.

It should also be pointed out that on many of these measures China scores higher than India. According to most projections, this situation is also likely to remain unchanged in the near future. Burma and Afghanistan are unlikely to play any major role in the region in the foreseeable future due to their continuing political and economic problems.

Macro Comparisons

How do Pakistan and India compare on aggregate indicators of size, population, economic strength, urbanization, resource potential and infrastructure availability? While some data are not as current as one would like, these comparisons are likely to hold for the past few years also.

TABLE 6.1 Macro Comparisons Between India and Pakistan

	Area (000 km^2)	Population (m)	GDP (m US$)	International Reserves	No. Cities > 500000
India (I)	3,288	797.5	220,830	11,512	36
Pakistan (P)	796	102.5	31,650	1,441	7
Difference (I-P)	2,492	695	189,180	10,071	29
Ratio (I/P)	4.1	7.8	7.0	8.0	5.15

Source: *World Development Report, 1989.* The World Bank, Wash., D.C.

In Table 6.1, five indicators are compared for 1987. These refer to the total area and population, GDP, international reserves and number of large cities. On all indicators India scores from 4 to 8 times as high as Pakistan (ratio I/P). Even in the extreme case when an equivalent amount of area and economic might of Pakistan are subtracted from the Indian indicators (difference, I-P), India is still left with a sizeable amount of area, production capability, external reserves and number of large cities. This is not to imply that, in the case of all-out hostilities between the two countries, Pakistan can at best destroy an equivalent area and economy in India. This will obviously depend on a large number of factors. However, these comparisons do point to sizeable disparities between the two countries.[3]

Table 6.2 compares the availability of various infrastructure stocks for transportation, communication, and energy in the two countries. In terms of absolute numbers, India is again seen to score 3 to 15 times higher than Pakistan. On per capita basis, however, this disparity is greatly reduced. For example, in 1983-84, Pakistani per capita availability of telephones and passenger cars was marginally higher than India's.[4] However, it must be noted that stock availability and use efficiency are two separate issues, the latter being more important, especially in crisis situation. A paucity of needed data, however, makes it virtually impossible to compare the two countries on efficiency indicators.

Looking at mineral reserves, oil refining capacity and electricity generation except for known reserves of natural gas in 1981, the Indian reserves and capacities are many magnitudes higher than Pakistan's. However, what proportions of these reserves and capabilities can be mobilized and made available to the military sector in either country at the time of a major crisis remains an open question. Reserves in the ground and production capacities must be evaluated in conjunction with capabilities for timely transportation to targeted sites, under different scenarios for hostilities between the two countries. Nonetheless, most available indicators do show the indigenous capabilities for rebuilding the extraction, production and transportation equipment and infrastructures to be more developed, numerous and widely available in India. These could have significant impacts during protracted hostilities between the two countries.

TABLE 6.2 Macro Comparisons Between India and Pakistan: Infrastructure

	Pakistan (1)	*India (2)*	*Ratio (2)/(1)*
Telephones/1000 Persons	511,000 (1984)	3,487,900 (1984)	7.0
	5.4	4.7	0.9
Roads (km)/Unit Area	103,428 (1985)	1,545,891 (1982)	15.0
	0.13	0.47	3.6
Railways (km)/Unit Area	8,775 (1984)	61,230 (1981)	7.0
	0.011	0.019	1.7
Ships Registered Tonnage	78 (1986)	736 (1986)	9.4
(gross tones)	434,079	6,540,121	15.1
Ports	1	9	9.0
Major Airports	3 + 25 (1985)	4 + 78 (1985)	3.0
Commercial	72,000 (1985)	825,000 (1983)	11.5
Vehicles/1000 persons	0.7	1.1	1.6
Mineral Reserves:			
Coal (m tons)	102 (1979)	26,331 (1981)	258.1
Crude Oil (m tons)	13 (1981)	471 (1981)	36.2
Nat gas (b mt^3)	450 (1981)	420 (1981)	0.93
Uranium (tons)	N.A.	46,090 (1984)	–
Petroleum Refining			
Capacity (m tons)	6.4 (1984)	37.8 (1984)	6.0
Electrical Capacity (MW)	5,010 (1984)	47,690 (1984)	9.5

Source: *The World in Figures* (Boston: G.K. Hall & Co., 1988).

TABLE 6.3 A Comparison Between Pakistani and Indian Border States

	Area km²	Population 1986 (m)	Population Density 1986 (People/km²)	Percent Urban	Percent Hindu	Percent Muslim	National Highway 1981 (km)	State Highways 1981 (km)	Railways 1981 (km)	Power Generation 1985-86 mil KWH
Gujarat	196,024	37.7	192	31.1	89.5	8.5	1,424	9,158	5,635	12,934
Haryana	44,212	14.8	335	21.9	89.4	4.0	655	3,166	1,501	1,206
H.P.	55,673	4.7	84	7.6	95.8	1.6	589	3,251	256	1,247
J. & K.	222,236*	6.7	30	21.0	32.2	64.2	593	688	77	870
Punjab	50,362	18.5	333	27.7	36.9	1.0	977	1,900	2,139	5,763
Rajasthan	342,239	39.2	100	20.9	89.3	7.3	2,521	7,273	5,614	3,326
Total	910,746	121.6	133.5	24.7	78.5	21.5	6,759	25,436	15,222	25,346
Pakistan	796,000	1,025	1,287	31	-	-		103,428	8,775 (1984)	50,101 (1984)

We have compared Pakistan with the six combined border states of India—J & K, Haryana, Himachal Pradesh, Punjab, Gujarat and Rajasthan—along a variety of indicators (Table 6.3)[5] Essentially, what these comparisons show is that, on many indicators related to area, population and its distribution, production and infrastructure, these six states of India together constitute an equivalent Pakistan. Total annihilation or loss of these states, while a devastating blow, will still leave India with sizeable economic and military strength. Whether this will be an acceptable level of damage for India cannot be debated in this short chapter.

Physical Geography

At the outset it must be recognized that the division of the subcontinent between India and Pakistan on any physical geographic basis is a purely artificial one. Both countries are integral parts of the same landmass, sharing similar geographic features, climate, flora and fauna. The Himalayan mountain ranges and the Indus Plains cut across the boundaries of both nations; so do five major rivers and tributaries.

Pakistan covers an area of 310,403 sq. miles of which 183,840 sq. miles in the north and west form mountain terrain and table lands. Pakistan shares a 1400 mile-long border with India in the west, 590 miles with Iran to the southeast and nearly 1200 miles with Afghanistan in the northwest. In the south the length of the coastal boundary is approximately 500 miles.[6]

Based on the physical features alone, the country can be divided into five major regions; the Himalayas, the Hindu Kush and the western mountains, the Baluchistan Plateau, the Patwar Plateau and the Salt Range, and the Indus Plain. These regions can be further subdivided along many physical characteristics, e.g. elevation, climate, soils, flora and fauna, etc.

The Himalayas comprise five ranges, three of which—the Central or Great Himalayas, the Inner Himalayas (Ladakh range) and the Trans Himalayas (Karakoram Ranges) are mostly under Indian control, the remaining two—the Sub Himalayas and the Lesser Himalayas—are within Pakistani territory.

The Indus Plain is perhaps the most interesting physical feature of Pakistan from a security-strategic perspective. It is in this plain— stretching all along the length of Pakistan from Arabian Sea to the

Himalayas, along the Indus River—where most of Pakistan's mineral, economic, political, social, cultural and human wealth and resources are located.

The Indus plain forms the western limit of the Indo-Gangetic plain, stretching all the way to the eastern parts of India. It can be further divided into the Upper Indus Plain—with major tributaries of the Indus, Jhelum, Chenab, Ravi and Sutlej, and the doabs formed by them—and the Lower Indus Plain, with only the Indus running through a flat area. The Sind Plain, the Indus Delta and the Karachi Plain form parts of this latter region. The two plains are narrowly separated where the Suleiman Ranges approach the Indus River near Mithankot in Pakistan.

Among the five tributaries (rivers), the flows of Ravi, Beas and Sutlej were allocated to India in 1960, while Chenab, Jhelum and Indus flows are exclusively under Pakistani jurisdiction and use.[7] Nearly 60% of the flow in the Indus system is concentrated in three rainy months—June, July, August—necessitating the construction of an elaborate system of dams, reservoirs and canals in the Indus valley. Rainfall in Pakistan is insufficient and erratic, reducing its usefulness for agriculture. Much of the rainfall takes place in the late summer months and most of it is evaporated and transpirated by the high temperatures. Consequently, Pakistan is highly dependent on the three river flows and the elaborate storage and distribution system in the Indus Plain.

In contrast to the narrowness and concentration in Pakistan, the physical features of India—its rivers and tributary systems, land use pattern, irrigation networks, intensity of cropping, and distribution of mineral resources—all show a much more dispersed distribution. In comparison with Pakistan, India also possesses many more minerals, and larger reserves for each of them. Indian energy resources—coal, oil and gas—are mostly located far from the post 1971 Pakistani territory, and their reserves are estimated to be many magnitudes higher than Pakistan's. This dispersed pattern of resource in India, however, does imply much more energy and other resources being consumed in transportation to targeted areas. A sizeable portion of India's transportation capacity, especially the railways, is tied up in these movements.

Climate and Weather. Pakistan lies on the western margin of the monsoon region. Winds in winter are NE to SW, and SW to NE in summer. In the winter months, due to low temperatures over land, a high pressure area is established over Pakistan, with the pressure generally decreasing from north to south. This draws winds from NE to SE, but mostly along a N-S corridor. During summer the high land temperatures create a low pressure area in southwestern Pakistan, attracting winds from the Indian Ocean. Some cyclonic storms also migrate to this low pressure area from the Bay of Bengal across northern India.

Winter winds in India are characterized by E-W and SW-NE flows, while the summer flows are predominantly from W to E and SE-W. Only a few circular and W-E flows during the summer are noticeable near the upper Himalayas. As Rashid Naim has pointed out in Chapter 2, these wind patterns imply time-bound possibilities for nuclear, chemical or biological weapons use between the two countries. Essentially, India must carry out such attacks during the summer months, while the least damaging time to itself for Pakistan would be the winter months.

However, due to the nature of these prevailing winds both countries must also consider the possibility of some radioactive, chemical or biological agents being carried beyond the boundaries of the adversary. Given the narrowness of Pakistan, such agents released during an Indian attack on Pakistan's western frontiers could be carried over to Iran and Afghanistan, and possibly the southern USSR. Similarly, agents released by a Pakistani attack on northern and eastern boundaries of India could be transported to Nepal, Bangladesh, Burma and the PRC.

The wide ranging fallout from the Chernobyl disaster, and more locally from the Bhopal chemical gas spill in India, are two clear reminders of these possibilities. The Chernobyl disaster also points to the longevity of ground level nuclear radiation and its long term effects on flora, fauna, and ground water supplies. Similarly, the Bhopal accident has highlighted the longevity of human suffering as a result of chemical exposures and inhalations. Of course, the specific impacts of any nuclear, chemical, or biological warfare between the two countries will depend on the size, scope and intensity of explosions, and their timing and locations.

Coastlines and Islands. Other noteworthy features of the physical geography of India and Pakistan are the coastlines and islands, and the associated Expanded Economic Zones (EEZs) of the two countries. Clearly, Pakistan has a much shorter shoreline compared to India. Also, since Pakistan's shoreline has opening to only one ocean—the Arabian Sea—it is presumably much easier to monitor than the Indian coastline with openings into the Bay of

Bengal, the Indian Ocean and the Arabian Sea. Given India's current and projected naval strength, it is clear that India is more vulnerable to a surprise naval infiltration and attack. The ease of moving in and out of India by sea has been clearly and consistently demonstrated by the many smuggling operations carried out daily on the eastern and western coasts of India.[8]

The maritime jurisdictional claims of Pakistan cover an area of 92,900 sq. km, with a 200 nautical miles fishing zone and EEZ. The Indian claim, the the other hand, stretches to nearly 587,000 sq. km with the same width of the fishing zone and the EEZ, requiring a much larger naval force to monitor and control this vast ocean territory.

However, an important feature missing in Pakistan's physical geography is islands, whereas the Indian territory incorporates a cluster of islands on the west, the Lakshwadeeps, and a string in the Bay of Bengal, the Andaman-Nicobars. While these islands do make India's monitoring and interdiction tasks that much more extensive and difficult, they also provide India with a distinct advantage. These cluster of islands are ideal sites for surveillance of the western and eastern oceans and coastlines, respectively. The Andaman-Nicobar islands, due to their solid geological formations, can also be developed as major air and naval bases, and, more importantly, as potential ballistic missile bases. The distances of these islands from the Pakistani territory (approximately 3000-3500 km) places them well out of range of the Pakistani aircraft and any ballistic missiles Pakistan is likely to develop or acquire in the near future. India could conceivably station a second-strike force on and around these islands, far out of reach of the Pakistani weapons. In case India were to acquire a truly long range missile capability, missile bases on these islands would also greatly enhance India reach in Southeast and East Asia, and as far as the Australian continent.

The Lakshwadeep Islands, on the other hand, are within 1500 km of Pakistani territory. From a strategic view point they would seem to be a better site than the Andaman-Nicobars for air, naval and missile bases. However, these are essentially coral islands unsuitable for deep drilling or heavy infrastructure construction. They do, however, provide a prime location for surveillance and early warning systems.

Economic Geography

The economic-geographic aspects examined here include the locations and spatial distributions of mineral wealth, agricultural production, energy production and power transmission, irrigation systems, other physical infrastructures—roadways, railways, seaports, and airports—and, finally, populations in the two countries. For most military-strategic calculations, the economy of Pakistan, and the various infrastructures supporting it, are all located within a 450 km wide corridor from the Indian border, stretching from the Indus Delta in the south to the lower Himalayas in the north. Except for some mineral and energy production (and reserves) in the Baluchistan and NWFP provinces, most agricultural and industrial production, transportation and consumption in Pakistan is confined to this narrow geographical area. Karachi being the only major seaport with access to the Arabian Sea, nearly all of Pakistan's external trade is concentrated in this port. And, Karachi is only within 150 km of the Indian border.

Admittedly, Pakistan has openings to Afghanistan, Iran and the PRC through road and rail connections, also air, yet accessibility to these channels at a time of major conflicts with India will depend on the stands these countries adopt toward the combatants. Thus, Pakistan's vulnerability to an all-out Indian attack from land, air and sea would seem to be clearly underlined by this unique geography.

India, on the other hand, enjoys a clear advantage over Pakistan in all the aggregate economic geography aspects examined here. Besides its size, India's production capacity and infrastructures are much more dispersed. A very high proportion of India's natural resources, agricultural and industrial capacity are located far from the India-Pakistan border. Among the major urban agglomerations dominating the economic and industrial landscape in India, many— except Delhi-Meerut, Kanpur-Lucknow, Ahmedabad-Baroda and possibly Bombay-Pune—would, currently, seem to be beyond the reach of Pakistani aircraft and missiles. In a worst case scenario, destruction of the above urban agglomerates, while a devastating blow, will still leave India with sizeable resources, production capabilities and infrastructures to reconstruct a viable economy.

Figures 6.1 and 6.2 show the distribution of the main population concentrations (urban areas) in Pakistan and India; 1981 statistics being the most comprehensive and reliable for both countries, maps based on these data clearly highlight the imbalances

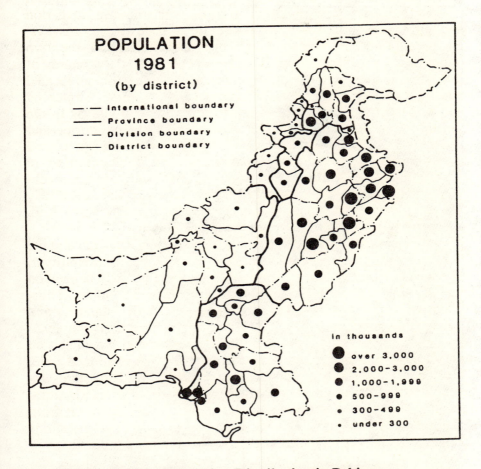

FIGURE 6.1 Urban Population Distribution in Pakistan.
Source: Ashok K. Dutt and M.Margaret Geib, *Atlas of South Asia* (Boulder: Westview Press, 1987).

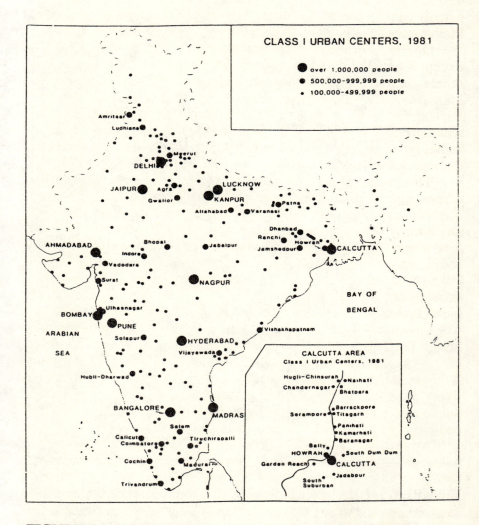

FIGURE 6.2 Urban Population Distribution in India.
Source: Ashok K. Dutt and M. Margaret Geib, *Atlas of South Asia* (Boulder: Westview Press, 1987).

between the two countries. Once again, it is seen that, except Quetta, all the major urban centers in Pakistan are situated within the 450 km wide corridor east of the Indus River. And, within this narrow band, a majority of these centers are clustered in the Upper Plain close to the India border.

On the other hand, the major urban agglomerations in India—except Chandigarh, Ahmedabad, Jaipur, New Delhi, and a few others—all are currently beyond the reach of aircraft and missals known to be in the Pakistani arsenal. Obviously, a sizeable all-out nuclear, chemical or biological first strike, or a surface conventional weapons attack, would still cause a lot of damage and havoc in India, however a first or second strike by India would be far more damaging for Pakistan.

This concentrated economic geography of Pakistan and its wide dispersion in India also have many implications for weapons acquisition/production, targeting strategies, and the verification of any arms control agreement by and between the two countries. The long distance separating Pakistan from many counter-value targets in India, and their much larger number, must necessarily impel Pakistan to acquire long distance penetrating capabilities—aircraft, missiles and satellite-based systems, as well as nuclear submarines based systems—*if* it is to threaten India in a substantial way.

Given its lack of depth, Pakistan may also explore the possibility of basing some of its nuclear weapon system in a third country or countries. Some Middle Eastern countries, Iran and/or Afghanistan, China, and possibly Indonesia, would seem to be likely sites for such bases. However, this possibility opens up a whole new scenario for regional and international security, much too complex and hypothetical to be rigorously analyzed here.

Among the various options for Pakistan then, long range ballistic missiles with conventional and/or nuclear, chemical and biological warheads, and such weapons based on nuclear submarine and/or surface ships, would seem to be the more plausible and feasible ones. Among these, the land-based systems imply very long warning/reaction times for most targets in India; only the sea-based systems are more likely to achieve the full benefits of a surprise attack. Among the latter, long-range nuclear submarine-based weapons would seem to be the best alternative, allowing access to the east and west coast cities of India as well as most interior cities in the mid and southern regions. Access to these interior cities will, of course, depend on the ranges of such weapons and the locations of the submarines and/or ships at the time of attack.

Lessons from Past Hostilities

India and Pakistan have fought three wars on their northern and western borders in 1948, 1965 and 1971. These increasingly violent wars have, presumably, been fought to settle territorial disputes, yet, to date, nothing has been fully settled. Neither country has been able to gain and retain any new territories, except in Kashmir in 1948. Admittedly, Bangladesh was created in 1971 out of the old East Pakistan, yet it can hardly be characterized as a territorial gain for India.

At best, a status quo is maintained along most of the post-1971 common borders, while low level hostilities claiming many lives have continued for four decades along the Line of Actual Control (LAC) in Kashmir. The recent hostilities on the Siachen glacier are the latest example of this low level attrition.

Clearly, a comprehensive analysis of the experiences of four decades is beyond the scope of this chapter; postmortem analyses are available elsewhere. Here, we only point to some salient features which may have a bearing on future hostilities between the two countries. Once, again, a geographical perspective will guide our observations.[9]

All the wars between the two countries were undeclared, but signalled well in advance. This raises question about the larger politico-military objectives of these costly campaigns. Is the primary interest and objective then to maintain the status quo obtaining since 1948? If so, to what greater purpose? Neither side has gained or retained much new territory over the past four decades, despite all hostilities.

As each war has flared and subsided, the politico-military focus has continued to shift away from the original theater—from Kashmir in 1948 to Punjab in 1965, and to Multan-Sind-Kutch region in 1971.

The larger political objectives in any of the three wars have never been clearly spelled out. The defensive directives, albeit political in nature, have included "no territorial losses" in Punjab in 1971 and beyond, and similar directives in the J & K sector in 1948 and 1965. A result of these directives has been the creation of a hard, forward-defended Zone of Defense on both sides, stretching continuously along the border. On both sides, an essentially linear belt has, consequently, been given tremendous depth. This has tied down the offensive assets on both sides in a virtually static, holding and defensive pattern. Yet, both sides continue to adhere to an offensive military doctrine.

Recently, some offensive high-value capital hardware assets have been built up, but their composition, structuring and weaponry seem to be entirely oriented to warfare in the souther plains. Thus, even if a major surprise thrust were achieved by either side it will only prolong hostilities until the status quo is restored once again.

While both sides may have considered a jugular option, i.e., capturing the whole of Punjab for India and capturing the Indian territory up to New Delhi for Pakistan in order to secure full control of Kashmir, neither has yet pursued it with any intensity, and for good reasons. Among the many dangers of these options, if exercised, besides their very high costs given the hard Zones of Defense, is a very real danger of the breakup of the rest of the polity in the defeated country. This danger would seem to be greater in Pakistan, but the possibilities exist on both sides. In any case, a recognition of the problems of governing and maintaining any occupied and hostile territories may have led to more sober thinking. Hopefully, both sides have also learned new lessons from the recent Soviet experience in Afghanistan and the Indian experience in Sri Lanka.

Both countries have important and unresolved domestic, ethnic, linguistic and inter-regional conflicts. Despite the different forms of governance from time to time, the overriding concerns for both India and Pakistan in the security arena will continue to be internal cohesion and national survival.

As long as China can exercise a check on India, and the USSR on China, neither India nor Pakistan will consider itself sufficiently deterred or totally vulnerable, no matter what the indigenous military capabilities of the other side. The three extra-regional actors in the drama —the U.S., USSR and PRC—are hardly likely to allow the total defeat and/or dismemberment of either country. This places obvious limits on how far each country can go in its offensive.

Despite an active state of hostilities and the three wars, both countries have, in the past, bilaterally limited their options in terms of troop commitments and the duration of hostilities. A consensus seems to exist on both sides that neither can achieve decisive outcomes in any available time frame. This also allows for the shifting of blame for any politico-strategic failures on to the military by the politicians, and vice versa, on both sides.

During four decades of hostilities and the considerable loss of life and hardware, neither Delhi nor Islamabad has undertaken serious countervalue strikes against the other. Despite all the rhetoric, population centers have not come under serious attack. It is difficult to visualize an Iran-Iraq type of "war of the cities" between the two countries, except in the case of all-out hostilities. However, the acquisition of ballistic missiles might change this scenario in the future.

Also, despite these conflicts, the Indus Waters Treaty of 1960 has held. There may be a lesson here for any future arms accord, verification regime and/or regional cooperation system. Maybe the World Bank or some other international or multilateral financial agency should be made party to a multilateral nuclear verification system also!

Finally, despite the invocation of external threats and talk of a "two front" war, neither country has yet experienced simultaneous hostilities on its borders. The Chinese and Soviet restraint in 1965 and 1971, despite their close cooperation and friendship treaties with the two regional actors, must be noted. Nor have the other smaller countries in the region actively supported either side militarily.

In sum, it would seem that despite all the hostilities and military preparations, there is an inherent incompatibility between the political objectives and political will, strategic aims and operational directives, and a confusion about the ultimate mission of the armed forces, in both India and Pakistan. There is a reluctance to "go all the way," and a propensity to seek some kind of cease-fire within a short time frame. There is no evidence of serious contemplation of a jugular option or of countervalue strikes. Occasionally, there has been a high profile encouragement of peripheral blood-letting of no serious politico-military consequences.

Would the introduction of nuclear weapons, change this status quo? Assuming that all problems relating to the development and production of tested weapons and accurate delivery systems; their deployment, basing and targeting; C^3I and command structures; domestic and world opinion; and pressures against military nuclearization, are smoothly resolved, can either or both countries overcome the chaos, confusions and incompatibilities existing in their politico-strategic military objectives and directives? Or, do these questions not really matter? Is it sufficient to have crude and untested bombs, attached to inaccurate delivery systems, with no sophisticated C^{3}I in place to deter the enemy and deny him/it any politico-strategic-military advantages?

Perceptions of Nuclear Threats in South Asia

Figure 6.3 presents a schematic diagram of perceived threats and the justification offered for "going nuclear" in the South Asian region. Clearly, the now mostly forgotten Chinese explosion of a

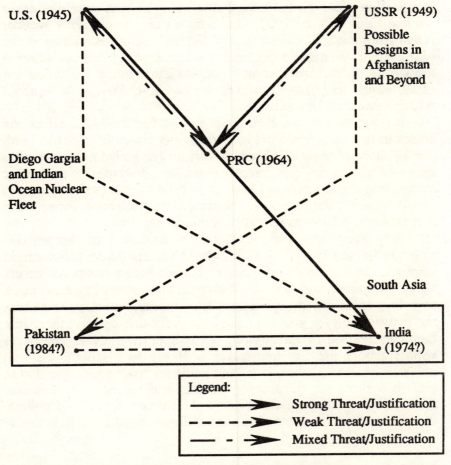

FIGURE 6.3 Perceived Nuclear Threats and Justifications in South Asia.

nuclear device in 1964, following on the border war with India in 1962, can be identified as the precipitating event leading to the potential military nuclearization of South Asia. Some recently released CIA documents reveal the strong reverberations this explosion had caused in the Indian subcontinent almost instantaneously, and the actions taken subsequently.[10]

Since the late 1960s, the perceptions guiding the Chinese military-nuclear program have focused on the Soviets, with a weaker and changing emphasis on the U.S. nuclear arsenal. The "bomb-lobby" in India has justified its calls for going nuclear by pointing to a possible and strong Chinese threat. And, similar justifications vis-à-vis India have echoed in Pakistan since the Indian nuclear explosion of 1974. In India's case, a relatively weaker threat from the U.S. base in Diego Garcia and occasional presence of the American nuclear fleet in the Indian Ocean has been added to the strong threat/justification. The Pakistani bomb-lobby, on the other hand, may have pointed to possible Soviet designs in Afghanistan, and beyond.

It must be remembered that, except for the U.S., all of the actors in this nuclear drama have on-going boundary disputes with one or more of their neighbors. All four have also participated in major hostilities on their borders. And, the geography of the region shows that these countries share some of the longest borders on earth. Absent genuine and concerted multilateral efforts, these disputes are unlikely to be resolved in the near future.

While highly reductionist, this formulation of the nuclear impetus in South Asia does highlight certain basic problems in implementing any regional nuclear or conventional weapons accord. Unless perceived and/or claimed internal and external threats can be somehow managed through a multilateral arrangement, undercutting the justification for going nuclear, it is very difficult to visualize a denuclearization of the region. Cost-benefit analyses, however sophisticated, are by themselves unlikely to dissuade the two potential nuclear powers, India and Pakistan, from going ahead with their programs for developing nuclear and ballistic capabilities. How far these countries can go in this direction will, of course, depend on their future economic and military capabilities.

The Future Economic and Military Capabilities
of China, India and Pakistan

Any attempt to project the economic and military might of a country is always fraught with fundamental limitations associated with data accuracy, the level of aggregation, and the validity of estimation methods. These limitations become more problematic and the resulting projections more inaccurate as the time frame is lengthened. With these inherent limitations in mind, in Table 6.4 we present the latest RAND (1989) estimates for China and India for the three decades, 1980 to 2010, for four indicators of economic and military potential.[11]

According to these estimates, China's decadal GDP growth rate vis-à-vis India's GNP growth rate is likely to be 1.72 to 1.18 times higher over the next three decades, leading to a Chinese GDP nearly three times as high as India's by the year 2010. In other words, Beijing will control an economy with total production equivalent to three Indias, a mere two decades from now. In the interim period also, the Chinese economy will be nearly two and a half times as large as India's. Even if the Chinese economy were only twice as large as India's by 2010, this suggests a need for serious thinking in Delhi about the comparative military burden each country is capable of sustaining in the future.

The projections for military spending and military stocks, including weapons and structures, further highlight these disparities. By 2010, the projected annual military spending in China ($218 billion, in 1986 U.S. dollars) is expected to be more than four times India's, while the Chinese military capital stock is projected to be proportionately even higher—a ratio of six to one.

Clearly, according to these projections, India cannot hope to match the Chinese economic and military might over the next three decades. This is not to imply that changes in the world economy which favor/disfavor the two countries disproportionately, possible domestic turmoil, changes in the political will and capabilities of the leaders in these countries, and unforeseen technological and structural changes, among many other factors, will not have serious impacts on this scenario. However, these estimates do point to a basic disequilibrium in the possible and sustainable military efforts by these two Asian giants, over the next three decades.[12]

What these estimates point to, for the nuclear-ballistic comparisons between India and China, is that, barring some totally

TABLE 6.4 Long Term Economic and Military Projections: China and India

		1980s	1990s	2000s	2010s
GNP (Billion 1986 U.S. $)					
China*		793	1,520	2,395	3,791
India		408	598	897	1,330
	Ratio	1.94	2.54	2.67	2.85
GNP Growth Rates (Decade Ending)					
China		6.6	6.7	4.7	4.7
India		3.3	3.9	4.1	4.0
	Ratio	2.0	1.72	1.15	1.18
Annual Military Spending (Billion 1986 U.S. $)					
China		45	53	120	218
India		12	24	36	53
	Ratio	3.75	2.21	3.33	4.11
Military Capital Stock (Billion U.S. $)					
China		211	236	392	785
India		21	42	81	131
	Ratio	10.05	5.62	4.84	6.0

* Gross Domestic Product
Source: *Long-Term Economic and Military Trends 1950-2010*, RAND Note N--2757-USDP (Santa Monica: RAND Corporation, 1989).

unforeseen developments, the latter is likely to retain a substantial superiority over the former. However, what proportion of China's military might can be exclusively devoted to the China-India theater remains an open question—too complex and riddled with probabilities to be meaningfully tackled here, especially in light of the ongoing and incredible changes within the USSR.

According to 1988 SIPRI estimates for current Chinese nuclear forces, even if China were to slow down its nuclear buildup in the future because of economic problems and/or other imperatives, it will still have sizeable superiority over India in the number and size of weapons and delivery systems.[13] The current best estimates for Indian production of nuclear weapons, by the end of the century, place an upper ceiling of 200.[14] Also, India has only recently tested a 1500 km range missile. Clearly, India cannot hope to achieve anything resembling parity with the Chinese arsenal and delivery capabilities in the foreseeable future.

For comparisons between India and Pakistan, similar projections for Pakistani economic and military potential are, unfortunately, not available. However, given the much smaller base of Pakistan's economy vis-à-vis India's, a similar disequilibrium between these countries can be safely projected to remain in the foreseeable future. Once again, the proportional allocation of India's military might exclusively to the India-Pakistan theater is an open-ended question. However, India's clear superiority in total military effort, for a long time to come, cannot be denied.

The main conclusion to be derived from these comparisons is that, over the next three decades, the China > India > Pakistan hierarchy in absolute and relative military efforts is most likely to remain. During this period, Pakistan vis-à-vis India and India vis-à-vis China can only hope to mount a weak nuclear deterrent, without much hope of radically transforming the hierarchy. A questionable first-strike advantage against the strong threat, for either Pakistan or India, is therefore likely to prove a very costly gamble. But, perhaps a weak deterrent is sufficient to raise the stakes for an aggressor to an unacceptable level.

Defense Production in Pakistan and India

Pakistan currently imports nearly 80% of it defense equipment from the U.S., China and West Europe. The remaining 20% is produced by fourteen organizations grouped within the state-owned Pakistan Ordnance Factories. The private sector firms—nearly 800 companies, based mainly in and around Lahore and Karachi—contribute a mere 5% to the indigenous manufacture, mainly producing equipment for the army. The navy and air force requirements are virtually all met by imports and licensed/joint production.[15]

Defense analysts have identified five main shortcomings of the Pakistani defense production enterprise. These are (1) absence of a developed technological infrastructure to sustain sophisticated weapons production, (2) very low priority to indigenous R&D—only 0.4% of the defense budget allocated, (3) a lack of commitment to invest in and develop the private sector's defense production capability, (4) need to import almost all of the materials and technologies, and (5) cumbersome bureaucratic procedures.

Among these shortcomings, only (2), (3) and (5) can be rectified in the short term, (1) and (4) can be adequately addressed only over the long term. Given the recent changes in the political system and the budgetary difficulties Pakistan currently faces,[16] it is not clear how adequately and quickly these problems can be solved.

Yet, despite these limitations, Pakistan has made significant strides in nuclear, space and missile technology development. Pakistani scientists and engineers have shown that, despite many adverse circumstances, they can hold their own in these high-technology sectors. However, total indigenization and self-sufficiency still remain elusive in every sector. The very low utilization rates for nuclear reactors; the blowing up of centrifuges at Kahuta; the need for Chinese collaboration/support in nuclear, space and missile technologies; and the very high share of imports in defense procurements, all point to certain inherent limits on achieving complete technological and production autonomy in defense endeavors. From a distance it would seem that, in Pakistan, islands of high-tech R&D and show-case excellence float on a sea of some very basic incompetencies, making for a very lop-sided indigenous base to mount an elaborate production and deployment program for high-tech weapons. Also, in one crucial area—computers and electronics—available evidence does not show any highly developed capabilities.

All of the above observations about Pakistani defense production apply to the Indian case. India does, however, have a more developed defense R&D and production system. Under state guidance and control, 36 ordnance factories, nearly forty defense R&D labs and agencies, nine major defense public sector undertakings and, increasingly, many private companies, including large business houses, provide India with an elaborate indigenous infrastructure on which to base defense production. From ammunition to tanks, small frigates to aircraft carriers, indigenously designed and produced computers and software, and, most recently, the Light Combat Aircraft (LCA) project, India seems increasingly capable of satisfying her defense needs indigenously. However, here too, the frequent cost overruns and delays, abandonment of projects midstream, massive purchases of weapon systems and technologies from abroad, loose quality control and below standard performance of equipment, political-bureaucratic-interagency fighting, and the on-going "guns versus butter" controversies would seem to be the rule rather than exceptions.

Yet, despite all the problems and bottlenecks, the Indian defense industry seems increasingly more capable of indigenously supporting a protracted war. The recent strides made in some high-tech sectors—electronics and computers,[17] telecommunication and avionics, among others—and the fact that India today has a large scientific and technological manpower base, with more joining the pool everyday, must also be taken into account while assessing India's technoscientific and production capabilities in the defense sector. Despite a state-controlled defense industry, perhaps India's real strength lies in its democratic polity and mixed economy which, however slowly and inefficiently, occasionally allow for the emergence of scientific excellence and entrepreneurship.

Spatial Organization of Defense R&D and Production

What of the spatial distribution of arms production in the two countries? With the belief that for a counter-force strike either side must take into consideration the actual locations of defense related R&D and production enterprises in the other country, we now proceed to highlight some salient features of the geography of arms production in the two countries.

Our data for Pakistan are woefully inadequate. We are forced to assume that most defense R&D and production in Pakistan takes place in and around the major urban centers—Karachi, Lahore and Rawalpindi-Islamabad—and all of it within the 400 km wide corridor east of the Indus River. Since most of Pakistan's industries, institutions of higher learning and research, and most of the transportation, communication and power infrastructures are located in this corridor, this assumption seems to us to be a reasonable one.

If the above spatial characterization of Pakistan's defense R&D and production is reasonably correct, it does point to a very concentrated geography, vulnerable to ballistic missiles or an all-out conventional attack. The small number of such enterprises also means relatively easy targeting by an adversary with a few long range weapons. The outcome of any such attack will, of course, depend on its strength and sophistication, and the ability of Pakistani surveillance and countering mechanisms, however a concentrated geography does make for increased vulnerability.

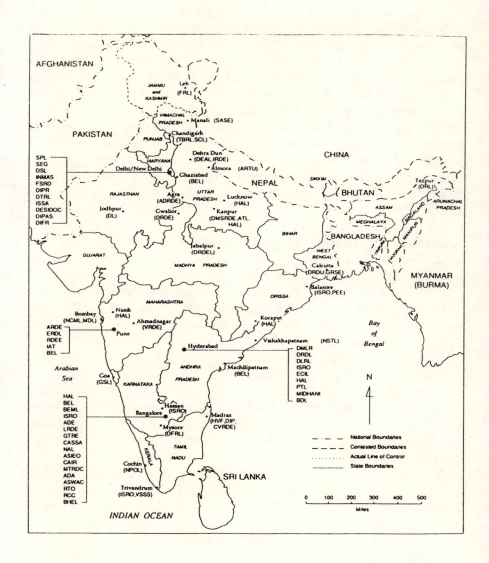

FIGURE 6.4 Major Defense Related Public Sector Enterprises and Laboratories.

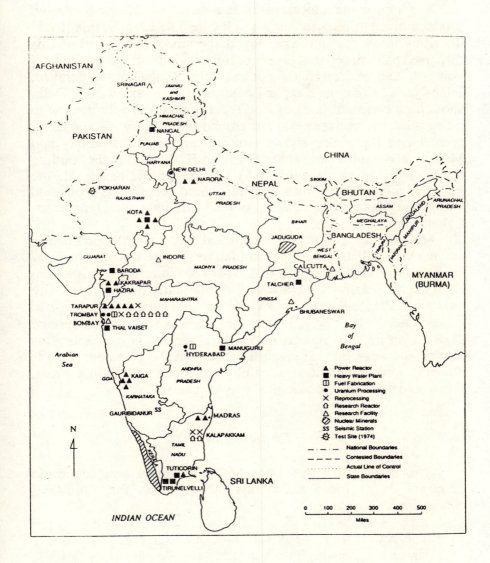

FIGURE 6.5 Nuclear Establishments in India (Existing and Planned).

Source: Leonard S. Spector, *The Undeclared Bomb* (Cambridge, Ballinger: 1988).

The approximate locations of India's major defense R&D and production enterprises are shown in Figure 6.4. Clearly, this spatial distribution is characterized by dispersion. Yet, within this dispersed pattern, certain clusters or military-industrial complexes, if you will, can be identified. For example, Bangalore, Hyderabad, Pune-Nasik, Koraput, Kanpur-Lucknow, Calcutta and New Delhi show high concentrations of R&D and production activities, with many other enterprises scattered around the country. The nuclear complex in India also shows two clusters around Bombay and Madras, and a third band stretching from Hyderabad in the south to Calcutta in the east (Figure 6.5). Interestingly, nearly all the facilities within the Bombay cluster would seem to be replicated within the Madras cluster also, as well as within the Hyderabad-Calcutta corridor.

Most of the clusters of conventional defense R&D, production and nuclear-ballistic development (and production) would currently seem to be outside the reach of land-based aircraft and missiles in the Pakistani arsenal. However, this situation could radically change if Pakistan were to acquire/produce long-range ballistic missiles and/or base her conventional /nuclear weapons on surface ships and/or nuclear submarines. In the absence of a verifiable arms accord and cessation of hostilities between the two countries, if Pakistan were to develop a credible deterrent to the Indian threat, this would seem to be one logical way to proceed.

Conclusion

After this bird's-eye view of the physical and economic geographies of India and Pakistan we reach the following conclusions:

- The wars between Pakistan and India have not served any larger and meaningful political or strategic objectives. Except for the creation of Bangladesh in 1971, neither country has been able to make any territorial gains despite the very high human and other costs. Whether any domestic benefits have been derived by either side from these wars remains an open question.

- Geography and territorial disputes lie at the heart of regional hostilities and dictate offensive and defensive preparedness between the two countries.
- The physical and economic geographies of the two countries will continue to dictate all arms production, procurement and strategic-military decision making in the two countries. These geographical aspects also have an obvious bearing on the basing and targeting of nuclear weapons.
- While both countries may decide to go openly nuclear, India (with regard to China) and Pakistan (with regard to India) can only hope to mount a weak nuclear deterrent in the foreseeable future. Whether this will radically change the conventional military equations is an open question.
- As long as an outside power can exercise checks on the degrees of freedom of its adversary—the USSR on China, China on India, the U.S. on Pakistan—neither India nor Pakistan will feel sufficiently deterred or totally vulnerable, no matter what the offensive or defensive capabilities of the other.

As for the future post-Cold War era, with a relative decline in the global reach of the superpowers, who will and can persuade India and Pakistan from launching a nuclear arms race? In particular, will the on-going conflicts within the USSR and a possible unwillingness on its part to come to India's help in the event of a major war, and a similar scenario for Pakistan vis-à-vis China and the U.S., inevitably force India, followed by Pakistan, to go overtly nuclear? But, perhaps, wiser counsel will prevail and the much-needed regional cooperation in the emerging global economy would impel the two states to turn away from the brink and the abyss.

Notes

1. Most subsequent references to Pakistan in this chapter are to the post-1971 state.

2. The World Bank, *World Development Report, 1989* (Washington, D.C., 1989).

3. Pakistan does score marginally higher than India for GNP per capita. However in strategic calculations, the absolute size of an economy is much more important than per capita availability. The U.S.-USSR case is a good example.

4. In the past 3-4 years, however, the Indian telecommunications and automobile industries have shown very high growth rates. Most likely, India now scores higher on per capita basis for these infrastructures also.

5. Himachal Pradesh and Haryana are strictly not border states. However, their nearness to Pakistan impels us to include them in this comparison. Their inclusion also leads to some interesting results.

6. K. U. Kureshy: *A Geography of Pakistan* (Karachi: Oxford University Press, 1977).

7. Indus Waters Treaty, 1960. See A.A. Michel, *The Indus River: A Study of the Effects of Partition* (New Haven: Yale University Press, 1967), for the details and functioning of this treaty.

8. Here it is interesting to point out that costs for the U.S. Air Force and Navy for patrolling the sea coast and oceans have been estimated at U.S. $7,000 per hour. However, even with the most modern equipment and systems only 10% of the traffic is properly identified and intercepted.

9. For this section, we have relied heavily on a report by an *Indian Defense Review* research team (undated)."A Case for an Irradiated Landscape." Also see Sumit Ganguly, *Origins of War in South Asia* (Boulder: Westview Press, 1986).

10. Roberta Wohlstetter, *The Buddha Smiles: Absent-minded Peaceful Aid and the Indian Bomb* (Washington, D.C.: Energy Research and Development Administration, 1977).

11. For the nature of data and estimation, see *Long Term Economic and Military Trends, 1950-2010*. RAND Note N-2757-USDP (Santa Monica: RAND Corporation, 1989).

12. It must be pointed out that the Indian economy has shown a new vitality during the second half of the 1980s, breaking through the "Hindu growth rate" of the earlier two decades. The economic modernization program in China, on the other hand, has clearly run into problems lately, possibly with adverse long-term effects for military efforts also.

13. *SIPRI 1988 Arms and Disarmament Yearbook* (Oxford: Oxford University Press; SIPRI, 1988).

14. Carnegie Endowment for International Peace, *Report of the Carnegie Task Force on Nonproliferation and South Asian Security* (Washington, D.C., 1988).

15. Mushahid Hasan, "Slow Growth of Pakistani Industry," *Jane's Defense Weekly*, September 17, 1988.

16. Akmal Hussain, "Pakistan's Budget: Difficult Choices," *Times of India*, July 31, 1989.

17. Joseph Grieco, *Between Dependence and Autonomy: India's Experience with the International Compute Industry* (Berkeley: University of California Press, 1984).

7

The Verification and Control
of Fissile Material in South Asia

Jon Neuhoff and Clifford Singer

Previous chapters have described possible consequences of nuclear war involving South Asian countries and have given political perspectives on the prospect of verifying understandings aimed at controlling this threat. The present chapter presents a more technically oriented perspective on South Asian nuclear programs of potential military interest. We begin with a general review of nuclear materials production and the particular capabilities of India and Pakistan. This review concentrates on one of the most difficult steps in nuclear weapons manufacture, fissile materials production, leaving aside questions of construction, testing, and delivery. Those familiar with the production of nuclear materials in South Asia[1] may wish to skip to the final part of this chapter. Here we survey the general gamut of arms control verification technologies to see what problems and opportunities might be relevant to the South Asian context. It is argued that a number of regionally applicable arms control technologies exist, but an excessive emphasis on technological issues in a predominantly political problem would be a mistake.

Nuclear Capabilities in South Asia

Historical Perspective

The nuclearization of South Asia began more than three decades ago, with India initiating nuclear research before the end of World War II.[2] Homi Bhabha, a pioneer in Indian nuclear research, stated in 1944, "When nuclear energy has been successfully applied for power production, in, say, a couple decades from now, India will not have to look abroad for its experts but will find them ready at hand."[3] In succeeding years, Indian scientists imported and then produced nuclear power stations. The Indian Atomic Energy Commission (IAEC) was founded in 1948 and helped promote atomic research and the advancement of knowledge in nuclear physics.[4] In the early 1950s, the groundwork was laid for an Indian nuclear explosives program, and research and development received large support from the government.[5] In 1969 the development of nuclear explosives was an important part of the Indian nuclear program.[6] This culminated in a 1974 test of India's nuclear explosion at Pokhran.[7] Pakistan pressed for a nuclear program as early as 1964-1965,[8] and accelerated its program with the establishment of the Pakistan Atomic Energy Commission (PAEC). By 1972, a research program relevant to the potential production of nuclear weapons was reportedly underway.[9]

As a basis for understanding the potential for development of nuclear weapons in South Asia,[10] we include here a brief discussion of nuclear materials and production methods. We then review facilities available for nuclear materials production in South Asia.

Nuclear Materials—Use and Production

The materials used in nuclear weapons are technically difficult to produce and, therefore, expensive to obtain. Moreover, a sizable amount of research is needed if a country wishes to manufacture a nuclear weapon.   Both India and Pakistan have committed considerable time and energy to nuclear research and have made great strides in their technology base. Six special nuclear materials are of particular importance in this context: uranium, plutonium, heavy water (D_2O), tritium (^3H), lithium, and beryllium.[11] Each nuclear material will be discussed along with its production and use.

Uranium. Uranium is a radioactive, metallic element (atomic number 92; natural average atomic weight 238.03).[12] As found in nature, uranium is a mixture of three isotopes (i.e. three types of uranium nuclei with the same number of protons but different number of neutrons): ^{238}U (99.2745%), ^{235}U (0.7200%), and ^{234}U (0.0055%).[13] While ^{238}U comprises the majority of natural uranium, the isotope of primary interest in nuclear materials production is ^{235}U. ^{235}U is fissile (i.e. it will split into two parts when hit with a very low energy neutron with the accompanied release of neutrons and a large amount of energy). The neutrons created in the fission event can induce more fissions in ^{235}U, thereby causing a chain reaction.[14] Thus, an enormous amount of energy for nuclear power or nuclear weapons can be liberated from a small amount of uranium.

Natural uranium is mined from the earth and can be used, for example, in a reactor known as CANDU (**C**anadian **D**euterium-**U**ranium).[15] India relies primarily on this form of reactor for its power production. The advantage of this fuel is that it doesn't need conversion to fissile plutonium or enrichment to higher concentrations of ^{235}U and can be used immediately,[16] greatly reducing the cost of the fuel cycle. While ^{238}U cannot sustain a chain reaction, it has several potential uses in nuclear weapons.[17] ^{235}U can be used in both fission and thermonuclear weapons (since thermonuclear weapons need a fission explosion to ignite the fusion reaction). Uranium needs to be enriched to greater than 20% ^{235}U, and preferably greater than 90% ^{235}U, for fission weapons.[18] By enrichment is meant the increase in concentration of ^{235}U in uranium. Uranium enriched in ^{235}U to concentrations of about 3% or more can also be used as a fuel for light-water reactors (LWR). Extremely high enrichments have been used for some naval reactors.[19] There are several ways to enrich uranium, of which, in the present context, the ultracentrifuge process is the most relevant.

The ultracentrifuge process for enriching uranium separates out ^{235}U in uranium hexafluoride (UF_6) by subjecting this gas to a strong centrifugal force in a rotating cylinder. The heavier isotopes of uranium (i.e. ^{238}U) are forced to the outer edge of the cylinder and separated out from the light isotopes (i.e. ^{235}U). The enriched product can then be collected. One usually sets up a cascade of centrifuges to pass increasingly enriched gas through multiple stages. Each gas centrifuge can only hold a certain amount of UF_6, thus requiring many centrifuges to produce weapons-grade uranium.[20]

Plutonium. Plutonium is a radioactive, chemically reactive, metallic element which poses a significant toxicological hazard.[21] Plutonium is produced in a nuclear reactor by neutron absorption in ^{238}U and then purified through chemical separation processes.[22] The isotope of primary interest is ^{239}Pu. ^{239}Pu produces slightly more neutrons per fission than ^{235}U, and, therefore, has a smaller minimum ("critical") mass needed to sustain a fission chain reaction.[23] As a nuclear reactor containing ^{238}U operates and quantities of ^{239}Pu are made by neutron capture and subsequent radioactive decay to ^{239}Pu, heavier isotopes of plutonium (^{240}Pu, ^{241}Pu, and ^{242}Pu) are also gradually produced. The rate at which these isotopes build up depends upon the design of the reactor, operating power, and the length of time the fuel remains in the reactor.[24] These isotopes are not desired in a weapons program. ^{240}Pu, in particular, has a higher spontaneous fission rate and is more radioactive than ^{239}Pu.[25] Weapons-grade plutonium is defined, in the United States, as containing less than 7% of the major isotopic contaminant, ^{240}Pu.[26] (This convention for definition of "weapons grade" should not be taken to imply that plutonium with higher concentrations of ^{240}Pu may not be used in nuclear explosives, however.)

Heavy Water (D$_2$O). Deuterium (^{2}H), a stable isotope of hydrogen, occurs in ordinary water with a natural abundance of approximately one part in 6500 of the element hydrogen.[27] Deuterium is purified to high concentrations in the form of heavy water through processes which increase the proportion of deuterium to hydrogen in water (H$_2$O) far beyond the natural occurrence.[28] Heavy water can be produced in large quantities at purity levels of 99.75%.[29] The application of heavy water is mainly for moderating the speed of neutrons in a reactor to increase the ratio of fission to other neutron capture events,[30] e.g. in a CANDU-type power reactor or smaller reactors such as the Indian Cirus reactor. A minor use of heavy water is as a source of deuterium for nuclear weapons. For this purpose, deuterium is in the form of a gas or as solid lithium deuteride.[31]

Tritium (^{3}H). Tritium can be formed by the absorption of neutrons in lithium in or deuterium. Tritium can be used in small amounts to enhance the yield/weight ratio of a fissile weapon.[32] The production of tritium takes place in a reactor where, for example, a ^{6}Li nucleus absorbs a neutron with the release of tritium and a helium nucleus.[33] Its production is also a byproduct of the operation of reactors moderated with heavy water. Extraction of tritium from heavy water reduces the level of tritium containment needed in a power reactor and also can provide a source of tritium in quantities which could be significant for weapons production. The relatively short half life (i.e. the amount of time it takes for one-half of the material to decay away) of tritium of 12.5 years means it must be replenished periodically.[34]

Beryllium, Lithium, and Other Materials. Beryllium metal, a toxic element, is found as the single isotope ^{9}Be in nature and is therefore much easier to obtain than other nuclear materials for which a single isotope is desired. Beryllium is used as a neutron reflector and multiplier.[35] Although isotope separation is not required to obtain ^{9}Be, the need for a unique isotope in these applications defines it in some sense as a nuclear material. Because a significant fraction of the available supply of purified beryllium is used in nuclear research and development applications, there may be some interest in monitoring production and use of this material. Lithium, the lightest of all metals, is not found free in nature but always in conjunction with other elements.[36] As found in nature, lithium is in the form of a mixture of two isotopes: ^{7}Li (92.58%) and ^{6}Li (7.42%).[37] The enrichment of lithium in ^{6}Li might also be monitored or controlled as part of a nuclear verification regime. There are some "non-nuclear materials" (i.e., materials for which special isotopes are not needed) such as gold, titanium, and tungsten, which may be of particular use along with the "nuclear materials" in nuclear weapons programs.[38] These materials have many other uses and relatively lower costs than most "nuclear materials," so they are not of particular interest in the present context.

We now examine the production complexes in India and Pakistan which could possibly produce the nuclear materials described above. As will be seen, the nuclear programs of these countries are quite different in size, but contain many qualitatively similar facilities.

Nuclear Materials—South Asian Production Facilities

There is one obvious contrast between Pakistani and Indian programs which could be relevant to weapons production—Pakistan emphasizes uranium enrichment while India has a much larger plutonium production rate. This is seen in the facilities that exist and are planned in these two countries.[39] The status of each country's nuclear program is of interest because these facilities have the technical potential to produce nuclear weapons materials.

India relies a great deal upon heavy water reactors of the CANDU type. Indian reprocessing capability is also quite extensive and represents a major production capacity. The building of a tritium plant, whose location is unknown, indicates a potential for advanced nuclear weapons materials production.[40] India has also imported beryllium from a West German company, Degussa, in 1984.[41]

Regarding future operating plans, India shares with many other countries a history of such plans not all coming promptly to fruition. For example, there has been serious concern over the Madras nuclear power plants. Both units have been in and out of the Tamil Nadu power grid since December, 1988. Madras II may have to be scrapped entirely, while Madras I may operate at a reduced capacity because of major heavy water leaks. Madras II has severe leakage problems at its end shields, and also had the wrong fuel rod cut out of it, possibly damaging the geometry irreversibly. A normal fuel rod was cut out and two dislodged fuel rods were left in the reactor core. The problems have been turned over to the Bhabha Atomic Research Center; a solution hasn't been found yet.[42] This could have serious repercussions for the Indian nuclear power program. Nevertheless, the Indian nuclear program comprises an extensive potential for the production of nuclear weapons materials.

Pakistan relies primarily upon uranium enrichment for a near term weapons program. The Kahuta complex is the center of the Pakistani program. Pakistan has also imported beryllium.[43] With respect to a tritium plant,[44] Pakistan appears not to have the equipment available to extract tritium from its CANDU reactors.[45] Reports of a research reactor operating in Pakistan have not been publicly confirmed.[46] Pakistan is not planning as many nuclear power plants as India is, perhaps partly due to difficulties finding a supplier for its Chashma reactor because of proliferation concerns.[47]

Summary of Production Potentials

There has been a fairly dramatic shift over the past decade or two from an imported to an indigenous nuclear materials technology base in South Asia. This is particularly true of India but also increasingly true of Pakistan. It is in this sense that "the genie is already out of the bottle" with respect to one of the most serious obstacles to nuclear weapons production potential in South Asia. Moreover, a substantial number of Indian and Pakistani nuclear facilities are partially or completely free of international "safeguards" concerning the use of the products they produce.

A second point is that India already has a large unsafeguarded plutonium production and reprocessing capability. Thus, controls on gross production capacity are unlikely to have much impact in South Asia except in the context of the kind of massive arms race in which Pakistan is unlikely to be willing or able to compete.

A third point is the breadth and variety of nuclear materials facilities whose presence in South Asia has been inferred by various authors. Not only have a wide variety of reactor types and a substantial number of reactors been constructed; but uranium enrichment, heavy water, tritium, and beryllium processing units also provide additional potential complications. This may present both a problem and an opportunity. The problem is that a comprehensive arrangement concerning all of these facilities could be complicated. The opportunity is that the variety of available facilities allows many different routes for taking initial steps. It is to the range of such possible alternatives that we now turn.

Technical Constraints on Various Political Options

We limit ourselves here to nuclear materials and their assembly into nuclear weapons. Delivery modes are considered elsewhere. We examine three broad classes of options with respect to nuclear weapons developments in South Asia. Roughly organized in ascending degrees of technical difficulty, these include (1) confidence building measures, (2) controls on nuclear materials production, and (3) controls on use of stockpiled nuclear materials. As pointed out by Burns, no method in any of these areas will lead to absolute confidence in detection of all nuclear weapons related activities. Consequently, no end of objections will be raised by those who take absolute confidence as a necessary standard. It is assumed here that a genuine desire to take some steps related to nuclear weapons development may come to exist amongst the relevant parties, in a framework that allows for the possibility that increased security due to the measures taken will outweigh the risk that the measures are not 100% effective. Without this assumption, discussion of technical issues is purely academic.

We concentrate primary on nuclear materials, operationally defined here as elements whose isotopic composition is customarily controlled. This is because control of isotopic compositions is generally much more expensive (and correspondingly easier to monitor) than ordinary chemical processing. Materials are considered in three groups: (1) plutonium, uranium and heavy water, (2) tritium and lithium, and (3) other materials used with natural isotopic concentrations, such as beryllium, heavy metal tampers, centrifuge materials (including maraging steel and lighter weight high strength materials), and manufactured weapons components. For each class of materials, we ask what is technically feasible in the South Asian context in the way of confidence building measures, production control, and control of already produced materials.

Classes of Possible Measures

Confidence Building Measures. Confidence building measures could, in principle, lie in an extremely wide range, from one time perfunctory visits of facilities to total and complete disclosure of all potential weapons-related activities and stockpiles. In between lie agreements concerning off site monitoring, on-site non-intrusive monitoring, on-site monitoring with process stream sampling, and notification procedures and exchanges of data.

Off-site monitoring possibilities include satellite surveillance by commercial companies, by third party governments, or by the participants themselves. Agreements relevant to satellite monitoring could include procedures for notification of activities which could be relevant to nuclear weapons construction, testing or storage. The avoidance of otherwise nonproductive activities whose sole purpose would be to disguise nuclear activities could also be classified as a pure confidence building measure, as this would put no practical constraint on nuclear development. Airplane overflights can be a less expensive alternative to monitoring. Intermittent or permanent observations from outside an agreed exclusion boundary could provide more continuity. More remote ground based observation points for radiochemical assay or nuclear explosion monitoring have also been discussed.

On-site non-intrusive monitoring activities include human and/or video camera visual inspections and nondestructive assay techniques for reactor fuel burnup and/or isotopic concentration of purified nuclear materials.[48] On-site intrusive monitoring activities include sampling of uranium enrichment and/or reactor irradiation product reprocessing streams.[49] Neutron activation analysis using sufficiently large neutron fluences to impact operations might also be classified as an intrusive on-site monitoring scheme. Again, prohibition of activities whose sole purpose is to interfere with on site monitoring schemes might be classified as a pure confidence building measure. An example would be shielding of processed nuclear materials beyond normally accepted radiological safety practice for the sole purpose of complicating their detection or nondestructive isotopic assay.

Data exchanges are a particularly important potential type of initial and/or continuing confidence building measure. Exchanging lists of some or all nuclear relevant facilities, with or without accompanying technical data, could be useful. Notification of reactor refueling schedules and other activities potentially relevant to nuclear weapons production might also be useful confidence building measures. In the context of a formal confidence building agreement, there could be procedures for evaluating third party governmental or private information, and/or procedures to protect privileged data and individuals who disclose potential violations. With or without a formal agreement, meetings and/or exchanges involving technical or administrative personnel could be useful in some contexts.

Controls on Nuclear Materials Production. If South Asian countries become parties to an agreement limiting production of nuclear materials relevant to weapons construction, monitoring measures more systematic than those employed for confidence building may be essential. This consideration requires examining in turn the three classes of nuclear weapons relevant materials defined above. In the past, mostly in the context of the Nonproliferation Treaty and IAEA and Euratom safeguards, emphasis has been placed on nuclear materials accounting in production of fissile isotopes, especially those of plutonium. Heavy water utilization is also relevant here. In the South Asian context, comparable emphasis would presumably have to placed on materials accounting during enrichment of uranium in ^{235}U. The second class of materials defined above, containing tritium and lithium, is also of potential concern in the South Asian context. Other materials will be discussed briefly after we deal with these two classes of nuclear materials.

While development and implementation of procedures related to IAEA safeguards have produced a significant technological and bureaucratic base for monitoring fissile materials, we assume here that India and Pakistan will remain disinterested for the foreseeable future in simply applying for extension of IAEA monitoring. If this assumption is incorrect, then comprehensive submission to IAEA procedures would provide a reasonably well understood level of confidence concerning diversion of fissile materials for unsafeguarded uses. The main problems specific to the South Asian context would be the special difficulties associated with continuous refuelling of CANDU reactors and the challenge of devising a system for monitoring a previously uninspected gas centrifuge uranium enrichment facility. If IAEA bureaucracy and methods are not used, however, an even more complicated interplay between indigenous and third party fissile isotope production monitoring technology may need to be examined. It is to this problem that we now turn our attention.

First, we consider the somewhat familiar ground of monitoring plutonium production and recycling. An upper limit on possible plutonium production rates is determinable from the total thermal power output of all known reactors.[50] This is determinable in principle by infrared detection from satellites, but the required resolution and coverage make this impractical in the South Asian context in the foreseeable future. Permanent ground based observation posts could set better limits. Total Indian thermal reactor power production is already so high that such limits would probably be of limited practical political utility there, but they might be of some interim use when applied to Pakistan if other measures were used in India. Monitoring of heavy water inventories can be of some additional help in estimating rough limits on plutonium production potential.

Assuming large plutonium production rates, the more relevant question is what the isotopic concentration of the plutonium is, and how much plutonium of various isotopic concentrations is being reprocessed for various purposes. This issue is complicated by the fact that high Pu-239 fractions (94% or higher) are desirable for weapons producers in order to limit spontaneous neutron production (and to also limit other radiation that complicates materials handling), but some lower grade plutonium may also be usable. Here we assume some agreement has been reached about the fate of various grades of reprocessed plutonium, and we examine the materials accounting implications.

While direct nondestructive assay before reprocessing of the plutonium isotope concentrations after uranium irradiation is impractical, useful information on the isotopic concentration can be obtained nondestructively by estimating the overall burnup from the radiation spectrum emitted by the irradiated fuel. After reprocessing, the plutonium isotopic concentration can be assayed nondestructively even if the material is sealed in casks of a size which would normally be used for shipping or storage. In combination with fairly extensive monitoring by scales, sealed cameras,[51] inspection, and record keeping, a reasonably accurate inventory of plutonium isotopes can be obtained. With continuously refueled CANDU reactors, however, such monitoring could consume considerably more skilled labor than it would on a batch reloaded reactor (Two batch loaded reactors are under IAEA safeguards at Tarapur in India at least until 1993.)[52] In the South Asian context, it might be decided simply to put an upper limit on the amount of plutonium which might be diverted over a specified time without detection. This amount of in-principle-divertible plutonium would presumably be chosen so as not to be of major significance compared to unsafeguarded plutonium already reprocessed. If so, this could considerably simplify the technical problem of timely detection of a significant diversion problem compared to the smaller detection limits which are the goal of IAEA safeguards inspection. (The IAEA aims to be confident of detecting diversions of 8 kg or more of plutonium from safeguarded facilities.)

If India persists with its stated plans of moving from CANDU to plutonium fast breeders to ^{233}U breeders based on thorium irradiation,[53] a comparably difficult problem of accounting for similar amounts of ^{233}U could eventually arise. This would probably take many years to become a significant technical problem, but the question of a feasible solution might arise in negotiations.

Monitoring of ^{235}U enrichment facilities presents a somewhat different kind of problem, for which IAEA experience is less extensive. A general review of problems involved in monitoring gas centrifuge enrichment facilities is given in *Uranium Enrichment and Nuclear Weapon Proliferation* by Krass, et al.[54] A key technical decision in this area for detailed materials accounting would be the degree of access to centrifuge enrichment areas. Centrifuges in these areas are connected in a cascade. Levels of inspection include nondestructive assay of inputs and/or outputs, sampling thereof, access to centrifuge rooms for visual inspection of the cascade arrangement, and/or nondestructive assay or sampling of the cascade.

Substantial technical progress in nondestructive assay of uranium isotopes has recently been made.[55] However, previous experience with repeated safeguards inspection is limited, perhaps due in part to concerns about disclosure of centrifuge setups which producers have found to be adequate. While industrial security might be of some concern in the South Asian context, perhaps equally important is that access to centrifuge areas could reveal information about the extent and possibly the enrichment levels aimed for in previous work. Any mismatch between enrichment levels deduced from centrifuge arrangements and previous public statements could entail a perceived political cost. In the absence of a complete confidence building regime concerning previously accumulated stockpiles, revelation of the number and appearance of existing centrifuge casings might also provide unwanted release of information concerning possible existing stockpiles.

Stockpiles

Even assuming a genuine willingness by participating parties to make progress, one of the most vexing problems is likely to be the question of how to deal with the possibility of existing stockpiles of fissile material. These stockpiles may consist of uranium with natural, low, or high enrichment in ^{235}U; unreprocessed plutonium and also reprocessed plutonium with various possible concentrations of ^{239}Pu; and to a small extent irradiated thorium and reprocessed ^{233}U. Even without delving into speculation about details of past production, it is obvious that India's total stock of safeguarded and unsafeguarded plutonium greatly exceed Pakistan's stockpile of plutonium and enriched uranium. Whether this is of any real significance is a political question, but the question of how to implement any agreement concerning existing stockpiles raises challenging technical problems.

The question of fissile material stockpiles basically has not been addressed in other contexts, largely because complex technical discussion of nuclear arms control has been dominated by negotiations between the U.S. and the USSR, where delivery vehicles are more of a limitation than are fissile materials stockpiles. In the South Asian context, however, the amount of fissile material potentially available for weapons construction has at least until recently been more of a limitation that the number of aircraft available to deliver nuclear weapons. Under some conceivable agreements or understandings, this might continue to be the case. Then the level and disposition of stockpiled fissile materials may loom large in peoples' minds.

Given unrestricted access to all possible storage locations, nondestructive assay of stockpiled fissile materials would probably be a reasonable goal. The remote detection of well shielded uranium or plutonium metal (which might in principle be anywhere in an entire country) seems totally out of the question, however. A detailed understanding concerning stockpiled materials must therefore rely on (1) trust between the Indian and Pakistani political leaders, and confidence that they have effective and continuing control over disposition of fissile materials, (2) exhaustive interviews with the entire spectrum of people who may have handled fissile materials in any form potentially relevant to weapons production, along with a climate of moral or practical incentives for enough people to disclose activities indicating a pattern of maintaining stored weapons and/or weapons production potential, or (3) a less ambitious goal of limiting the number of actual or potential weapons to an implicitly or explicitly stated maximum, along with fairly stringent controls on potential weapons assembly and/or delivery systems.

Herein lies a fundamental problem, imposed by the technical difficulty of detecting weapons grade nuclear materials already through the production process. To approach any significant controls on weapons grade materials. India and Pakistan face a significant dilemma. Either (1) they must accept unprecedented extensive surveys and mutually imposed controls over fissile materials stockpiles or less extensive assurances with considerable potential uncertainty, or (2) they agree to disparate levels of stockpiled materials under similar constraints, or (3) they enter into very difficult negotiations concerning an approach to acceptable higher levels of fissile materials stockpiles. This latter approach might be perceived to be complicated by the extensive nuclear weapons capabilities of up to five or six other nuclear powers. It seems clear that local adoption of IAEA type production safeguards could provide only part of the solutions to this dilemma. Either considerable imagination and ingenuity will be required here, or South Asia will have to be content with confidence building measures and/or delivery vehicle controls, perhaps combined with fissile materials production controls which at best may help to prevent vast overbuilding of actual or potential nuclear arsenals.

Tritium, Lithium, and Nuclear Testing. Reports of activities related to tritium technology in South Asia raise an additional complication. By replacing ^{238}U target atoms by lithium enriched in ^6Li, U.S. weapons material production reactors were reportedly capable of producing comparable numbers of tritium atoms in place of plutonium atoms (and, therefore, about two orders of magnitude less tritium by weight). By estimating U.S. tritium production history[56] and comparing to the number of weapons likely to contain tritium, it can be concluded that several grams of tritium are incorporated to boost the yield of these weapons. In the context of limitations but not elimination of nuclear weapons potential in South Asia, increased explosive power deliverable with a limited amount of fissile material and/or delivery systems might appear significant. However, if it is not imported, the tritium would have to be produced and purified at a limited number of facilities. Since tritium has a half life of 12.5 years to radioactive decay, reasonable production controls or disclosure could put an increasingly stringent upper limit on the amount of tritium available for use in nuclear weapons. The difficulty of non-intrusive assay and the relatively small masses needed for practical use, however, suggest that attempts to control this use of tritium could also be problematic.

Another significant concern with tritium boosting of fission weapon yields is that absence of previous testing would leave considerable uncertainty in how effective this method would be. From the weapons designer's point of view, careful preparations for a very limited number of tests might be perceived as compensating for the risk and expense of maintaining a fission boosting option. A similar situation exists with respect to optimizing the yield of pure fission weapons and the more complicated option of developing fusion weapons based on lithium deuteride. Especially in the context of an arms control agreement or confidence building measures concerning the number of available delivery systems, limitations on detectable yield tests or preparations for such a test might be quite significant.

Other Materials. While collection of special isotopes in sufficient quantities is a major task in constructing nuclear weapons, the remainder of the weaponization process also involves significant numbers of people and potentially detectable industrial activity. While materials such as beryllium and such as high atomic number tampers can be used in nuclear weapons, they also have other uses in sufficiently large quantities that their acquisition is not an unambiguous indicator of nuclear weapons design and production activities. Taken as a whole, however, the parts of the weaponization process not involving special isotope production could in principle be subject to the the same kind of confidence building and monitoring measures suggested above.

Conclusion

Verification of nuclear weapons restrictions in the South Asian context raises unique problems. Many of these problems were not successfully addressed in the early stages of weapons development by the presently declared nuclear weapons states. Moreover, they have not yet come to the forefront in the regions where less political impetus for controls may exist or where potentially weapons-relevant programs have not yet developed as far. Thus, while experience from IAEA activities relevant to the Nonproliferation Treaty (NPT) is important, the South Asian context raises additional problems. Notable among these are (1) the control of existing stockpiles of fissile materials in quantities potentially adequate to produce many nuclear weapons, and (2) research and development activities on fusion boosting and thermonuclear weapons which may proceed even in the absence of the kind of ongoing nuclear weapons testing program conducted during the comparable phase of development by the presently declared nuclear weapons states. Present IAEA experience has some relevance to these issues, but it is primarily concerned with the detection of unauthorized production of fissile materials and international transfer of these and other materials related to fissile materials production. In an ambitious weapons control regime, the inventory and control of presently stockpiled materials would present unique problems. In a regime less ambitious than the present NPT, control of improvements in potential for increasing the explosive yield potentially achievable with a given amount of fissile material would also present major challenges. In these two problematic areas, we have been more able to identify potential difficulties than to suggest convincing remedies. Verification methods for the control of fissile material production and very low yield testing, while also problematic, should be relatively easier to effect.

All of this suggests that predominantly technical solutions to the problem of nuclear armament may need less emphasis in South Asia than has previously been the case in other contexts. Extensive person to person contacts, including technical and administrative personnel, may be as important in confidence building and/or arms limitation measures as are technical measures to monitor nuclear materials production, preparation and execution of nuclear tests, weaponization programs, and delivery systems.

Notes

1. Leonard S. Spector, *The Undeclared Bomb* (Cambridge: Ballinger, 1988), p. 91.

2. K.C. Pant, "The Indian Nuclear Power Program," *Energy* Vol. 9, 1984, p. 773.

3. "The Nuclear Options: Danger Ahead," *Imprint* (New Delhi) 1986, p. 12.

4. Pant, "The Indian Nuclear Power Program," p. 773.

5. Ravindra Tomar, "The Indian Nuclear Power Program: Myths and Mirages," *Asian Survey*, Vol. 20, No. 5, 1980, p. 518.

6. Spector, *The Undeclared Bomb*, p. 82.

7. David Albright and Tom Zamora, "India's, Pakistan's Nuclear Weapons: All the Pieces in Place," *Bulletin of the Atomic Scientists*, June, 1989, p. 24.

8. Stephen P. Cohen, "Solving Proliferation Problems in a Regional Context: South Asia," paper presented to the Aspen Strategy Group Summer Workshop on Responding to the Proliferation of Nuclear, Chemical, and Ballistic Missile Capabilities, 1989, p. 1.

9. Albright and Zamora, and Spector, *The Undeclared Bomb*, p. 121.

10. David Albright, "Pakistan's Bomb Making Capability," *Bulletin of the Atomic Scientists*, June, 1987, p. 30; Albright and Zamora, p. 20; Spector, *The Undeclared Bomb*, pp. 81-82.

11. Thomas B. Cochran, William M. Arkin, Robert S. Norris and Milton M. Hoenig, *Nuclear Weapons Databook, Vol. II: U.S. Nuclear Warhead Production* (Cambridge: Ballinger, 1987), p. 31.

12. R. C. Weast, ed., *Handbook of Chemistry and Physics, 69th Edition* (Boca Raton: CRC Press, 1988-1989), p. B-39.

13. *Chart of the Nuclides* (San Jose: General Electric, 1984), p. 47.

14. Kosta Tsipis, "The Physics of Nuclear Weapons," in Jack Dennis, ed., *The Nuclear Almanac* (Reading: Addison-Wesley, 1984), p. 197.

15. Alan V. Nero, *A Guidebook to Nuclear Reactors* (Berkeley: University of California Press, 1979), p. 109.

16. *Ibid.*

17. Tsipis, p. 202.

18. Cochran, et al., p. 31.

19. *Ibid.*, p. 71.

20. *Ibid.*, p. 130.

21. Weast, p. B-28.

22. Cochran, et al., p. 58; Tsipis, p. 200.

23. *Ibid.*, pp. 202, 198.

24. Cochran, et al., p. 135.

25. *Ibid.*

26. *Ibid.*, p. 136.

27. *Ibid.*, p. 86.

28. *Ibid.*

29. *Ibid.*

30. Nero, p. 118.

31. Cochran, et al., p. 90.

32. Milton M. Hoenig, *The Tritium Factor: Tritium's Impact on Nuclear Arms Reductions* (Nuclear Control Institute and American Academy of Arts and Sciences, 1988), p. 58.

33. Cochran, et al., pp. 62, 90.

34. *Chart of the Nuclides*, p. 22.

35. Weast, p. B-9, B-10; Cochran et al., *Nuclear Weapons Databook, Vol. II*, p. 91.

36. Weast, p. B-23.

37. Cochran, et al., p. 90.

38. *Ibid.*, p. 92; Tsipis, pp. 197, 199, 200, 202; E.J. Moniz and T.L. Neff, "Nuclear Power and Nuclear Weapons Proliferation," *Physics Today*, Vol. 31, No.: 4, April, 1978, p. 21; Albright and Zamora, p. 20.

39. For lists and descriptions of Indian and Pakistani nuclear facilities and capabilities see Spector, *The Undeclared Bomb*, pp. 111-115, 150-151; "World List of Nuclear Power Plants," *Nuclear News*, August, 1989, pp. 82-84; Dieter Braun, "Pakistan's Nuclear Development Programme," *Defence Journal* (Islamabad) Vol. 14, No. 9, 10, 1988, pp. 10-17. For the most recent comprehensive list of Indian and Pakistani nuclear facilities see Jon Neuhoff and Clifford Singer, "Verification and Control of Fissile Materials," in *Towards a Nuclear Verification Regime in South Asia*, a study for the Los Alamos National Laboratory, LANL subcontract no 9-SC9-C4353-1 (Urbana: University of Illinois, April, 1990), pp. 169-184.

40. Albright and Zamora, p. 20.

41. S. Engleberg, "German Atomic Sale Challenged," *New York Times*, Feb. 1, 1989.

42. "Kalpakkam—Powerless Performance," *India Today*, June 30, 1989.

43. Albright and Zamora, p. 20.

44. *Ibid.*

45. *Ibid.*

46. Leonard S. Spector, "Monitoring Nuclear Proliferation," Manuscript, October, 1989, p. 6.

47. Braun, p. 14.

48. M. Ouyang, "An Iterative Correction Method for Nondestructive Plutonium Waste Assay," *Nuclear Technology* 71, 1985, p. 506.

49. W. Beyrich, W. Golly, G. Spannagel, P. DeBievre, W.H. Wolters, and W. Lycke, "The Assay of Uranium and Plutonium in Reprocessing Input Solutions by Isotope Dilution Mass Spectrometry: Results of the Isotope Dilution Analysis Measurement Evaluation Method," *Nuclear Technology* 15, 1985, p. 73.

50. *Report of the Carnegie Task Force on Nonproliferation and South Asian Security* (Washington, D.C.: Carnegie Endowment for International Peace, 1988).

51. Harry Anderson, Fred Coleman, Christopher Dickey, and Jane Whitmore, "Sandia Keeps Eye on Nuclear Facilities," *Monitor*, July, 1985, p. 27.

52. "World List of Nuclear Power Plants," *Nuclear News* August, 1989, p. 82.

53. Pant, p. 773.

54. A.S. Krass, P. Boksma, B. Elzen and W. Smit, *Uranium Enrichment and Nuclear Weapon Proliferation* (New York: Taylor & Francis, SIPRI, 1983).

55. D.W. Swindle, "Application of the Limited Frequency-Unannounced Access Strategy Measurement Technology in Gas Centrifuge Enrichment Plants" (in press); N. Cooley, L. W. Fields and D.W. Swindle, "Results from Uranium Deposition studies for Development of a Limited Frequency-Unannounced Access Inspection Strategy for Gas Centrifuge Plants" (in press); K. van der Meer, "Enrichment Verification on UF_6 in Low Pressure Process Pipes: An Application of the Two-Geometry Method," *Eleventh ESARDA Annual Symposium on Safeguards and Nuclear Material Management* Luxembourg, May 30- June 1, 1989.

56. T.B. Cochran, W.M. Arkin, M.M. Hoenig, and Robert S. Norris, eds., *Nuclear Weapons Databook Vol. III: U.S. Nuclear Warhead Facility Profiles* (Cambridge, MA: Ballinger, 1987), p. 92.

8

Sensing the Threat—
Remote Monitoring Technologies

Vipin Gupta

The spread of nuclear weapons beyond the superpowers coincides with the global spread of remote sensing technologies that can be used to verify limits on such weapons. India and Pakistan are exemplary of proliferation in these two politically-linked areas of technology. Both countries are capable of becoming official nuclear powers and both countries have access to remote sensing systems that could be useful in verifying compliance with existing and possibly future bilateral arms control agreements.[1]

Remote sensing technologies are based on a variety of techniques to obtain information about a particular area or event without being in direct contact with the region of interest. These technologies are most useful in gathering and processing information that cannot be acquired in any other way due to physical, financial, or political obstructions. These technologies are also used as an economical or complementary means of acquiring and processing information.

Theoretically, remote sensing technologies are the ideal means of gathering intelligence data given the current nationalistic world order. Remote sensing can transcend barriers without physically transgressing a country's boundaries—the ultimate assault on a nation's sovereignty. Although remote sensing is still a form of intrusion, it is a subtle one that is difficult to define.

Furthermore, it is a tolerable form of intrusion since the only way to stop the cognitive intrusion is to disable the sensor platform. Remote sensing can even become an acceptable form of intrusion in a situation of reciprocity and mutual benefit.

As shown by the experience of the superpowers, the advantages of remote sensing can be fully utilized in monitoring clandestine or highly sensitive activities. Remote sensing systems can detect such activities by acquiring and processing vast amounts of timely information. Once the activities are detected and identified, the monitoring system can provide surveillance for as long as the user desires.

The Regional Significance of Remote Sensing

Remote sensing technology is particularly suitable in South Asia where an antagonistic relationship between India and Pakistan clearly exists. It is a region that has been historically plagued with border conflicts and thus legitimate bilateral forms of physical intrusion (e.g. on-site inspections) do not exist.[2] It is a region where the nuclear capabilities and intentions of each side are highly dynamic and ambiguous. And finally, it is a region that consists of recently active participants in the formation of bilateral security arrangements including nuclear arms control.

The political and strategic dynamics in South Asia have created a huge demand for reliable and timely information about the other side's nuclear intentions and capabilities. The problem is that the political process of obtaining such information has not been able to keep up with the increasing technical difficulty of acquiring such information.

Until political solutions such as on-site inspections are negotiated and implemented, remote sensing is the only means of at least partially accommodating the regional demand for nuclear information. It is a short-term technical solution to a technical problem.

Furthermore, it is a solution whose implementation is independent of political efforts to obtain reliable forms of data exchange. From a verification perspective, this is particularly advantageous. Each country can develop the national technical means (NTM) to verify various types of bilateral agreements before and during the respective negotiations.

This greatly reduces or eliminates the complications of establishing a follow-on verification agreement outlining which NTM technologies are acceptable and which are not.[3] Figure 8.1 shows the theoretical role of remote sensing in simplifying the

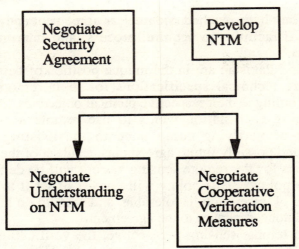

FIGURE 8.1 The Negotiating Process with Simultaneous Development of NTM.

sequential negotiating steps between two nations with developing monitoring systems. By simultaneously developing national technical means and negotiating a security agreement, the technical infrastructure would exist to provide the necessary information to verify compliance to the prospective agreement.

The "dual-track" approach will also ease nationalist resistance towards a transition from a unilateral security approach to a bilateral security arrangement. Remote sensing technologies can act as an indigenous buffer between a country's own lack of information and reliance on its adversary for reliable and relevant information (data exchanges) or access to information (on-site inspections).

Should negotiations collapse, the monitoring system would not lose its purpose. It could still gather the same information it would have with the presence of an agreement. The only difference would be the use of the information. Instead of verifying compliance, the information could be used for crisis management and for other diplomatic purposes including the reestablishment of negotiations.[4]

Remote Sensing and Verification Policy

As noted earlier, India and Pakistan are in the infant stage of developing bilateral security arrangements and remote sensing systems. They have reached one nuclear agreement and both have the technical facilities to acquire, process, and interpret remote sensing data.[5]

India and Pakistan are in the unique position of being able to shape future technical specifications for their remote sensing systems according to their respective political objectives.

Assuming each nation wants to use remote sensing as a component of verifying compliance to the existing bilateral agreement and possibly future agreements, a subset of the technical specifications for the remote sensing system will be derived from verification policy. This policy will consist of what to look for, what degree of uncertainty is tolerable, and what to do in response to perceived noncompliance to the agreement.

From a remote sensing perspective, the verification process consists of seven steps as shown in Figure 8.2.[6] Three components of the verification process are purely technical in operation.

The interpretation of data is a grey area. On the one hand, it is a technical component because it utilizes steps defined in the scientific method. On the other hand, it is a political component because the policymakers specify the acceptable error tolerances and types of data needed to formulate solid conclusions.

To illustrate this point, consider the U.S. monitoring experience. During the supposed missile gap era, the Air Force had to assess the ICBM capability of the Soviet Union. At the time, the U.S. was concerned about its nuclear security given Soviet space advances such as Sputnik. As a result, the rigid technical parameters for identifying an ICBM in a U-2 photograph were relaxed, resulting in highly overestimated ICBM counts by the Air Force. As one photoanalyst put it, the USAF thought ". . . every flyspeck on film was a missile."[7]

This chapter will place the technical steps shown in Figure 8.2 in their South Asian context and explore how remote sensing technologies can be used to fulfill the technical aspects of potential Indian and Pakistani verification policies. I will then look at the types of future remote monitoring architectures that can fulfill these policies and how other nations can contribute to a verification regime. Finally, given their present status, I will estimate how long it would take India and Pakistan to develop and deploy their own comprehensive remote sensing system.

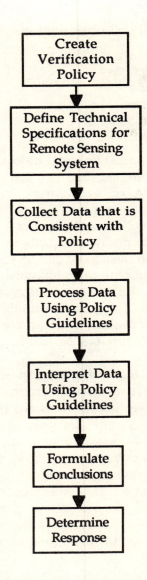

FIGURE 8.2 Verification Process for Remote Sensing.

Remote Sensing Technologies for Verification

To apply remote sensing technologies for verification purposes in South Asia, one has to have a general idea of what the political objectives and associated technical specifications could be. In general terms, the political objectives can be categorized as the following:

- Production Restrictions
- Testing Restrictions
- Training Restrictions
- Deployment Restrictions
- Employment Restrictions

By coupling the general political objectives with the relevant remote sensing technologies, one can see how each technology could be used in South Asia.

For example, the recent "no attack" on nuclear facilities agreement falls in two of these categories. The ban on attacking nuclear facilities can be considered an employment restriction. The disclosure clause within the accord can be considered a production restriction. Compliance with the employment restriction could be verified by monitoring the communications between pilots during practice or actual sorties. Compliance with the production restriction can be verified by using cameras to detect construction of new large facilities and photointerpreters to assess the function of such facilities.

Remote sensing technologies can also be categorized. Specifically, there are two distinct groups for data acquisition: passive sensors and active sensors. Passive sensors detect reflected or emitted energy from a particular site. In general, the energy is either electromagnetic, acoustic, or seismic. The sensors are only capable of receiving energy and thus cannot emit their own signals and analyze the echo signals.

Active sensors emit a signal and infer information on the site from the reflected signal. The advantage of such a system is that it is autonomous. It does not depend on the sun or a specific event such as a nuclear explosion to obtain useful information.

Photoreconnaissance Satellites

In very general terms, photoreconnaissance satellites take pictures of Earth sites from space. The term "photoreconnaissance" implies the presence of electromagnetic (light) sensors such as cameras or light-sensitive semiconductors that can see in the visible part of the electromagnetic spectrum.[8]

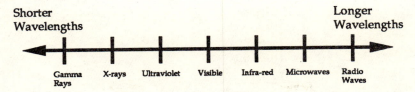

FIGURE 8.3 Electromagnetic Spectrum.

Because its orbit is located in a fixed plane and the Earth rotates under it, a photoreconnaissance satellite is capable of taking pictures of vast portions of the Earth's surface. This is its principle advantage. It can cover more area than aircraft in less time.

Photoreconnaissance satellites can be used to verify any of the five general restrictions. Its comprehensive utility comes from the fact that each step requires outdoor activity.

Even though such satellites cannot see through walls, the satellite can take pictures of what goes in a hidden site, what exits the site, and what is stored around the site. Such information could reveal just as much about the purpose of a site as a proverbial blueprint of the site. Even objects such as storage boxes can reveal the contents within it. Cratology is one of the most important derived disciplines of photoreconnaissance.

This black box approach is a powerful method of detecting clandestine activities (See Figure 8.4). It may not reveal as much direct information as desired, but it is important to remember that the absence of particular information can reveal just as much about a particular activity as the visible presence of the activity.

From a South Asian perspective, this is a particularly important point since both countries are already active in concealing their nuclear activities. Should they reach a nuclear agreement in the future, it will be more difficult to discriminate between legal and illegal activities because both countries have already blurred the line of distinction. As a result, more evidence would be needed in order to make a substantive conclusion.

Even in an environment of active concealment, information (or the lack of) provided by photoreconnaissance satellites could indicate the presence of suspicious activities. Once suspected, other proximate and remote monitoring assets could be used to positively reveal illegal activity.

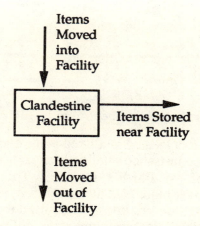

FIGURE 8.4 Black Box Approach to Remote Monitoring.

It is possible for the photoreconnaissance satellite to provide exclusively enough information to verify compliance or prove noncompliance. Whether the satellite can actually provide enough information depends on the type and extent of the activity, the ground resolution provided by the satellite, and the overflight frequency.

For example, SPOT's 10 meter resolution image of the Israeli Dimona reactor was sufficient to reveal that the reactor was built on a plateau that appears manmade. According to former technician Mordecai Vanunu, a secret nuclear weapons production facility is located within this hill. Independent of the logical inference from Mr. Vanunu's ultimate fate, the SPOT image could not confirm his assertions. However, if SPOT existed in the early 1960s during the secret construction of the facility, SPOT could have provided enough information to determine whether an extensive underground facility existed.[9]

The ground resolution provided by a photoreconnaissance satellite is widely considered the primary performance parameter. Its value determines how much detail one can see from a specific image taken at a specific time.[10]

Objects smaller than the ground resolution may be detected, but cannot be identified. For example, in an image with one meter resolution, one could not read the headlines off a newspaper. However, the headline may appear on the image as a black dot.

The value of the ground resolution depends on two main factors: the sensor and the scene. To see fine details in a scene, the sensor must have as many line pairs per mm or pixels per mm to map each detail in the scene. It also must have as large a focal length (f) as possible because that reduces the demagnification suffered by the image projection.

The hardware and image geometry is not sufficient though. The sensor cannot see an object unless it receives a sufficient amount of energy (in this case, visible light) from the objects in that scene. The incident energy on the sensor can be enhanced by increasing the aperature D. This also has the added benefit of reducing diffraction (blurring) effects.

One can also expect higher resolution if the sensor is as close to the scene as possible (i.e., H is as small as possible). High contrast in the scene also enhances the resolution.

From this simple analysis, the optimal specifications for a high-resolution photoreconnaissance satellite become apparent:

- Create an array of very small, sensitive sensors
- Orbit satellite as close to the ground as possible
- Make the satellite length (f) as long as possible
- Make the satellite width (D) as wide as possible

In short, one needs to design high resolution sensors, put them in a satellite the size of a bus, and place the satellite in an orbit that is

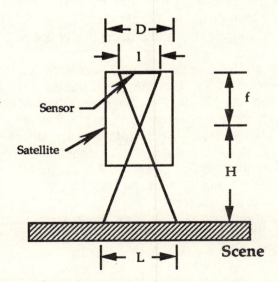

FIGURE 8.5 Image Projection Geometry (not to scale).

as close to the Earth's surface as possible. The fact that there are U.S. Keyhole (KH) spy satellites with the listed characteristics is no coincidence.[11]

Such satellites represent optimal designs given current levels of technology and current launch capabilities. For verification purposes, less powerful satellites can be sufficient. The SPOT satellite, for example, has a focal length that is approximately 20% of the focal length of U.S. KH satellites and is approximately 10% of the weight of U.S. KH satellites.[12] Yet, it has provided verification-relevant information including pictures of the Kahuta enrichment plant in Pakistan and the Indian nuclear test site in the Rajasthan desert.[13]

This raises the question concerning what ground resolution is needed to detect and identify various verification-relevant sites and objects. Such information would be integral to the design of the sensors. The most common reference for such information is the *McDonnell-Douglas Corporation Reconnaissance Handy Book*.[14] However, recent experience with commercially available images reveals that the numbers in the handy book are, in many instances, an order of magnitude too low.[15] This is good news for India and Pakistan because sensor specifications can be less stringent than what was initially anticipated.

Table 8.1 integrates the handy book data with the empirical data from commercial data analysis. The table shows the resolution thresholds for detection, general identification, and precise identification of various sites and objects that could be of interest in a verification regime.

Detection implies that the site or object is shown on the image by at least one pixel or dot. It cannot be identified, but its location is defined. General identification implies that the site or object can be seen and classified. For example, an image might show an object with four wheels. Such an object could be generally classified as a vehicle. Precise identification implies that the site or object can be classified into a more specific category. For example, a picture of a vehicle with four wheels, no roof, and a foldable windshield could be precisely classified as a jeep.

For verification purposes, all three levels of photointerpretation need to be fulfilled. Consequently, for a particular verification mission such as a ban on medium-range missiles, photoreconnaissance satellites must be able to perform within the respective thresholds outlined in Table 8.1.

TABLE 8.1   Thresholds for Various Sites and Objects (in meters)

Site or Object	Detection	General Identification	Precise Identification
Aircraft	10	10	5–10
Airfield Facilities	80	30	5–10
Bridges	30–80	20–30	5–20
Buildings/Plants	30	10	1.5–5
Coasts/Beaches	80	30	3
Large Command Centers	80	10–30	5–10
Missile Sites	80	30–80	10
Nuclear Weapon Components	2.4	1.5	.3
Ports/Harbors	80	20–30	5–6
Radars	10	10	.3–5
Railways	80	10	5
Roads	80	80	5–30
Rockets and Artillery	30–80	10–20	.15–5
Supply Dumps	80	10	10
Surface Ships	20	20	10
Surfaced Submarines	30	10–20	1.5–5
Terrain	–	80	5–30
Troop Units	6	2	1.2
Vehicles	5–6	.6	.3

Of course, it is important to emphasize that the thresholds are not absolute—especially for monitoring in South Asia. Since India and Pakistan are already actively concealing their nuclear work, these efforts can alter the values shown in Table 8.1. India and Pakistan can make monitoring in the visible region more difficult by (1) reducing the amount of energy emitted by site and (2) decreasing scenic contrast.

These techniques can be countered through a variety of data processing algorithms. Numerous electromagnetic bands of the same scene can be combined to bring out hidden features and the contrast can be digitally enhanced.

India and Pakistan can conceal their activities not only by hiding when the satellite is looking, but also by performing their clandestine activities when the satellite is not looking. By predicting when the satellite will fly overhead, the illegal activity could cease until after the overflight.

To counter this, the satellite must have high temporal resolution as well. That is, the satellite must be able to fly over particular areas in relatively short time intervals such as once or twice a day. The temporal resolution can be increased in three ways. First, by adding more satellites to the system in various orbits, the temporal resolution of the system would be enhanced since there would be more "eyes" in the sky.

Second, the sensors can be designed to see to the left and right of its flight path (oblique imaging). The French SPOT satellite has this capability. As a result, it can take pictures of sites within an 850 km total field of view. If it did not have such an off-track capability, it could only take pictures of sites within a 60 km total field of view.[16] The increased peripheral view of the satellite's eyes enables it to revisit sites at shorter time intervals.

Third, the satellite can be designed to perform frequent and sophisticated orbital maneuvers. This way, it can rely on its own propulsion to get a closer look and also complicate efforts to predict the next time it passes overhead.

The U.S. KH-12 satellite, for example, was specifically designed to enhance its maneuverability. Although its dry weight is comparable to previous U.S. KH satellites, it contains an additional 3600 kg of fuel for its maneuvering rockets.[17]

Technically, it is clear why photoreconnaissance satellites are highly suitable for verification purposes. However, such satellites do have two inherent technical disadvantages; they cannot see through clouds nor can they see objects that are concealed by large scenic features such as the thick canopy of a jungle.

In South Asia, this technical deficiency could complicate verification efforts during the monsoon season or in dense tropical forests along the western Indian coast.[18] To compensate for the technical limitations of visible sensors, additional data should also be acquired from other parts of the electromagnetic spectrum. Each image would represent a piece of the jigsaw puzzle containing unique information about the overall picture.

Infra-red Sensors

The range of the infra-red (IR) part of the electromagnetic spectrum is approximately 40 times greater than the visible part of the spectrum. There are three distinct parts of the infra-red range that can be observed from space—the near, middle, and thermal part. The near portion is adjacent to the visible region. Near IR sensors can detect much greater contrasts in natural features such as vegetation, soil, water, and snow. The technical reason for the greater contrast is that the IR reflectance properties of these features are more distinct than in the visible region.[19] Consequently, inconsistencies in natural features are sharply shown in near IR images.

The verification implications of this technology are significant. Near IR sensors are ideal for detecting sites and objects that are camouflaged in areas such as Indian jungles. The resolution may not be adequate to identify the object, but it can pinpoint areas that require constant surveillance and the use of a variety of identification techniques such as the black box approach.[20] In short, near IR sensors cannot identify a needle in a haystack, but can detect a chameleon in a corn field.

In addition, near IR sensors can provide a limited degree of coverage at night and on cloudy days. Because the scenic contrast is greater, less light is needed to reveal details in the image.

Middle IR sensors are particularly suitable for verifying adherence to missile testing restrictions and missile employment restrictions (e.g. ban on attacking cities). During peacetime, such sensors would be most useful for verifying a limit or ban on short or medium-range missile tests in South Asia.

Burned rocket fuel emits intensely in the middle IR region. Indeed, the energy levels emitted are high enough to saturate or even damage a sensor in low Earth orbit (LEO).

Compared with other logistical parts of a missile test such as test preparations and warhead retrieval, the risk of detection and identification is highest when the actual test takes place. Although the resolution is an order of magnitude worse than in the visible region, space-based sensors in geostationary orbit can still record the missile trajectory and estimate the launch location. This is why U.S. early-warning satellites are in such orbits—continuous coverage without any significant sacrifice in performance.

Because India and Pakistan are near the equator, the missile IR signatures will be particularly salient since the missiles will be well within the line of sight of middle IR sensors in geostationary orbit.

Thermal IR sensors are suitable for the detection and identification of heat sources. The sensor can be used to verify compliance with production, testing, and deployment restrictions.

For example, thermal sensors can be used to determine whether or not a nuclear weapons production plant is active. If it is active, the data can be used to estimate how much weapons-grade plutonium or tritium is being produced and whether it is within specified limits.

Thermal sensors could also be used to reveal the presence of a "hot" mobile missile unit traveling under a "cold" forest canopy. Or the sensors could reveal the presence of heavy equipment operating under darkness to conceal secret nuclear testing preparations.

These sensors need to be located on platforms in LEO since the heat difference between the object and the background may be relatively low and since the signature may be weak and difficult to resolve.

Based on the experiments conducted for the Carnegie Endowment Nonproliferation Project, it is clear that there are many technical problems with using commercially available thermal sensors.[21] LEO thermal sensors with resolutions on the order of 100 meters are not adequate for pinpointing the heat source unless the source is surrounded by a cool background. In urban areas or facilities with multiple heat sources, this is typically not the case.

It may be possible to enhance the resolution by placing the sensor on aircraft instead.[22] The plane could then scan along the border or coastline. The effective range would be limited to approximately 330 km provided the sensors were properly cooled while in operation.

This range could cover significant portions of India and Pakistan. Approximately 70% of Pakistan's land area lies within 330 km of the international border with India or international waters. Approximately 35% of India's land area lies within 330 km of the international border with Pakistan or international waters.[23] All of Pakistan's nuclear facilities except the Chashma fuel fabrication plant lie within this thermally exposed area. All of India's nuclear facilities except the Kota power reactors and Narora power reactors lie within this thermal detection region.[24]

Radio Receivers

The best remote way of assessing activities inside a building or military vehicle is to monitor communications. Radio waves can be intercepted from ground-based, air-based, or space-based receivers. The geography of the India-Pakistan conflict is compatible with all three types of receivers. Space-based receivers are of particular interest though because such systems, if in geostationary orbit, can provide continuous coverage over all of South Asia.

Space-based receivers for electronic interception are still in the research phase within each country. The ability of space-based receivers to pick up electronic signals depends on the antenna size. For remote sensing purposes, the antenna size should be between 25 and 100 meters in diameter.[25] To fit into a launcher, the satellite is folded up like an umbrella. When boosted to its orbit, the satellite opens up into a large parabolic dish, begins receiving signals, and starts to locate transmitters.

Radio receivers can be used to verify compliance for all five general restrictions. Its comprehensive utility stems from the fact that all stages of the nuclear weapons process requires some form of communication. Of course, sensitive messages will most likely be sent through "secure" lines which cannot be tapped or where the message is encoded. Nonetheless, if one can receive the encoded message, decryption algorithms can be utilized.

Even if a message cannot be decoded, the message still may be of use. The size of the message and frequency of transmissions can reveal the amount of activity at a particular site. The duration of secure conversation can reveal the imminence of some bigger activity to come.

The environmental context of the transmission can reveal its content and thus simplify decryption efforts. For example, if a message is transmitted from a radar installation immediately after a satellite within its sight suddenly changed to a new orbit, one can infer the message concerns the satellite's orbital transfer.

Electronic surveillance is particularly useful to monitor missile activities or nuclear testing activities. Typically, test sites constantly emit radio waves. High or very low levels of transmissions can reveal the imminence of a test.

Gamma and X-ray Sensors

Although these two sensors represent distinct parts of the electromagnetic spectrum, the two are linked to one primary verification purpose—detection and identification of above-ground nuclear tests. This includes atmospheric testing and outer space testing. Nuclear tests are the only events that can be remotely monitored in this way.

Like any object, a nuclear bomb releases energy throughout the electromagnetic spectrum. For physical reasons, the explosion releases intense bursts of gamma rays and x-rays. Since there are no other natural events on Earth that emit such light at energy levels comparable to even subkiloton explosions, it is relatively easy to identify the event.

The United States took advantage of this unique nuclear signature by deploying the VELA satellite in synchronous orbit shortly after the signing of the Limited Test Ban Treaty. X-ray and gamma ray sensors are now deployed on the U.S. Global Positioning System (GPS) which, when fully deployed, will provide continuous worldwide coverage.[26]

Bhangmeters are also used to detect surface and atmospheric nuclear tests. Sensitive in the visible region, bhangmeters record the characteristic double flash caused by a nuclear explosion. Correlated with x-ray and gamma ray data, bhangmeter data can confirm that a nuclear event has taken place. Furthermore, the origin of the test can be pinpointed and the yield can be estimated.

A complicating variable in South Asia is the possibility of collaboration with existing nuclear powers for nuclear tests. There have been assertions that Pakistan has received nuclear design assistance from China.[27] One could envision cooperation in the future including a joint atmospheric nuclear test. Should this occur, Pakistan could circumvent a nuclear testing treaty by disguising its test as a Chinese one.

Remote sensing could provide evidence of a joint effort by monitoring the assembly and transport of the test bomb or by monitoring the movements of Pakistani nuclear scientists. Whatever the countermeasure, it is clear more techniques or political efforts (such as China's signing of the LTBT) would be needed to verify compliance with nuclear testing limitations in the atmosphere or in space.

Other Technologies for Monitoring Nuclear Tests

Setting collaboration issues aside for the moment, it is important to point out a variety of other technologies that can be used to monitor atmospheric tests. These technologies utilize quick and simple methods of monitoring for atmospheric tests.

Atmospheric sensors can search for large disturbances in the atmosphere caused by nuclear explosions. Electrical ripples in the ionosphere or acoustic waves from the explosion site could be recorded. With this data, the location of the disturbance could be estimated. Aircraft could be dispatched to the area to take air samples in order to find nuclear products such as cesium and strontium.[28]

India already has experience in such an exercise. In 1980, Indian scientists collected fallout samples from a Chinese test.[29] One can infer that the data may have been used for weapons design purposes.

Oceanographic Sensors

It is also important to be able to monitor nuclear tests in the ocean. The primary sensor would be acoustical. Similar to passive sonar technologies used in submarines, these sensors would be positioned at specific locations throughout the Indian Ocean including the Arabian Sea and Bay of Bengal. One can envision a network of sensors as elaborate as NATO's array in the GIUK gap.

Naval ships could be used as mobile sensors, since each side already monitors the movements of the other's naval ships. Trailing ships could be used to ensure that they are within listening distance should a nuclear test take place. If a suspicious activity is detected, the ships could then inspect the relevant site and take a series of water samples for fallout analysis.

Seismic Sensors

An underground test is the least visible method of nuclear testing because most of the evidence is entombed within the Earth. Furthermore, the underground test can be performed at just about any location since the Earth's crust is a much safer, less destructive medium to test in compared with the atmosphere, space, or underwater.

The principle method of detecting and identifying underground tests is through seismic monitoring. The explosion transfers some of its energy into the Earth, generating seismic waves that can be recorded remotely.

Seismic detection consists of the recording of a suspected test and an estimate of the location of the test. Seismic identification consists of the use of various techniques to identify the seismic event as a nuclear explosion. Four main pieces of information are needed to identify an explosion:[30] location, depth estimation, surface wave to body wave ratio, and Variable Frequency Magnitude (VFM).

The location of the event can immediately rule out the possibility that the event was caused by a nuclear explosion. If the event originated from deep in the ocean floor where there was no naval activity and where there were no acoustic signatures similar to an explosion, the possibility of a nuclear event can be ruled out.

Depth estimation is often a clear indicator of whether or not a seismic event was created by a nuclear explosion. If the origin of the signal was, for example, 70 km below the Earth's surface, one could reasonably conclude it was a natural seismic event. In general, seismic events that are below 15 km are definitely caused by natural movements in the Earth's crust. The deepest hole drilled into the Earth's crust was 10 km deep. The deepest hole for a nuclear explosion was 2 km deep.[31]

If either India or Pakistan are determined to have a secret nuclear test and are willing to drill a hole at least 10 km deep, the country's drilling operations become more vulnerable to detection because of the longer time required to drill the hole. The utility of such an operation is dubious as well, considering there are two other techniques for identifying a nuclear explosion.[32]

Checking the ratio of surface waves to body waves is a useful discriminator between earthquakes and explosions. This ratio reveals the dynamic differences between an earthquake and nuclear explosion. An earthquake is the seismic release of energy caused by the sliding of two plates against each other. As a result, earthquakes tend to emit more surface waves (shear waves in particular) than body waves.[33] A nuclear explosion generates seismic waves that spread out spherically in all directions. The dynamic is similar to the circular waves generated by dropping a rock in a pond. As a result, nuclear explosions tend to emit more body waves than surface waves.

This method of discrimination is most powerful when the source and receiver are less than 2000 km apart.[34] This is fortuitous for South Asia because each point in both India and Pakistan can be observed within this range provided the sensor arrays include detectors on the ocean floor.

Consequently, India and Pakistan can take full advantage of regional (<2000 km) seismic characteristics. Regional seismic waves are exponentially stronger than teleseismic waves (>2000 km). In addition, the receiver can collect a wealth of high frequency signals representing explosion characteristics that are inaudible at teleseismic distances.

The superpowers can only acquire such regional data over the other's respective territory by using in-country seismic stations. As neighbors, India and Pakistan inherently have the technical advantages of deployed "in-country" monitoring stations without the political disadvantages of negotiating, installing and maintaining "in-country" stations.

The Variable Frequency Magnitude method identifies an explosion by analyzing the seismic signal at two distinct frequencies. This technique takes advantage of the fact that an explosion- generated signal contains higher frequencies in its body wave than an earthquake-generated signal. The ratio of magnitudes at each frequency for each signal establishes a clear distinction between explosions and earthquakes.

In an indirect way, these identification parameters are also applicable for discriminating between chemical and nuclear explosions. Explosions in the kiloton range are definitely nuclear. It is simply impractical and dangerous to use thousands of tons of chemical explosives for industrial purposes. Furthermore, neither India nor Pakistan would want to be falsely accused of setting off a nuclear device.

Subkiloton explosions, however, can be difficult to tag as nuclear or chemical. A limited amount of discrimination can be performed by using seismology to locate the sites where chemical explosions most often occur.[35] This can be determined by calculating the frequency of explosions in the area over an extended time period and correlating the seismic information with photoreconnaissance data.

Research is also being conducted to look for unique seismic signatures of small chemical explosions. Some types of chemical explosions such as ripple explosions are common for mining purposes and could contain seismic information revealing its dynamic differences with nuclear explosions.[36]

Radar Systems

It is often desirable to have an autonomous "searchlight" which can be used to provide surveillance under the same environmental conditions at all times. Radars can provide such surveillance. These systems are particularly useful when an object or site is obstructed from view by clouds or lack of natural light.

Radars are active systems and thus require large amounts of power to operate. This is the principle sacrifice for having an all-weather monitoring capability.

Mechanically steered ground-based radars can be used to monitor compliance with missile testing, aircraft training and deployment, and general employment restrictions. If operating close to the border, these radars can be used to detect and identify missile tests. Even though an image of the object cannot be produced, the missile can be identified by observing its velocity and trajectory characteristics. Missiles have significantly higher accelerations and ascent angles than aircraft. In addition, missiles can travel to higher altitudes.

Radars can be used to monitor practice sortie missions and look for characteristic maneuvers simulating atomic bombing missions.[37] If a phased-array radar is used, it can track hundreds of different objects at the same time. The phased-array radar is capable of multiple tracking because it steers its beam electronically. Because it does not depend on a rotating emitter and receiver dish, it can scan its entire field of view in microseconds. One radar could monitor the maneuvers of squadrons of aircraft.

Such a radar has powerful battle management capabilities as well. From a verification perspective, these capabilities are necessary to monitor employment restrictions such as a ban on attacks against each country's capital. Satellites cannot provide the necessary coverage to monitor such rules during wartime. Radars, however, can provided the systems are well protected with air and missile defense systems.

Both of these radar systems do have one principal limitation. Each type cannot see distant objects hidden by the curvature of the Earth. Over-The-Horizon (OTH) and airborne radars can compensate for this deficiency.

As shown in Figure 8.6, airborne radars can extend the line of sight to areas close to the Earth's surface and under the field of view of a ground-based radar. An airborne radar such as a U.S. AWAC operating at a cruising altitude of 9.2 km (30,000 ft) can extend the field of view by 330 km. Its operating altitude also enables it to locate low flying aircraft and cruise missiles.

As stated earlier in regard to thermal IR sensors, such radars could skirt along the periphery of each country scanning 70% of Pakistani territory and 35% of Indian territory. The critical scan region would most likely be the Indian-Pakistani border. Since the radar is most suitable for monitoring of aircraft, the radars can provide early-warning and, if necessary, battle management.

For verification purposes, the radar can be used to verify compliance with deployment and employment restrictions. If a mutually agreed fighter free zone has been established as a confidence building measure, airborne radars can be used to monitor compliance with such an agreement. During wartime, the radars could be used to ensure mutual restraint on attacks against nuclear facilities. Such wartime verification (or rather, warning) could be an integral part of any future crisis management in South Asia.

Over-The-Horizon radars would be of principal utility for deep territorial monitoring. Operating at high frequencies, OTH radars can see aircraft and missiles in flight that are hidden by the curvature of the Earth. The high-frequency signal is reflected by the ionosphere back to the Earth. The return signal is then reflected back to the source. Figure 8.6 shows an OTH radar scanning for aircraft activity around a ground-based radar.

OTH radars would be most suitable for Pakistan. Pakistan could monitor Indian missile and rocket activities in southern India as well as Indian Air Force (IAF) activities in central India and along

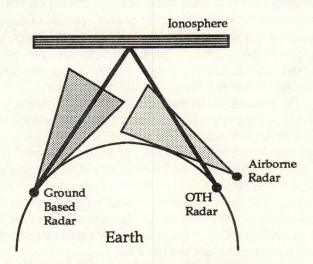

FIGURE 8.6 Coverage of Different Radar Systems.

the eastern coast. Without OTH radars, Pakistan would suffer a coverage disadvantage with respect to India. As a substitute, Pakistan would have to use reconnaissance aircraft. This would be a more difficult way of monitoring the eastern Indian coast since a Pakistani aircraft would have to fly around the Indian peninsula before scanning could begin. To perform such a mission and return without refueling, a reconnaissance aircraft would have to travel approximately 9250 km. Even U.S. and Soviet strategic bombers do not have such a range.[38]

India would also benefit from the use of OTH radars. OTH radars would provide India with full air coverage of Pakistan. It is important to add that OTH radars operate very well in coastal states such as India and Pakistan. If deployed near seawater, OTH radars can reflect signals off the sea as well thereby enhancing the strength and directionality of the emitted and return signal.[39]

Besides being used for aircraft and missile monitoring, radars can be designed to produce pictures of features on the Earth's surface. In order to get resolutions between 1 and 100 meters, these radars operate as synthetic aperature radars (SAR). The large synthetic apertures are created by the motion of the platform with respect to the ground.

The principle advantage of a SAR is that it provides an all-weather imaging capability that is independent of natural light conditions. SARs can be placed on LEO satellites or aircraft. SARs are particularly useful on satellites because such platforms provide comprehensive coverage in a relatively short period of time.

Depending on the region of interest, aircraft could provide adequate coverage. The U.S. TR-1 aircraft, for example, is equipped with a SAR and can map 450,000 sq km per hour and can see objects 900 km away from the aircraft.[40] Travelling along the Pakistan border and Indian coastline, this aircraft could image 90% of India in eight hours provided it had a sufficient amount of fuel. It could image all of Pakistan in 2.5 hours.

If based in low Earth orbit, an Indian or Pakistani SAR could acquire microwave images and immediately transmit them to the ground receiving station. This method of data transmission is possible because an SAR scanning in South Asia can simultaneously be within the line of sight of a receiving station. Direct transmission would greatly reduce the lag time of data reception as experienced by aircraft and would eliminate the need for large on-board data storage or complementary relay satellites.

Compared to the superpowers, India and Pakistan are at a significant advantage in this respect. Because the United States and Soviet Union are not regionally located, they can only transmit directly to a ground station through relay satellites.

It is important to note that a real-time link to the satellite does not mean interpreters could then immediately see radar pictures of any site in either country. All SAR data needs to be processed. Thousands of mathematical calculations must be performed to get a picture of each point. SAR data requires more data processing than any other form of remote sensing data. The amount of area covered further increases the amount of time needed to process all of the data.

To minimize data processing time, SAR data should only be used to produce pictures of areas that cannot be imaged in any other way or areas that require an additional piece for the overall jigsaw puzzle.

South Asian Monitoring Architectures

Remote sensing technologies are only regulated by the laws of physics. To serve any useful purpose, these technologies need to be configured into an overall system architecture. This technical architecture holds the system together by acquiring, combining and categorizing information, maintaining sensor platforms, and designing more advanced systems. This architecture also optimizes various parameters that take advantage of fortuitous environmental conditions such as good weather and low seismic background noise.

Each technology that has been discussed needs to be linked to the overall monitoring system. Third-party systems need to be considered as well for integration. The end result should be a skeletal structure of a South Asian remote monitoring system designed and optimized for verification purposes.

Remote Sensing Satellite Networks

India and Pakistan have working experience with commercially available remote sensing data. In addition to purchased commercial satellite images, both countries have their own ground receiving stations for SPOT and Landsat data.[41] Pakistan's is located in Islamabad and India's is located in the southern city of Hyderabad, in Andhra Pradesh. These stations can receive regional data directly from the satellites when they pass overhead. Data processing and analysis can then follow immediately. Compared with placing orders with the managing companies, EOSAT or SPOT Image, the lag time between the need for the data and the reception of the data can be reduced by weeks or even months.

In addition to having access to commercial data, India has its own remote sensing satellite. Known as IRS, this satellite has two sensors; each one can see in the visible and near IR region. One sensor has a spatial resolution of 73 m and the other has a spatial resolution of 37 m.[42] IRS spatial resolution is comparable to the U.S. Landsat series and the sensors are similar to SPOT sensors.[43]

The principle advantage of IRS is that India has full control of the satellite's functions and orbit. India does not have to wait in line for service nor does India have to sign any licensing agreements. In addition, India's access to remote sensing information is not at the mercy of foreign government or company budget cuts that shut down the information service.

Further enhancing its autonomy, India has its own data analysis, photographic processing, and reproduction facilities.[44] To avoid lines for deploying satellites, India has its own space program that is capable of launching payloads of approximately 800 kg into low Earth orbit.[45] Pakistan does not have its own satellites nor its own fully operational launch facility. Pakistan is in the research phase in both of these endeavors.

Nonetheless, even though India is ahead in building its own remote sensing system in space, both countries are still in the infant stage of development. Serious system design issues remain and short-term and long-term objectives with respect to verification need to be defined.

To remotely verify compliance with any of the five restrictions stated earlier, remote sensing satellites would be needed. The question is how many satellites are needed, what sensors should be placed on each platform, where should the satellites be deployed, and how can the satellites be deployed.

If both countries play their technical cards correctly, the space-based system architecture shown in Table 8.2 could prove sufficient for verification purposes. The proposed architecture would provide each country with an all-weather multispectral imaging capability from space and continuous coverage for monitoring communications, missile testing, and nuclear testing. The system would also provide redundancy should a satellite malfunction.

As shown in Table 8.2, the imaging satellites are divided into two principle types—high resolution and low resolution. This specifically refers to the sensors that can see in the visible region and SARs that can see in the microwave region. Based on the data in Table 8.1, the low-resolution sensors would have a resolution between 30 meters and 80 meters. Its primary mission would be the detection of suspicious activity. To fulfill its mission, the detection platform should also have thermal IR sensors and a SAR with 30–100 meter resolution.

The high-resolution sensors should have resolutions between .3 and 5 meters. The high-resolution platform should carry near IR sensors, thermal IR sensors, and a SAR with 1—10 meter resolution. In addition, the high-resolution platform should be able to rotate its sensors. With this capability, the satellites could take pictures at various angles, providing the ability to point the sensors at suspicious sites and the necessary data for three-dimensional imaging.

One low-resolution platform would work with one high-resolution platform. Each platform would be configured in different orbital planes so that the high-resolution platform could fly over the same area that the low-resolution platform flew over a few hours earlier.

Once deployed in this manner, the satellites would operate as a pair in a search-and-track mode. For technical reasons, the low-resolution platform would have a large field of view (see Figure 8.7). Taking advantage of this, the platform would take pictures of

TABLE 8.2 Space-based System Architecture for India and Pakistan

Purpose	*Sensors*	*Orbit*	*No. of Satellites*
Imaging	Visible, Near IR, Thermal IR, SAR	LEO (Polar)	2 – Low Resolution 2 – High Resolution
Above-ground Nuclear Test Monitoring	Visible, x-ray, gamma ray	Geostationary	2
Electronic Interception	Radio	Geostationary	2
Missile Test Monitoring and Early-Warning	Middle IR	Geostationary	2

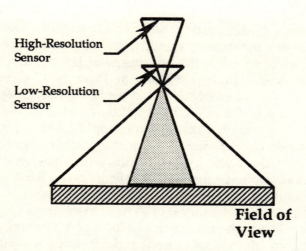

FIGURE 8.7 Field of View of High and Low-Resolution Satellites.

an area comparable in size to Sri Lanka. The data would be directly relayed to a ground station for analysis. Since India and Pakistan are adjacent to each other, no relay satellites would be needed because the satellite would take pictures while it was within the line of sight of the country operating it or just before it would come into view of a ground-based or ship-based receiving station on the next revolution.

Before the high-resolution satellite approached the area, photointerpreters would examine the data and detect suspicious activities. A few hours later, the coordinates of these sites would be relayed to the high-resolution satellite in order to catch the potential violator "in the act." Using the relayed information, the satellite would move its sensors to take a closer look at the suspicious activities. It must do this because the high resolution sensor does not have as large a field of view as the low-resolution sensor (see Figure 8.7).

Once in range, the high-resolution sensors would take more detailed pictures of the detected activities. Whether it images all of the recorded anomalies in one pass depends on the number and distribution of suspicious activities. The data is then relayed to the ground station for processing, analysis, and interpretation.

Figure 8.8 illustrates the search-and-track method for monitoring a ban on short-range missile deployments. The method optimizes the technical features of each type of sensor through

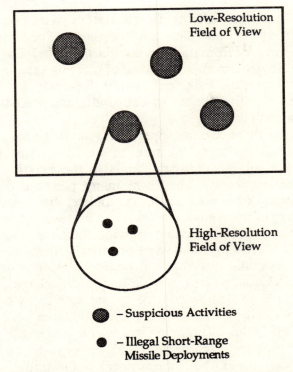

FIGURE 8.8 Search-and-Track Method (View from Satellite over Scene).

combination. Neither satellite alone could provide enough data for verification purposes.

Like the SPOT satellite, a satellite pair could revisit an area every four days.[46] If this revisit period is considered too long, it can be reduced by deploying the second satellite set in a different orbit. With two sets of high and low resolution satellites in operation at the same time, the revisit period could be reduced to one or two days.

By combining commercially available images with their own network, India and Pakistan could operate an even larger space-based system, capable of multiple visits per day. To take full advantage of commercial satellites as well, both countries would have to distribute their LEO assets in a way that minimizes spatial and temporal overlap.

It is even possible for India and Pakistan to obtain direct or indirect access to images from other nations including the

superpowers.   After all, it is consistent with superpower
nonproliferation policy and there are precedents.   The United States
has provided imagery from military satellites to Israel, England, and
Canada.   The Soviet Union is suspected of offering satellite imagery
to Argentina during the Falklands War.[47]   Recently, the U.S. may
have provided satellite images to both India and Pakistan during
their 1990 Kashmir crisis.

Some form of access to superpower intelligence resources
would enable India and Pakistan to build on not only the
commercially available network, but also the existing military
reconnaissance network.   There are many possible degrees of
assistance ranging from none at all to complete, direct access to all
satellite imagery of the region.

For instance, the U.S. could provide Pakistan with its own
military satellite.   Using the design of older systems such as the
KH-1, the U.S. could develop and deploy photoreconnaissance
satellites for Pakistan as part of a military aid package.   Pakistan
would then have exclusive control of the satellite's operations
including daily orbital maintenance and exclusive access to the
imagery,[48] altering this information in a way that does not seriously
compromise electronic-gathering and decryption techniques.
Nonetheless, there could be circumstances in the future where the
superpowers consider acceptable the risk of compromising ELINT
(ELectronic INTelligence) capabilities.

The Soviet Union could make a similar satellite arrangement
with India.   Or the Soviet Union could provide images at digitally
degraded resolutions of a few meters.   Such resolution would be
very useful to India and, at the same time, would protect Soviet
secrets and exclusive access to higher quality images.

A lesser form of cooperation could be indirect.   Instead of
providing the images, the superpowers could use their own
intelligence resources to process and interpret the images.   They
could then provide India or Pakistan with hints concerning where to
search and what to look for.

America and the Soviet Union could also provide information
gathered from electronic interception.   There is precedence for this
level of international cooperation as well.[49]   However, the sources
of such information and the associated decryption capabilities would
be difficult to conceal.   There is no technical way of packaging or
altering this information in a way that does not seriously
compromise electronic-gathering and decryption techniques.

Nonetheless there could be circumstances in the future where the superpowers consider the risk of compromising ELINT (ELectronic INTelligence) capabilities acceptable.

Table 8.3 lists third-party systems that could be integrated into India's or Pakistan's satellite architecture.[50] Whether these systems are actually included depends primarily on political and diplomatic factors.

At the very least, third-party systems can discourage illegal endeavors. India and Pakistan have several reasons for not being

TABLE 8.3 Third-Party Systems for South Asian Verification

Country	System	Civilian, Military	Resolution (meters)	Spectral Region	Likely Client	Likely Access to Data
U.S.	KH Series	Military	.3	Visible, Near IR	Pakistan	Direct if degraded; Indirect
U.S.	ELINT Series	Military	–	Radio, Microwave	Pakistan	Indirect
U.S.	Missile Launch Detection	Military	–	Middle IR	Pakistan, India	Indirect
U.S.	Landsat series	Civilian	80, 30	Visible, Near IR	Pakistan, India	Indirect
USSR	Cosmos Series	Military	.3	Visible, Near IR	India	Direct if degraded; Indirect
USSR	ELINT Series	Military	–	Radio, Microwave	India	Indirect
USSR	Missile Launch Detection	Military	–	Middle IR	India	Indirect
USSR	KFA	Civilian, Military	5	Visible	India	Direct
France	SPOT	Civilian	20, 10	Visible	Pakistan, India	Direct
Canada	RADAR SAT (SAR)	Civilian	25	Microwave	Pakistan, India	Direct
Japan	ERS–1 (SAR on board)	Civilian	25	Visible, Microwave	Pakistan, India	Direct
Japan	MOS–1	Civilian	.9	Visible	Pakistan, India	Direct

held responsible for starting an arms race in South Asia. Should either country violate an arms control agreement, it would undermine the country's professed non-nuclear stance. An Indian violation would undermine its legitimacy as a regional power and its leadership in the non-aligned movement. A Pakistani violation would damage its ties with the United States and would place the country against a superior Indian nuclear force.[51] Third-party systems can deter noncompliance because the violator can never be certain if a third-party witness will publicly testify against him or her or will secretly provide evidence to his or her adversary.

An additional method of acquiring data from third-parties is through their manned space programs. The United States and Soviet Union regularly conduct manned missions into LEO. Through political agreements to take Indian or Pakistani astronauts on-board for remote sensing purposes, India and Pakistan could occasionally acquire high-resolution images of South Asia. They would be able to take high quality pictures because manned mission orbits are typically closer to the Earth's surface than the orbits of remote sensing satellites with long projected lifetimes.[52] With respect to the Indian satellite IRS, the U.S. space shuttle can be 750 km closer to the Earth. If an Indian astronaut used the IRS sensors to image the Earth from the shuttle, the resolution would be 10 meters instead of 37 meters.

For practical reasons, manned missions would not be a systematic verification approach. Nonetheless, it can be a useful component and could foster further international cooperation in space and remote sensing.

Satellite Design

Once a space-based system design has been defined, the next step is to design the sensors. Table 8.2 lists the different types of sensors that are needed for particular applications. India and Pakistan can base their sensor designs on their past experience with other remote sensing data and the objects that need to be monitored.

For instance, based on their Landsat and SPOT experience, they can infer what type of sensor parameters are needed to obtain certain types of data. In fact, they can acquire a significant amount of public information on Landsat and SPOT designs and use this information to assist their own efforts.

Once each country has come up with a design, the machining technologies need to be developed. These technologies are critical for the construction of sensitive components such as the mirrors and on-board calibration systems.

For missile detection purposes, they can use their experience with their own short and medium-range missile programs to design middle IR sensors that can detect such missiles. For above-ground nuclear testing, they can, ironically, use their own bomb models to predict x-ray and gamma ray emissions. Based on the predictions, they can design the sensors accordingly.

For electronic interception, the principle design parameter is size. Large parabolic antennas need to be designed to collect and integrate weak radio emissions. Furthermore, for logistical reasons, these antennas must be designed to fold up in order to fit in a rocket payload and reopen when deployed.

For SAR design, India and Pakistan can obtain past U.S. SAR data from SEASAT, SIR-A, and SIR-B or current data from Canada's RADARSAT. India could obtain SAR data from the Soviet ALMAZ radar or possibly Soviet RORSATs. With experience handling existing data, India and Pakistan can not only design the radar, but also develop techniques for timely processing of the massive amount of SAR imaging information.

Launch Facilities

Once satellites have been designed and developed, they must be boosted into orbit. Based on the U.S. and Soviet experience with multisensor remote sensing satellites, the booster must be able to lift at least 3000 kg.[53] The miniaturization of electrical components has not significantly reduced the weight of satellites.

Neither Pakistan nor India has such as lift capacity. In the long-term, they have to develop their own launch capability. The Soviet space program is the best model for India's and Pakistan's rocket development.[54] That is, each country should develop crude, low technology boosters, produce them at high production rate, and use them at high annual launch rates.

In the short-term, India and Pakistan could contract out for a lift capability. The United States, Soviet Union, France, and China are all prospective candidates for boosting Indian and Pakistani satellites. In the past, India has worked with three of these countries (U.S., France, and Soviet Union) to boost their satellites.[55]

All four nations have experience with boosting remote sensing satellites in LEO and geostationary orbit and all four have solicited for satellites to deploy in space.[56] The privatization of the U.S. space industry and the ever growing Japanese space program could open up even more space opportunities for India and Pakistan.

Air-Based, Sea-Based, and Ground-Based Systems

The design of air-based, sea-based, and ground-based systems is simpler than a space-based system. However, the amount of resources needed to establish them is of the same order of magnitude.

India and Pakistan would need airborne radars similar to the U.S. AWACs and airborne SARs similar to the TR-1. These platforms are needed for tactical verification missions such as monitoring compliance with aircraft training restrictions and artillery deployments along the Indian-Pakistan border.

As a complement to these systems, both countries need advanced computer hardware and software to process the information. These systems are as important as the radars. For example, using 1984 SAR data processing hardware and software, it would take 1 hour of computer time to process a 10000 sq km image. This translates to 360 hours or 15 days of computer time to process SAR data of 90% of India and 5 days to process SAR data of all of Pakistan. With the most advanced systems, the computer time can be cut down to 15 hours and 5 hours respectfully.

To scan the entire Indian coast, Pakistan must develop extensive refueling capabilities to support its reconnaissance aircraft. As an alternative, Pakistan could design high-altitude SAR balloons towed by navel vessels. This approach would alleviate the fuel problem, but it would also increase the amount of time required to scan the area. Furthermore, Pakistan would lose the element of tactical surprise which is a critical component of a verification regime that is dependent on sampling rather than continuous coverage.

For sea-based monitoring, both countries can utilize their naval resources. As stated earlier, passive sonar technologies can be readily applied for monitoring nuclear testing activities at sea.

Unfortunately, these technologies cannot be used to verify a ban on nuclear weapons at sea. As the superpowers have learned through experience, there are no current remote sensing technologies that can reliably verify a ban on nuclear weapons at sea.[57]

To monitor missile and aircraft activities, India and Pakistan need an extensive ground-based radar network. Specifically, India and Pakistan need to deploy a mix of conventional, phased-array, and OTH radars to ensure complete and continuous coverage of the adversary's air space. With such a network, each nation could verify missile or aircraft restrictions with a high degree of confidence.

Seismic Monitoring System

Pakistan has four known seismic stations and India has 19 known seismic stations.[58] One of Pakistan's stations and two of India's are part of the Worldwide Standardized Seismograph Network (WWSSN).[59] WWSSN stations have common sets of instruments so that the quality of the data is the same.

Seismic stations worldwide are very well networked and they routinely exchange data with each other. *As a result, a basic infrastructure to monitor a ban on underground nuclear tests in South Asia currently exists.*

Technical assistance also exists. There are several international sources of seismic data and analysis on underground nuclear tests. In addition to the U.S. Geological Survey, geological institutions in other countries such as Sweden and Norway routinely monitor and report on nuclear tests worldwide. The Swedish Ministry of Defense annually publishes reports on nuclear testing.[60]

As noted earlier, in order to obtain regional seismic coverage in South Asia where the source to receiver distance is less than 2000 km, sensor arrays have to be placed on the ocean floor. Specifically, Pakistan would have to place sensors around the Indian peninsula. The sensors could then be linked to a receiving station by underwater cable. Or Pakistan could deploy ships to collect batches of seismic data. The former approach is more efficient in data collection and the latter approach is less vulnerable to sabotage.

In the area of regional seismic monitoring, India and Pakistan could lead the way in the design of effective regional seismic systems. As stated earlier, because of their geographic proximity, India and Pakistan will primarily be monitoring for seismic events within a 2000 km radius of the receiver. A significant amount of seismic research still needs to be done for monitoring within this range.[61]

Because the superpowers have dominated seismic research efforts, most research has been done for teleseismic (>2000 km) monitoring. However, there is now interest in in-country stations for both the United States and Soviet Union.

The technical parameters and variables inherent in South Asian seismic monitoring would be similar to the dynamics that would be experienced by in-country stations. In exchange for teleseismic data originating from South Asia, India and Pakistan could provide invaluable data and research on short-range seismic dynamics. With such an exchange, the superpowers could use South Asia's empirical data and first-hand experience to design in-country networks and India and Pakistan could use traditional teleseismic techniques as well to verify compliance with a ban on nuclear tests in South Asia.

Conclusions

India and Pakistan are on the verge of joining the nuclear club. They have already entered the bilateral nuclear arms control club and now are entering the adjoining verification club. I have outlined the membership requirements to this last club.

As with their covert nuclear programs, India and Pakistan need to coordinate a comprehensive remote monitoring program. With respect to verification, both countries need to determine how remote sensing technologies can contribute to their security and how the systems can be developed and deployed.

The United States made this assessment in 1954 under the Eisenhower Administration.[62] A decision to develop and deploy an extensive remote monitoring and support system followed shortly thereafter. Nine years later, the system was built.

India and Pakistan can build their own systems within nine years as well provided each government embarks on a Regional Verification Initiative. Such an initiative would require a political commitment comparable to the 1954 Eisenhower decision, an economic commitment comparable to Reagan's Strategic Defense Initiative, and a technical commitment comparable to the Manhattan Project.[63]

A Regional Verification Initiative would also require a parallel commitment to nuclear arms control in order to preclude system designs that are optimal for offensive military missions and to prevent military spin-offs from civilian technical endeavors. For example, without a mutual commitment to limitations on missile flight tests, there could be no identifiable distinction between Indian and Pakistani space programs and ballistic missile programs.

The nine year estimate is partially a function of the level of foreign assistance offered directly or indirectly to India and Pakistan. India would need indirect aid such as access to advanced technologies from the United States, Europe, and Japan. Pakistan would need direct assistance because Pakistan's indigenous defense industry currently cannot handle the Herculean tasks associated with a verification initiative, especially the space components.

Pakistan could seek direct assistance from its close allies such as the United States and China, or Pakistan could solicit for satellites from other nations. For example, consistent with their arms export policy and economic interests, France or Brazil could custom design intelligence-gathering satellites for Pakistan and sell them for a profit.[64] Creating a remote sensing market would extend the technical aspects of a South Asian verification initiative beyond the region thereby transcending the inherent industrial limitations of the area.

The U.S. experience in designing a remote sensing system is a reasonable basis for assessing the feasibility of a similar effort in South Asia. Even though India and Pakistan do not have the technical or human resources that the United States had in 1954, both countries have and are familiar with post-1954 technologies. They can use revolutionary technologies such as semiconductors and optical data storage that were not available in 1954.

Like the U.S. pool of German scientists and U.S. Army electrical engineers in 1954, India and Pakistan have their own pool of missile experts and remote sensing experts. Furthermore, they are in the fortuitous historical position where they can learn from other nations' successes and failures in their respective programs and realize which routes will hit dead ends. Analogous to Japan's economic history, India and Pakistan can take remote sensing concepts from the superpowers, modify them, improve them, and build on them.

As noted earlier, the nine year time scale assumes each government will allocate the necessary funds to build a remote monitoring system or will receive financial aid from other nations.

It is difficult to estimate the total cost because the overall architecture would be significantly different from existing ones.

However, one can estimate the cost of some of the main components. Based on the cost of U.S. satellite systems, India and Pakistan will each have to allocate approximately U.S. $4.2 billion to build all of the satellites shown in Table 8.2.[65] Based on the cost of U.S. radar installations, India and Pakistan will each have to allocate approximately U.S. $1.8 billion to build a comprehensive ground-based radar network.[66] In addition, money would have to be appropriated for building and maintaining the following:

- Space Launch Capability
- Airborne Radar Systems
- Seismic Arrays
- Sonar Arrays
- Data Processing and Analysis Facilities

Considering the enumerated cost estimates, it is clear that the space-based component of the remote sensing system would be the largest investment with no guarantee of a security return. Like most political and technical endeavors, the risk is unavoidable. However, the overall investment can be reduced (in the short term) through the introduction of creative alternatives. The emerging NATO-Warsaw Pact model of "Open Skies" is a relevant example.

Chemical weapons are considered the poor man's nuclear bomb. Air monitoring can be considered the poor man's verification instrument. The development and operational costs of airborne platforms are comparable to the cost of building and maintaining a new airline or squadron of fighter aircraft, a burden that is much less cumbersome than an intensive space program.

Airborne monitoring can be an effective short-term substitute for satellite monitoring. It is an internationally mature science. Because aerial surveillance is performed 1-25 km above the sites of interest, it can provide images with as much scenic detail as U.S. satellite imagery.[67] As part of a South Asian "Open Skies" agreement, aerial surveillance can be performed throughout Indian and Pakistani territory. It could be used to provide close looks at critical sites and facilities. Coupled with commercial satellite data, aerial monitoring could be effectively used to investigate suspicious activities detected by large-scale visual sweeps.

Of course, the effectiveness of airborne monitoring primarily depends on the degree of airborne intrusion that is politically legitimized. Issues such as inspection quotas, methods of transit to sites, aircraft maintenance, while in a host nation, notification times, permissible sensors, and data distribution would have to be included in the Open Skies agreement to each party's satisfaction.[68]

India would be most concerned with the permissible sensors and data distribution since Pakistan could obtain direct technical assistance from the United States and thus gain a qualitative edge in imagery. Pakistan would be most concerned with the quotas and aircraft maintenance while in the host nation. Because India is larger than Pakistan, Pakistan would require a greater number of inspections in order to have the same spatial probability of verifying compliance. In addition, Pakistan would require aircraft refueling within India in order to monitor activities in portions of eastern India.

As with the acquisition of nuclear weapons, the creation of a verification system is not an end in itself. The key to real security is the lack of physical threats and psychological reassurances. Arms control can eliminate threats. Verification regimes can provide the psychological reassurances. Both go hand in hand.

Bilateral arms control and verification in South Asia is consistent with U.S. nonproliferation policy. It is a fresh regional approach for obtaining nuclear security in South Asia. Like the decision to "go nuclear," South Asia will ultimately make the decision on whether or not to "go arms control." Remote sensing will not make arms control in South Asia certain. But it will make it possible.

Notes

1. Although their suspected nuclear weapons capabilities have been extensively publicized in the United States, India's and Pakistan's remote sensing capabilities have not. Nor have the technical issues of remotely verifying the disclosure clause (Article II) in their agreement to prohibit attacks against the other's nuclear facilities been addressed.

2. Indeed, territorial claims between the two countries remain unresolved. Rodney Jones, "India's Nuclear Strategy: A Threat to World Peace?" *Nuclear, Biological, and Chemical Defense and Technology*, Vol 1, No. 2, 1986, p. 68.

3. One can imagine the metaphysical need to verify the restrictions in the verification agreement.

4. The U.S.-Soviet experience in negotiating a comprehensive nuclear test ban is exemplary of how tenuous the link between monitoring systems and verification can be at times.

5. The details of each side's remote sensing capabilities will be discussed later. Though their capabilities are not as extensive as those of the superpowers, each has its own satellite receiving station and seismic monitoring networks.

6. The origin of some of these steps can be traced to Allan Krass' book, *Verification: How Much is Enough?* (London: Taylor & Francis, 1985), pp. 8-10.

7. W.E. Burrows, *Deep Black: The Secrets of Space Espionage* (New York: Bantam Press, 1986), p. 96.

8. There are satellites that contain additional electromagnetic sensors such as gamma ray sensors and x-ray sensors. I shall use the traditional definition of "photoreconnaissance" and will discuss later the other type of sensors that can fit on space-based platforms.

9. Leonard Spector, *Nuclear Proliferation Today* (New York: Vintage Books, 1984), p. 119.

10. Ground resolution is also considered the primary performance parameter for sensors that can see in other parts of the electromagnetic spectrum.

11. Burrows, p. 241.

12. Michele Chevrel, Michel Courtois, and Gilbert Weill, "The SPOT Satellite Remote Sensing Mission," *Photogrammetric Engineering and Remote Sensing*, Vol. 47, No. 8, August, 1981, p. 1164.

13. Peter Zimmerman, "From the SPOT Files: Evidence of Spying," *Bulletin of the Atomic Scientists*, September, 1989, p. 25.

14. Bhupendra Jasani and Toshibomi Sakata, eds., *Satellites for Arms Control and Crisis Monitoring* (Oxford: Oxford University Press, 1987), p. 15.

15. This includes my own experience in analyzing satellite data. Peter Zimmerman comprehensively addresses the Handy Book's accuracy. Peter Zimmerman, "A New Resource for Arms Control," *New Scientist*, September 1989, pp. 38-43.

16. Off-track viewing can also be used to create three-dimensional pictures of a site. This technique is one of many counters to concealment tactics. Michele Chevrel, et al., p. 1168.

17. John Pike, "Verification and Space Weapons," paper presented at the Technologies of Arms Control Verification Course at Imperial College, London, U.K., September 1988, p. 5.

18. *Webster's New World Atlas* (New York: Prentice Hall Press, 1987), p. 15.

19. Krass, p. 30.

20. Near IR sensors are often placed on platforms with visible sensors. Working with low-resolution cameras, near IR sensors perform wide area searches for suspicious activities. If detected, the suspicious activities are singled out for a closer look with high-resolution sensors.

21. Leonard Spector, "Monitoring Nuclear Proliferation," Manuscript, 1989, p. 22.

22. *Ibid.*, p. 23.

23. *Webster's New World Atlas*, p. 118.

24. I correlated the World Atlas political and geographic map with a map of each nation's nuclear facilities. David Albright and Tom Zamora, "India,

Pakistan's Nuclear Weapons: All the Pieces in Place," *Bulletin of the Atomic Scientists*, June, 1989, p. 23.

25. This is based on U.S. electronic interception satellites. Pike, pp. 30–32.

26. Krass, p. 79.

27. Albright and Zamora, p. 21.

28. Fallout sampling could also be used to detect and identify underground nuclear tests. As the U.S. and Soviet Union have experienced, fallout sometimes leaks out of the hole and crosses international borders.

This is even more likely in South Asia. India and Pakistan have little or no working experience with underground testing. Furthermore, India's Pokhran test site and Pakistan's suspected Chagai Hills test site are only 240 km and 570 km from the international border. Keeping a released fallout cloud from crossing the border would be difficult and would largely depend on the seasonal wind patterns.

29. Albright and Zamora, p. 26.

30. Paul Richards, "Seismic Methods of Verifying Test Ban Treaties," Department of Geological Sciences, Columbia University and Lamont-Doherty Geological Observatory, pp. 16-18.

31. Lynn Sykes and Jack Evernden, "The Verification of a Comprehensive Nuclear Test Ban," *Scientific American*, October 1982, p. 49.

32. Even the use of existing holes drilled for tapping oil sources would not be advantageous for the same reason.

33. Body waves primarily travel deep below the Earth's surface.

34. Richards, p. 18.

35. Of course, seismology cannot reveal efforts to disguise a nuclear explosion as a chemical explosion. Other sensors including nuclear emission sensors would be needed to monitor potential masking sites such as mines and quarries.

36. Ripple explosions are a series of small chemical explosions. *Seismic Verification of Nuclear Testing Treaties*, OTA-ISC-361 (Washington, D.C.: U.S. Government Printing Office, May 1988), pp. 85–86.

37. The tactics of atomic bombing can be considered a separate military discipline. Lewis Dunn, *Controlling the Bomb: Nuclear Proliferation in the 1980s* (New Haven: Yale University Press, 1982), pp. 42–43.

38. *Soviet Military Power* (Washington, D.C.: U.S. Government Printing Office, 1987), p. 36.

39. Kosta Tsipis, *Arsenal* (New York: Touchstone Books, 1983), p. 248.

40. Krass, p. 49.

41. "Satellite Ground Receiving Station Opens," *FBIS-South Asia*: Islamabad Domestic Service in English, August 17,1989. Leonard Spector, "Keep the Skies Open," *Bulletin of the Atomic Scientists*, September 1989, p. 16.

42. Jasani and Sakata, p. 18.

43. For additional details of Indian remote sensing and space launch capabilities see Akhtar Ali, Chapter. 9 in this volume, note 32.

44. *Ibid.*, p. 154.

45. *Ibid.*, p. 70.

46. Chevrel, et al., p. 1169.

47. Jeffrey Richelson, "Military Intelligence—SPOT is not enough," *Bulletin of the Atomic Scientists*, September 1989, p. 26.

48. To prevent conflicts with other U.S. security interests, the U.S. could include an electrical switch on the satellite so that it would be "on" when the satellite was over South Asia and "off" when it was over other areas such as the continental U.S. or Diego Garcia.

49. Peter Wright, *Spycatcher* (New York: Dell, 1987), pp. 188–194.

50. Part of Table 8.3 is based on data from Jasani and Sakata, eds., p. 15.

51. A.F. Mullins, "Proliferation in South Asia: The Military Dimension," (Livermore: Lawrence Livermore National Laboratory, Manuscript, n.d.), p. 6.

52. If placed too close to the Earth, a satellite will eventually fall because atmospheric drag will slow it down. Manned missions are usually of short duration or utilize boosting in order to counter drag effects.

53. This was the weight of the U.S. KH-1 satellite. Compared to other satellites of its kind, the KH-1 was a light satellite.

54. The U.S. satellite program is the best model for India and Pakistan. Each country should develop multisystem satellites with lifetimes on the order of one or two years.

55. Jasani and Toshibomi, p. 35.

56. *Ibid.*, p. 31.

57. Such deployments could be detected through the interception of communications. However, this is not a systematic method of assessing whether or not the seas are nuclear free.

58. These stations routinely report to the U.S. Geological Survey. *Seismic Verification of Nuclear Testing Treaties*, p. 65.

59. *Seismic Verification of Nuclear Testing Treaties*, p. 64.

60. Richards, p. 3.

61. *Ibid.* p. 21.

62. Burrows, pp. 69-72.

63. A Regional Verification Initiative could contain cooperative components. For example, India and Pakistan could build a satellite receiving station that was optimally located for both nations. The station could be run jointly with no restrictions on access to imagery and the use of data processing and interpretation facilities. To preclude division within the jointly operated station, Indian and Pakistani personnel could be organized into small, working groups assigned to a variety of projects.

64. Leonard Spector originally proposed that Pakistan could contract out for a satellite. Workshop on Verifying a Regional Nuclear Agreement, University of Illinois at Urbana-Champaign, November 15, 1989.

65. The estimates are in constant 1987 dollars and are based on the cost of the U.S. Vela, KH-9, KH-11, Rhyolite, and DSP-I satellites. Pike, p. 3.

66. This assumes the construction of three early-warning radars, three phased-array radars, two OTH radars, one ship-based, phased-array radar, and two spacetrack radar. Pike, p. 3.

67. Michael Krepon, "Open Skies: Money in the Bank," *New York Times*, February 19, 1990.

68. To see how the NATO-Warsaw Pact model addresses these issues see "Open Skies: Basic Elements," *NATO Review*, December, 1989, pp. 27-28.

9

A Framework for Nuclear Agreement and Verification

Akhtar Ali

Let me at the outset predict that there is no immediate prospect for a nuclear agreement between India and Pakistan. Indeed, there does not seem to be any pressing need for one, however desirable this might be. Many proposals are there, a number of them tabled by Pakistan. The real inhibiting factor appears to be the Indian elite's romance for military power and the "Bomb" and the not-yet-ready-for-the-marriage syndrome between India and Pakistan. There is no frenzy in the air, despite a not very pleasant political climate between the two countries. The initiatives, launched by Prime Ministers Benazir Bhutto and Rajiv Gandhi have succumbed to the political instabilities of both countries.

On the other hand, the two states are not likely to jeopardize a rather tricky nuclear equilibrium, which may not exactly be a balance. Indeed, two years back I wrote my second book on the subject asking the question in its title, *South Asia: Nuclear Stalemate or Conflagration?*[1]

Two years have passed and it is heartening to note that nothing of a rash nature has happened. The stalemate persists, and may well continue for quite a while. Indeed, stalemate might sound like a negative term, perceived as belittling by the Indian elite while the Pakistan elite may declare it to be a success, creating pressures for the other side to annul it. And since a stalemate can be resolved by dialogue, surrender or even conquest there may be merit in avoiding its resolution. There is usually a tremendous desire on the part of

265

the parties to a stalemate to change the status quo, either by dialogue, surrender or conquest. The best alternative for India and Pakistan may be stalemate. Yet, there could be movement in the direction of containing or capping the evolving nuclear capabilities in the two countries in a multilateral context if the current superpower arms control initiatives are successful. In a post-proliferated context, one could also conceive of certain kinds of bilateral agreements to stabilize or contain the nuclear competition. However, the right moment may not have come for such agreements, not because of willingness on the part of the two countries but because a declared nuclear deployment has not taken place. So, although South Asia has elements of a post-proliferation environment, there are no deployed nuclear forces or even nuclear doctrines. Such alarmism has utility in the sense that it is directed towards the decision-makers in the U.S. and other Western countries and creates pressures for more appropriate policies. While governments (especially the U.S. and other Western states) have many sources of information to verify the accuracy of news and statements (indeed for many they are the source themselves) the elite in the affected countries have no access to such facilities. Even if the information is impartial from the perspective of the competing parties, the information is believed selectively by the recipients. Thus, Pakistanis might give more credence to the views of India preparing to make a second nuclear explosion or a thermonuclear one, while ignoring equally alarming news about the nuclear activities of their own country, on the grounds that they are inspired the "anti-Muslim" media. Indians do the same, understanding that the West favors client states such as Pakistan and acts against a "non-aligned India." So even a balanced activism may create pressures instabilities.

Despite the loud, though often legitimate, concerns of many critics, the nuclear status in the subcontinent has come to be seen as stable. India exploded its nuclear device in 1974 and has not indulged in a provocative nuclear act since then, although its nuclear capabilities have increased. Pakistan announced the commissioning of its uranium enrichment facility at Kahuta in 1984, and, contrary to many forecasts, has abstained from rashly demonstrating its nuclear muscles. With the passage of time, people in the subcontinent seem to be getting used to the existence of the dangerous capabilities across the border. The much talked about preemption by either country has not taken place, and has indeed been averted by an agreement not to attack each other's nuclear facilities. Thus, there is a sufficient empirical evidence (15 years in India and 5 years in Pakistan) that an undeployed rudimentary nuclear competition may be stable, although one could still speculate that a deployed rudimentary nuclear competition may be unstable.

Indeed, the sources and agents of instability, if any, came from outside the region in the form of alarmist forecasts by the nonproliferation community. Year after year, their forecasts have proved incorrect. So people have learned to live with not only dangerous nuclear capabilities, but also with all kinds of alarmist and half-verified information. The nonproliferation community in the U.S. needs to adopt a less activist approach in favors of a more realistic effort, at least in so far as South Asia is concerned. Although South Asia has survived such campaigns, it is not certain that it will be able to do so in the future, and thus the need of some transparency between the two countries.

The arms control debate in the U.S. has been skeptical of verification largely because of the closed Soviet sociopolitical system, while the USSR has opposed verification on the grounds that U.S. interest in "intrusive" verification stemmed from desires to collect intelligence. Because *glasnost* and the increasing transparency of the Soviet Union has enabled the latter to drop its objectives to verification activities which were earlier considered unduly intrusive, cheating and break-out scenarios are given much less credence. Indeed, verification is being dubbed as the "last resort" of the hawks, who oppose arms control *per se*. Certainly increasing technological capabilities have played a role in enhancing the credibility of verification.

Meanwhile, the global understanding of the politics of a near-nuclear or threshold-nuclear environment has matured. In the early seventies, many bizarre scenarios were offered of how a country could circumvent or cheat the IAEA safeguards system, and thus acquire a few kilograms of fissile material and convert it into a nuclear weapon, and possibly smuggle it into a major U.S. city, forcing America into submission. But the evidence is that those countries that have acquired fissile material have not "immediately" converted it into a bomb, let alone threatened to detonate it on an adversary. It has also been seen that fissile material has been obtained from unsafeguarded dedicated facilities rather than diverted from recognized civilian safeguarded programs.[2]

It is now generally acknowledged that a few bomb-equivalents of fissile material, untested and unaccompanied by an overt deployment and delivery system has hardly any political value, while bizarre scenarios at least for the purpose of the countries in question (Pakistan, India, Argentina and Brazil) have receded into the background.[3]

Thus more realism on the part of the American academic-policy circles and among the non-proliferationists and the rehabilitation of confidence in IAEA safeguards is a welcome development which would ultimately go a long way towards finding a solution to the nonproliferation issue.[4] Considerable developmental work has gone into new safeguards technologies in the meantime, e.g., on-line safeguards, etc. With the implementation of new safeguards technology, IAEA's material accounting safeguards methods are expected to improve even further. However, it is expected that no safeguard regime or technology can be absolutely fool-proof against small diversions of questionable political value.

It is a welcome development that the Pakistani point of view is better understood now than in the late 1970s and early 1980s. For a considerable time, the Indo-Israeli axis had belabored the following two themes:[5]

• The Islamic Bomb syndrome, which attempted to project a larger political and strategic context to Pakistan's nuclear efforts than a strictly South Asian one.
• The Indian bomb-lobby, for a considerable period, succeeded in popularizing the view that Pakistan's nuclear effort antedates that of India, that it was an independent one and that it was not a consequence of India's nuclear activities, especially the latter's nuclear explosion in 1974.

Neither themes is now generally accepted. It is recognized that Pakistan's nuclear efforts have a purely South Asian character and have emanated solely as a reaction to India's nuclear activities. There is a greater appreciation of legitimate Pakistani security concerns with an Indian nuclear monopoly. The two countries have gone to war three times and a consequence of the last conflict was that Pakistan was divided into two. India's political attitude toward its smaller neighbors other than Pakistan have also induced within the international community a more realistic and meaningful perception of the geopolitics in South Asia. India's military acquisitions and preparations are increasingly perceived in a larger threat context than South Asia. All of these factors, largely of India's making, led the world community, especially U.S. policymakers, to a more sympathetic (or less-hostile) attitude toward the modest Pakistani nuclear program.

Furthermore, Pakistan's policymakers have consistently attempted to prevent the nuclearization of the region and have lobbied for many nonproliferation proposals.[6] In all, six proposals have been made by Pakistan over a period of more than a decade. These have enjoyed support irrespective of the type of government ruling in Pakistan—democratic or military. Indeed, the military rulers have shown more readiness for a nuclear agreement. Pakistan's proposals have included:

- Establishment of a Nuclear Weapon Free Zone NWFZ in South Asia (1974).
- Joint declaration renouncing nuclear weapons (1978).
- Mutual inspection of nuclear facilities (1979).
- Simultaneous adherence to the NPT by both countries (1979).
- Simultaneous acceptance of IAEA Safeguards, in case there is an ideological or philosophical reservation to the NPT (1979).
- Bilateral/regional nuclear test ban (1987).

India's response has varied from ambivalence to irritation.[7] There are many reasons for India's lack of interest, indeed opposition. First, a large lobby, finds all such proposals to be variants of the NPT, which Delhi finds discriminatory. Indians argue that nuclear weapons are a global problem and thus should be tackled at a global level. Second, there are nuclear weapons in the region, e.g., Chinese nuclear capability and the traffic of U.S. naval ships carrying nuclear weapons into the Indian Ocean has been cited in India—notably the *USS Enterprise* episode. Third, dealing with Pakistan is perceived as belittling and tantamount to being equated with smaller powers. Fourth, there is a romanticization of the role India could play in the world. In this folklore, nuclear weapons are at center stage. Finally, nuclear weapons are an important currency of power; India, as a large country, is entitled to having such power projection capabilities for political purposes in the region and beyond.[8]

Linkage of Global Arms Control Agreements

Admittedly, India's nuclear program has been partly motivated by the spiraling nuclear arms race between the two superpowers. Nehru was a genuine supporter of disarmament. It is certainly not he who gave approval to a weapon-based nuclear program, which culminated in the 1974 explosion and subsequent related activities. Immediately after signing the NPT, and thereby undertaking to enter into serious negotiations for worldwide nuclear disarmament, the two superpowers entered into expanded nuclear and conventional arms races. Not only were the promises made under the NPT put aside, but the multi-lateral context of disarmament negotiations, although for partially understandable reasons of technical expertise, sensitivity and others, was considered spurious. Half-hearted arms control measures were taken in a bilateral context but led nowhere. In this context, the incentives for weaponization by lesser powers were accentuated. However, the situation has begun to change. It may have a dramatic impact on the regional nuclear scene. The process started with the INF treaty, which is being successfully implemented. It may be that present nuclear restraint in South Asia is partly traceable to the INF treaty, which for the first time resulted in meaningful reduction of nuclear weapons.

If the post-war nuclearization was led by the super powers, they must also take the lead of denuclearization. In an atmosphere of global reductions in tension and armaments, it would be difficult for regional elites to push their militaristic ambitions and over-zealous expansive politics. Further, the domestic popular base for weaponization may shrink. Despite this optimistic forecast, it is not plausible that India would agree, before 1995, to enter into any meaningful regional nuclear arrangement (other than certain CBM understandings). It is imperative that certain multilateral initiatives be undertaken which could be implemented on a global scale and thus eliminate the discrimination bottleneck. The following proposals might lure India and other threshold nuclear states (TNS) into binding agreements, which would not totally denuclearize them but could help contain and cap their nuclear capabilities. These are:

- Put all nuclear material production facilities in the world, without any distinction or discrimination between nuclear weapon states and non-nuclear weapons states, under IAEA safeguards.
- Ban the production of weapon grade fissile materials under IAEA safeguards without distinction or discrimination.[9]
- A Comprehensive Test Ban Treaty, prohibiting all nuclear tests on a global scale.

A global IAEA safeguards regime seems to be the most feasible, of the three, although expensive. A differentiated material accounting approach, risking discrimination sensitivities, may reduce its costs. With all such ongoing negotiations on the reduction of nuclear weapons, weapon grade fissile material may become redundant. Global cessation of HEU and plutonium production might be opposed by non-nuclear weapon states with active breeder and reprocessing programs, e.g., France, Germany and Japan. West Germany has problems maintaining even a conventional nuclear power program in the face of active domestic political opposition, and the French breeder program has entered into technical difficulties. An agreement might be possible if the major countries involved are convinced of the arms control or nonproliferation advantages of the proposal and even the TNS may agree under global moral and political pressure. This still does not solve the problem of existing fissile material stockpiles in the TNS, but would at least arrest any increase in such inventories.

Fortunately or unfortunately, nuclear power has acquired new appeal in the wake of evidence of the greenhouse effect. In the U.S., the nuclear industry has still to come up with a demonstrably safer and environmentally more acceptable nuclear technology. But domestic opposition to nuclear power is practically non-existent in Japan and France. In other countries of Western Europe, convincing greenhouse arguments may mellow the not too-strong resistance to nuclear power. In the circumstance of a revival of nuclear power, reprocessing and breeders may also acquire a new appeal, and thus resistance to proposals for the cessation of HEU and Pu production. However, it is conceivable that since safer commercial breeder technologies are not currently in sight, an agreement could be reached on the proposal as it would not hamper the development of conventional nuclear power.

For a variety of reasons a CTB offers the maximum opportunity to cap and contain proliferation for the TNS which are non-signatory to NPT. For over thirty years, a CTB has remained on the active arms control agenda of successive U.S. presidents. Most initiatives were thwarted because of differences on verification, its type, frequency and duration, etc. Moreover in the U.S., the reliability of verification regimes has often been questioned. However, now that the Soviet Union has come to see on-site inspection as more acceptable, there is in the U.S. a renewed emphasis on the need to continue testing. The arguments range from reliability, effectiveness, R&D, and even that explosions attract new blood to the waning weapon designer community.[10] The fact of the matter is that President Reagan wanted to launch a massive arms-build up program, for which testing was obviously required for developing new types of weapons.

The CTB concept offers the following merits for wider acceptance:

- It is comprehensive and non-discriminatory (unlike the NPT which divides the nations into nuclear haves and have nots).
- It does not restrict the development of civilian nuclear technology.
- It is much less intrusive in terms of verification.
- It has a much wider global acceptability than the NPT.
- It has been assumed to be the collateral obligation of NWS under NPT article VI.[11]

India has supported the idea of a CTB and it is expected that it would sign such a treaty. However, India might have supported it knowing that it would not be signed by the superpowers, providing India an excuse not to sign the NPT or any other non-proliferation proposal. The counter argument is that CTB has never been a weak case. Its chances of success have always been rated as considerable.

India may be able to avoid signing a CTB, even if the superpowers reach an agreement—if China does not accede. Beijing has historically opposed any attempt to cap the evolution of capabilities of new nuclear states. It has even opposed the NPT. Until the Tienanmen Square episode, however, it was understood that PRC had begun to act cooperatively with respect to the NPT.[12] However, India should have many incentives to sign a CTB. It is politically very difficult to ignore an agreement which it has been advocating for a long time; further, a CTB would leave India with a degree of freedom, in terms of its ability to enhance its dual-use nuclear capabilities, which a nonproliferation regime does not permit. India would thus have a rather mixed status, whereby on the one hand it is enhancing its capabilities but on the other hand is not able to demonstrate them. This is the kind of situation, which to my judgement, matches rather closely with the mind set of Indian elite policymakers.

It is understood that if India determines that developing and deploying an overt nuclear force is in its national interest, going back on earlier promises may not be seen as too large a to pay. But if an Indian leadership wants to restrain its nuclear program while still retaining freedom for technological open-ended development, the Indian bomb lobby would find it difficult to oppose a CTB.[13]

CTB Verification Prospects

We have earlier argued that the verification issue has considerably different dimensions and perspective in a small nuclear force environment where the issue is less complicated and thus more amenable to agreement. In the context of CTB verification, the following should be kept in mind:

- Geographical contiguity offers a locational advantage for seismic monitoring stations.
- Additional stations would be available in other countries of the region i.e. Bangladesh, Nepal and Sri Lanka.
- There would be certain overlaps in an almost global monitoring system for a CTB.
- CTB opponents in the U.S. have argued that low yield (1-5 KT) explosions could escape monitoring. With the existing nuclear know-how of the TNS including India (In fact India is the only country which has the experience of having conducted

at least one explosion), low yield explosions are probably not technically feasible and are therefore irrelevant in the present circumstances.

A CTB's political feasibility and wider acceptance (excluding the U.S.) is its major strength, if not the only one.[14] It is clear that it may not prevent nuclear proliferation in the sense that the NPT is meant to, but a CTB would certainly reduce the pressures to proliferate, and freeze the status quo in the TNS. For acquiring and deploying a credible nuclear force, many nuclear explosions are required. The fact that there have been 1700 nuclear explosions in the postwar period and that the main residual reason for American resistance to CTB is the perceived need for testing, is testimony enough for the slowdown impact of the treaty on horizontal and vertical proliferation.[15]

The move by NNWS parties to LTBT for converting the latter into a CTB is an interesting one. While it is premature to make a judgement on the prospects of such a move, the three depository NWS (i.e. the U.S., the UK and the USSR) have concurred on the convening of the amendment conference. While the peculiar amendment mechanism providing the NNWS with leverage is a source of irritation and even perhaps embarrassment to the NWS (especially the U.S.), the very peculiarity may be instrumental in leading some of the most problematic states, like India to accept and abide by a test ban agreement.[16] There is considerable political support for a CTB in the U.S., in the form of a strong and favorable public opinion, and sizeable support in both the Senate and the House. Except for Reagan, successive U.S. presidents have sought an agreement on CTB. It is quite possible that after a successful CFE and START, the residual opposition of the Joint Chiefs of Staff and the weapons labs might become manageable, paving the way for a CTB agreement.

The Role of Nuclear Power

Technology and trade control policies of the industrialized countries have a mixed record of success and failure. There is no doubt that such policies have largely constrained the nuclear programs of both India and Pakistan. Although India's nuclear program is largely self-contained, it does require some critical inputs from abroad. Heavy water has been a major source of difficulty despite having erected several heavy water production plants. Most of these have severe operational and safety problems and work intermittently at very low capacity utilization rates. At the end of 1989, India has an installed and operating nuclear capacity of 1360 MW and another 1320 MW is under various stages of construction, expected to come on-stream by 1997. It is alleged that, except RAPP I and RAPP II, whose safeguarded heavy water is imported from Canada and the USSR respectively, the rest of the capacity could not have been brought into operation without illegally or secretly importing heavy water.[17] It is doubtful that India will have an operating nuclear power capacity of more than 3000 MW by the year 2000. Until recently the predictions were that 5000 MW could be achieved by the end of this century as against a target of 10,000 MW.

The story of Pakistan's nuclear power program is even more dismal. In the wake of the oil price shock of 1974 and the consequent world-wide euphoria for nuclear power, Pakistan drew up a rather grotesque and unrealistic plan of installing 20,000 MW of electrical power, almost one reactor per year on the average, by the turn of the century.[18] Pakistan later revised these figures to a more realistic figure of 6000 MW of nuclear power. Over the last fifteen years, Pakistan has invited bids for a 900 MW light water reactor. No bidders have turned up, largely as a result of quiet American opposition, as it is well understood that the financial package required to implement a project of this size could be arranged without the considerable interest and support of American dominated world capital markets and multilateral financial institutions.[19]

Pakistan suffers from an acute shortage of energy, especially electrical power. One of its major conventional (hydro) energy projects (Kalabagh Dam), projected to come on stream in the early 1990s to provide 3600 MW of electrical power, has been a subject of furious domestic controversy involving differential resource and environmental impacts of the project on different provinces.

Thus India and Pakistan face considerable power shortages; outages and brown-outs are common in both.[20] However, it is

difficult to convincingly demonstrate that the power shortages are
due to the restrictive trade and control policies of Western countries.
Power wastage, leakage, inefficiency and lack of financial resources
to sufficiently invest in power projects are the main reasons in the
short and medium term, but energy resource scarcity could be a
major bottleneck in the long run—and thus the rationale for nuclear
energy. Indeed it may be argued that had capital-intensive nuclear
technologies been adopted, the financial crunch might have been
greater.

Paradoxically, dedicated fissile material production capabilities
have increased over time in both countries. Nuclear trade controls
could not hamper Pakistan's uranium enrichment project at Kahuta,
and India has installed new reprocessing facilities. India's installed
reprocessing capacity has reached a figure of several hundred kg of
Pu per year, most of it installed in the 1970s and 1980s. The
empirical evidence, however scanty, is that trade and technology
controls have hampered the erection of civilian nuclear facilities
rather than the establishment of dedicated dual-use nuclear facilities.

The question is, would Pakistan have been more amenable to
international pressures, had it been in the midst of a burgeoning
nuclear power program, where continued operations would have
depended on foreign inputs and assistance? As for India, it has
consistently refused to enter into a dependency relationship even at
the expense of substantially slowing down its nuclear power
program. The situation may, however, be changing as recent
economic policies seem to be more efficiency-oriented than
autarchic.

Those Pakistanis who argue for a bomb capability for Pakistan
oppose the installation of nuclear power plants as it would enhance
the foreign leverage on Pakistan's nuclear activities. Thus there is a
need for a more differentiated policy requiring separate yardsticks
for TNS, as distinct from those countries whose nuclear industries
are not so relatively well developed. Although this issue appears
academic under the present circumstances of stagnating and even
decaying nuclear power industries in the West, the question may yet
become relevant. As we have discussed elsewhere, there are signals
for the rehabilitation of nuclear power in the U.S. due to an almost
certain existence of the greenhouse effects of burning fossil fuels.
Furthermore, serious R&D is continuing for small and safe reactors.

It is expected that the technology may be ready for commercial operation by the turn of the century. Such smaller and safer reactors would make a lot of sense in the developing country environment, as opposed to the existing 1000 MW standard, too large for a typical grid system in a developing country.[21]

In those TNS which are denied nuclear power reactors, the only possible and useful work left for their large nuclear establishments appears to be the involvement in precisely those nuclear activities which technology denial policies aim to discourage. It would be a more pragmatic policy to enhance dependencies by supplying nuclear power facilities to such TNS, while restricting such technologies to other less-developed countries, at least until the political problems are resolved.

Verification and Intrusiveness

Intrusiveness should not be a significant factor in the verification regimes of the threshold nuclear states.

Neither secrecy nor espionage arguments apply, at least not so severely, to the threshold nuclear states. These countries are relatively more open, albeit with varying degrees of freedom, and should not fear the social or political consequences of large scale and frequent visits of foreign inspectors, or even the permanent stationing involved in an elaborate verification system. Nor are these countries at the frontiers of technology, where there could be legitimate fears of the leakage of industrial secrets. However, in a bilateral verification regime, competitive arguments do apply, e.g., enrichment technology is at a relatively advanced stage in Pakistan, while reprocessing has a similar comparative status in India. But the reciprocal nature of verification inspection should have a balancing impact on the leakage calculus. The intrusiveness argument should not be entertained with any seriousness in the TNS environment.

But non-intrusiveness could be useful in a situation where the two rival countries do not reach a political agreement on a bilateral or multilateral verification scheme which involves on-site activities. In such a case, a non-intrusive verification infrastructure (satellite or seismic monitoring) provided by a multilateral framework (e.g. Canada's PAXSAT) could be useful as a confidence building measure, defusing a potential arms race among regional rivals.

Verification Technologies and
Institutional Arrangements

Four types of monitoring and verification are applicable to TNS environments, including India and Pakistan: (I) nuclear material accounting-based IAEA safeguards, (II) remote-sensing, (III) seismic monitoring, and (IV) on-site inspection.

For NNWS, IAEA-type safeguards are usually adequate to verify that no diversion of nuclear materials is taking place for any possible military applications. In order to be effective, full scope safeguards, i.e., monitoring all stages of movement of nuclear materials, are essential. NWS are not subject to this kind of nuclear material accounting, nor does any known bilateral arms control agreement involve such a scheme. But in a TNS environment, where several unsafeguarded nuclear materials producing facilities have been in operation, the threat of secret and undeclared military activities contrary to a formal agreement or a voluntary restraint framework may exist. Such a threat could exacerbate adversary suspicions, possibly instigating a declared or secret development and/or deployment of proscribed weapon systems. Types II, III and IV provide a way to deal with such situations. These technologies and procedures have been extensively involved in superpower arms control practice and negotiations. Ideally, in a TNS environment, all four techniques would be required to various degrees and levels of intensities. Types I and IV are intrusive and require cooperative behavior of the participatory states in a bilateral or multi-lateral context. Type I has earned the encomium of being a variant of NPT safeguards. It is highly unlikely that in the immediate future, India would subscribe to these.

Type III does not technically require cooperation between participatory states, although provisions for cooperative verification would be very effective and desirable. Earthquake monitoring systems are in place in both India and Pakistan and a great degree of international cooperation and interaction exists in this field in the form of data flow and analyses. It may not be out of place to suggest that the relevant inexpensive and widely available monitoring assets already exist.[22] We have discussed other relevant aspects elsewhere in reference to a CTB.

In the following, we will take up the application of remote-sensing technologies for arms control verification and for maintaining a confidence-building regime. Although these technologies and the associated hardware are very expensive, there could be a number of channels through which the TNS, including India and Pakistan, could have access. Except for the superpowers, NTM and, all other schemes are at various stages of evolution and the last one, involving the SAARC organization, is proposed here. Although national remote sensing capabilities are at various stages of development, and while India has already lofted a satellite in this respect, the performance and capabilities of such systems would remain inadequate for the purpose under discussion for a long time to come.

The Threat of Transparency

While open skies offer a unique means of promoting and acquiring transparency, it could be a double edged sword because of inability of sensors to see inside buildings, under water or underground, environmental and weather limitations, orbital and coverage constraints, data processing and other limitations on technical expertise, budgetary constraints, and camouflage and deception.

In a technologically less sophisticated monitoring theater, undue suspicion could arise from a false sense of confidence in monitoring capabilities. Despite highly sophisticated monitoring apparatus, assisted by collateral intelligence collection programs, the U.S. still demands on-site inspection for monitoring compliance with many kinds of arms control agreements. A multilateral framework in a much less sophisticated monitoring environment may generate "false transparency" and could be a source of instability. Before suggesting or transferring any technological panacea, an explicit delineation of the limits of such a system seems highly advisable. Also, a third-party system of interpretation services might be necessary in a situation where indigenous capabilities are still evolving, as with India and Pakistan.

Space based remote sensors are being increasingly used for both civilian and military purposes. These have played a significant role in promoting transparency and building confidence in superpower context. It is expected that their roles would expand to other geographical areas. A possible arms control or confidence-building regime in South Asia could involve one or more of the following;

- Co-operative use of superpower NTM.
- UN based ISMA (International Satellite Monitoring Agency) concept.
- Multilateral treaty-specific (Canadian) PAXSAT concept.
- Use of and reinforcement of commercially available remote sensing facilities.
- SAARC-based civilian remote sensing.

Finally an anti-thesis is in order. If monitoring and verification technologies do not give reliable results and prove to be excessively expensive, resource-allocation debates in the TNS may conclude that "a cheap and dirty nuclear deterrent may be handy."[23]

Cooperative Use of Superpower NTM

The superpowers have been known to be cooperating with each other through their national technical means in monitoring and preventing nuclear proliferation. Attention to a possible South African preparation for an underground nuclear test was initially drawn by the Soviet space monitoring infrastructure, which in turn was followed up by the U.S.[24] NTM have also been used at an informal level in the form of leakages to the press, regarding the creeping nuclear capabilities of India and Pakistan, which have in turn brought about pressures on the two countries.[25] The feasibility of a quasi-formal mechanism of the two superpowers involving India and Pakistan as recipients of data and information, in a more reliable and organized manner, in bringing about and maintaining a confidence-building regime should be investigated. A quadrilateral, diplomatic information flow would diffuse the pressures which may be generated over time due to misinformed suspicion regarding the shifting technological spectrum in the two countries. The credibility of this system would depend on the degree or lack of political opportunism or bias displayed by the two superpowers and as well as the degree of openness in terms of sharing and disclosing their capabilities. An evolving transparency between the two superpowers should further facilitate matters in this respect.[26] This would not require, often unavailable, cooperation between India and Pakistan, in the form of a bilateral or a multilateral treaty, agreement or arrangement.

An International Satellite Monitoring Agency (ISMA)

The idea of an ISMA, operating under the auspices of the UN, was first proposed by the French president Giscard d'Estaing. In fact the idea is not new; it has been discussed since 1961 in one form or the other, for enhancing transparency and thus stability and security. A UN study was conducted in 1982[27] to examine the feasibility of the proposal,concluding that it could be done and that there was no legal problem in satellite monitoring, as satellites operate beyond national airspace limits. France, Sweden and Canada and Switzerland have shown substantial interest in this issue. The superpowers have not shown much interest in the proposal for many reasons. Although the proposed monitoring structure would observe military activities around the globe, its political attractiveness, economic justification and viability would depend on U.S.-Soviet cooperation. The satellite system has been pursued, though, with substantial commitment by Canada, which has come up with a slightly different framework named PAXSAT (discussed below).

While the UN framework is particularly efficacious for global acceptance, it poses regarding the confidentiality, of sensitive installations of the major powers. Regionalization of the agency framework has thus been proposed. France has been particularly interested in a European Space Agency, which, interalia, should perform the monitoring task. There is a divergence of opinion on the functions and responsibilities of ISMA; some would restrict its functions to surveillance and data gathering for confidence-building, transparency and verification monitoring of arms control agreements, while others would extend it to assessment functions and even crisis monitoring and management. The developing countries have proposed that civilian remote-sensing functions may also be included, while others argue against the over-lapping of functions.[28] The nature of the debate indicates that the proposal is still at a preliminary stage and much work needs to be done to bring it to the level of implementation. An evolution and sustenance of the recent amiable political climate between the two superpowers, and consequent agreements on arms control and confidence building may give a new acceptability to the ISMA concept, within or outside the UN framework. Moreover, while the need for on-site inspection has been largely accepted by the Soviet Union, the U.S. may have little incentive left for downgrading the value of satellite monitoring in arms control verification. Indeed a mix of OSI and satellite monitoring might ultimately prove to be a technically, economically and politically acceptable verification regime.

Thus, if and when a global satellite monitoring system is brought about in an ISMA framework (or some other arrangement), it could be utilized for South Asia, and indeed even adopted for a conventional-weapons agreement. Insofar as the collection and dissemination of data is concerned, a formal agreement between India and Pakistan may not be required. The most attractive aspect of an international approach would be its economics; such services could be charged to the participating or recipient countries on a marginal basis or such costs could be picked up by the extra-regional sponsoring parties. An alternative concept of ISMA, in my view, could be a confederation of regional agencies like the proposed ESA, PAXSAT or SAARC.

Canada's PAXSAT

Advancements in commercial remote sensing technologies and the emergence of a whole set of possible arms control proposals among the superpowers, European countries and in other parts of the world have motivated Canada to introduce the PAXSAT concept, in the wake of stagnation of the ISMA proposal. The third party verification concept has received support from major European countries such as France, Sweden and Switzerland. Although the focus of the proposal is Europe, it is not restricted to the latter alone. The initiators of the proposal are discounting the umpire role of third party (non-superpower) verification, possibly to ward off the opposition of the affected countries. The ultimate strength of such a system might indeed be precisely this role. PAXSAT would provide a context of specific multilateral arms control agreements rather than being open-ended.[29] It would also permit implementation of verification procedures by treaty parties themselves, rather than a supra-national organization. Although open to the superpowers, a PAXSAT arrangement would enable independence from them.

Canada is one of the two original major suppliers of nuclear technology to South Asia. All of the unsafeguarded Indian power reactors are of Canadian CANDU design. Canada is thus motivated to play an active role in promoting verifiable nuclear arms control agreements. Indeed, South Asia might be a test-bed for the development of more elaborate structures and technologies for Europe.

Use of Commercial Satellites

The surveillance and military uses of commercial satellites are rapidly evolving. SPOT's coverage of Chernobyl and the use of LANDSAT data by the publishers of *Soviet Military Power* have enhanced the awareness and significance of such capabilities. Although the U.S. LANDSAT has been in business since the early 1970s, commercial satellite imagery has been advanced by the start-up of France's SPOT in early 1986. Currently SPOT, LANDSAT and (Soviet) SOYUZKARTA provide earth-imagery services of resolutions in the range of 10- 20 meters, 30-80 meters, and 5-10 meters respectively.[30] Japan also intends to enter this business, with their latest ERS-1 launched in 1988, with a 25 meter resolution. In all, some 24 such satellite systems are planned for launch during 1990-2000. Commercial success will depend on time schedules and resolution, in addition to pricing. Military or surveillance uses are more demanding in terms of scheduling and resolution. For such surveillance and verification uses often a resolution of less than a meter could be required, depending on the nature of object/target and the purpose of the exercise. In some cases, resolution requirements may be relaxed, i.e., 1-5 meters.

The necessary technology now exists, and it is outside superpower control. How soon it could be converted into a service depends on market forces. Verification requirements could certainly develop the required market pressures for the installation of such services and capabilities. Global competition would bring prices further below the not-very-high level today and may put verification capabilities within the economic reach of major regional states.

However, investments would have to be made in ground equipment and data-processing facilities. Indeed such investments have already been made by India and Pakistan. Ultimately, a mix of commercially available international and national facilities could provide dual-use civil and military services.[31]

SAARC Remote Sensing and Verification

The substantial remote sensing interests, involvement and capabilities of India and Pakistan have been described elsewhere.[32] There is a genuine case for cooperation among the regional countries in civilian remote sensing, as resource bases, environment and meteorological factors spill beyond political boundaries of the countries. The differential in expertise of India and Pakistan and the relatively much lesser capabilities in other countries of the region, e.g., Bangladesh, Nepal and Sri Lanka, would indeed make regional cooperation more meaningful and realistic. The world community is increasingly aware of the deteriorating global ecology, and any major international initiative in this respect would have to enlist the cooperation of South Asia, where alone one billion people live. There is a case for promoting and supporting regional remote sensing in terms of financial aid and technology, over and above the present levels of such flows from the industrialized countries, especially the U.S. We have argued elsewhere for the need to integrate South Asia, particularly India and Pakistan, closely to the world system, for channeling and providing alternative routes for fulfilling national ambitious and aspirations. Hopefully, if an initiative is taken in this respect by the U.S., SAARC regional remote-sensing could be one of the most important and significant projects. In such a scheme of things, one would expect that the acquisition of relevant verification sensing, data gathering, and analysis hardware and software assets, which have a high degree of overlap with civilian applications anyway, would be promoted. Indeed a mix of PAXSAT, an American initiative, commercial satellites, a SAARC system and the national capabilities of the region could bring about greater transparency, whether for an arms control verification regime or as a CBM measure. It is highly desirable that a feasibility study be commissioned, in the near future, to examine and work out the salient features and requirements of such a system.

Post-Proliferation Agreements

No-first-use pledges or policy announcements do have a stabilizing role, diffusing the pressures for preemption. In a SNF environment lacking a second strike structure, no-first-use could have even more significance.[33] A "no first-use" pledge or agreement is actually a nuclear non-aggression pact, and therefore has to be preceded by a conventional non-aggression pact. Pakistan has made a proposal to India for signing a pact on non-aggression, to which India has made a counter proposal of signing a treaty of friendship, the latter requiring some stipulation. Negotiations are underway for a mix of the two proposals. It is inconceivable that a country would abide by non-use pledges or agreement if an adversary is marching into its territory using conventional weapons. A nuclear no-first-use agreement could spell out the specific conditions (i.e., conventional attack, possibly specifying certain technical conditions) under which adherence to the agreement would not be expected. In this manner conventional peace may be brought about by nuclear weapons.

In a post-*glasnost* environment with a liberated Eastern Europe and an effective confidence-building regime in place in Europe, the need for first-use, on the part of NATO or the U.S., may wither away. Already, the classic doctrine of "massive retaliation" has been watered down by the doctrine of flexible response. The most plausible argument against no-first-use, is that if nuclear deterrence brings peace, more may be better; why dilute it with such pledges, when there are inherent pressures against usage due to the soberly understood consequences of even a limited nuclear war. In a SNF environment, circumscribed by a hierarchical world order, where the superpowers and major industrial states manage world affairs to a large degree, the political pressures in favor of non-usage, and having to bear the stigma of initiating a nuclear conflict should be the major restraining elements.

Pakistan's situation in the subcontinent is almost similar to that of Western Europe vis-à-vis the Soviet Union. One should therefore anticipate Pakistani inhibitions regarding a no-first-use pledge once nuclearization actually takes place in South Asia. One may question the rationale of diluting the deterrence advantage, when the menace of nuclear weapons has been invited anyway, against international advice and pressure. The Indian bomb-lobby's eagerness towards "no-first-use" should be understood in this context.[34]

While it may be very problematic to bring about a force structure compatible with a credible and reliable no-first-use for a variety of reasons, an evolving SNF environment could implement a mutually agreed force structure. Although there can be no absolute guarantee of "no-first-use" (except by reciprocal control of each other's permissive action links, which is preposterous), any mechanism which elongates the period between the decision to use nuclear weapons and their actual use, and possibly provides early warning of such an event, would create pressures against the break-out from the no-first-use pledge or agreement. The following mechanisms are possible:

- Ban development and production of ballistic missiles of a certain payload, range or design.
- Ban land and sea deployments of missiles.
- Cooperative installations of early warning systems on the other's nuclear-capable craft (ballistic and aerodynamic).
- Separating warheads from delivery vehicles and the installation of EW on warhead storage facilities.
- Finally, deployment of nuclear delivery vehicles (missile silos) away from bordering regions (e.g., 500 km away).

India is in the midst of implementing an ambitious space program which has been discussed elsewhere. It has successfully launched an IRBM (*Agni*) with a range of 1500 km. India has persistently claimed that its space program is for peaceful purposes,[35] and has consequently enjoyed U.S. (NASA) assistance. However, with mounting successes, Indian incentives to loudly emphasize and reassure world opinion of its peaceful claims are growing weaker. The satellite launch vehicle is not exactly a working ballistic missile or a prototype. Substantial, though not insurmountable, problems are to be solved for the development of re-entry vehicles and guidance and control systems. Because of technological and political problems with its ballistic missile development program, India is expected to be content for some time with a satellite launching capability. This would cater to the prestige requirements. Thus the idea of a mutually agreed ban on the production of ballistic missiles may be politically feasible from the point of view of India's acceptability criteria. The proposal does not interfere with keeping the nuclear option open, does not hinder technology processes and promotes a "no-first-use" regime, and thus creates stability. Indeed this has a nonproliferation dimension in terms of bringing about qualitative limits on delivery capabilities. The shortcoming of the proposal is its intrusive, almost permanent stationing of inspectors at production facilities and the continuing possibilities of clandestine facilities.

A ban on missile deployment achieves the same result as a ban on development and production; in addition it may be easier to verify with much less intrusive means. Indeed, satellite monitoring and limited challenge on-site inspection might be adequate for reliable verification. The ban on deployment at sea raises other verification problems. It should be noted, however, that under this scheme of things, there is no restriction on nuclear weapons deployment on aircraft, with consequent perils and opportunities. With the installation of a cooperative early warning system at the appropriate products, equipment and facilities of the adversary, the regime may become more credible and thus possibly stable. *However, it should be noted that, in so far as a ban missile production is concerned, the time for initiating negotiations for an agreement is now, for Indian development of reentry vehicles can be prevented at this stage.* Even for a ban on the deployment of ballistic missiles, one could argue for an early initiation of negotiations, as such an agreement may discourage the related developmental activities. It is obvious that India would not accept such limitations in a purely disarmament context. A highly coordinated political-economic package may possibly bring India round to a negotiating stance on any proposal meant to limit its nuclear dreams, activities and ambitions. This aspect has been discussed in detail elsewhere.

Installation of an early warning system could be implemented as part of a missile production or deployment ban, or independently. In the latter case, EW could be installed on ballistic missiles themselves, aircraft and warhead storage sites. The fourth proposal, separating warheads from aircraft and ballistic delivery vehicles, may be too intrusive in terms of verification, although mechanisms for early warning against mating of warhead and vehicles could be automated to a substantial degree. Lastly, deploying nuclear delivery vehicles away from borders would also be useful for cooperative deployment of ballistic missile defense (BMD) systems.[36] It should be noted that to implement such proposals, active superpower technical assistance may be required, in itself a limitation of sorts.

Arms Control as Legitimation

While arguing or striving for a nuclear agreement, one should keep in mind the legitimizing role of such agreements. In the superpower context, many argue that most of the arms control treaties have permitted even higher ceilings on weapon systems, than there would have been without an agreement. The INF is the only agreement which has resulted in any meaningful reduction of nuclear weapons. On the other hand, this stigma on arms control may disappear with successful negotiation and implementation of START. Nevertheless, in South Asia, the process of negotiation of a nuclear agreement (and most probably with some kind of an interaction or influence of outside powers, especially the superpowers), may bring out in the open and thus legitimize some capabilities which are considered objectionable by the international community. One should therefore ask; is the risk and uncertainty of an ambiguous nuclear regime better than the certainties of declared nuclear capabilities?

Persuading India

There is an almost total impasse on the subject of a nuclear agreement in South Asia. India, it appears, has neither an incentive nor the inclination to enter into such agreements. Indeed there is no pressure on it to begin negotiations. Only a well-timed and coordinated diplomatic offensive by the superpowers, or the U.S. and other major industrialized countries with Soviet support could induce India to move in this direction. Such a campaign would have to be a balanced one, incorporating disarmament measures, a technology-economic package, and diplomatic and political pressures.

Fortunately, the superpowers are moving in the direction of disarmament. With START, CFE, a chemical weapons ban and even possibly a CTB, militarization and nuclearization may become less fashionable. This would give Washington and Moscow some moral authority to argue for disarmament elsewhere. India may also join other global agreements such as global cessation of the production of fissile material or global IAEA safeguards, as discussed above. At some stage, multilateralization (as opposed to the current bilateral process) of disarmament negotiations becomes imperative. India could be encouraged to play a leading role in this. In such a process, it would be politically very difficult to sustain a belligerent, uncompromising stance. This would also make irrelevant the argument of the necessity of possessing nuclear weapons in order to have a place around the negotiating table. One would also hope, in an environment of global disarmament that political pressure to divert resources from the military sector to the more pressing economic needs of a largely poor populace, could alter India's course.

A Technology-Economic Package

Despite an abundance of mutual-admiration clubs in the subcontinent, proposing toasts to India's industrial and scientific achievements and its rising middle class, and to Pakistan's high regional per capita income ($350), there is uneasiness about South Asia's relative backwardness. The economic miracle of ASEAN is often cited with admiration but also with a sense of loss and deprivation. Mr. Rajiv Gandhi's recent economic policies of liberalization, as opposed to protection and autarchy, point in this direction. Given the influx of seed resources, it may be possible to duplicate the miracle of ASEAN in South Asia, and unleash a process which could satisfy the aspirations of regional elites. Until now, with a $150 billion budget deficit in the U.S. and similar fiscal problems in most of the Western countries, talk of major economic initiative in a generally low-priority region has been unrealistic. With the expected reduction in military expenditures, and even the emergence of Eastern Europe as a major focus of economic aid, one might reasonably expect that such an initiative could be launched by the mid-1990s. Environment, social services, natural resource management, and aid and trade in commodities and technology could be the major focus of an international effort to integrate the region. In a number of areas, enlightened self-interest of the donors would also be served.

The participation in a regional technology-economic package should be made conditional on a quid-pro-quo in the nuclear/military area. Strong diplomatic pressure and persuasive efforts involving the two superpowers and the major industrialized countries, after progress in the aforementioned two areas, would be necessary in melting away the resistance of recalcitrant elements within the Indian political system.

The Pakistan Question

Once India is brought to terms with some arrangement for nonproliferation, the Pakistani side will resolve itself automatically, as Islamabad has expressed its readiness to enter into any binding agreement which is uniformly applicable to both countries. America's nonproliferation policies towards Pakistan have been largely successful in preventing Pakistan's nuclearization to a similar level as that of India, although single-issue activists may argue otherwise. There is merit in continuing with this policy and avoiding sharp discontinuities.

While critics of Washington's policy complain of a lenient attitude toward Pakistan, the fact is that severe diplomatic and psychological pressures have been applied to Pakistan, despite the risks of hurting the Afghan policy. Indeed, a realistic consideration of Pakistan's security needs (culminating in two significant military-economic aid packages) has been the single most effective factor in grappling with Pakistan's nuclear situation. Washington's nonproliferation policies have succeeded in that Pakistan has refrained from staging a demonstration of what it has been capable of doing since the early or mid-eighties (India exploded its nuclear device not long after acquiring the requisite capability, as have all other nuclear powers). If there has been a failure, it is of technical approaches to an intrinsically political problem. The political approach has worked, and it may be the only approach which has the potential of success. An isolated and insecure country may be much less sensitive to international public opinion and more prone to rash and last-resort-like actions, while an integrated and confident country may behave more sensibly and responsibly.

While Pakistan has many reasons to adopt a very cautious attitude in relation to its nuclear activities, it is almost certain that it would resist any formulation that singles it out and ignores or disregards the activities of other countries in the region. Indeed, some consideration should be given to a country which has traditionally supported the efforts to contain communism, and much to the chagrin of powerful rulers and elites among Muslim countries to its west, has played a regional stabilizing role. It is one of the few countries east of the Suez that could be counted upon to play a constructive and active role in advancing often compatible U.S.-Pakistan interests and aims in the larger surrounding area, however anachronistic it may sound in today's political environment.

Notes

1. Akhtar Ali, *South Asia: Nuclear Stalemate or Conflagration?* (Karachi: Research on Armament and Poverty, 1987).

2. Understandably, there had been a great interest on the part of countries like Israel to discredit the IAEA safeguard system. In order to maintain its nuclear monopoly, Israel raided and destroyed the Iraqi Osirak nuclear facility, which was under IAEA safeguards. Furthermore, Iraq is a signatory to NPT. To justify its actions it was necessary to destroy the respectability of IAEA safeguards and the NPT itself.

3. The Israeli example tends to counter this thesis. But a number of peculiarities of the Israeli situation should be kept in mind. Israel has had a dedicated nuclear fuel cycle capability for more than two decades. It has been assisted directly by France, and by implication, the U.S. In light of recent revelations about U.S. assistance to the French nuclear program, such possibilities acquire even new dimensions. For all practical purposes it has an overt nuclear capability, apparently reserved as a last resort weapon. Indeed Israel's claimed capabilities have been regarded more as a part of a disinformation campaign, in so much that the Vanunu incident is understood to have been master-minded by Israelis themselves. If the claims of possessing 200 nuclear weapons are correct, then a substantial percentage of this figure should have been imported from one of the existing nuclear powers in the form of material or even the final product. A figure of 200 weapons cannot be derived from available data on Israeli input-output of its nuclear systems.

4. A recent conference of nonproliferation specialists at the Carnegie Endowment for International Peace, Washington, D.C., has recommended an enhancement of the IAEA budget. Many among them would not have supported

such a proposal several years back, due to alleged politicization of IAEA which ensued in the wake of Israeli attack on the Osirak reactor.

5. For a related discussion see Palit and P.K.S. Namboodiri, *Pakistan's Islamic Bomb* (New Delhi: Vikas, 1979), K. Subrahmanyam, *Nuclear Myths and Realities: India's Dilemma* (New Delhi: ABC, New Delhi, 1981), and Steven Weissman and Herbert Krosney, *The Islamic Bomb*.(New York: Times Books,1981). The Libyan connection has been noted. Much capital has also been made of Pakistan Prime Minister Z.A. Bhutto's, statement that Pakistan "will make the bomb if we must eat grass." Certain excerpts form his book *If I Am Assassinated* (New Delhi: Vikas, 1979), also provided material to fuel such speculation. A Saudi link has also been cited, which obviously is much less scary to the Western Nations. In his recent paper, "Rashomon in South Asia," (Urbana: manuscript, 1989) Stephen P. Cohen suggests Islam as a political factor in Bhutto's nuclear ambitions i.e. "to establish Pakistan's position as one of the leading and most advanced states of Islam." This is a much diluted remnant of the militaristic Islamic Bomb syndrome, which may recede into the background further with the passage of time.

6. Except for occasional rhetorical and even naivete of some of its diplomats and bureaucrats, Pakistan has consistently adopted a pro-NPT stand. Nor does it make a big issue about discrimination, the inequality of the world political system, or offer exaggerated definitions and conceptions of sovereignty.

7. Interestingly enough, during Prime Minister Rajiv Gandhi's visit to the U.S., President Reagan asked him to dissuade Pakistan from going nuclear, which was perceived by a jubilant lobby in India as encouragement to attack Pakistani facilities. Later clarifications by U.S. authorities explained that the President had actually meant to ask Gandhi to pay heed to the Pakistani proposals and if these were a bluff, then to call the bluff.

8. For an elaborate discussion of this view point, see K. Subrahmanyam, *Nuclear Myths and Reality* (Delhi: ABC, 1981). While it is possible to come up with a certain mix of formulae and arrangements to meet most of the Indian objections to the concept of nonproliferation, especially in the evolving political environment between the East and the West, it may be very difficult to come to terms with the romanticism of the Indian elite.

9. Harold A. Feiveson, Frank von Hippel and David Albright, "Breaking the Fuel/Weapons Connection," *Bulletin of the Atomic Scientists,* March 1986, pp. 26-31.

10. For an elaborate discussion on these arguments, see Steve Fetter, *Towards a Comprehensive Test Ban* (Cambridge: Ballinger, 1988). In a recent lecture at MIT, Center for International Studies, in November 1989, Dr. Ray Kidder, a renowned weapon designer from Lawrence Livermore, rejected all of the arguments for testing, except for the development of nuclear weapons.

11. Although strictly speaking, NPT article VI only requires "pursuing negotiations for nuclear disarmament" and that there is no express mention of CTB. But the history of NPT negotiation and the subsequent deliberations on the issue have made CTB synonymous with the NWS obligations under article

VI. It should be noted that all NPT review conferences i.e. 1975, 1980 and 1985 have maintained this position.

12. In June 1982, at the second UN special session, the Chinese foreign secretary said: "Small and medium sized countries are all entitled to take what ever measures they deem necessary to maintain their defence capabilities for resisting aggression and safeguarding their independence." A clearly anti-arms control stance. But by 1987, Beijing began to work actively at the Conference on Disarmament in Geneva. Beijing signed the Outer Space Treaty and joined IAEA. A successful agreement on START further meet the requirement of the PRC for supporting or entering into nuclear arms control agreements. On the other hand, recent Chinese-Romanian flirtation convey a threat of a possible turn about in PRC's recent policies. See John Prados, "China's New Thinking on Nuclear Arms," *Bulletin of the Atomic Scientists*, June, 1989, pp. 32-35. Also see Alastair Johnson, "China Enters the Arms Control Arena," *Arms Control Today*, Vol. 17, No.6, July/Aug 1987.

13. Rajiv Gandhi personally favored a slow down on nuclear matters. His five-continent-initiative was approved despite the opposition of the pro-bomb factions in the government. The latter do not support a CTB as they recognize that it would prohibit the tests so vital for the development of nuclear weapons.

14. UN voting patterns, however, reveal an element of ambivalence among the TNS. Pakistan has consistently voted in favor of all the ten resolutions tabled at the UN General Assembly between 1984-86. India has favored three times and abstained on seven, while Argentine has abstained on six and Brazil on five. Resolutions 40/80B and 41/46B which are supported by India actually are for converting LTBT into a CTB. More research is required on the rationale of India's abstentions; the professed logic may enable us to speculate on the eventual behavior of India on a putative CTB agreement (for a discussion of UN voting patterns, see Fetter).

15. One could argue that Israel has acquired a convincing nuclear capability, while it has conducted only one test, if the Vela satellite signatures can be ascribed to an Israeli nuclear explosion. One has to keep in mind, however, that Israeli nuclear doctrine is one of "last resort," facing rather inferior states in terms of military and technological capabilities. India's nuclear motivations are more of prestige and politics. It wants to project and demonstrate power. Continued testing in itself would provide such advantages, beside being a requirement for improving the quality and reliability of a stockpile.

16. The LTBT has now 116 parties. More than one-third of the parties, including the three depository nuclear states (the U.K., the U.S. and the USSR) can convene an amendment conference which has already been done. A simple majority including the three NWS, would be required to approve the amendment, as a consequence of which the amendment would come into force for all the signatory parties.

17. It is inconceivable that imports could have come illegally from Canada or the U.S., although illegal imports may have been possible from Western Europe, e.g. Norway, which interestingly enough has a large heavy water production capacity. The PRC is not a member of either NPT or the supplier's

club. It is very plausible that secret imports came from PRC. For a rather convincing and indignant discussion of India's illegal and secret imports of heavy water, see Gary Milhollin, "Heavy Water in India: A Study," unpublished paper by The Wisconsin Project on Nuclear Arms Control, Jan., 1986.

18. These plans were made with the assistance of and in collaboration with an IAEA study. The IAEA had done similar studies for other developing countries. All such forecasts put together and many other safety and environmental concerns created a backlash against nuclear power, as every potential MW of nuclear power was multiplied by a factor of n bombs per MW-year to arrive at a potential bomb population. Indeed a figure of 20,000 MW of nuclear power rationalized Pakistan's efforts to acquire a complete nuclear fuel cycle capability.

19. There has been some quiet French interest in the project. Some negotiations have been reported regarding a package deal which sorts out the still pending issue of the financial compensation involved as France backed out from a commercially binding agreement to supply a reprocessing plant, while Pakistan had invested substantial civil works costs for the project.

20. Pakistan's power shortage problem is more acute than that of India, as considerable portion of its electrical output is hydro-based. Lower water levels in winters bring down the capacity to just half of peak capacity This problem seems to be common in many parts of the world. For a detailed discussion see *Energy Economist*, June 1989, p. 4, "Is Hydropower Becoming Less Efficient?"

21. Indeed, some demonstration plants may be built in the 1990s, if not on U.S. soil, then in Europe or Japan. Today the nuclear power industry is much less dependent on politics and policies in the U.S., than it was in the 1970s. France, Switzerland, Sweden, Japan, and the Soviet Union have either acquired complete nuclear fuel cycle capabilities or have perfected individual parts of the cycle and in a cooperative arrangement could handle nuclear power activities independently, as opposed to the 1960s and early 1970s, when most of these countries were dependent on the U.S. for nuclear fuel and reactor cores.

22. See relevant discussion by Vipin Gupta, Chapter 8.

23. Skepticism has been shown by a number of writers in India; see chapter XII (Mutual Inspection and Verification) in R.R. Subramaniam, *India, Pakistan, China; Defense & Nuclear Tangle in South Asia* (New Delhi: ABC Publishers, 1989), pp. 145-51.

24. Richard K. Betts, "A Diplomatic Bomb? South Africa's Nuclear Potential," in Joseph A. Yager, ed., *Nonproliferation and U.S. Foreign Policy* (Washington, D.C.: Brookings,1980), p. 300.

25. Interestingly, the idea has received support in India, Pakistan and the U.S. e.g. see author's book *South Asia; Nuclear Stalemate or Conflagration* p.158; also K. Subrahmanyam "Our Nuclear Predicament," *Strategic Analysis*, Oct 1985, who argues for only U.S.-Pakistan verification, a rather non-serious proposition; and most importantly Stephen P. Cohen, "Solving Proliferation Problems in a Regional Context: South Asia," in Joseph P. Nye, Jr., et al., eds. *New Threats: Responding to the Proliferation of Nuclear, Chemical and Delivery Capabilities in the Third World* (Aspen: Aspen Strategy Group, 1990).

26. Sharing satellite imagery and the collateral intelligence information is not new. The U.S. has cooperated in this respect with Canada, the UK and Israel. Indeed Israel's Entebbe and OSIRAK operations could not have been successfully completed without such support from the U.S. See Jeffrey Richelson, "Military Intelligence: SPOT is not enough," *Bulletin of the Atomic Scientists*, September, 1989, pp 26-27; also Amos Perlmutter, Michael Handel and Uri Bar-Joseph, *Two Minutes over Baghdad* (London: Valentine Mitchell, 1982), p.103. However the reliability and certainty of such support could be questionable. The USSR supplied satellite intelligence data to Argentina in Falkland war, but did not provide such support to Egypt during the 1973 war, although the Soviets monitored the conflict intensely. Anwar Sadat had complaints about it, see his autobiography, *In Search of Identity* (New York: Harper & Row, 1977), p.260. Reportedly, there are plans to retire the SR-71 Blackbird, largely due to the availability of better, up-to-date satellite technology. Such systems could be profitably shifted to non U.S.-Soviet Union contexts. See Lonnie Brodie, "Can the U.S. afford to retire the SR-71 Blackbird?" *Defence Electronics*, September, 1989, pp. 57-60.

27. UN, *Study on the Implications of Establishing an International Satellite Monitoring Agency* (New York: UN A/AC 206/19, August 6,1981). An abundant literature exists on the technological and political aspects of satellite monitoring, e.g. see (a) Bhupendra Jasani and Toshibomi Sakata, eds., *Satellites for Arms Control and Crisis Monitoring*, (Oxford: Oxford University Press, SIPRI,1986), p. 176; (b) Allan S. Krass, *Verification: How Much is Enough?* (London: Taylor & Francis, SIPRI, 1985), p.271; (c) K. Tsipis, D. Hafemeister & P. Janeway, eds., *Arms Control Verification: The Technologies that Make It Possible* (Wash., D.C.: Pergamon-Brassey's, 1986)

28. C. Voute, "Agreement and Disagreement on an International Satellite Monitoring Agency," *International Journal of Remote-Sensing*, Vol. 5, No. 2, 1989, pp.479-83. Also see, Torliev Orhang, "An International and Regional Satellite Monitoring Agency," and C. Voute, "A Space Policy for Peace," in Joseph Rotblat and Sven Hellman, *Nuclear Strategy and World Security* (London: Macmillan, 1985), p. 392.

29. For details of the proposal see Ministry of External Affairs, Canada, "PAXSAT Concept: The Application of Space-Based Remote-Sensing for Arms Control Verification" *Verification Brochure*, No. 2, 1986 and F.R. Clemison, "PAXSAT and Progress in Arms Control," *Space Policy*, May, 1988.

30. The Soviet resolution claims have been contested. Instead the analysis showed that Soyuzkarta's resolution is closer to 20m. See James W. Rawles, "Commercial Imaging Comes Down to Earth," *Defence Electronics*, April, 1989, pp. 47-57.

31. See Michael Krepon, "Peacemakers or Rent-a-Spies," *Bulletin of the Atomic Scientists*, Sept., 1981. In the same issue see Leonard Spector, "Keep the skies open." Also see Ann B. Flonni, "Remote Sensing and Diplomacy," and J.E. Thomas, "Impact on the Military," both in *Technology in Society*, Vol. 11, 1989.

32. Space activities in India and Pakistan date back to the 1960s. Indeed, India has a very large dual-use space establishment, which has acquired substantial satellite launching capabilities, recently earning it the status of an IRBM-capable country. There are a number of extremely informative articles on this subject. For an extensive analysis of how India acquired a missile capability with foreign help including the U.S. see Gary Milhollin, "India's Missiles— With a Little Help from Our Friends," *Bulletin of the Atomic Scientists,* Nov. 1989, pp. 31-35. Also see Aaron Karp, "Ballistic Missiles in the Third World," *International Security,* Winter 1984-85, Joe D. Pumphrey, "Status of Third World Ballistic Missile Technology" (manuscript, Weapon Systems Division, Defense Intelligence Agency, Sept. 1986, released by National Security Archives, Washington, D.C).

India has indigenously developed many satellites. India's Department of Space employs 16,000 persons and had a budget of $267 million in 1988. From 1963 through 1986, India's space program has cost it $1.1 billion. Projected expenditure for the period (1987-95) approaches $3 billion (Incoming telegram from New Delhi, U.S. Department of State, dated 8/22/88, declassified and procured by National Security Archives, Washington, D.C.). Apart from communications and meteorology, remote-sensing has enjoyed substantial support with the obvious potential of military observation and battle management roles (Stephen F. Von Weleck, "India's Space Policy," *Space Policy,* November, 1987, pp. 326-334. A National Remote Agency has been formed with headquarters in Hyderabad, with a major earth resource assessment function. In March, 1988, the first of a series of Indian Remote Sensing Satellites, the IRS-IA, was launched by the Soviet- Union (Telegram, 8/22/88, National Security Archives). The Indian Space Research Organization (ISRO) had indigenously developed this satellite, which now functions satisfactorily in a polar sun-synchronous orbit of 904 km. Indeed, barely after a month, ISRO arranged a presentation to NASA of an image from IRS-IA Satellite. NASA and ISRO have a cooperative data exchange program. Source: NASA released document, signed Richard Barnes, release date April 22, 1988 (NSA Archive). The satellite has three cameras; one of 72.5 meter resolution and a swath of 148 km, and two of 36.25 resolution each and a combined swath of 145 km.

Although Pakistan's space program originated around the same period as India's, it has stagnated and lacks any significant capabilities in terms of satellite/rocket production and launching. Its rocket launching is limited to sounding rockets of 30-50 kg and a range of 200-500 km. An experimental low cost satellite has been indigenously developed and launched aboard an Ariane launch vehicle. A number of other plans are on paper. However, a considerable infrastructure which is relevant to verification exists, including ground receiving and data-processing and analysis. SPOT, LANDSAT and NOAA imagery is received by the ground stations and processed. These are cooperative arrangements with many international space research and remote-sensing agencies including India's (Salim Mehmud, "Pakistan's Space Program," *Space Policy,* August 1989, pp. 217-227).

33. Frank Blackaby, Jozef Goldblat and Sverre Lodgaard, *No First Use* (London: Taylor and Francis, 1984), pp. 9-10. In 1982 the Soviet Union formally pledged itself not to be the first to use nuclear weapons, adding a caveat that its actual implementation would depend on the policy of others. Moscow had made a repeated declaration four years prior to this announcement that it would not use nuclear weapons against non-nuclear and nuclear-free countries. No-first use issues have been discussed in detail by the authors in largely a superpower context. Three possible situations of nuclear use are discussed: (1) surprise preemptive attack or first-strike; (2) escalation of a conventional war to the nuclear level—generally understood to be the most likely mode of first-use; and (3) as a reprisal to a nuclear attack. See also the discussion of no first use pledges by Susan Burns, chapter 4

34. K. Subrahmanyam, "Our Nuclear Predicament," *Strategic Analysis*, Oct 1985, pp. 230-240.

35. See, Indian Parliament, *Debates, Rajya Sabha,* Vol. 115, No. 16, Aug 1980, Col. 158.

36. For details see the author's *South Asia: Nuclear Stalemate or Conflagration*, pp. 65-71.

10

Regional Proliferation: Issues and Challenges

Brahma Chellaney

The nonproliferation debate has been raging since the 1974 Indian detonation of a nuclear device in the Rajasthan desert. But, nearly 17 years after the detonation, this debate has shifted markedly from ways to halt the spread of bomb technology to a search for practical ways to contain regional nuclear competitions in South Asia, the Middle East and Latin America. Nowhere is this emphasis more apparent than in analyses on South Asia. There is now less interest in issues relating to control of sensitive nuclear and missile technologies, and more interest in finding ways to manage the South Asian nuclear arms race through a regional verification regime. This regime would have to be outside the fold of the NPT because of the unwillingness of regional rivals to sign the treaty and also because of the way the current patchwork international nonproliferation system is structured.

This emerging focus on regional containment is both an acknowledgement of the strategic realities that have evolved since the 1970s and the general direction in which countries like India and Pakistan appear relentlessly headed. Stephen Cohen's chapter reflects this new realism. The emerging focus is also an indirect admission of the failure of the international nonproliferation system to check the spread of nuclear-weapons capabilities in the Third World or provide a framework for evolving regional agreements. The nonproliferation regime has sought primarily to apply a technical approach to proliferation, with the policy of technology denial being a cornerstone of the system. In the short run, such a policy did create significant delays and problems in nuclear work in a country like India, which had been one of the principal targets of the Nuclear Suppliers Group. However, the long-run effects of the policy have been to promote indigenous development of nuclear and fuel-cycle technologies in the Third World.

The underlying assumption of the regime that proliferation could be effectively contained through denial of sensitive technology[1] has been shattered by the rapid technological advances by India, Pakistan and several other non-NPT countries in the past one decade. The technical approach to proliferation, the pivot of Carter administration policies on full scope safeguards and export controls,[2] traditionally has overlooked a key question: Can the indigenous forces of technology in the Third World be contained? For example, India—which already has the world's largest pool of scientific manpower after the superpowers—produces hundreds of trained nuclear engineers, scientists and technicians every year,[3] and it may appear almost inevitable that this burgeoning nuclear manpower pool would accelerate the country's nuclear development and expand its weapons-related capabilities. Technological momentum is already creating sophisticated systems in India and Pakistan with an important bearing on regional—and Asian—security. It is this momentum which has helped catapult India into what is perceived as the role of a regional superpower through an awesome defense buildup and an increasingly assertive military role.[4]

The evolving focus on regional nuclear containment, reflected in the nonproliferation policies of the superpowers[5] as well as in the proposals of interested third parties such as Australia,[6] is an acknowledgement that the proliferation issue cannot be tackled without dealing with its political dimensions. Attempts now are being made to bridge the technical approach to nonproliferation (which is almost punitive in character) with a political approach to the problem that necessarily will have to emphasize diplomacy and cooperation. Nuclear export controls alone cannot achieve much. A cooperative political approach is needed to help evolve a South Asian nuclear agreement. Political issues, in any case, are expected to dominate the international nonproliferation debate as the 1995 expiration of the NPT draws closer. Proposals to renew and extend the NPT—which has remained unchanged for more than 12 years—will bring out in the open the politics of nonproliferation.

The Nuclear Landscape

The expanding nuclear programs of India and Pakistan will sharply increase subcontinental inventories of weapons-usable materials over the next decade. India admits its stockpile of fissile materials outside the scope of IAEA safeguards is likely to grow by thousands of kilograms as commercial reprocessing and recycling of plutonium in the nuclear power program expands substantially in the coming years.[7] Pakistan has sought to complete three reprocessing facilities, including one at Chasma with a 100-ton capacity, although it has no unsafeguarded spent fuel to reprocess and appears unlikely to have such fuel in the near future. Clandestine import of such technology and equipment enabled Pakistan to build the Kahuta enrichment plant but concern over its program has been increased by the testing of a "triggering package" for nuclear devices[8] and the purchase of tritium technology.[9] China, another key player on the South Asian proliferation landscape, has launched an ambitious program to expand its nuclear armory[10] and has made important strides in recent years: it has acquired a MIRVed surface-to-surface missile capability[11] and conducted its first successful ballistic missile launch from a nuclear submarine.

After repeated denials by Pakistan for years that it was seeking to acquire nuclear weapons, the Pakistani Army chief now has acknowledged that his country's nuclear program is designed to provide "a meaningful deterrent" to India.[12] The nuclear military capability of India, which likewise has denied working on nuclear weapons, flows from its rapidly expanding civilian atomic power program.[13] An indication of this expansion is the setting up of a Center for Advanced Technology (CAT) at Indore to spearhead research in lasers, fusion and other advanced technologies.

Although China's modernization program is aimed at cutting the military's size and qualitatively improving weapon systems, Beijing's nuclear arsenal is expected to double between 1986-96. There has been concern in India over nuclear deployments in Xinjiang and Tibet,[14] whose annexation by China in the 1950s removed an important buffer state between the world's two most populous nations. China's deployment strategy involves constant movement and concealment of nuclear forces in order to avert a surprise attack, but one study by two well-respected U.S. weapon experts suggests in a map that the major missile deployment area is located in Tibet near the border with northeastern India.[15]

Although India and Pakistan have aircraft that are capable of delivering nuclear weapons to targets inside the other country, advances in missile technology in both nations are strengthening rival delivery capabilities. A subcontinental ballistic missile race seems to have broken out. Pakistan, whose space-related activities until the mid-1980s were restricted mainly to launching sounding rockets from a range near Karachi, tested two short-range SSMs, *Haft I* and *Haft II,* in February 1989. *Anza,* a shoulder-fired SAM also has been tested and may now be in service.[16] Pakistan's dedicated missile program may have benefitted from design and technology assistance from its close ally, China, which has emerged as the leading missile exporter in the world. India has made major advances in military research and development in recent years, including the 1989 test-launch of the country's first IRBM, the 1200-mile range *Agni,* or Fire. In addition, India has test-fired a shorter-range SSM, the *Prithvi,* which like Agni can carry a nuclear payload; *Nag,* a sophisticated anti-tank missile; *Trishul,* a SAM likely to be introduced into service by 1991; and an ASM, *Akash.* Having surprised the world in 1989 by placing a civilian satellite into orbit, India has a latent ICBM capability, although it should be noted that its civilian space program has suffered serious setbacks in the last few years. Its rapid strides in the missile field, however, are the result of the "dual use" of civilian space technologies.

The Emerging Picture

With both India and Pakistan armed with weapons-usable fissile materials and nuclear delivery capabilities, the trend toward nuclearization of South Asia may seem irreversible. The recast of the nonproliferation regime in the 1970s—making safeguards a major political and security instrument of the leading nuclear powers—did little to stem proliferation trends in South Asia. In fact, the major advances in the Pakistani nuclear program occurred after this recast of the regime, with trial runs at Kahuta not starting until 1984.[17] Although Chinese assistance and the dovetailing of U.S. nonproliferation policy to geopolitical interests under Reagan may have contributed to Pakistan's rapid nuclear development, one important explanation also lies in the way nuclear activity was conducted. Pakistan concentrated its efforts and resources in building dedicated weapons-related facilities independent of its nuclear power program, emulating China and Israel. Nonproliferation efforts were earlier directed at deterring India and Pakistan from acquiring weapons capabilities, but in 1990 that appears clearly like a muffed goal. Not only is there sufficient evidence to show that both rival nations have such capabilities, but there are growing indications that the two may be headed toward a subcontinental arms race. The proliferation of ballistic missile systems in the region is one such indication. The improvements in that have taken place through the 1980s have infused a sense of confidence among the political and scientific leaders on the subcontinent.

This is reflected in the Indian decision to not only export military hardware but also explore the possibility of selling civilian nuclear power technology to overseas clients. The Indian Department of Atomic Energy (DAE), which is studying the feasibility of such exports, says it already has received inquiries from several Third World countries, including Sri Lanka, Malaysia, Libya and Bangladesh, about possible Indian nuclear sales.[18] Vietnam, which has a nuclear cooperation agreement with India,[19] is another nation interested in Indian exports. The DAE believes the Indian-designed 235-MWe CANDU reactor, which conceivably could be sold with complete fuel-cycle technologies, will be attractive to many Third World countries because of their small electricity grid structures. China, whose nuclear cooperation with Pakistan is controversial, is another potential nuclear exporter. The likely emergence of several second-tier suppliers outside the framework of the international nonproliferation regime[20] could not only promote greater South-South cooperation in the civilian nuclear power field, especially if costs of goods and services are more competitive than those of the established suppliers, but also make it more difficult for the regime to continue in its present core structure beyond 1995.

The technological momentum in India and Pakistan can only accelerate in the 1990s, and three possible stages or scenarios can be visualized in relation to the South Asian nuclear competition:

- India and Pakistan retain present policies of calculated nuclear ambiguity but continue to strengthen weapons capabilities and various component programs of a nuclear deterrent.
- India and Pakistan build limited nuclear arsenals for deterrence but no nuclear arms race breaks out in the subcontinent.
- India is involved in a dual nuclear arms race in South Asia with China and Pakistan.

The policies of calculated nuclear ambiguity will continue for some time to come on the Indian subcontinent. It is advantageous for both Pakistan and India to maintain such policies. For India, it would be premature to give up its peaceful nuclear posture if it cannot counter the Chinese nuclear threat. Although India had the distinction of building Asia's first research reactor, Apsara, in the mid-1950s, the country's nuclear-explosive program began in earnest only after the 1964 Chinese nuclear test. In recent years, Indian security planners have placed heavy emphasis on developing long-range delivery capabilities, a need reinforced by the disadvantage of geography. While China can strike India's main Gangetic plain even with short-range missiles from Tibet, the world's highest plateau which overlooks India, New Delhi would need to have missiles with a range of more than 2,000 miles in order to hit major military and urban-industrial targets in the Chinese heartland. China's ground-based missiles can all be transported by and fired from trailers, and Beijing may be seeking to further enhance capabilities by converting all its land-based missiles from liquid to solid fuel.[21] Although China's land-based missiles have deterred the Soviet Union, the improvement in relations and the resolution of the border dispute between the two countries is seen to have increased the Chinese threat to other Asian countries, particularly India[22]—a threat underlined by the upgrading of nuclear war-fighting exercises in recent years.

For Pakistan, a policy of nuclear ambiguity has the advantage of being able to strike two birds with one stone. First, it ensures continuance of the close strategic cooperation with the United States without a cutoff of hundreds of millions of dollars in aid every year.

Second and more importantly, it provides Pakistan status and some
benefits of deterrence without the evidence or a declaration of
weaponization. The value of deterrence in Pakistan's security is
now debated publicly. According to Pakistan's General Beg, "Both
the nuclear option and the missiles act as a deterrent and these in turn
contribute to the total fighting ability of the Army, which then
[further] acts as a deterrent to the enemy."[23]

Any evident weaponization by either side, however, could
quickly lift the veil from present policies of nuclear ambiguity and
precipitate a subcontinental arms race. A Pakistani nuclear test, for
example, would place Indian policymakers under intense domestic
pressure, forcing them to respond with an overtly nuclear military
program. Indian government leaders have warned repeatedly that
any evidence of Pakistani weaponization would spur a major change
in India's nuclear policy. Superpower nonproliferation policies,
therefore, have been directed at restraining Pakistan from carrying
out an underground test or overtly engaging in a weapons program.
This has been seen as the key to lengthening the fuse and
maintaining stability in South Asia. As Pakistan's ally, the United
States has had to assume the responsibility of restraining Islamabad,
although Washington's aid program and reluctance to impose
congressionally-mandated nonproliferation conditions are viewed to
have actually contributed to the progress of the Pakistani nuclear
program.[24] This pressure, however, is deeply resented by Pakistan
which contends that its program is merely a response to the 1974
Indian nuclear detonation. While it is true that the India factor has
provided the major impetus to the Pakistani program, it also is true
that, left to itself, India appears to be in no hurry to overtly
weaponize—at least until it has acquired the technical capabilities to
build a credible deterrent to China.

Although ambiguity in policy is tactically advantageous for both
sides, only a short step separates it from the next stage of small
nuclear arsenals. Even without entering this second stage, each
side's technical capabilities are being incrementally strengthened.
India has dozens of major research and development projects under
the umbrella of the Defense Research and Development Organization
(DRDO), the Bhabha Atomic Research Center (BARC) and the
Indian Space Research Organization (ISRO); seen together, these
projects look like components of a nuclear deterrent program. An

inherent advantage in a policy of ambiguity, in fact, is that it provides time and cover to catch up on key technologies. But such policies hide more than they reveal so it is very difficult to know if either country (or both) has all the nuclear-weapon components (or even some bombs) in the basement.[25] In any case, all indications seem to point to the subcontinent being on the brink of weaponization.

The stage already may have been set for the emergence of four nuclear giants in Asia sharing disputed frontiers: China, India, Pakistan and the Soviet Union. This will have a profound impact on the global power structure and the shape of international political alignments. The world has no experience of more than two nuclear-armed nations sharing frontiers, and the convergence of four such states in Central-South Asia could lead to a new delicate power equilibrium in the region and force the revision of present deterrence strategies and theories.

Central-South Asia, where the borders of the four nations converge, has historically been the gateway to power in Asia. It was this area of the ancient Silk Road, close to the Hindukush mountain range, that was the gateway to a host of invasions of South Asia, China, Russia and Persia by different rulers through history, including the Aryan conquest of the subcontinent about 1600 BC.[26] In the new multipolar world that is likely to emerge in the 21st Century, South Asian nuclearization could place Asia at the center stage of world power. Japan, the continent's economic giant, could contribute to this power shift by emerging as a major political and military power. Japan is expected to acquire a formidable nuclear military potential from its civilian nuclear power program. Within the next thirty years, Japan would be able to extract more plutonium than the quantity now contained in the combined superpower nuclear arsenals.[27] Like India, Japan's breeder program would be able to absorb only a limited quantity of the available plutonium and create stockpiles of separated plutonium far in excess of commercial needs. Significantly, Japan and India today have the largest and second largest civilian nuclear power construction programs in the world, respectively, and both are strongly emphasizing breeder technology—which carries the highest proliferation risk—as a means of overcoming scarce uranium resources.

The China Factor

Any discussion of nonproliferation strategies in South Asia must take the China factor into account in several ways, since it holds the key to the issue. This is apparent from a brief survey of the regional dynamics of proliferation.

The Indian nuclear-weapons capability drive was not fuelled by a need to checkmate Pakistan. India, with its superior conventional strength, does not need nuclear weapons to counter a non-nuclear Pakistan. A nuclear rivalry with Pakistan would not only be strategically and militarily disadvantageous to India but be inconsistent with its long-term security interests and ambitions in the region. Nuclearization of the subcontinent would blunt India's superiority in conventional forces and undermine its strength as an emerging Asian power by creating balancing powers in a subcontinental deterrence framework. It would tie India down regionally.[28] An important foreign policy objective of India, therefore, would be to impede or slow down the Pakistani nuclear program. In fact, Pakistan was almost peripheral to Indian nuclear planning in the 1960s and most of the 1970s. Conversely, however, nuclear weapons can play a key role in Pakistani security plans to counter the growing military dominance of India in the region. The acquisition of nuclear weapons could be seen by Islamabad as providing a deterrent against an Indian invasion or a further Indian-supported breakup of Pakistan. This is underscored by the official argument that nuclear-weapons capability would provide Pakistan "a meaningful deterrent."[29] Pakistan has a far smaller nuclear program and capability to produce weapons-usable fissile materials than India, a gap that is expected to widen further in the 1990s, but that does not deny it the ability—in the short or long run—to build a small nuclear deterrent against India.

India has retained its nuclear option primarily to counter what it perceives to be the intimidating nuclear might of China,[30] although Pakistan's nuclear-weapons capability drive may have prompted India to accelerate work on its program. The emerging strategic realities indicate that the China-India rivalry is expected to intensify in the 1990s; China indeed believes India will remain "one of its most likely foes over the next couple of decades."[31] The component programs of India's current military R&D drive indicate that the capabilities that New Delhi wants to acquire are mainly geared to meeting the challenge from Beijing. An example is India's quest to develop an ICBM capability by the late 1990s. India does not need such capabilities against Pakistan because almost all Pakistani, economic urban targets are within the striking radius of its attack fighters. Building a minimal but credible nuclear deterrent seems to be the overall goal of the Indian R&D drive.[32] Various component programs are being pursued separately with the intention of later coalescing them into an effective deterrent. Fissile material production is an important priority area. Although India is likely to have large stockpiles of separated plutonium in the next fifteen years, these inventories could grow even larger if breeder technology is successfully introduced. That would help narrow the fissile-material production gap with China, which already possesses a nuclear armory bigger than the combined French and British arsenals.[33]

American analysts often tend to gloss over or underestimate the China factor in their writings on the subcontinent. A good example of this is a wide-ranging study on the nuclearization of South Asia in which as many as eighteen American scholars participated; the study examines the China factor briefly under a self-explanatory subtitle, "The Role of Outside Powers."[34] The treatment of China as an outside element in South Asian developments muddles analytical thinking. As long as the proliferation issue is reduced mainly to an analysis of the Pakistan-India rivalry, with passing references to China, we will continue to miss a key link in the chain reaction of South Asian proliferation. Any set of proposals derived from such analysis will be viewed by New Delhi as unrealistic and unacceptable. In fact, proposals for bilateral nuclear cooperation in an India-Pakistan framework have in the past been met with disdain in New Delhi. It needs to be recognized that South Asian proliferation has been a triangular competition, and China cannot be divorced from this affair. In the same way the Pakistani nuclear weapons capability drive was a reaction to the 1974 Indian detonation, the Indian nuclear-explosive program was a response to the Chinese test in Lop Nor a decade earlier.[35] This triangular equation in South Asia has been strengthened by close Sino-Pakistani strategic ties since the 1950s and by increasing international evidence of Chinese nuclear and missile technology

assistance to Islamabad.[36] The assistance has included transfer of
weapon designs to Islamabad[37] and, according to some accounts,
even testing a Pakistani device at Lop Nor.

There are several reasons why Americans underrate the China
factor. One may be that they have usually been trained in the Soviet-
American deterrence model, with its two rival and balancing forces.
There is an innate tendency to extend this analytical straitjacket to
conflicts elsewhere (Argentina versus Brazil, India versus Pakistan,
China versus the Soviet Union) and view situations in black and
white perspectives, giving short shrift to other possible actors or the
large grey areas that may be locked in. Second, American analysts
may be prisoners of their own definition of South Asia. Having
divided the world into a number of regions, some policymakers and
scholars find it analytically problematic to introduce an "outside"
country into their regional framework. China is not seen as part of
South Asia.[38] A third reason, of course, is that viewing China as a
key player in the South Asian proliferation picture just complicates
matters and makes it difficult to come up with practical, simple
proposals. China is an established nuclear weapons state and will
be most reluctant to accept any conditions that would tie it down. In
the common American analysis, therefore, China cannot be treated at
par with India and Pakistan in any South Asian anti-proliferation
framework. Its role can only be peripheral, confined to providing
"assurances."

This propensity to treat China in a separate class by itself is
reinforced by that country's strategic importance in U.S. policy, as
reflected in the whittling away of human rights-related sanctions
against Beijing by President Bush and the controversial Sino-U.S.
nuclear cooperation pact signed during the Reagan Administration.
Reagan was forced to delay approval of the pact for almost a year by
congressional pressure, triggered by convincing evidence on
Chinese aid to Pakistan in designing and developing nuclear
weapons.[39] However, the pact—which permits sensitive nuclear
technology to be sold to a country that has refused to accept the NPT
or embrace the nonproliferation regime and the MTCR—was
approved in late 1985 after the Administration informed Congress
that Beijing had agreed to terminate nuclear assistance to Pakistan.
That assurance has been belied by evidence that shows Beijing's
nuclear assistance to Islamabad has not only continued but been

supplemented with missile technology transfer. Pakistan's *Anza*, for instance, is said to be a copy of a Soviet-model Chinese SAM.

The reluctance to deal squarely with the China factor is a shortcoming of many chapters in this book. Although some do mention the significance of the China-India strategic relationship, most sidestep the larger complexities of the problem. Cohen, who knows the subcontinent better than most American scholars, does begin promisingly in Chapter 1 by saying the Indian-Pakistani and Chinese-Indian nuclear relationships cannot be separated and that "any 'regional' approach which does so will be crippled from the start." Having said so, however, his concluding chapter deals scrimpily with the Indian-Chinese relationship and proposes bilateral conventional arms control agreements and regional nuclear and missile verification measures in a Pakistan-India context. There appears to be a willingness to recognize the importance of the China-India equation but an unwillingness to deal with it.

China has been central to Indian security planning. This is reflected in defense strategies, the military R&D drive and the size of the armed forces. Conversely, however, the Indian subcontinent has not been the strategically most significant region in Chinese security planning. India's humiliating rout in the 1962 war with China is deeply embedded in the Indian psyche. No event in independent India cast more influence on national planning or on the shape of long-term goals and strategies. India's emergence from the 1962 defeat as a mighty regional power with the world's fourth largest military machine is as much a response to the rout as it is a product of a seemingly inexorable militaristic drive sparked by the war. In Indian analysis, the war came to be seen as a negation of India's pacifist policy enshrined in the "Panchsheel" doctrine of Nehru. Following the Chinese nuclear test in 1964, Prime Minister Lal Bahadur Shastri is believed to have ordered work to begin on an Indian nuclear-explosive capability. A combination of events—the death of the head of the nuclear program, Homi J. Bhabha, in a 1966 plane crash and the political instability following the appointment of an inexperienced and initially feeble leader, Indira Gandhi, as prime minister—ended India's hopes for an early nuclear breakthrough. But even before the NPT went into force, the Indian project appeared to be back on stream. The U.S. State Department warned New Delhi in 1970 that the development of peaceful nuclear-explosive devices would be "tantamount to the development of nuclear weapons."[40] Why India waited until 1974 to detonate its first nuclear device is a question most analysts still find difficult to address.

China still inspires awe (if not dread) among Indian policymakers and intellectuals. China is viewed as a demon not to be disturbed or pricked. That unspoken policy was observed until 1987, when India decided to flex its military muscles by carrying out large-scale military maneuvers along the frontier with China. There were some border clashes and the two countries went to the brink of war until a political dialogue helped defuse the crisis. Indian officials generally are very discreet in their statements and comments on China. Much of the Indian rhetoric is targeted on Pakistan, in part because the 1947 partition of the subcontinent still has a highly emotive and political significance. Some of the prickly problems between Pakistan and India, like trans-border terrorism and smuggling and a dispute over interstate river water sharing, are a consequence of the borders having been drawn in 1947 without any consideration to geography or national security interests of the new states. Historically and racially, Indians and Pakistanis have been one people, and to those dwindling number of Indians still nurturing visions of reunification it has not been lost that Pakistan's raison d'etre for independence—religion—has been overtaken by events, with India now having a larger Moslem population than Pakistan.

Because China is seen as a major military threat, Indian defense policymakers have always been concerned about the possibility of having to fight a a war simultaneously on both the Chinese and Pakistani fronts. Indian force deployments along the frontiers undergird this concern. Although the exact troop deployment picture is supposed to be a national secret, it is widely acknowledged that the deployments are nearly in the ratio of 50:50 along the Pakistan and Chinese fronts, with several additional divisions being available for immediate movement to strengthen one or both borders in the event of war. This estimate is backed by the International Institute of Strategic Studies' own deployment estimates.on the number of divisions in each of India's five Army commands.[41] The mighty Himalayas, however, provide a far more secure border with China than the fertile plains, desert land and swamps that make up the major stretch of the India-Pakistan frontier.

The fixation on a China-Pakistan "axis" in Indian security planning has played a role in New Delhi's rejection of a Chinese proposal to convert the present line-of-control into the international boundary between the two countries. The proposal, presented at the Chinese-Indian border negotiations with the blessing of Deng Xiaping, involved India accepting the Chinese annexation of Aksai Chin, Demchok and Shaksgam[42] in the Kashmir region in return for Beijing giving up its claim on India's northeastern Arunachal Pradesh state.[43] New Delhi has been reluctant tom surrender its claim over Aksai Chin because of its immense strategic importance, even though India does not have the military might to recover lost territories. The determination not to seek compromises on strategic territories also is a major factor in the silent war India has been waging with Pakistan over the control of Siachen glacier; a major Indian aim apparently is to deny Pakistan additional common border with China.[44]

Although China has never opened a second front during an India-Pakistan war, this "failure" to come to the rescue of its close ally, especially in 1971, has been cited in the Pakistani debate as a reason why Pakistan should develop a nuclear deterrent against India. China's assistance to Islamabad, however, may indicate that Beijing itself is encouraging Pakistan to develop its own full-fledged deterrent to independently counter India.

A major reason why China may have balked at intervening in the 1971 conflict, however, was the fear of the Soviet Union opening a front on the north. But with the resolution of the Chinese-Soviet border dispute and a gradual improvement in bilateral relations, the importance of the Soviet factor in Chinese and Indian security calculations has declined. The value of India's "Soviet card" has been further eroded by receding Soviet global commitments and and Moscow's preoccupation with domestic problems. However, the *glasnost* that fostered the Azeri and Tajik Islamic unrest could easily have a fallout across the Soviet Union in western China, where millions of Moslems already are restless and one province—Xinjiang—has imposed new measures to deal with "counterrevolutionary" ethnic rebellion.[45] A wave of Islamic fundamentalism could easily sweep through Xinjiang, home of six million Turkish speaking Uighur Moslems, in much the same way as the resurgence of Islamic militancy in neighboring Kashmir. With the ethnic rebellion in Tibet continuing to challenge Chinese rule, the spread of Islamic unrest in central-south Asia could exacerbate political and security problems in an area where the borders of the Soviet Union, India, China and Pakistan converge.

The Politics of Nuclearization

The importance of nuclear weapons in the world today is tied intrinsically to their political value. Nuclear weapons are not instruments for fighting wars and their military value actually derives from the political effects of the existence of nuclear arsenals, including their ability to define and shape political stability between rival nations and blocs. The political significance of nuclear weapons flows from the fact that they enable "mutual kill"[46] and are revered as such. More widely, these weapons signify power in relations between states. In military history, nuclear arms are the first truly political weapon system since the dawn of warfare. It therefore seems natural that they bestow immense political clout to their holders. It also may seem no coincidence that the five established nuclear powers in the world today are the permanent members of the UN Security Council. Nuclear weapons, indeed, have acquired a halo as instruments of power and influence in international politics and in relations among nations. The failure to see them in this wider light will reduce the value of any analysis on the process of nuclearization, and the incentives for it, in some major Third World countries.

National security concerns and threat perceptions of nations are no doubt a key factor in the process of proliferation. But a major motivating force can also be a desire to seek or enhance international prestige. In fact, two comprehensive studies on the origins of the British and Chinese nuclear programs show that a key motivating force for both was an intense national desire to gain international status as important political and technological powers.[47] The two countries believed that their success in developing their first weapons "would in itself validate the potency of their defense and technological capabilities and advertise their future military potential.

It would bring recognition from friend and foe alike."[48] Another key component of nuclearization can be nationalism.

Nationalism is a potent force behind the Indian and Pakistani programs. This is evident from the national consensus in the two countries on nuclear policy. The rapid technological advances by Pakistan in recent years are a symbol of national pride in a country which has had to overcome major political, technical and industrial obstacles and has mounted a program with a dedicated team. Pakistan is showing the world—as China did in 1964—how a country with limited technical resources and a narrow industrial base can acquire nuclear-weapons and ballistic missile capabilities. The fact that there has been a foreign input in the Pakistani program does not detract from its successes; not one of the established nuclear powers developed its weapons capability in a completely indigenous manner. Zulfiqar Ali Bhutto, who initiated the Pakistani program, said at his trial by the Zia ul-Haq military regime that, "We all know that Israel and South Africa have full nuclear capability. The Christian, Jewish and Hindu civilizations have this capability. The Communist powers also possess it. Only the Islamic civilization was without it, but that position was about to change."[49] Today, Pakistan is emerging as a technological leader of the Muslim world— its nuclear program is a visible symbol of Islamic scientific pride.

India is often cited as a Third World example of how national priorities and long-term planning have been shaped by nationalism. Self-reliance and an emphasis on science and technology have been the cornerstones of Indian planning since independence resulting in the growth of powerful forces of technology in society. However, unlike China, the goals of Indian research and development have not been clearly defined because of a lack of proper political leadership or because research has not been pursued in tandem with the country's five-year plans. At times scientific research has been carried out without any plans to translate it to uses for the benefit of society. But scientific achievements become symbols of national pride. After the first IRBM was successfully tested, Dr. Kalam said: "*Agni* is a technological strength. Strength respects strength. Weaklings are not honored. So we should be strong."[50] The Indian nuclear program, whose origins date back to the 1940s, needs to be understood in this context of nationalism.

In some ways nationalism and the quest for international respect and prestige can be invisibly connected with the problems and challenges of nationhood. The rigors of nation-building after historical periods of weak and divisive internal rule and then colonization can provide a strong nuclearization incentive. To political and scientific elites, this incentive could come from a determination not to fall prey again to the ravages of foreign rule and from an internal desire to get over the ignominy of the past. Nation-building in such circumstances carries a propensity to demonstrate military prowess. This has been true of both China and India, two of the world's oldest civilizations. Mao Zedong "had long regarded a country's independent capacity to display, deploy and commit its armies as a vital component of its sovereign independence. He dreamed that China would acquire the unshackled ability to mobilize and use effective military power, for only that power would distinguish the new state from its humiliated predecessors. Consistent with that dream, "Mao ordered work to begin on a nuclear weapons program.[51] These historical and strategic considerations also have played an important role in Indian security planning. In fact, India's massive naval buildup has been spurred by arguments that the major security threats in Indian history have always emanated from the sea.[52] According to this analysis, invaders who cam by sea, like the British, French, Portuguese and Dutch, ruled and left as foreigners and therefore never had the interest of the Indian subcontinent at heart, while those who came by land (such as the Moghuls) assimilated into the local society and became Indians in every respect. The rigors of nation-building also can come from a problem of national or historical identity. Pakistan (along with Israel, South Africa and Taiwan) belongs to that "class of nations whose survival is debated, whose legitimacy is doubted and whose conventional security apparatus may be inadequate to cope with the pressures of hostile neighbors."[53] This in itself is a powerful incentive to weaponization.

Most of the chapters in this book do not examine South Asian proliferation in this wider dimension. The unidimensional emphasis on national security and threat perceptions, although important, robs the analyses of some of the significant elements that are involved in the process of nuclearization. Perceived security threats always are a key factor in promoting proliferation, just as a perceived U.S.

nuclear threat was a spur to the Chinese program, but they are only a shield behind which some other crucial elements are ensconced. No analysis on a country's military policy can be complete without examining these other factors. For example, national security concerns and threat perceptions cannot explain America's largest-ever peacetime military buildup during the Reagan years, when more than $2.2 trillion were spent—at the rate of $30 million per hour—on military expansion and modernization. As Reagan and his advisors acknowledged, this buildup had more to do with political power projections, in particular the desire to reinforce and perpetuate America's role as the most powerful nation on the globe, and the perception that strength guarantees peace and respect. Political factors, similarly, are important in South Asia especially because two of the three nations we are dealing with are the world's largest.

The Politics of Nonproliferation

It is significant that China, India and Pakistan perceive the nonproliferation regime as discriminatory and designed to institutionalize superpower nuclear dominance. This is a view that is widely shared in the Third World. It is equally significant that the intellectual leadership of the offensive against what is perceived as nuclear apartheid has been provided by China and India, the two countries that also are likely to spearhead the opposition to the renewal of the NPT. The philosophical underpinnings of the debate against "atomic colonialism" have been provided by a famous Chinese government statement: "It is absolutely impermissible for two or three countries to brandish their nuclear weapons at will, issue orders and commands, and lord it over in the world as self-ordained nuclear overlords, while the overwhelming majority of countries are expected to kneel and obey orders meekly, as if they were nuclear slaves. The time of power politics has gone forever, and major questions of the world can no long be decided by a few powers."[54] Although Pakistan officially has maintained its position that it is willing to sign the NPT despite its discriminatory character if India also agreed, this is seen more as a cat and mouse game within the framework of regional political power. Nationalistic fervor, however, is sharpening the criticism by many Pakistani intellectuals of the structural inequity of the NPT regime.[55]

The central concern of the nonproliferation debate in the West has been the perceived destabilizing role of proliferation. It is assumed that emergence of new nuclear-weapons states will pose a grave threat to the "systemic stability" that has characterized international relations since World War II.[56] However, from a Third World perspective, this so-called international systemic stability that has been the core focus of Western deterrence theorists might be seen as chimerical, especially when viewed against the backdrop of dozens of past and present conflicts in the Third World. There is nothing "international" about this stability, which has been strictly limited to relations between the two blocs. Having raised the political and military costs of aggression through "overkill" to such an extent as to preclude direct confrontation between themselves, the superpowers have gone about since the 1950s carving out regional spheres of influence, fuelling regional conflicts with aggressive arms-sale policies, and fighting proxy wars in the Third World.[57] Nuclear weapons have helped make the superpowers and their allies feel secure, but the freedom these arsenals have given them may actually have made nations outside the alliances feel insecure. So what appears as international stability to the two blocs and to deterrence theorists like Thomas Schelling may be systemic instability to the Third World. The receding role of Gorbachev's Soviet Union as an assertive global power might contain Soviet adventurism in the Third World, but as Panama and Nicaragua show it may do little to change Washington's innate inclination toward interventionism, an impression reinforced by a classified Bush Administration guidance to military commanders.[58]

Against this background, the Third World may be seen to have little stake in preserving the present world political order, which was created at a time when many such countries were still colonized or were struggling with the problems of nation-building after decolonization. Many of the intractable interstate disputes in the Third World (including the China-India-Pakistan boundary question and the Middle East conflict) are rooted in colonialism, in particular the colonially-demarcated boundaries that bore no stamp of history or no regard for geography and local security considerations. Underdevelopment itself is a manifestation of colonization. A corollary of that argument is that much of the Third World (although interested in preserving the current nuclear peace) may have little respect for the present nuclear order, which is viewed as protecting the superpower geopolitical interests and hegemonic influence in world affairs and preserving bipolarity in the international system.

The politics of nonproliferation is compounded by the fact that it is a predominantly American subject with much of the literature emanating there. Although this may have to do with the intellectual richness of the United States, which today has become the global center of art and learning, two obvious issues undergird the politicization of the subject. One is the way "proliferation" is defined or accepted, in particular the way certain developments are seen or not seen as a proliferation threat or viewed as a low-magnitude threat. That judgment quite often is colored by perceptions of U.S. strategic interests, giving many the impression that nonproliferation may just be a tool of foreign policy. It is widely acknowledged that the United States has contributed to the spread of nuclear-weapons technologies to Israel and South Africa and, as recent evidence suggests, even provided secret technical assistance to the French nuclear program. Strategic considerations helped mute criticism in and outside Congress of the obvious proliferation implications of the controversial nuclear pacts signed with China and Japan during the Reagan Administration. The same considerations also have helped win waivers for Pakistan of the nonproliferation provisions of U.S. law and prompted transfer to France of U.S. treaty obligations to provide fuel to India's Tarapur plant. In American literature, the list of "proliferation concern" countries is made up almost entirely of Third World nations, including several who have signed the NPT;[59] there is little discussion of the growth of fissile materials and other significant nuclear developments in some non-weapons states in the advanced industrial world.

The other issue is the unidirectional approach to nonproliferation, the focus on horizontal proliferation, to the virtual seclusion or underestimation of the main problem, the vertical proliferation of superpower strategic weapons. As the U.S. plans to build numerous new weapons systems shows, the strategic arsenal buildup will continue despite the receding Soviet and Warsaw Pact threat. And without additional arms-control agreements, START will make little difference to the current doctrine emphasizing construction of sophisticated high-yield warheads "designed to deliver maximum destructive power with minimum bulk and weight."[60] Far from accepting the concept of minimal nuclear deterrence, the greater nuclear powers are determined to arm themselves with more and more sophisticated weapon systems.

Set against these policies, the framing of acceptable nonproliferation proposals for South Asia or any other region becomes problematic. Any Western argument that Pakistan's enrichment program with a comparatively minuscule production capacity is a threat to world peace could be an invitation for an attack on its ethnocentric character. The fact that India declines to enter into any kind of nonproliferation arrangement with Pakistan and thereby is willing to live with any threat from that program to its security makes any Western-sponsored regional verification proposal alien in nature if it is not tied to a larger global disarmament idea.

The politicization of nonproliferation also comes from the attempt to deter the spread of technologies that would have an adverse impact on the present capabilities of the greater nuclear powers to police the seas or intervene in regional conflicts without incurring significant military and political costs. A case in point is the issue of non-nuclear weapon states using atomic power for naval propulsion. There is concern that nuclear submarine projects involving unsafeguarded reactor fuel and plutonium wastes would seriously undermine the international nonproliferation regime[61] even though the NPT itself permits such "non-proscribed military activity." Although this issue is seen as a major challenge to the regime, technological advances have increased the importance of nuclear submarines in modern warfare. A nuclear-powered attack submarine (SSN) is much better placed than a conventional diesel-electric attack submarine (SSK) in speed, maneuverability and survivability—qualities that attract the SSN to countries with large coastlines like India, Brazil and Canada. Moreover, the cost difference between a top-of-the-line SSK and an SSN has narrowed to a point that an on-nuclear weapon state may easily feel more secure by investing in an SSN project.[62] The 1982 Falklands war testified to the might of an SSN, armed with conventional torpedoes, in modern warfare.

There has to be a proper balance between nonproliferation concerns and the rights of countries to use military technology for national defense. Criticism of the SSN projects in India[63] and Brazil could be construed as support for the perpetuation of the technological superiority and military dominance of the established nuclear powers.

The central objective of nonproliferation should be to make this world a safer place not just in the short run but also for future generations. Due to the intrinsically political nature of the subject, nonproliferation scholarship needs to walk a tightrope. An emphasis on one issue to the exclusion of others or the advocacy of positions that would impinge on the technological and military development of nations could blur the distinction between independent scholarship and representation of U.S. or Soviet strategic interests. Also, proliferation should clearly be defined and analyzed as the vertical and horizontal spread of nuclear weapons. This is important because for the first time the continued vertical proliferation of weapons is being explained as a response to prospective horizontal proliferation. President Bush, for instance, has cited a "threat" to the United States from the spread of nuclear-weapons capability to new countries.[64]

Regional Verification:
Incentives and Disincentives

The need for nuclear transparency and cooperation in South Asia is evident from several perspectives: the uneasy relations between Pakistan and India and India and China, the expansion of nuclear programs and conventional forces in the region, and the sharp escalation in terrorist-related violence. The growth of ethnic, sectarian and separatist violence, which has given South Asia the dubious distinction of having the world's highest incidence of terrorist violence, has important nuclear safety implications especially when viewed in the context of nuclear safety standards in the region.[65] A nonproliferation framework for South Asia, however, raises several questions and challenges. These relate to the role of established nuclear powers, the extent of a regional framework, the inclusion and exclusion of activities within such an arrangement, the technical means of verification, and the political will to achieve goals.

The strongest political incentive to the establishment of such a regional framework can be provided by major agreements between the superpowers to work toward minimum nuclear deterrence. That is the key to any anti-proliferation proposal gaining all-party acceptance in South Asia. The idea of complete nuclear disarmament may be difficult to realize because technical knowledge in nuclear weaponry cannot be wiped out. But there are no technical restraints to reducing the tens of thousands of weapons in the arsenals of the nuclear powers in order to achieve a minimal effective deterrent.[66] What is needed is the political will to go from "overkill" deterrence, which involves a constant campaign to build more and more sophisticated weapons, to minimum deterrence, preferably with a freeze on technological improvements. A first step in that direction would be a joint U.S.-Soviet halt to fissile material production especially since the addition of more plutonium and uranium to the superpower inventories cannot enhance the deterrent effect of their forces.[67] A tritium production cutoff alone could revolutionize arms control because it would force the superpowers to reduce their arsenals at the rate at which tritium decays—5.5 % yearly.[68] The erosion of the Soviet threat to the United States is providing challenging opportunities for rapid cuts in strategic armories.

The superpowers, in fact, have a legal obligation under the NPT to negotiate "effective measures relating to cessation of the nuclear arms race at an early date and to nuclear disarmament"—an obligation which has remained on paper for 20 years. They also are committed to end "all test explosions of nuclear weapons for all time," a pledge that the United States and Britain refuse to honor. In a 1988 report to Congress, Reagan argued that the United States may need to expand its nuclear testing program even after strategic-arms reduction agreements were reached with the Soviet Union;[69] this position has been backed by the Bush Administration. The only other country that has refused to support a Comprehensive Test Ban is France, which is not a signatory to the NPT or the Partial Test Ban Treaty. A recommendation to convert the PTBT into a total test ban has received strong support in the UN, but the refusal of some nuclear powers to accept a CTB could put the renewal of the NPT "into jeopardy."[70] Some countries have already expressed their opposition to the extension of the NPT, while some others are seeking to make their continued membership conditional.[71] A CTB (a proposal supported by both India and Pakistan) could be a key instrument in halting the spread of nuclear-weapons capability to new countries. The development of reliable weapons in India and Pakistan will be stymied by such a ban, which would also limit the options of the two countries. The global and regional linkages of proliferation become even more apparent when one examines superpower nuclear targeting and the deployment of nuclear forces of outside powers in the Indian Ocean. Such an examination also suggests that the threat of nuclear arms being used in South Asia cannot be eliminated just by Pakistan and India abjuring the manufacture of atomic weapons. Each superpower has targeted the major hotbeds of tension in the world, including the Indian Ocean region, with four of the five established nuclear powers employing as many as 3,000 warheads to target areas mainly in the Third World.[72] The deployed weapons include the sea-launched cruise missile (SLCM). An example of how battlefield nuclear arms could play a role in Third World war plans is a U.S. Army decision to set up light divisions armed with 155mm nuclear-capable guns "for the express purpose of creating a force to respond to crises in the Third World.[73]

Any South Asian nonproliferation proposal cannot overlook the fact that much of the ocean region around the subcontinent bristles with nuclear weapons as a consequence of superpower naval buildups in the 1980s. This arms race began after negotiations on a proposal during the Carter Administration to demilitarize the Indian Ocean and declare it a zone of peace broke down following events in Iran and Somalia. Today, the northwest quadrant of the Indian Ocean has became a favored deployment area for the superpowers, with even the French maintaining a sizable ocean presence and the Chinese showing interest in a role in the region.[74] The strategic importance of the Indian Ocean has been such that at one stage it was the "fastest-growing area of military competition between the United States and the Soviet Union."[75] Tactical weapons that make up the bulk of the deployments in the Indian Ocean raise the specter of nuclear fighting in the region. Nonproliferation initiatives need to be pursued in tandem with proposals aimed at lessening this threat. One such proposal could be the denuclearization of the Indian Ocean, an idea that might be supported by China. Denuclearization would, of course, not turn the Indian Ocean into a zone of peace, a major proposal of India. Such a political incentive, however, will make an important contribution to creating a South Asian climate conducive to the pursuit of nonproliferation.

The political incentives just discussed will need to be supplemented with technical incentives. Although such incentives could include technology transfers for safety-related or other non-weapons use, the most important technical incentive to nonproliferation is the availability of reliable technology for verification of regional agreements. This is a key to the issue but its very demands present a problem. The political will to accept a regional anti-proliferation framework can spring only from available technical measures being widely accepted as adequate to prevent cheating. Technology for verifying any set of nuclear restraints may be seen reliable, however, only if it has been tested in a practical setting. Because the nuclear situation in South Asia is unique in many ways, a number of technical measures that have been suggested may be found wanting. Satellite-based technologies can help only in monitoring outdoor activities. Indoor activity and research needs to be observed perforce by on-site monitoring. But as Singer and Neuhoff point out, there are no easy or complete technical solutions to the South Asian problem. A major problem is how to account for all the existing inventories of fissile material. Nations may not declare all the plutonium, uranium and tritium they have produced. If all the available fissile materials cannot be brought under some sort of verifiable system of accounting, secret weapons could still be produced.

If we do not address this problem but focus our attention instead on a cutoff of further fissile-material production, we then may be admitting small nuclear forces are likely to emerge on the subcontinent. A production cutoff would, of course, eliminate the possibility of a nuclear arms race. But such a proposal may be unacceptable to Islamabad because it would lock Pakistan into perpetual inferiority in South Asia as a result of its very small fissile-material inventory and production capability at.present.

This leads us to two possible anti-proliferation models for South Asia, each with six principal features:

Model I

- Nuclear weapons capabilities but no nuclear weapons on the subcontinent.
- Agreements on verifiable mutual restraints between India and Pakistan.
- India, China, and Pakistan sign a treaty pledging not to attack each other and not to use, or threaten to use, nuclear weapons.
- An India-Pakistan ban on underground nuclear testing.
- An India-Pakistan agreement to limit production of fissile materials to the specific fuel needs of civilian nuclear power and research reactors.
- Denuclearization of the Indian Ocean and Tibet.

Model II

- Small nuclear forces in India and Pakistan but no arms race.
- Treaty-incorporated pledges by China, India, Soviet Union, and Pakistan not to use, or threaten to use, nuclear arms against each other.
- Treaty signed by the established nuclear powers banning deployment of permanent forces in the Indian Ocean or the forward deployment of nuclear armed battlegroups or submarines in a zone adjacent to South Asia.
- A non-aggression treaty and confidence-building measures among China, India, and Pakistan including notifying troop movements, military maneuvers and nuclear accidents.
- Conventional arms control and border-deployments agreements between India and Pakistan and between China and India.
- Acceptance of a CTB by the established nuclear powers and major cuts in superpower nuclear arsenals.

Model I, which may be viewed as an ideal, could incorporate most of the nonproliferation proposals that have been floated in different fora. Model II presents a more likely (although pessimistic) picture of the emerging South Asia and U.S. strategic realities. There are at present too many major political and technical constraints for the first model to work. Most of these have been discussed at length above. Of the three main players in the South Asian proliferation game, only one—Pakistan—is ready to seek agreements within such a framework. And this willingness appears rooted in political and military realism: Pakistan does not have, and is unlikely to have, the resources to compete with India. The other players, India and China, as the world's two largest nations, see themselves in a bigger-than-the-region role and, therefore, Model I is a mismatch for them. To India, any arrangement within the framework of this model would mean acceptance of parity with Pakistan and a freeze on its power projection. Proposals for regional agreements within a subcontinental framework, such as the idea of a nuclear weapons-free zone, have therefore been treated with contempt in New Delhi,[76] since they give free rein to India's other principal rival, China.[77]

Two major political disincentives to South Asian nonproliferation are continued vertical proliferation by the superpowers and the way they have turned the Indian Ocean into a zone of military competition. Although some major arms-control agreements are expected to emerge in the next five years as a follow-up to START, U.S. actions in spearheading the opposition to a CTB, developing new major strategic systems, and declining to accept the concept of a minimal nuclear deterrent are important disincentives to making nonproliferation a globally accepted path.

Conclusion

Major advances in nuclear and missile programs on the subcontinent are a result of a technological momentum that is likely to gain further force in the 1990s. This momentum itself has been spurred by nationalism, expanding forces of technology and a national policy consensus in India and Pakistan. The task of drawing an acceptable nonproliferation agenda for South Asia, consequently,m is becoming increasingly difficult. South Asian proliferation is a major challenge to the legitimacy of the present international nonproliferation regime, whose very survival in its present form has come under a cloud. When nonproliferation initiatives were launched in the late 1970s, the situation on the subcontinent was very different. Pakistan had no enrichment capability. India had exploded a nuclear device but it had no reliable delivery capabilities or the ability to indigenously manufacture components and materials for a weapons program. Today, nonproliferation efforts constitute in some ways an attempt to shut the stable after the horses have bolted.

South Asian nuclearization nonetheless is spurring significant changes in the thrust of nonproliferation efforts. The earlier thrust on technology control and denial as the main nonproliferation instrument is giving way to a dominant political approach. The ascendancy of the more political approach over the technical approach is reflected in the emerging emphasis in policy and research on regional nuclear containment. With the failure to prevent the indigenous development of weapons-related technologies, the focus of the new thrust is on ways to block or manage a nuclear arms race through regional political cooperation and agreements.

The need for South Asian political cooperation and nuclear transparency is self-evident in a region which today has the world's highest level of terrorist-related violence. The expansion of rival nuclear programs on the subcontinent, the growing nuclearization of the Indian Ocean by outside powers, and China's ambitious weapons-buildup program have significant implications for regional security and nuclear safety. These developments are compounded by Pakistan-India and China-India border tensions and disputes which are centered on Kashmir, a region which is adjacent to the frontiers of another nuclear power, the Soviet Union. Although the territorial control of Kashmir is divided among Pakistan, India and China, it remains the main focus of regional disputes, with the resurgence of Islamic separatist militancy in the Indian-controlled Kashmir adding a new dimension to the territorial issue. The nuclearization of the subcontinent, however, may be an augury of the likely emergence of four nuclear powers with their borders converging in central-south Asia. such a development is bound to have a major impact on regional and global alignments and the world power structure.

Despite the possibility that present trends might be irreversible, it still may be feasible to prevent a subcontinental nuclear arms race and forestall the emergence of India and Pakistan as full-fledged nuclear powers. But there remains a failure to fully comprehend the dynamics of regional proliferation and local sensitivities. First and foremost, nonproliferation proposals will succeed only if they originate locally and reflect a genuine concern and desire among political leaders. Any proposal seen to be associated with outsiders will not receive serious consideration. This sensitivity has been reinforced by more than two decades of American public pressure on India and Pakistan to sign the NPT and accept international inspections on all facilities.

Subcontinental sensitivities also have been bruised by concerns in the United States that Pakistan and India could use nuclear arms in a conflict; implicit in such concerns is the assumption that India and Pakistan are weak and irresponsible or not as strong and responsible as the established nuclear powers.[78] South Asia, however, has a record of responsibly conducted wars. Strikes in all conflicts involving Pakistan, India and China have been restricted mainly to military targets, avoiding the large-scale civilian and industrial destruction as has occurred in wars elsewhere. Cooperative bargaining and dialogue between countries in the region have built an element of stability despite high levels of rhetoric and difficult and emotions-rousing political problems. The India-Pakistan agreement not to attack each other's nuclear facilities is an example of such bargaining. Against this background, Western concerns seem misplaced, and it could also be argued that weaponization need not necessarily have a destabilizing effect in South Asia.

The formulation of anti-proliferation strategies for South Asia is handicapped by underplaying the China factor. India's nuclear-weapons capability drive was a response to Chinese nuclearization; India has had no incentives to weaponize against a non-nuclear Pakistan because it always has had far superior conventional forces. China is an integral member of the South Asian proliferation triad, an involvement underscored by international documentation of Beijing's assistance to the Pakistani weapons program. China's nuclear threat to India has been reinforced by Beijing's current ten-year program to double the size of its nuclear armory by 1996. Beijing, therefore, needs to be part of any regional proposal to resolve the proliferation program.

Evolving strategic realities indicate that the Chinese-Indian rivalry may intensify as the world's two most populous nations seek to carve out a bigger role for themselves in Asia. The ongoing naval buildup programs in both countries, in particular the emphasis on creating large blue-water navies, are a signal of an emerging Indian-Chinese competition in the Indian Ocean and the waterways of

Southeast Asia. These buildups also are a challenge to the U.S. and Soviet strategic interests in the region.

The legitimacy of horizontal nonproliferation strategies would be enhanced if the established nuclear powers accepted and practiced vertical nonproliferation. Far from working toward minimum nuclear deterrence or vertical nonproliferation, the nuclear powers are still committed to producing large numbers of highly sophisticated weapons every year despite START. No anti-proliferation strategy can succeed in South Asia if the neighborhood still bristled with nuclear arms. An end to the big-power military competition in the Indian Ocean and the ocean's denuclearization will be important moves to promote nonproliferation on the subcontinent. An initial step in that direction could be a ban on the forward deployment of nuclear-armed submarines and aircraft-carrier battlegroups near the subcontinent.

The single most effective nonproliferation proposal for South Asia, however, is a CTB, a proposal that is supported both by India and Pakistan. A test ban would emasculate the Indian and Pakistan programs and block a nuclear arms race on the subcontinent. India and Pakistan, parties to the PTBT, would have little incentive to build arsenals of untested weapons if their current underground testing options were blocked by a CTB. This is underscored by official U.S. arguments on the importance of testing in nuclear deterrence. A total test ban is the only available political and technical route to a halt of both vertical and horizontal proliferation. Such a ban, however, may not completely block horizontal or vertical proliferation if tested weapon designs were transferred from one country to another.

Nonproliferation specialists need to bear two important points in mind when they examine South Asia. One, no nation has ever relinquished its nuclear option voluntarily or through a regional pact after having acquired a nuclear-weapons capability. In that sense, we are dealing with a unique situation because of the existence of sizable stocks of fissile materials outside the scope of IAEA safeguards. A pact like the South Pacific Nuclear-Free Zone Treaty, therefore, provides no model for South Asia. We can only discuss possibilities of a "weapons-control"—not a "weapons-free"—verification regime. A second point is that once the technical jinni is out of the bottle, technology alone cannot suppress it. In other words, complete technical solutions to the South Asian problem are not available. A CTB, however, offers an unrivalled path to stopping both horizontal and vertical proliferation globally, especially if it is coupled with a international ban on ballistic missile flight-testing. A total test ban also would be a first step in two other directions: minimum nuclear deterrence and shedding nuclear weapons of their aura as instruments of power and influence in world politics.

In the interim, it will be in the interests of India and Pakistan, and India and China, to work out some regional arrangements to clear the "air of mutual suspicion" and encourage the development of confidence-building nuclear transparency. Such steps obviously would have to go hand-in-hand with other confidence-building measures such as notifying each other of troop movements, military maneuvers and nuclear accidents. Chinese-Indian and Pakistani-Indian cooperation could also make a significant contribution to the promotion and strengthening of nuclear safety. The escalation of terrorist violence has given rise to concern over the safety of the dozens of nuclear facilities and the transport and storage of weapons-useable materials on the subcontinent. India and Pakistan need to upgrade physical-security systems and anti-terrorism safeguards at facilities and storage sites and closely monitor transport of fissile materials. All the countries in the region should ratify the Convention on the Physical Protection of Nuclear Material, which has been designed to deter international nuclear terrorism.

An India-Pakistan framework for periodic discussions on nuclear and conventional military matters would be an important follow-up step to the pact abjuring attacks on each other's nuclear installations. That agreement encouraged an element of nuclear transparency by requiring each party to inform the other of the exact location of all its nuclear installations and whenever new facilities are built.[79] Because of the secrecy surrounding the location of many of China's nuclear facilities and deployed missiles, a China-India framework for periodic discussions on nuclear and conventional issues would make an equally significant contribution to allaying mutual suspicions and fears. Indian-Chinese and Pakistani-Indian exchanges of nuclear-related information and reciprocal site visits are other important confidence-boosting measures the three countries could consider.

The outside nuclear powers also have a safety-related role to play in South Asia, although not in the immediate future, if there are signs of weaponization in India and Pakistan. These powers, particularly the United States and the Soviet Union, could provide help in developing the necessary technical and political conditions for stable deterrence, besides seeking to regulate the competition and trying to influence the development of nuclear doctrines. Their role would mainly involve providing assistance in building effective command and control systems and transferring technology to help secure weapons and prevent their unauthorized use. The safeguarding of weapons through multilayered protection systems would have to be an important priority. This task would include incorporating advanced protective systems consisting of "permissive action links" (PAL) devices with limited-try and command-disable functions into weapons and setting up nuclear emergency search teams (NESTs) on the lines of the U.S. Department of Energy's NEST teams to find and render harmless stolen weapons, improvised nuclear devises or weapons-usable materials.[80] China's own weapons probably need to be safeguarded with PALs.

South Asia's nuclear programs have bared the inadequacy and ineffectiveness of the current international nonproliferation regime, They therefore signal the need for change in the system. As the renewal of the NPT becomes an international issue, the regime's obsolescence will grow more apparent. But before the NPT unravels completely, policymakers and scholars must devise a new regime that is more realistic and widely acceptable.

Notes

1. A succinct analysis of the evolution of this policy is in Lawrence Scheinman's *The International Atomic Energy Agency and World Nuclear Order* (Washington, D.C.: Resources for the Future, 1987).

2. By the time Reagan succeeded Carter, the United States had no nuclear cooperation with the six leading "proliferation concern" countries: India, Pakistan, Israel, South Africa, Brazil and Argentina.

3. In one year, between 1987-88 and 1988-89, the Indian Department of Atomic Energy's scientific and technical manpower increased 2,181 to 20,109 (Government of India, Department of Atomic Energy, *Annual Report 1988-89*). India's main nuclear research complex, the Bhabha Atomic Research Center, which produces 250 nuclear scientists annually, also trains scientists from other

Third World countries including Vietnam, Malaysia, the Philippines and Tanzania.

4. The emergence of India as a major military and industrial force is discussed in detail in Brahma Chellaney, "Passage to Power," *World Monitor*, February, 1990, 24-32.

5. There appears to be a new policy focus in Washington and Moscow on employing high-powered diplomacy to pursue nonproliferation objectives. A case in point is the diplomatic pressure on Beijing to deter missile exports by China, which refuses to be part of either the nuclear nonproliferation system or the Missile Technology Control Regime. Moscow took the first step toward embracing the Western missile regime by sending its senior arms control negotiator Viktor P. Karpov to Washington in September 1988 for high-level discussions that represented the first U.S.-Soviet effort to jointly explore cooperation in curbing the missile race. Nonproliferation issues have figured prominently in the superpower summit meetings since the INF agreement. This is promoting closer superpower cooperation on nuclear and missile nonproliferation.

6. Australia, with the apparent backing of the United States, has promoted the idea of a regional nuclear agreement between Pakistan and India.

7. Steven R. Weissman, "India's Nuclear Energy Policy Raises New Doubts on Arms," *New York Times*, May 17, 1988. Based on an interview with the head of India's Department of Atomic Energy.

8. U.S. House of Representatives, *Hearings on U.S. Aid to Pakistan before the Subcommittee on Asian and Pacific Affairs of the Committee on Foreign Affairs*, October 22, 1987. Testimony of Ambassador Richard T. Kennedy.

9. Mark Hibbs, "U,S, Repeatedly Warned Germany on Nuclear Exports to Pakistan," *Nuclear Fuel*, March 6, 1989, and "Prosecutors Link tritium Plant to Pakistan Weapons Program," *Nuclear Fuel*, May 1, 1989

10. Chong-Pin Lin, "China: Nuclear Wild Card," *The New York Times*, July 29, 1988.

11. SIPRI Yearbook 1988, *World Armaments and Disarmament* (New York: Oxford University Press, 1988), pp. 52-54.

12. Mushahid Hussain, "Pakistan 'Responding to Change'," *Jane's Defense Weekly*, October 14, 1989, p. 779, interview with General Mirza Aslam Beg, Chief of Staff of the Pakistan Army.

13. This underscores the interlink between peaceful and military uses of nuclear technology as though they were two sides of the same coin. A country's civilian nuclear program can be peaceful only as long as such a strategy is desired by the political leadership or as long as the country is tied down by international treaty obligations. But since it is difficult at times even to draw a line between peaceful and military-oriented nuclear research work, treaty provisions can be breached willfully. The exclusion of fuel for nuclear submarines from the NPT safeguards system portends such a danger. What some analysts call a "loophole" in the nonproliferation system is actually an exclusion intentionally introduced as Article 14 in the NPT safeguards regime at the insistence of nations like West Germany and Japan. The danger to the regime

arises from the possibility that—in the name of using unsafeguarded fissile material in "non-proscribed military activity"—nations could stockpile unreasonably large quantities of highly-enriched uranium and defeat the system's very aim of deterring the spread of nuclear-explosive capability. The line between what is permitted and what is proscribed could easily blur.

In the Asian context, Japan's large civilian nuclear power construction program will yield huge inventories of weapons-usable plutonium in the near future. Tokyo would be able to have more plutonium under its control within thirty years than the amount now contained in the arsenals of the superpowers.

14. Western intelligence reports have mentioned the presence in Tibet of land-based missiles, all of which are trailer-transportable. The Dalai Lama, whose information is considered normally reliable because of the mass respect and support he enjoys in his Himalayan homeland, expressed his concern over the nuclearization of Tibet in an interview (Brahma Chellaney, "Militant Nationalism on the Rise in Tibet," *The Christian Science Monitor*, November 1, 1987). According to the Dalai Lama, new military bases and nuclear armament factories have been built in Tibet, which he said also was being used as a nuclear waste repository. The exiled Tibetan leader has called for making Tibet a nuclear weapons-free zone. The International Institute of Strategic Studies' *The Military Balance 1989-90* mentions substantial missile forces in the Chinese Military Regions bordering South Asia but does not provide exact deployment patterns.

15. William M. Arkin and Richard W. Fieldhouse, *Nuclear Battlefields: Global Links in the Arms Race* (Cambridge: Ballinger, 1985), p. 55.

16. International Institute of Strategic Studies, *The Military Balance, 1989-1990* (London: Brassey's, 1989), p. 150.

17. Leonard S. Spector, *The Undeclared Bomb* (Cambridge: Ballinger, 1988), p.150.

18. Brahma Chellaney, "Proliferation: The Nuclear Family Game," *World Paper*, Vol.10, No. 8, August 1988, pp. 1-2.

19. The two countries signed a protocol in August 1988 for increased cooperation on the peaceful uses of atomic energy.

20. This is discussed in detail in William Potter (ed.), *International Nuclear Trade and Nonproliferation: The Challenge of the Emerging Suppliers* (Lexington: Lexington Books, 1990).

21. SIPRI, *Armaments and Disarmament*, p. 53.

22. Jonas Bernstein, "Beijing's Nuclear Strategy Makes China a Major Player," *Insight*, August 22, 1988, p. 30.

23. Hussain, "Pakistan Responding to Change," p. 779.

24. Gerard C. Smith and Helena Cobban, "A Blind Eye to Nuclear Proliferation," *Foreign Affairs*, Summer,1989, pp. 53-54.

25. There is little hard evidence on the extent to which India and Pakistan may have gone. But there are several scholars and analysts who believe that at least in Pakistan some or all parts of nuclear weapons already may have been fabricated. According to one account, Pakistan has made most of the components and that it can quickly assemble weapons (Hedrick Smith, "A Bomb

Ticks in Pakistan," *New York Times Magazine*, March 6, 1988). According to another account, "Between late 1986 and mid-1988, convincing evidence emerged that Pakistan crossed the nuclear-weapons threshold and had acquired the essentials for its first nuclear weapons" (Spector, *Undeclared Bomb*, p. 120).

26. Richard Holmes, *The World Atlas of Warfare* (London: Viking Studio Books, 1988) and *The Harper Atlas of World History* (New York: Harper & Row, Publishers, 1987).

27. *The New U.S.-Japan Agreement* (Backgrounder: The Nuclear Control Institute, July 14, 1988). Also, Brahma Chellaney, "Fears over U.S. Plutonium Agreement with Japan," *The Age* (Melbourne), April 4, 1988.

28. There is an apparent recognition of this in Washington. Some questions, however, have been raised whether some important members of the U.S. administration view the Pakistani nuclear program as providing some strategic benefits to the United States like the Israeli weaponization. While addressing the Defense Policy Panel of the House Committee on Armed Services in 1987, General Crist, Commander-in-Chief CENTCOM, was asked "what impact would deployment of a Pakistani nuclear capability have on our military challenges and commitments in the area." General Crist's surprise answer was that such a Pakistani capability *"would present quite a great deal more deterrence to the Soviets* should they decide to move through Pakistan" (Hearings before the Defense Policy Panel of the Committee on Armed Services, House of Representatives, 100th Congress, First Session, March 11,13,17,18 This argument has been extended by some officials to imply that Pakistani nuclearization would not only be a deterrent to the Soviets but also serve to check India's ambitions to be the dominant naval and military power between the Persian Gulf and the Straits of Malacca. It now is admitted in Washington that India's growth as a regional power could challenge U.S. strategic interests in the Indian Ocean. American strategic interests in South Asia, however, have altered radically in the last three decades. For example, when the United States in 1964 was struggling to draft a nonproliferation policy, "with special attention to the problem of India," Secretary Dean Rusk contended that exclusion of India from such a policy may serve U.S. interests. Questioning a key assumption in the Thompson Committee's report, "Rusk said he thought a basic question was whether we really should have a nonproliferation policy prescribing that no countries beyond the present five might acquire nuclear weapons. Were we clear that this should be a major objective of U.S. policy? For example, might *we* not want to be in a position where India or Japan would be able to respond with nuclear weapons to a Chinese threat?" Glenn T. Seaborg with Benjamin S. Loeb, *Stemming the Tide: Arms Control in the Johnson Years* (Lexington: Lexington Books, 1987), p. 135.

29. Hussain,"Pakistan Responding to Change," p. 779. There appears to be a growing consensus in Pakistan in favor of weaponization. For example, General K.M. Arif, a former vice Army chief, told a seminar that weapons production would in the "national interest" of Pakistan. *Jang* (Lahore), August 10, 1989, p. 3.

30. To buttress its argument that its weapons program is defensive in character and should not be viewed as a threat by India, Beijing has cited its "solemn declaration" made after conducting its first nuclear test that "China will never at any time or under any circumstances be the first to use nuclear weapons." The significance of nuclear weapons, however, comes from not they being instruments of war fighting (which they are not) but in their threat value and the immense coercive power they are able to command over an adversary.

31. Tai Ming Cheung, "Command of the Seas," *Far Eastern Economic Review*, July 27, 1989, pp. 17-18.

32. M.G.K. Menon, Abdul Kalam and Raja Ramanna, who have played a pivotal role in military technology advances, are three of the principal leaders of India's military R&D program. Significantly, Menon (principal scientific adviser to the previous prime minister) and Ramanna (leader of the team that built the 1974 nuclear device) have been elevated to the Cabinet of Prime Minister V.P. Singh; this is the first time leading scientists have been appointed ministers. Kalam heads the missile program.

33. John W. Lewis and Xue Litai, *China Builds the Bomb* (Palo Alto: Stanford University Press, 1988), p. 2.

34. *Nuclear Weapons and South Asian Security*, Report of the Carnegie Task Force on Nonproliferation and South Asian Security (Washington, D.C.: Carnegie Endowment for International Peace, 1988), pp. 40-42.

35. The tests provided the necessary political impetus to put those projects into motion even though the Indians already had the expertise to extract plutonium from spent fuel before the Chinese detonation and the Pakistanis had been shopping for nuclear technology (according to a famous BBC documentary) before India's Pokhran test.

36. China signed a bilateral nuclear cooperation agreement with Pakistan in September 1986, and Chinese scientists have been visiting Kahuta. According to one account, "Pakistan's success owes much to Chinese help." *Foreign Report*, "Pakistan's Atomic Bomb," January 12, 1989, 1-3.

37. Smith, p. 38.

38. Henry Kissinger, speaking in a television interview in 1988 about the changing power equilibrium in the world, said he expected China to emerge as a major power in "northeast Asia" and India to become an important power in "South Asia." A viewer unfamiliar with Asian geography may not have realized that actually the two countries are neighbors sharing a long border.

39. Warren H. Donnelly, "Implementation of the U.S.-Chinese Agreement for Nuclear Cooperation," U.S. Library of Congress, Congressional Research Service, March 1, 1989, Issue Brief 86050. Also, Leslie H. Gelb, "Pakistan Links Peril U.S.-China Nuclear Pact," *New York Times*, June 22, 1984, and "Peking Said to Balk at Nuclear Pledges," *New York Times*, June 23, 1984.

40. The warning was contained in a classified aide-memoire to the Indian government that said the use of plutonium derived from the civilian program in nuclear-explosive devices would be incompatible with bilateral agreements. The aide-memoire was declassified September 19, 1980 by the Bureau of Oceans and International Environmental and Scientific Affairs, Department of State.

41. IISS, *Military Balance*, p. 159. According to the book, the Western Command facing Pakistan has seven divisions, while there are nine divisions in the eastern command in charge of the northeastern Indian border with China. There are seven divisions in the Northern Command, entrusted with safeguarding the frontiers with Pakistan and China.

42. This was part of the Pakistani-controlled Kashmir but was ceded to China.

43. In the 1962 conflict, Chinese troops seized control of this region but withdrew quickly.

44. Hundreds of troops have died in this combat at sub-zero temperatures on the world's highest battlefield. The Indians have suffered heavier casualties since they control the upper main section of the glacier, where breathing air contains less than half the normal oxygen content. Many of the victims simply perished in the blizzards. According to the Pakistani Army chief, "India has no strategic advantage in Siachen over Pakistan, only a political advantage of denying us 70 kilometers of common border with China." *Jane's Defense Weekly*, October, 14, 1989, p. 779.

45. Colina Mac Dougall, "Restless Moslem Fringe Worries Peking," *Financial Times*, January 30, 1990.

46. Thomas Schelling, *Arms and Influence* (New Haven: Yale University Press, 1966), and Bernard Brodie, ed., *The Absolute Weapon: Atomic Weapon and World Order* (New York: Harcourt Brace, 1946).

47. Margaret M. Gowing, *Independence and Deterrence: Britain and Atomic Energy, 1945-1952* (New York: 1974); Lewis and Litai.

48. Lewis and Litai, p. 229.

49. International Institute of Strategic Studies, "Nuclear Proliferation in South Asia," *Strategic Survey 1979* (London: IISS, 1980), p.16.

50. Chellaney, *Passage to Power*, p. 26.

51. Lewis and Litai, p. 35.

52. Brahma Chellaney, "India Bolsters its Naval Forces," Christian Science Monitory, Jan. 22, 1988.

53. Stephen P. Cohen, *The Pakistan Army* (Berkeley: University of California Press, 1984). This feeling is reinforced by a sense of challenge to Pakistan's very "raison d'etre."

54. Lewis and Litai, p. 36. The statement was issued after China declined to be a party to the Partial Test Ban Treaty.

55. As an example see the piece by Farhatullah Babar, "Nuclear Nonproliferation Issues: The International Context," *Strategic Studies* (Islamabad), Vol.10, No.4 and Vol.11, No.1, combined Summer and Autumn 1987 issue, pp. 21-25. Babar concludes by saying, "It should therefore be obvious to our policy planners that the current anti-proliferation strategy is motivated less by considerations of nonproliferation and more by a combination of political, commercial and other considerations. The Treaty is a hollow sermon, a criticism of non-nuclear weapon states, a misstatement, [and] an abdication of responsibility by the superpowers to perpetuate their technological, political and economic dominance of the rest of the world."

56. The only major dissenter to this theory has been Waltz, who argues that proliferation would upset neither systemic stability nor the bipolar nature of the international system. See Kenneth Waltz, *The Spread of Nuclear Weapons: More May Be Better*, Adelphi Paper No. 171 (London: Institute for Strategic Studies, 1981).

57. Robert Jervis contends that nuclear weapons will preserve the nuclear peace but they cannot "prevent—and, indeed, may even facilitate—the use of lower levels of violence. It is then not surprising that some observers attribute Soviet adventurism, particularly in Africa, to the Russians' ability to use the nuclear stalemate as a shield behind which they can deploy pressure, military aid, surrogate troops, and even their troops in areas they had not previously controlled." See: "The Political Effects of Nuclear Weapons," *International Security*, Vol.13, No.2, Fall 1988, pp. 80-90.

58. Patrick E. Tyler, "New Pentagon 'Guidance' Cites Soviet Threat in Third World," *Washington Post*, February 13, 1990.

59. As an example see Leonard S. Spector with Jacqueline R. Smith, *Nuclear Ambitions: The Spread of Nuclear Weapons, 1989-1990* (Boulder: Westview, 1990).

60. David Albright and Christopher Paine, "Making Warheads: A Case Against Producing Nuclear Material," *Bulletin of the Atomic Scientists*, January, 1988, p.47.

61. See, for example, Ben Sanders and John Simpson, *Nuclear Submarines and Nonproliferation: Cause for Concern*, Occasional Paper Two, Program for Promoting Nuclear Nonproliferation, (Southampton: Center for International Policy Studies, University of Southampton, July, 1988). The lease of an old Soviet SSN to India was severely criticized by the U.S. State Department on nonproliferation grounds.

62. This is mentioned in an official Canadian military journal. See the issue, "A New Submarine for Canada," *Wings* (Calgary), 1988. Canada, however, has decided for the time being not to proceed with the development of SSNs.

63. The dispatch of the nuclear-powered U.S. aircraft carrier, *Enterprise*, to the Bay of Bengal during the India-Pakistan 1971 war made bare India's naval vulnerability and thus may have contributed to the country's naval buildup program. The *Enterprise's* threatening presence played no mean role in hastening the withdrawal of Indian troops from newly created Bangladesh.

64. *New York Times*, "Mr. Bush on Defense: Too Much, Too Late," January 30, 1990.

65. This is discussed in length in Paul Leventhal and Brahma Chellaney, "Nuclear Terrorism: Threat, Perception and Response in South Asia," *Terrorism*, Vol.11, 1990, pp. 447-470.

66. A blueprint for achieving minimum nuclear deterrence suggests 1,000 strategic weapons for each superpower and perhaps 200 each for China, France and Britain. Richard Garwin, "A Blueprint for Radical Weapon Cuts," *Bulletin of the Atomic Scientists*, March, 1988, pp. 10-13.

67. For a discussion of proposals in U.S. Congress to halt Soviet-American fissile material production and the verification issues they raise, see Warren H. Donnelly and David Cheney, "Proposals for Ending U.S. and Soviet Production of Fissile Materials for Nuclear Weapons," Library of Congress, Congressional Research Service, Issue Brief IB89141, November 9, 1989.

68. J. Carson Mark, Thomas D. Davies, Milton M. Hoenig and Paul L. Leventhal, "The Tritium Factor as a Forcing Function in Nuclear Arms Reduction Talks," *Science*, Vol. 241, September 2, 1988, pp. 1166-1168. Also, Nuclear Control Institute and American Academy of Arts and Sciences, *The Tritium Factor* (NCI-AAAS, 1989).

69. Michael R. Gordon, "Reagan Links Fewer Nuclear Arms to More Tests," *New York Times*, September 30, 1988.

70. William Epstein and Glenn T. Seaborg, "An Amended Nuclear Pact Holds Hope of Total Ban," *Los Angeles Times*, August 5, 1988. For an account of the technical arguments put forth by the anti-CTB lobby in the United States see Jack F. Evernden, "Lies That Stopped a Test Ban," *Bulletin of the Atomic Scientists*, October, 1988, pp. 20-24.

71. Kathleen Bailey, "A Nuclear Weapons Turning Point: Proliferation Could Surface as Old Alliances Sink," *The Christian Science Monitor*, February 12, 1990.

72. Arkin and Fieldhouse, *Nuclear Battlefields*, pp. 132-137.

73. *Ibid.*

74. Tai Ming Cheung, pp. 16-20. A senior PLA officer has cited his Navy's Indian Ocean voyages as an example of expanding Chinese seapower. Bradley Hahn, "Third-Ranking Maritime Power—And Growing," *Pacific Defense Reporter*, October 1988, p. B13.

75. Arkin and Fieldhouse, p. 135.

76. India has presented to the United Nations a three-phase arms control proposal under which nuclear-threshold states would "undertake not to cross the threshold" if the nuclear-weapons states cut the size of their arsenals, ended arms testing and production of weapons-grade materials, and agreed to work toward complete nuclear disarmament by 2010. This idea has been supported by the Five-Continent Six-Nation Peace Initiative, of which Sweden, Tanzania, Greece, Argentina, Mexico and India are members.

77. China's entry into the South Asian nonproliferation arena would be an "interference" and a "deviation" from its established foreign policy, according to the Chinese representative at the South Asian nonproliferation workshop organized by Pakistan's Institute for Strategic Studies *Strategic Studies*, "Special Issue: Nuclear Nonproliferation in South Asia," Vol. 10. No. 4 and Vol. 11, No. 1, 1987, p. 156.

78. An example of how any regional dispute can be viewed as a potential nuclear conflict is the editorial, "The Nuclear Edge," in *Washington Post*, on February 4, 1990. Although the unrest in Indian-controlled Kashmir has not triggered a major conventional mobilization in either India or Pakistan, the *Post* concluded that Kashmir has started to "become shorthand for a Third World dispute with a nuclear edge."

79. However, as of mid-1990, the two countries had not yet exchanged formal documents to put the agreement into effect.

80. For discussion of civilian and military nuclear security measures, including the use of permissive action links, see Burns, chapter 4 of this volume.

11

Policy Implications

Stephen Philip Cohen

This chapter expands the discussion of the relationship between verification, arms control and nuclear proliferation and it offers a number of policy-related suggestions.[1]

The Stages of Proliferation and Verification

How can we refine our understanding of the stages of proliferation in South Asia, and link this to the verification process? Adapting Louis Dunn's distinction between prevention, containment, and management of proliferation, we conceptualize proliferation as a three stage *process*.[2]

Stage I: Prevention or Renunciation

Some states either have no capacity to develop nuclear weapons or have taken a firm political decision not to do so. These are at *Stage I* of the proliferation process. Here, the full range of formal verification technologies can be applied with relative technical ease to single states. One hundred and forty-one countries fall into this category, and have subscribed to the Nonproliferation Treaty and IAEA verification services. A few NPT parties (e.g. Libya, North Korea, and Iraq) are suspected of harboring plans to acquire nuclear weapons. For states at Stage I verification must provide evidence that a state is fulfilling its commitment not to acquire nuclear weapons, or that a state still lacks the capacity to do so. Technically, this could be accomplished by informal means even if a state has not signed the NPT and does not allow the IAEA to inspect its facilities (Brazil and Argentina are not NPT signatories but have made it possible for others to confirm the non-military status of their nuclear programs).

Stage II: Ambiguity

Dunn writes of containment, but from the perspective of proliferating states the key concept is their *ambiguous* nuclear status. Here there is uncertainty both as to the will and the capacity of a country to acquire nuclear weapons.[3] Sometimes called the "option" (a term virtually invented by Indians in the mid-1960s), Stage II nuclear status can be ambiguous in several respects. There may be uncertainty as to whether it represents a real stopping point, a temporary halt in the proliferation process, or merely a transition to declared or overt nuclear status. There may even be uncertainty as to whether a country has covertly acquired a few nuclear devices. Stage II also has a time dimension: uncertainty with regard to how long it would take to weaponize a nuclear program—is the program a legendary screwdriver turn away, or is a weapon some months or years in the future?

In Stage II of proliferation, the role of verification is quite different from Stage I. Instead of proving a negative, arms control arrangements have to do two things. First, they must outline the contours of a state's overall nuclear *potential*. Second, such agreements must provide some indication as to the *time* it would take for a state to acquire a significant nuclear weapon capability. Indicators that a state does not have the intention of quickly weaponizing can be especially useful here. Since it is so critical to the India-Pakistan situation we will further refine the notion of ambiguity below, and introduce the idea of *designed ambiguity:* the conscious and structured manipulation of a state's ambiguous nuclear status.[4]

Stage III: Declared Status

The chief purpose of verification in a *Stage III* situation (especially in the case of India and Pakistan, where two states might declare their weapons status at about the same time) is to ensure *stability*. Here, verification arrangements must confirm adherence to stated limits on numbers and deployment arrangements, and the existence of a reliable command and control system. Evidence of a lack of incentive or capability of striking first are essential here to ensure stability. This would be of greater importance in South Asia than other regions of the world since India and Pakistan have high-value targets across their common border, and Pakistan's airfields are especially vulnerable to preemptive attack. If these states were to weaponize, their relationship would be more similar to that of the U.S.-Soviet strategic contest than to any other regional nuclear balance in the world. Even the India-China relationship is more stable, since the distances are much greater, the intensity of divisive issues is weaker, and the likelihood of escalation from a conventional war is smaller. However, the India-China nuclear relationship does have a greater potential for interaction with U.S.-Soviet-Chinese nuclear calculations.

Designed Ambiguity, Transitions and Stability

Three important problems are suggested by this discussion. The first is the further refinement of the notion of nuclear ambiguity—especially ambiguity by design. The second is the transition from ambiguity to weaponization—from Stage II to Stage III. The third is the relationship between ambiguity and stability.

Designed Ambiguity

When a state has achieved Stage II, and possesses an ambiguous nuclear program, and tries to manage its ambiguous status, then we can say that it has achieved *designed* ambiguity. It is important to know whether a country has reached the status of nuclear ambiguity deliberately or by accident. Does it attempt to manage (or manipulate) its ambiguous status, or does it pay little attention to what others think of its program? This, of course, implies an audience—another attentive state or states. In South Asia we have the unique situation of two states achieving designed ambiguity—and their audience consists in large part (but not entirely) of each other. *This is an historically unprecedented situation.*

India devised the policy of designed ambiguity after the Chinese nuclear test of 1964, and designed ambiguity was adapted by the

Pakistanis after their nuclear program acquired a near-military capability in the mid-1980s. The Indians first called their policy the option strategy, later they and the Pakistanis began to talk of uncertainty or ambiguity as the core element of their nuclear policies.[5] These options—the game of reveal and conceal—applies to both intentions and capabilities. It has been so well-played by both states over such a long period that there is little doubt that they have created a unique nuclear relationship of managed, or designed ambiguity. Both sides believe that designed ambiguity enhances their security by preserving the nuclear option and by allowing the political and strategic exploitation of the advantages of being a nuclear power without incurring the costs and risks of actually deploying nuclear forces.

Compared with the American and Soviet record over the same years (from about 1965), this regional record of unilateral and reciprocal restraint under a policy of designed ambiguity is quite impressive. There was only one nuclear test, no evidence of an assembled (or deployed) weapon, and only recently, rudimentary development of a missile delivery capability. There have also been several confidence-building agreements, and no evidence that either has side seriously contemplated a preemptive strike on the other's nuclear facilities. Both India and Pakistan have been willing to let the other develop civil nuclear systems which have direct military implications. They can do this because of their own interest in protecting the good name of the option strategy, and because each has demonstrated some restraint in weaponizing civilian-based dual use technologies.[6] This approach has led to a considerable overhang of nuclear and missile capabilities. This overhang must be part of any regional nuclear arrangement, whether bilateral or multilateral, and it must be factored in to any American policy directed towards India or Pakistan.

The central challenge facing American nonproliferation policy in South Asia is to formulate policies which will be effective in this context of designed ambiguity, especially since both regional states seem to find the situation at least acceptable (and Pakistanis find it highly desirable). We will elaborate this below, but the basic policy options open to the United States are to attempt to *reverse* this situation, *maintain* it, or move it *forward* to one of declared nuclear status.

However, India and Pakistan face a larger set of choices. Not only must they decide whether to move ahead to declared nuclear status or move back to a situation of unambiguous non-nuclear status, but also how they want to *manage* their ambiguous nuclear status. Indeed, their understanding of the role that ambiguity plays in the decisions of others (especially decisions involving the prevention of accidental war, but also decisions which would help keep costs down), is one of the biggest questions they face. Participants in this project disagree strongly on the ability of India *and* Pakistan to perpetuate a situation of designed ambiguity. As we have noted, their record on nuclear matters is quite good. Balancing this, their record of managing conventional arms balances is uneven. At least two regional wars were caused by Pakistani miscalculations of Indian capabilities and responses.

The interactive quality of regional relations is central to an ambiguous nuclear relationship. Indians are confident of their own ability to manage nuclear ambiguity but they must remember that they are at the mercy of the Pakistani political process to make restrained and balanced decisions. Since they often deride Pakistan as an unstable and unpredictable state, they should be doubly concerned about entering into an intimate competitive nuclear relationship with Islamabad, let alone Islamabad plus Beijing.[7] In these matters, the stability of a nuclear balance of terror (and therefore, the security of each state) can be no greater than the quality of decision-making in the least responsible state, and it can sometimes be a good deal worse, as the Cuban Missile Crisis shows.[8]

Above all, Indian and Pakistani leaders must reflect carefully upon the criteria that will determine whether they move to Stage III proliferation, and whether this movement will be fast or slow, whether they will seek a minimum deterrent or a continually expanding one, and how elaborate, reliable, and costly their command and control systems must be. What will shape these decisions? Fear of the other state? Fear of falling behind? The desire for some political advantage that might accrue as a consequence of being a nuclear power? The habit of competition? Or the example of forty years of superpower competition?

The Transitions from Ambiguity to Certainty

Beyond describing the contours of an arms control agreement, and the time required to break out of such an agreement, Stage II verification must provide help in assessing a state's *intentions* since the most critical fact about ambiguity is the possibility of moving forward to a declared nuclear weapons capability. In the absence of a formal arms control agreement, verification of informal agreements and understandings, as well as confidence building measures (CBMs) of many types (even if they are trivial), may provide important clues as to the intention of a state. If the time needed to weaponize is very short, then stability requires a very high quality of assessment of intentions. Cooperation in CBMs may be the only way to provide such an assessment. Technical verification schemes on their own cannot tell us much about intentions, but they can provide supporting evidence that might verify public or private statements concerning a state's nuclear intentions. CBMs are of critical importance if they can demonstrate that a state's actions are in rough congruence with estimates of its intentions, both declared and undeclared. If a state can find ways of demonstrating this congruence in important areas their neighbors and others can be somewhat reassured that it is not moving ahead to weaponization.

Time is obviously a central issue for Stage II proliferation states, and especially important for India and Pakistan, since their nuclear systems would be born into a world where they could be immediately targeted by mature nuclear weapon states or by each other. If India or Pakistan were to do everything necessary to deploy a nuclear weapon except complete a few easy steps that would take a matter of minutes or hours—then verification of any arms control agreement that is achieved must be more intrusive, more detailed, and more reliable to provide the same degree of reassurance than if there are many steps before it can deploy a nuclear weapon, steps that would take days, weeks, or months. *For many reasons, this is a very dangerous period: states that believe that they are holding a short-tether option may look as if they possess an actual nuclear war fighting capability. If a state begins to look as if it has proliferated—that it has moved to Stage III—other states begin to make calculations of nuclear war fighting, and the risk of misinterpretation or misjudgment becomes very great.*

Ambiguity and Stability

One central question raised in one form or another by nearly every contributor to this book is: in the South Asian context, are ambiguity and stability inconsistent? If they are—as most of the American participants tend to believe—then the present designed ambiguity strategies of India and Pakistan could lead to disaster. But, from the perspective of informed regional experts, there are good reasons why Stage II nuclear ambiguity and stability may not be incompatible:

- The cost of an all-out nuclear arms race (involving missiles, extensive testing, second and third generation nuclear weapons, and so forth) would be very great for both states.
- There are potential strategic losses and uncertainties associated with plunging ahead. For India, entry into the "big league" of nuclear powers would still leave considerable uncertainty as to the specific, regional gains that this would produce. For Pakistan, the losses are self-evident: a regional arms race would seal its fate as a small, vulnerable state, albeit one with nuclear weapons. It would be vulnerable until (in the distant future) it could develop a seaborne nuclear delivery system, while India can now think of secure, second-strike retaliatory forces located beyond the range of any Pakistani missile or aircraft. It would probably lose the support of the United States, although the Chinese tie may continue to expand.
- For both states, there must be a nagging question whether nuclear weapons are propelled by their own logic. The U.S.-Soviet experience, and that of other nuclear states, suggests that NWS may start out with the notion of acquiring a finite "MAD"-like deterrent but are driven by many factors to seek larger war-fighting capabilities. Will this logic drive Indian and Pakistan systems well beyond any minimum deterrent, beyond their fiscal and technical capabilities?

This central core of ambiguity, circumscribes the limits of *nuclear* arms control possibilities in South Asia, although it powerfully suggests the need for other kinds of regional arms control arrangements. Any arms control agreement which precipitously removed ambiguity concerning Indian and Pakistani nuclear capabilities would be rejected by both states, and if accepted, might do more damage than good; but any proposal which strengthened ambiguity without reducing instability (at present or higher levels), or which encouraged one or both states to move to higher levels of weapons development or deployment is obviously undesirable. Therefore, we can narrow our search to proposals which: preserve a minimum level of ambiguity as to regional capabilities (since this is the bedrock of both Indian and Pakistani nuclear policy, at least for the moment); reduce instability, including the risk of accidental war; discourage movement to a higher level of weapons development, and take into account collateral symbolic, strategic, and economic interests.

Arms Control Proposals: An Inventory

Table 11-1, which follows this chapter, lists a number of major proposals, confidence-building measures, arms control proposals, and other other suggestions that are pertinent to the South Asian and—to a lesser degree—the India-China relationship. These have been graded according to their relationship to Stage I, II, or III proliferation. We are particularly interested in proposals which attempt to define, stabilize, and regulate the inherent ambiguity of Stage II proliferation. The following discussion of U.S. policy initiatives will be guided by this list. However, two points need to be made. First, any arms control or verification proposal must be weighed not only in terms of its immediate benefits in constraining or stabilizing South Asia's move towards weaponization, but also in terms of collateral damage to long-run prospects for arms control. Offering permissive action links to states which have yet to make a deployment decision may force such a deployment, may destabilize a regional nuclear balance, or may accidentally push it to a new level. On the other hand, moving to overt nuclear status may make it easier to verify that a stable regional balance exists, and to work out the details to ensure that stability can be preserved.[9] Second, some weapons systems, or dual-use technologies are easier than others to control—and verify that they are controlled. The ability of satellites to detect the movement of smaller and smaller military units, and to monitor the production of large-scale systems (missiles), and to monitor nuclear test sites is increasing rapidly. In five years, such capabilities will be commercially available to both India and Pakistan, and to outside groups that might wish to monitor regional nuclear developments. When coupled with additional seismic monitoring stations, and increased national technical means capabilities, it appears that all of the technical means to monitor several kinds of regional arms control agreements are either in place or can be acquired soon. Some kind of regional open-skies arrangement would be of considerable promise because of its relative inexpensiveness, availability, and flexibility.

Policy Implications for the United States

U.S. policy must address an anomaly: the shortest route to a successful nonproliferation effort in the South Asian case may not be via a primary focus on nuclear weapons.

Why is the "weapons first" approach wrong? It tends to ignore the deeper motives which drive India and Pakistan towards a Stage II policy of designed ambiguity. It ignores the domestic political pressures behind weaponization, the technical capabilities which make it easy for such states as India (although not, originally, Pakistan) to experiment with nuclear ambiguity and, above all, it ignores the special regional circumstances which shape the environment for weaponization. Ironically, it also tends to underestimate the political and moral restraints that do keep India and Pakistan from moving ahead to a Stage III declared nuclear capability, or even a covert nuclear capability. In the words of Geoffrey Kemp, summing up a recent two-year project on the spread of advanced military technologies to the Middle East and South Asia:

> The U.S. supports Pakistan in the furtherance of U.S. policy to contain Soviet influence, but, rather schizophrenically, threatens to cut Islamabad off because of its nuclear weapons program. Pakistan cherishes its relationship with the U.S. as a means to acquire the equipment to deter Indian aggression, but India's intransigence on bilateral disputes and overwhelming nuclear superiority have forced Pakistani leaders to seek nuclear weapons in order to stay in the game. And finally, Pakistani nuclear weapons, which are not overly threatening to the far larger and stronger India, are a constant source of annoyance to New Delhi because they spark efforts by the U.S. to reduce India in stature to Pakistan's level, and thus interfere with India's goals of achieving parity with China and eventual great power status. Separating out nuclear weapons in this case is nearly impossible as each country's interest in them is the result of factors that are only related when taken in their entirety. Until analysts are prepared to discuss all the factors relating to the military balance, discussions on arms control will remain hopelessly unrealistic.[10]

Most of the chapters in this book make the same point even where they differ on specifics: nonproliferation policy *is* regional policy, the two cannot be separated. The U.S. made an exception to Europe in formulating its nonproliferation policies in the 1950s and 1960s, and more recently has regularly excluded Israel (and to some degree, Pakistan) from broader nonproliferation calculations.[11] By and large, these policies have worked in that generalized proliferation has not taken place. I am not sanguine about the future—Leonard S. Spector may be correct in characterizing the current period as the "lull before the storm"—and I do believe that new strategies will be required to deal with a Stage II situation of designed ambiguity, but in South Asia, at least, these will have to be different policies than those designed to deal with a Stage I situation of pre-nuclearization.[12]

These remarks do not imply a narrowing down of the range of policies available to influence proliferation in South Asia. Indeed, they *broaden* our understanding of what is useful. Nonproliferation policy, arms control, and "confidence building measures" are so closely related that they may be different names for the same thing. In a Stage II environment of designed ambiguity, the chief objective of arms control must focus on the last two of the classic goals of arms control: to reduce the probability of war and the destructiveness of war, not the first classic goal, to eliminate or reduce a particular type of weapon. Although nuclear weapons are different in that they are true instruments of mass destruction, the world has enough experience in managing and handling them so that fear of these weapons must not paralyze our willingness to contain rather than completely eliminate them.

In South Asia arms control must encompass a wide range of strategies, policies, and confidence building measures.[13] Here, as in the Middle East, nuclear proliferation is a process that can be influenced, slowed, and perhaps guided, but it would be naive to claim that it can be stopped. This view is gaining wider acceptance. In summarizing another project on the spread of nuclear weapons and advanced military technologies to the Middle East and South Asia, Joseph Nye has written that "in a sense, all of arms control is a confidence and security-building measure. By increasing transparency and communication among adversaries, worst case analyses are limited and security dilemmas are alleviated. . . . [a]greements on incidents at sea, crisis centers . . . have been scorned by some experts as the junk food of arms control, [b]ut the classical distinctions between reductions of arms and measures to build confidence and security have begun to blur."[14] Thus, by probing deeper into the regional roots of proliferation, and by moving to management and containment, rather than focussing entirely on elimination, *we may broaden the definition and increase the complexity of the problem, but we gain considerably in the range of instruments available for policy.*

What are some of the lessons to be drawn for policy? First, we should not be restricted to traditional arms control proposals. The regional peace *processes* (well-underway between India and Pakistan and India and China) may be the most effective form of arms control. Second, we should be willing to consider *any* proposal, idea, confidence-building measure, or partner. Proliferation has complex, diverse origins; managing proliferation will require a wide range of policy instruments. Third, we should simultaneously make policy for the short run (the next few years) and the longer-run (beyond the renewal date of the NPT, i.e. 1995). Containing regional proliferation will require sustained attention, not a quick-fix, or a solution drawn up according to a simple formula.

Six Strategies

There are at least six different strategies that the United States *could* pursue with regard to proliferation in South Asia.

First, vigorous pressure on India and Pakistan to force compliance with the NNPA and the NPT, and other international agreements (such as MTCR) to get them back to Stage I status. Essentially backed by denial tactics, "getting tough" is now supported by fewer members of the nonproliferation community, in and out of the government.[15] These tactics did not work in the past; they are unlikely to lure India and Pakistan into the NPT. Both countries have long since passed the point where strong pressure would slow down or stop their nuclear programs, such pressure is now more likely to accelerate them. Even if the U.S. were willing to sacrifice other regional interests, getting India and Pakistan back to a pristine non-nuclear status is highly improbable. No one can take away knowledge once acquired.

Second, the U.S. could support an alternative NPT that might accommodate the demands of India and Pakistan (and a few other non-NPT signatories), and induce them to restrain or contain their nuclear programs.[16] In effect, India and Pakistan would be admitted to the NPT as weapons states (or near-weapons states). This could put the NPT structure at risk, but it might help limit their transfer of nuclear technology to other near-NWS. My own view is that diluting the NPT is both unfeasible and undesirable. The NPT has its flaws, but 141 countries find it useful, and its credibility is likely to grow as the U.S. and the Soviet Union increasingly fulfill their part of the NPT bargain by engaging in substantial arms reductions.

Third, the U.S. could push India and Pakistan to move to overt, declared nuclear-weapons status. Trading proliferation for the elimination of ambiguity, uncertainty, and risk would allow several states to work directly with India and Pakistan in perfecting their nuclear command and control systems, and making arrangements with existing nuclear NWS. But it is too early to consider these steps yet while a chance of avoiding the overt nuclearization of India and Pakistan remains.

Fourth, the U.S. could abandon its historical regional policy and make a choice: throwing its support to India or Pakistan and adopting tough measures against the other. This would mean the nuclearization of one state, but the effective containment of the other (although in the case of India, the U.S. would have to enlist Chinese support as well). But this policy is also seriously flawed. It would not work, in that both states have passed the point of no-return as far as their nuclear programs are concerned, and second, it does not match up with other important American interests. However, a regional approach (albeit one that did not treat the two states identically) would probably make it possible for both to accept restraints and limits. A global approach would make it easier still: thus, for tactical reasons, it would be preferable that a regional freeze be part of a larger, region-by-region strategy that would include Israel, South Africa, and other near-nuclears.

Fifth, the U.S. could continue its present policy of passive support for whatever regional agreements or confidence building arrangements that emerge from Indo-Pakistani discussions or from unilateral steps taken by one or both states. Essentially, this is a strategy of waiting for regional normalization to prepare the ground for regional agreement—unsurprisingly, it is the position urged upon Washington by regional hawks who wish to press ahead with both nuclear and advanced delivery systems as fast as possible.

Sixth, the U.S. could adopt a modified, active, regional strategy that focussed on freezing or containing the Indian and Pakistani programs at Stage II, while protecting the NPT and other international arrangements. Such a policy would likely result in a number of small agreements outside the NPT which added up to a containment regime. These agreements could be bilateral, multilateral, formal or informal. This "freeze" policy should identify areas where India, Pakistan, the U.S. and other important states have common nuclear interests. From a regional perspective, these common interests can be visualized as a series of plateaus or meeting points where both countries can reach a better understanding of the risks and benefits of moving towards Stage III proliferation, and improve the stability of their present ambiguous nuclear relationship. This is not a new suggestion, although it runs against the grain of much of the arms control literature, and India's long-standing policy of calling for a total ban on nuclear weapons before considering regional arms control arrangements.[17] A nuclear freeze, plateau, or standstill all imply the same thing: a degree of understanding between the two states to pause before crossing certain important thresholds, and attempt to work out either a way of staying on this side of such thresholds, or more smoothly managing the new strategic relationship that would be created by crossing them.[18]

The remainder of this section further develops this sixth strategy.

The Outlines of a Nonproliferation Policy

Nine complementary policy recommendations emerge from this discussion, and from other chapters in this book. These can be grouped into three categories.

Short to medium-term efforts to encourage Indian and Pakistani policies to move in directions compatible with important American (but also, I believe, Indian and Pakistani) interests:

(1) The U.S. and other supporting states should encourage India and Pakistan to move in the direction of a nuclear freeze or plateau. This would not be an equal relationship between the two, because of asymmetries in their capabilities and (perhaps) intentions. However an increasingly stable regional nuclear relationship (probably achievable within the context of a Stage II policy of

designed ambiguity) should be a central objective of American policy. Whether the situation were formalized, or left informal, its critical parameters would have to be defined by some kind of verification arrangement. These parameters could include: no testing, no assembly, no deployment and no attack on nuclear facilities; they might also include at some point a halt to production of weapons-usable fissile materials. The plateau could also include an agreement not to produce missiles beyond a certain range.[19] It should be emphasized that this arrangement does not by itself meet India's concerns regarding China.

This policy acknowledges reality: that India and Pakistan could be de facto or near-nuclear states, but assumes that it is not in the interest of either state to become Stage III declared NWS. The U.S. must treat them seriously, not as nuclear pariahs, but as states edging towards significant nuclear and conventional military capabilities.

(2) The United States should begin the aggressive pursuit of assurances that India and Pakistan will not assist nuclear proliferation elsewhere. This is a policy goal that remains important whether or not India and Pakistan move to Stage III. It has profound implications for the Middle East and Northeast Asia, where Delhi and Islamabad have burgeoning scientific, military, and economic ties. America's goal should be an overt and public declaration of no-transfer, backed by suitable verification or monitoring mechanisms. Civil nuclear exports should be allowed only under IAEA safeguards.

(3) Expand and refine verification. There needs to be improved methods of verifying the continued status of designed ambiguity and a more explicit mechanism to ensure the non-transfer of nuclear technology. Some of this is already done by the United States (with regard to Pakistan). The verification service that the U.S. provides to India with regard to Pakistan could be extended to Pakistan with regard to India if Congress changed American law so that the president was required to certify that American assistance to Pakistan also had a restraining influence on Indian nuclear policy.

Since this may be a temporary arrangement (linked to the provision of military equipment to Pakistan), and it is certainly a flawed arrangement—since it cannot measure intentions—it would be in America's interest to support an international or multinational nuclear verification service which could issue regular statements about the status of both nuclear programs and their relationship with covert proliferation efforts elsewhere.[20] The question of intentions might best be left to regional countries to determine for themselves, as they would best understand the range of ambiguity necessary to maintain an option on both sides. Since the region covers more than India and Pakistan when it comes to nuclear matters, similar evaluations of China's nuclear capabilities vis-à-vis South Asia, especially India, would be essential; the Chinese themselves might find it to be in there interest to provide a better estimate of their *intentions*, as well.

(4) Efforts to contain regional nuclear programs must be part of the regional peace process, which should include efforts to stabilize conventional arms relations. The India-Pakistan-China nuclear triangle interacts with regional conventional arms balances. Pakistan's nuclear program was originally motivated by its conventional military inferiority, and since their de facto or nuclear status may tempt some regional planners to explore low-level or low-intensity warfare (safe in the knowledge that neither side dare escalate very far for fear of jarring the nuclear trigger), we may have to pay more, not less, attention to conventional arms acquisitions than in the past. For America this means restraint on the sale or provision of particularly destabilizing systems, and consultation with both countries before their sale. On the other hand, it may mean selling systems which strengthen defenses and increase early warning time, and which do not provoke preemption, and so forth. Verifiability could also be a criteria for determining which types of technologies and weapons were sold.

Linking nuclear containment to a broader peace process has another important advantage. It helps undercut the regional argument that nuclear arms control is "discriminatory."[21] If it is seen as part of a broader regional effort, regional nuclear restraint begins to look exactly like the U.S.-Soviet peace process where nuclear and conventional arms are on the negotiating table.[22]

Separately, the time is ripe for a different kind of conventional arms management strategy. It is technically, economically, and politically feasible to publish an annual "Regional Military Balance" report. An independent academic or non-governmental agency could assemble a group of retired officers, drawn from different countries (a team of retired Soviet, American, Indian and Pakistani officers would be an ideal group), and ask them to provide an assessment of regional arms balances. An accompanying study might discuss the economic and social impact of arms spending, particular programs, and so forth.

Such a group would make it difficult for hawks in either India or Pakistan to press for unrealistic or excessive defense demands, and would (presumably) provide assurances with regard to the essential stability of the India-Pakistan conventional arms balance (or imbalance, since India has a substantial lead[23]). On the other hand, it could provide warning of systems or trends which might be destabilizing. The "Regional Balance" study team would best be funded by a private foundation.

Longer term policies or actions which attempt to inform and enrich the policy debates within India and Pakistan.

(5) Assist regional states in verifying a freeze. We have discussed a wide-range of CBMs, technical "fixes," and other arms control measures which might help India and Pakistan stabilize their nuclear relationship. The United States and other governments should make available to India and Pakistan those monitoring systems which could help them verify the different components of a nuclear freeze, or standstill, discussed above. In some cases, these could be provided at cost. In other cases, civilian use would offset costs. India and Pakistan have already made extensive purchases of SPOT and other satellite output; these data, plus seismic data, can be routinely but rapidly fed to Indian and Pakistani receiving stations. Here, it is important to ensure that each side understands the complementarity of this information, and becomes aware of the images that it presents to the other, as a way of improving the transparency of their relationship. This is especially important in the case of nuclear testing and missile deployment—in both cases the verification task is simplified because a single deviation from a policy of restraint is an unambiguous and fairly detectable signal. One way to transmit information about relevant verification technologies would be through Indians and Pakistanis attached to the IAEA; indeed, they might be encouraged to undertake an independent assessment of regional verification technologies and possibilities. Their technical expertise, and national perspective would lend weight to such a study.

(6) Expand educational programs. In 1979, concluding a study of Indian and Pakistani attitudes towards nuclear weapons and nuclear war, I suggested that it was in the U.S. interest to:

sharpen the awareness of South Asians of the effects of nuclear weapons. Most Indians and Pakistanis have a schizoid view of such weapons; at one moment they regard them all as evil, destructive devices, which must be eliminated from the globe; at another they seem to believe that they are (to quote Jagjivan Ram) "nuclear bullets," simple extensions of conventional weaponry. Indians refuse to discuss the problems of deterrence which would arise should they go nuclear, as they are true abolitionists; Pakistanis want "only" four or five weapons, and seem unaware of how vulnerable this would make them to a serious Indian program.[24]

What was true then is true now. It remains very much in America's interest to share with a broader and increasingly democratic South Asian public a fuller understanding of the effects of nuclear weapons. There is a historical irony: India was one of the first governments to fund and publish a comprehensive study of the effects of nuclear weapons.[25] I recognize that there may be another side to educational efforts: some civilians and soldiers may come to see in nuclear weapons a device that produces "more rumble for a rupee," in Richard Park's telling phrase.[26] But in the long run it is important to help develop popular awareness of the enormous destructive power of nuclear weapons, their collateral damages, and their peculiar relationship to conventional arms. Such an educational effort may best be pursued by the private sector: sharing some of the films that have appeared on American and British television ("The Day After," "Threads") with Indian and Pakistani television networks would convey to millions of South Asians some of the horror of nuclear warfare. They might also come to appreciate some of the motives behind the nonproliferation policies of nuclear weapons states, which are dismissed out of hand by some Indians and Pakistanis as discriminatory and self-serving.[27]

Shape the context of regional decisions. Much more can be done to influence Indian and Pakistan nuclear decisions by shaping their strategic, political, and moral environment.

(7) Reinforce and strengthen international norms against proliferation, and especially the transfer of nuclear military technology or unsafeguarded nuclear materials. India and Pakistan are candidates for "breakout" exporter status. Every existing NWS appears to have aided another country's nuclear program. So far, India and Pakistan have subscribed to the norm of no-transfer, but whether or not they edge towards a Stage III declared nuclear status,

it will be important to strengthen the political barriers against such transfers.

(8) Reassess the tradeoff between nuclear proliferation and other American nuclear concerns. Existing NWS will have to treat regional proliferation more seriously, and weigh carefully the known advantages of restraining proliferation against the possible disadvantages of adjusting their traditional nuclear policies. This applies with particular emphasis to the United States. Does Washington want to continue boycotting regional civilian nuclear programs? Does it suit American interests to refuse cooperation with India and Pakistan on nuclear safety when we cooperate with the Soviets, Chinese, and Israelis? Given the fact that nuclear weapons are increasingly irrelevant to the security challenges of this new decade, and probably the next century, would suspension of the U.S. testing program (along with that of the Soviet Union and other NWS) hurt American interests, on balance, if there was concurrent Indian and Pakistani adherence to a CTBT?[28]

The U.S. should also hold out the prospect of civilian nuclear assistance in exchange for military nuclear restraint.[29] This restraint will fall short of Nuclear Non-Proliferation Act legal requirements, but the U.S. is the only nuclear weapons state (and one of the few countries in the world) to have imposed such restrictions on both its civilian arms sales and its diplomacy. A policy which links civilian nuclear aid (power reactors, talks on safety, and so forth) with formal Indian and Pakistani commitments to restraint would enhance American leverage without providing encouragement for the two countries to move to Stage III.

While it exaggerates in several places, the Department of Defense's study of security challenges to the United States over the next decade is correct in pointing to regional conflict as an expanded area of American interest. These conflicts do not require the kind of nuclear deployment policies so important (in the past) for Europe. Indeed, such deployments may create enemies out of neutrals, and neutrals out of friends.[30] Therefore, it is important that wherever possible the NWS begin to shape the international environment to make it easier for India and Pakistan to stabilize their own nuclear relationship. In the case of India, this must also mean the inclusion of China. There are a number of steps that could be taken unilaterally or multilaterally by existing NWS that would have an impact on regional decisions. One, of course, would be a CTB.[31] Another would be further (perhaps collective) negative security assurances: no nuclear weapon state would target or consider attacking a non-nuclear state with nuclear weapons. Finally, the NWS could consider declaring that they would not deploy nuclear weapons around South Asia (within less than, say, 1500 km, which matches up with the INF treaty) creating a de facto NWFZ for South Asia. This need not apply to weapon systems in transit through the Indian Ocean. Like other measures discussed here, it would be strategically marginal in an actual war-fighting situation, but it would make an impact on regional decisionmakers looking for ways to justify the leveling-off of their own programs in the face of hawks who cite the superpower and Chinese threats.

(9) Seek out and enlist new partners in the nonproliferation effort, especially regional states and Japan. India's and Pakistan's regional neighbors, Nepal, Sri Lanka, Bhutan and Bangladesh, have all expressed concern with the prospect of regional nuclearization. These SAARC members have a direct and legitimate interest in stopping regional proliferation; their political weight may seem to be tiny, but both India and Pakistan pay attention to them.

Elsewhere in Asia, Japan could be an important partner in influencing regional nuclear decisions. Not only does Japan have substantial economic investments in India and Pakistan, it is looking for areas where it can begin to exercise political influence. There is no residual anti-Japanese feeling in South Asia as there is in Southeast Asia (recent polls show that Indians regard Japan more favorably than either the U.S. or the Soviet Union), Japan has both a comprehensive civilian nuclear program and a firm and credible commitment not to acquire nuclear weapons, and Japan has the moral weight—as an Asian state and as a target of nuclear weapons—that no NWS possesses. Finally, Japan has a solid record on regional nonproliferation: it temporarily cut off aid to India after the 1974 test (the only other country besides Canada and the U.S. to do so), and it has recently tightened up its nuclear export provisions.

Implementing American Policy

It is important to address a few words to the American and South Asian policy communities about the implementation of policies we have discussed.

American policymakers can be insensitive to the nuances of influencing regional policies. In these matters, American statements, declarations, and demarches have often *strengthened* the hand of regional hawks. The cruder attempts to use technology denial as an instrument of policy, to ban exchanges and discussions on nuclear safety, and the derision of civilian nuclear programs and the dismissal of regional security concerns all make credible the accusation (which has powerful racial undertones) that Western, and particularly American, policy is discriminatory.

On the other hand, foreign concern with regional nuclear proliferation has made a difference in internal Indian and Pakistani nuclear debates. Practically, these governments are very concerned about access to international lending institutions and Western technology, and both societies are increasingly tied to America's society and economy. Further, there is a deep distrust of nuclear weapons in both states, especially among moderate politicians, academics, and intellectuals. American statements of concern over proliferation, when put in the context of a general desire to see the region achieve peace, stability, and growth have been taken seriously. Often, however, it is the tone, rather than the content, of American statements and discussions that alienates regional decisionmakers.

On balance, I believe that the pragmatic self-interest of India and Pakistan will ultimately shape their nuclear policies. There is

> a gradual realization, among government leaders and military planners in non-nuclear weapons states, that nuclear arms are simply not very useful instruments for achieving policy objectives. . . . The belief that the Soviet-American nuclear arms race has resulted not in greater safety for either participant, but only in greater burdens imposed by the constant development and maintenance of costly weapons systems is perhaps the single most influential force shaping this perspective. Moreover, the observation that the nuclear weapons states have obtained a monopoly of a certain type of force that they are generally incapable of using has also supported this view.[32]

This realization should lead regional decisionmakers to seriously consider the verification, arms control, and confidence-building measures discussed in this book. These are, above all, in the interest of regional states to pursue, most are also in harmony with the interests of other regional and non-regional states. Most of these measures have been developed in the context of forty years of U.S.-Soviet conflict, and the experience of other regions.

But it may be that South Asia is still dominated by what Akhtar Ali calls "the not-quite-ready-for-the marriage" syndrome, which has a number of roots. One is a hundred and fifty years of colonialism. Indian and Pakistani politicians and intellectuals are deeply suspicious of any proposals which emanate from outside their region—they are justifiably wary of foreigners bearing gifts.

However, post-1947 events have disappointed Indian and Pakistanis, although for different reasons. All Pakistanis are convinced that the U.S. has betrayed Pakistan three times (in 1947-1948, 1965, and 1971) and that Americans are really interested in an alliance with the bigger, more powerful India. Recently, American support for Israel, and Pakistan's close ties to both Iran and Saudi Arabia (as well as a renewed search for its own identity) has added an Islamic facet to Pakistani distrust of proposals made in Washington.

On the Indian side, there is a persistent feeling of neglect and regret: Indians firmly believe that because of their democratic traditions and size, the U.S. should have long ago become its major supporter. That the U.S. has not—the Indians *also* see American actions in 1965 and 1971 as a betrayal—breeds suspicion of proposals emanating from Washington. It also confirms the bizarre view, held by some, that America's objective is to weaken or contain the more powerful India, using Pakistan and China to undercut Delhi's power. It is easy for Indians to interpret calls for a regional agreement through such spectacles: they are seen as thinly disguised attempt to cut India down to Pakistan's size, to *equate* India and Pakistan.

I believe that these regional views of American policy and American interests are wrong. They are as misplaced, and as stereotypical as the view held by many outside the region that all of South Asia's problems stem from irrational and irreconcilable India-Pakistan hatreds.[33]

TABLE 11.1 South Asian Nuclear Arms Control Proposals

CBM, Agreement or Policy	Stage: I =non nuclear II = ambiguous III = declared	Remarks
India or Pakistan sign NPT.	I	U.S. and Soviet policy since 1968. Verification provided by IAEA.[34]
Simultaneous Indian and Pakistan adherence to NPT.	I	Proposed by Pakistan in 1979.
Simultaneous acceptance of IAEA safeguards.	presumably I	Proposed by Pakistan in 1979.
Mutual inspection of nuclear facilities.	I, II?	Proposed by Pakistan (1979); fixed duration inspection proposed by Carnegie Task Force; could be periodically renewed.
One additional facility under safeguards.	I, II	Proposed by Senate staff aide, Peter Galbraith[35]
Alternative or revised NPT.	I, II	Proposed by Gordon Thompson, et. al.[36]
South Asia or second tier NWFZ.	I, II	Proposed by Pakistan in 1974; historically opposed by India on grounds it would legitimize nuclear weapons. Opposed by Bhutan and Mauritius, supported by other S. Asian states.
Expanded South Asia NWFZ.	I, II	Would include PRC, USSR, parts of Indian Ocean. Also discussed by Galbraith.
Unilateral declaration renouncing nuclear weapons.	I, II	Both Indian and Pakistani statements becoming softer on nuclear weapons.
"No-first-make" agreement.	I, II	Proposed by Prof. R. V. R. Chandrasekhara Rao.[37] Would formalize status quo of non-assembled nuclear weapons. Verification of a no-first-make agreement would require extensive and intrusive monitoring methods.

(continues)

TABLE 11.1 *(continued)*

CBM, Agreement or Policy	Stage: I = non nuclear II = ambiguous III = declared	Remarks
Joint declaration renouncing nuclear weapons.	I, II	Proposed by Pakistan in 1978.
Negative assurances by NWS: no nuclear attack against non-nuclear country.	I, II	Already policy of PRC, Soviet Union.
NWS reach CTBT and N Arms reduction to be followed by regional agreement	I, II	Long-standing position of India.
Enlist support of smaller South Asian states.	I, II	Nepal, Bangladesh, Bhutan have all issued statements opposing regional nuclear proliferation.[38]
Comprehensive educational and information program in South Asia about effects of nuclear weapons.	I, II	Proposed by Cohen[39] to influence domestic debate in India and Pakistan on political, military and moral dimensions of nuclear weapons (films, site visits, literature).
Shuttle diplomacy to prevent or contain proliferation.	I, II	Begun by Michael Armacost and Donald Fortier in last half of 1985.
Engage Japan as non-proliferation partner.	I, II	Proposed by Cohen (1989).
Supply conventional weapons to ease security pressures.	I, II	U.S. policy to Pakistan since 1981, perhaps Soviet policy to India as well.
No deployment of nuclear weapons.	II	Verification relatively easy over time, difficult for short periods and small numbers.
Declaration of no assembly of nuclear device.	II	Current stated Indian and Pakistani policies.

(continues)

TABLE 11.1 *(continued)*

CBM, Agreement or Policy	*Stage:* *I =non nuclear* *II = ambiguous* *III = declared*	Remarks
Verification of non-assembly of nuclear device.	II	U.S. President must certify to Congress that Pakistan does not possess nuclear explosive device as a condition of continued military assistance; not required for India.
Multi-year, time bound nuclear freeze.	II	Cohen (1987), Yager (1989). Notion of time-bound agreement has not been sufficiently exploited in South Asian context, viewed as "camel's nose in the tent" strategy by some. But might be suitable for specific or limited agreements.
Renunciation of nuclear war fighting doctrine.	II	Indian leadership divided on theory of deterrence; very much a part of Pakistani thinking, especially armed forces.
Existing stockpile not to be used for NW.	II	If existing stockpiles were segregated and inspected, could put de facto limits on numbers.
Sign External NPT as NWS or near-NWS.	II, III	India and Pakistan fulfill most significant NPT obligations outside formal NPT regime but maintain present or enhanced nuclear status.
Bilateral or regional test ban.	(I ?), II III	See Carnegie Task Force report. Proposed by Pakistan (1987); would limit development of small, boosted, or thermonuclear weapons, and affect reliability of stockpile. See Gupta on regional seismic monitoring methods.

(continues)

TABLE 11.1 *(continued)*

CBM, Agreement or Policy	Stage: I =non nuclear II = ambiguous III = declared	Remarks
Notification of missile tests & space launches, near-border flights of dual capable aircraft.	II, III	See Burns, Chapter 4.
Exchange of observers at missile tests/space launches.	II, III	
Ban development, production, or deployment of MRBMs of certain design, range.	II, III	See discussion by Akhtar Ali, Chapter 9
Regional Nuclear Risk Reduction Centers	II, III	An important CBM, but could evolve into Joint Early Warning system.See Burns, Chapter 5.
Joint early-warning system.	II, III	See chapters by Gupta and Ali.
Separate warheads from their delivery vehicles.	II, III	Akhtar Ali (1989); major strategic differences between II and III; verification problems very difficult.
"Monitored Inactive Status" system on missiles.	II, III	Using tags and seals technology, India and Pakistan could verify inactive status of missiles, or static level of technology (MIRVs, etc.).
Ban boosted fission devices.	II, III	Probably could be verified by monitoring tritium, etc., and ban on testing.
No-first use agreement.	implies III	Proposed by Indian strategist, K. Subrahmanyam; less acceptable to Islamabad because of conventional weapons disadvantage.

(continues)

TABLE 11.1 *(continued)*

CBM, Agreement or Policy	Stage: I = non nuclear II = ambiguous III = declared	Remarks
No early first use agreement.	implies III	Would be easier to to verify than no first use, but conflicts with Indian conventional military doctrine of 1970s, and recent Pakistani doctrine of "offensive-defense," i.e. pre-emptive attack.
No deployment on aircraft or missiles.	III	Missile deployment would require miniaturized warhead design; within capabilities of regional nuclear designers?
Provide PALs to emerging NWS.	III	Proposed by Haass.
No nuclear targeting of civilian populations	implies III	Impossible to verify; many civilian centers co-located with significant military facilities; see Naim Chapter 2 for data.
Abstain from using nuclear alerts or threats for political signalling.	III	II, if there is covert deployment; very unstable if both sides have covert deployment. See Burns, Chapter 4.
Abstain from launch on warning policies.	III	Will be difficult for state with weakest command structure, Pakistan.
Avoid decapitation strikes.	III	Essential to ensure survival of C^3 capability on both sides, necessary for war termination. See Burns, Chapter 4.
Deploy nuclear delivery systems, esp. missiles, 500 km+ from border.	III	See chapters by Elhance and Ali; verification relatively easy if III

(continues)

TABLE 11.1 *(continued)*

CBM, Agreement or Policy	Stage: I =non nuclear II = ambiguous III = declared	Remarks
Global Nuclear "Freeze" on production of fissile material in whole world.	I, III?	Freeze language adapted by India in 1982 in UN General Assembly; would presumably eliminate possibility of nuclear ambiguity if NNWS accepted same verification as NWS, unless fissile material, etc. hidden away or secretly produced.
Regional INF Arms limitation agreement.	I, II, III	INF inspection procedures especially relevant to South Asia, could be adapted to permit production of peaceful nuclear materials or conventional military missile technology, but would include ban on testing of nuclear warheads necessary to ensure non-deployment of such warheads on shorter range missiles.
Hot Lines.	I, II, III	In effect since 1970s between sector commanders; would different system be required to deal with nuclear crises? Upgrade to use facsimile transmission, superior to voice communications. See Burns, Chapter 4.
No attack on nuclear facilities.	I, II, III	India-Pakistan agreement signed December 31, 1988; approved by Pakistani parliament, Indian cabinet. List of sites not yet exchanged.
No war agreement between India and Pakistan.	I, II, III	Originally proposed by Nehru in 1949, revived by Zia in 1981 at time of acceptance of renewed U.S. aid package. *(continues)*

TABLE 11.1 *(continued)*

CBM, Agreement or Policy	Stage: I =non nuclear II = ambiguous III = declared	Remarks
Alternate major military maneuvers in three year cycle: India, Pakistan, pause, and avert provocative maneuvers.	I, II, III	Proposed by Cohen, 1990, to both Indian and Pakistani armed services.
Joint Defense agreement by India and Pakistan.	I, II, III	Originally proposed by Pakistan in 1959, rejected by India.
Prior notification of troop movement, exercises.	I, II, III	In effect since 1966; See Burns, Chapter 4.
Joint patrolling of entire border.	I, II, III	Already being done on Punjab and Rajasthan border; extend to Kashmir ceasefire line? Might involve change in status of UN observer force, unlikely unless settlement of entire Kashmir dispute occurs.
Support of other NWS.	I, II, III	British historically very cooperative, French uneven, Soviets marginally useful, China positively harmful in their support of regional nuclear control.
No external transfer of military nuclear technology.	I, II, III	India has several civilian nuclear technology transfer agreements but has stated intention to limit these to peaceful purposes; would be hard to verify private or rogue Indian assistance.
No transfer of fissile material.	I, II, III	At II or III deployment abroad of nuclear weapons by India, or Pakistan could be problem.
Implement nuclear materials accounting system, enhanced physical protection and security of all nuclear facilities.	I, II, III	

(continues)

TABLE 11.1 *(continued)*

CBM, Agreement or Policy	Stage: I =non nuclear II = ambiguous III = declared	Remarks
Implement nuclear materials accounting system, enhanced physical protection and security of all nuclear facilities.	I, II, III	
One year moratorium on nuclear research activities deemed as threatening or destabilizing.	I, II, III	Carnegie Task Force; some easier to monitor (testing) others (fissile material production) more difficult; see Neuhoff/Singer,Chapter 7
Multilateral non-regional: restrictions on supply of nuclear technology, etc.to India and Pakistan.	I, II, III	codified in NPT, supplemented by London Suppliers Group.
Foreign support for civilian nuclear programs in exchange for nuclear restraint.	I, II, III	Proposed by Pakistanis to Cong. Stephen Solarz in 1989, later denied.
Joint India-Pakistan Military Commission.	I, II, III	In existence for several years. Flawed because of different political weight of army in each country.
Exchange of experts, information.	I, II, III	Especially important to avert misinterpretation at stage II; see Burns, Singer/Neuhoff, Carnegie Task Force
Site visits.	I, II, III	Depending on sensitivity of sites, could be important CBM.
International Verification Service.	I, II, III	Private, multi-national, or international service provides reasonably accurate information on status of regional nuclear programs.

Notes

1. I am grateful to Susan Burns, Arun Elhance, Nancy Gallagher and several workshop participants for comments on an earlier draft. This chapter—particularly its policy-related suggestions—are solely my responsibility.

2. Dunn describes measures to deal with proliferation, I have shifted the perspective to describe the stage of proliferation of a particular state or region. See Dunn, "Four Decades of Nuclear Non-Proliferation: Some Lessons from Wins, Losses, and Draws," in Joseph P. Nye, Jr., et al, eds, *New Threats: Responding to the Proliferation of Nuclear, Chemical and Ballistic Missile Capabilities in the Third World* (Aspen: Aspen Strategy Group, 1990).

3. But it should be emphasized that uncertainty or ambiguity is not the same as instability. American policy should try to first avert instability within the context of uncertainty that has been chosen by both India and Pakistan.

4. Thomas W. Graham uses the term "calculated ambiguity." See "Shiva and Allah: Nuclear Futures for India and Pakistan," The Wilson Center, Asia Program, Occasional Paper Number 28, 1986. "Deliberate" ambiguity has been used to refer to the Israeli nuclear weapons program. See Gerald M. Steinberg, "Deliberate Ambiguity: Evolution and Evaluation," in Louis Rene Beres, ed., *Security or Armageddon: Israel's Nuclear Strategy* (Lexington, Lexington Books, 1986), pp. 29-43.

5. President Zia told several visitors in June, 1988, that India and Pakistan had achieved a stable deterrent relationship based on uncertainty as to whether they each possessed nuclear weapons, and if they did, how many they had. See Cohen, "Our Bomb and Theirs: Reflections on McGeorge Bundy's *Danger and Survival,*" *Swords and Ploughshares,* Program in Arms Control, Disarmament and International Security, University of Illinois, April, 1989.

6. This reluctance is due in part to technical barriers, but primarily to a fear of antagonizing the suppliers of advanced technologies.

7. Historically, the same Indian strategists who have been most pro-nuclear have also been most contemptuous of the rationality of Pakistani political processes, and have argued that only a nuclear deterrent would keep Pakistani leaders from meddling in Indian affairs.

8. While we have characterized Pakistani and Indian policy as one of calculated or designed ambiguity, the first public exchange on nuclear policy between Rajiv Gandhi, and his successor, V.P. Singh, suggests some degree of hesitation and confusion, rather than designed ambiguity:

> Singh: "If Pakistan goes nuclear . . . we will have to take a second look"
> [at India's commitments not to make the bomb].
> Gandhi: "Don't you have any doubts?"
> Singh: "It is for Pakistan to prove its credentials."

9. This is the logic behind Shai Feldman's argument in favor of overt Israeli declaration of its nuclear capabilities; it has at least as much relevance to the India-Pakistan-China nuclear triangle.

10. *Powderkeg: Weapons Proliferation in the Near East and South Asia: U.S. Policy Dilemmas,* report of the project on Arms Control and the

Proliferation of High Technology Weapons in the Near East and South Asia,
forthcoming, Carnegie Endowment for International Peace, 1990, pp. 139-40.

11. Yet there are still discussions of American policy towards Pakistan—
and other states—which disregard the security considerations which led these
states to seek nuclear weapons to begin with. See Gerard Smith and Helena
Cobban, "A Blind Eye to Nuclear Non-Proliferation," *Foreign Affairs,* Summer,
1989.

12. There is a paradox associated with the development and implementation
of a regional nonproliferation policy, recognized by those in the policy
community. It is that the absence of American involvement in South Asia
lowers Washington's interest in regional proliferation, but a high interest in a
region creates an interest that competes with nonproliferation. This was most
evident in the Reagan administration, and even the end of the Carter
administration (where a high interest in proliferation was first supplanted by a
sudden regional interest—the Soviet invasion of Afghanistan).

13. CBMs are a special class of arms control measures. By their very
nature, CBMs can bypass the question of relative military capabilities and go
directly to the other side's assessment of intent, which is the real issue in South
Asia. CBMs are ultimately psychological: they demonstrate that a state does not
intend, or have the capability to initiate a conflict. Obviously, they are doubly
effective if the same state can demonstrate that it is prepared to meet a sudden or
unprovoked attack.

14. Joseph P. Nye, Jr., "Arms Control After the Cold War," *Foreign
Affairs,* Winter, 1989-90, pp. 42-60. Nye's article grows out of another
conference on the spread of new technologies, especially to the Middle East and
South Asia. See Nye, *New Threats.*

15. For a recent statement see G. Smith and Cobban.

16. See Gordon Thompson, *A Global Approach to Controlling Nuclear
Weapons* (Cambridge, : Institute for Resource and Security Studies, Occasional
Paper No. 2, October 1989).

17. This idea is discussed in several of my recent papers and articles. See
chapters in books edited by Kemp and Nye, referred to elsewhere in this chapter.
See Joseph A. Yager, *Nuclear Non-Proliferation Strategy in Asia,* Center for
National Security Negotiations, SAI Inc., CNSN Paper, Vol. 1, No. 3, July,
1989, pp. 43 ff., for discussion of a nuclear standstill in South Asia.

18. I conceive of the concept of "threshold" as a collection of smaller
agreements, arrangements, and practices which add up to a significant stopping
point. These are not to be seen as barriers, but the outcome of decisions taken
by different sets of national leaders pursuing their different national interests. It
so happens that these interests coincide at certain places.

19. Missiles without nuclear weapons are excellent first-strike systems in
the present South Asian nuclear context (they could be used to attack airfields
and runways with chemical or high-explosive warheads), and with nuclear
weapons they are excellent second-strike weapons of mass destruction. Hence,
they are doubly-destabilizing.

20. An "International Verification Center" might be the channel for
information from a number of sources. It could help stabilize relations between
amenable neighbors.

21. See below, however, for other important steps (negative assurances, NWFZ, etc.) that would further weaken the charge of discrimination.

22. Geoffrey Kemp has elaborated the notion of a linkage between a regional peace process and arms control in the forthcoming Carnegie study, and applied it to the Middle East.

23. Pakistani strategists have accepted the notion of permanent inferiority to India in conventional arms, and have even concurred in the term "balanced imbalance," but insist that such an imbalance be "fair." Presumably, they mean that India not flaunt its superiority, and that Pakistan retain a credible deterrent against a conventional Indian attack.

24. Stephen P. Cohen, *Perception, Influence and Weapons Proliferation in South Asia*, a report prepared for the Department of State, Bureau of Intelligence and Research (# 1722-920184, August, 1978) p.46.

25. Jawaharlal Nehru commissioned *Nuclear Explosions and their Effects* in 1954; it went into a second edition in 1956 (New Delhi: Government of India Ministry of Information and Broadcasting 1956).

26. The term appears in Stephen P. Cohen and Richard L. Park, *India: Emergent Power?* (New York: Crane Russak, 1979).

27. An informal survey in March, 1990 of the officers and directing staff of the Staff College, Quetta, indicated that most Pakistani officers were familiar with "The Day After," which had circulated in Pakistani video shops. Few of these officers favored Pakistan overtly becoming a nuclear weapon state.

28. Generally, Americans fail to understand that the Indian position (and that of many Pakistanis) on CTB is quite independent of their interest in a nuclear option or "going" nuclear. They strongly believe that the failure of the U.S. and the Soviet Union to achieve a CTB is morally as well as strategically wrong. American policy might consider the following. It would recognize that there are costs associated with a CTB agreement (it might make the modernization of American nuclear weapons more difficult, and might complicate somewhat the process of developing safer and more reliable devices, although one can imagine ways of ameliorating these problems). But in exchange, the U.S. and other nuclear weapon states would have erected a substantial barrier in the path of a few states that might want to develop *advanced* nuclear weapons, and of many more that might want to develop a primitive weapon. As one quid pro quo for a CTB India and Pakistan could be asked to take the lead in organizing a "new nuclear suppliers" group, which could adhere to existing, published, Nuclear Supplier Group guidelines. This would not necessarily weaken their preference for ambiguity, but it would help protect New Delhi and Islamabad against nuclear terrorism and theft, and might prevent the emergence of nuclear states which could threaten *their* interests. Alternatively, India and Pakistan could unilaterally begin adhering to NSG guidelines, leaving it to the nuclear weapon states to take the next step. My point here is simply that there is a great overlap of interest, and modest concessions by both sides could advance the security of both the existing NWS and regional states that wanted to maintain a nuclear option, but which were also concerned about disrupting an already fast-changing world order.

29. This was the essence of the proposal apparently put to Congressman Solarz by Pakistani officials in 1989. They later denied making the proposal.

30. See Commission on Integrated Long-Term Strategy, *Report,* and the report of the Commission's study group on Future Security Environment, 1989. This study has alarmed Indian strategists who read it—incorrectly—as a blueprint to threaten India. See the speech of the former Minister of Defense, K.C. Pant, to a Harvard audience in 1989, reprinted in *Defense Analysis,* New Delhi, Institute for Defense Studies and Analysis, 1989

31. Based on unclassified briefings by weapon designers given to a workshop at the University of Illinois in February, 1990—concerning the importance of testing to ensure the safety and reliability of the U.S. stockpile—I have concluded that overall American security would be *enhanced* if adherence to a CTB influenced proliferation decisions—even marginally—in states such as India and Pakistan.

32. Mitchell Reiss, *Without the Bomb* (New York: Columbia University Press, 1988), p. 268.

33. One place where Americans learn such an interpretation of South Asian politics is in the region itself. Pakistanis never tire of telling visiting American officials about the sly but limitless ambitions of Hindu-India. In Delhi, the same officials are regaled with stories of Pakistan's corrupt and irresponsible military dictatorship, and its crazed Islamic tendencies. The net result is sometimes a "plague on both your houses" or "they deserve each other" response back in Washington. The images of a region can affect policies towards its members: thus India and Pakistan have a common interest in minimizing mutual recriminations (especially to outsiders) and maximizing the image of a common regional concern for stability. They do not want to be type-cast as "crazy states," especially if they do declare themselves to be NWS.

34. For a recent study of the IAEA's role see Lawrence Scheinman and Nelson F. Sievering, Jr., *Non-Proliferation and the IAEA: A U.S.-Soviet Agenda* (Washington, D.C.: The Atlantic Council, 1990). For an attack on the NPT by a Canadian professor see Ashok Kapur, "Dump the Treaty," *Bulletin of the Atomic Scientists,* July, 1990.

35. "Nuclear Proliferation in South Asia: Containing the Threat," Staff Report to the Committee on Foreign Relations, U.S. Senate (Washington, D.C.: Senate Committee on Foreign Relations, 1988).

36. Thompson, "A Global Approach," and "Treaty a Useful Relic," *Bulletin of the Atomic Scientists,* July, 1990.

37. "India, Pakistan Racing to be Last," *Bulletin of the Atomic Scientists,* November, 1987.

38. The views of some officials and scholars from smaller regional states, as well as others, is found in the proceedings of a United Nations sponsored workshop on *Disarmament: Confidence and Security-building Measures in Asia* held in Kathmandu in early 1990. This includes a useful chapter on South Asia by William Richter, and a general discussion of confidence-building measures by a Soviet scholar, Henry Trofimenko (New York: United Nations, 1990).

39. "Perception, Influence and Weapons Proliferation in South Asia," Department of State, Bureau of Intelligence and Research, 1978.

Acronyms

ABM, Anti-Ballistic Missile Treaty
(1972),

ACDIS, Program in Arms Control,
Disarmament, and
International Security
(University of Illinois)

ASEAN, Association of Southeast
Asian Nations

AWACS, airborne warning and
control system

BARC, Bhabha Atomic Research
Center (India)

C3, command, control and
communication

C3I, command, control,
communication and
information

CBM, confidence building measures

CSBM, Confidence- and Security-
Building Measures Accords
(1986)

CTB, comprehensive test ban

CTBT, Comprehensive Test Ban
Treaty

DCL, direct communications link

DRDO, Defense Research and
Development Organization
(India)

EAM, emergency action message

EMP, electromagnetic impulses

ESA, European Space Agency

FBR, fast breeder reactor

FROD, functionally related
observable differences

GNP, gross national product

HEU, highly enriched uranium

IAEA, International Atomic Energy
Agency

ICBM, intercontinental ballistic
missile

IHE, insensitive high explosives

INF, Intermediate-range and Shorter
Range Nuclear Forces Treaty

INF, U.S.-Soviet Intermediate and
Shorter Range Nuclear Force
Treaty (1987)

IRBM, intermediate range ballistic
missile

ISRO, Indian Space Research
Organization

kT, kiloton (100 tons of dynamite equivalent)

LoW, Launch on Warning

LTBT, Limited Test Ban Treaty

LWR, light water reactors

MIRV, multiple independently-targetable reentry vehicle

Mt, megaton (one million tons of dynamite equivalent)

MTCR, Missile Technology Control Regime (1987)

NASA, National Air and Space Administration (U.S.)

NATO, North Atlantic Treaty Organization

NPT, Non-Proliferation Treaty (1968)

NRRC, Nuclear Risk Reduction Center

NTM, National Technical Means

NWFZ, nuclear weapons' free zone

OAS, Organization of American States

OPANAL, Organization for the Prohibition of Nuclear Weapons in Latin America

OSI, on-site inspection

OTH, over-the-horizon radar

PAL, permissive action links (on nuclear weapons)

PNE, peaceful nuclear explosion

PNET, Peaceful Nuclear Explosions Treaty (1976)

PWR, pressurized water reactors

R & D, research and development

SAARC, South Asian Association for Regional Cooperation

SALT II, Strategic Arms Limitation Treaty

SAM, surface-to-air missile

SCC, Standing Consultative Committee

SDI, Strategic Defense Initiative (U.S.)

SIPRI, Stockholm International Peace Research Institute

SLV, space-launch vehicle,

SSK, conventionally powered submarine

SSM, surface-to-surface missile

SSN, nuclear powered submarine

START, Strategic Arms Reduction Talks

TNS, threshold nuclear state

TTBT, Threshold Test Ban Treaty (1974)

Index